AF803094

NEW ASIAN REGIONALISM IN INTERNATIONAL ECONOMIC LAW

This book provides the first systematic analysis of new Asian regionalism as a paradigm shift in international economic law. It argues that new Asian regionalism has emerged amid the Third Regionalism and contributed to the New Regional Economic Order, which reinvigorates the role of developing countries in shaping international trade norms. To substantiate the claims, the book introduces theoretical debates and evaluates major regional economic initiatives and institutions, including the ASEAN+6 framework, APEC, the CPTPP and the RCEP. It also sheds light on legal issues involving the US-China trade war and the COVID-19 pandemic, as well as trade policies of Asian powers, the European Union and the United States. Hence, the legal analysis and case studies offer a fresh perspective of Asian integration and bridge the gap between academia and practice.

PASHA L. HSIEH is an Associate Professor of Law and the Associate Dean (Faculty Matters & Research) at the Singapore Management University Yong Pung How School of Law. He served as the Co-Chair of the Asia-Pacific Interest Group of the American Society of International Law and is an Executive Council Member of the Society of International Economic Law.

CAMBRIDGE INTERNATIONAL TRADE AND ECONOMIC LAW

Series editors

Dr Lorand Bartels, *University of Cambridge*
Professor Thomas Cottier, *University of Berne*
Professor Tomer Broude, *Hebrew University of Jerusalem*
Professor Andrea K. Bjorklund, *McGill University, Montréal*

Processes of economic regionalisation and globalisation have intensified over the last decades, accompanied by increases in the regulation of international trade and economics at the levels of international, regional and national laws. At the same time, significant challenges have arisen with respect to economic liberalization, rule-based systems of trade and investment, and their political and social impacts. The subject matter of this series is international economic law, in this contemporary context. Its core is the regulation of international trade, investment, finance and cognate areas such as intellectual property and competition policy. The series publishes books on related regulatory areas, in particular human rights, labour, environment and culture, as well as sustainable development. These areas are horizontally interconnected and vertically linked at the international, regional and national levels. The series also includes works on governance, dealing with the structure and operation of international organisations related to the field of international economic law, and the way they interact with other subjects of international and national law. The series aims to include excellent legal doctrinal treatises, as well as cutting-edge interdisciplinary works that engage law and the social sciences and humanities.

Books in the series

New Asian Regionalism in International Economic Law
Pasha L. Hsieh

Digital Services in International Trade Law
Ines Willemyns

Energy in International Trade Law: Concepts, Regulation and Changing Markets
Anna-Alexandra Marhold

Essential Interoperability Standards: Interfacing Intellectual Property and Competition in International Economic Law
Simon Brinsmead

Shareholders' Claims for Reflective Loss in International Investment Law
Lukas Vanhonnaeker

Transparency in the WTO SPS and TBT Agreements: The Real Jewel in the Crown
Marianna B. Karttunen

Emerging Powers in International Economic Law: Cooperation, Competition and Transformation
Sonia E. Rolland and David M. Trubek

Commitments and Flexibilities in the WTO Agreement on Subsidies and Countervailing Measures
José Guilherme Moreno Caiado

The Return of the Home State to Investor-State Disputes: Bringing Back Diplomatic Protection?
Rodrigo Polanco

The Public International Law of Trade in Legal Services
David Collins

Industrial Policy and the World Trade Organization: Between Legal Constraints and Flexibilities
Sherzod Shadikhodjaev

The Prudential Carve-Out for Financial Services: Rationale and Practice in the GATS and Preferential Trade Agreements
Carlo Maria Cantore

Preferential Services Liberalization: The Case of the European Union and Federal States
Johanna Jacobsson

Judicial Acts and Investment Treaty Arbitration
Berk Demirkol

Distributive Justice and World Trade Law: A Political Theory of International Trade Regulation
Oisin Suttle

Freedom of Transit and Access to Gas Pipeline Networks under WTO Law
Vitalily Pogoretskyy

Reclaiming Development in the World Trading System, 2nd edition
Yong-Shik Lee

Developing Countries and Preferential Services Trade
Charlotte Sieber-Gasser

WTO Dispute Settlement and the TRIPS Agreement: Applying Intellectual Property Standards in a Trade Law Framework
Matthew Kennedy

Establishing Judicial Authority in International Economic Law
Edited by Joanna Jemielniak, Laura Nielsen and Henrik Palmer Olsen

Trade, Investment, Innovation and Their Impact on Access to Medicines: An Asian Perspective
Locknie Hsu

The Law, Economics and Politics of International Standardisation
Edited by Panagiotis Delimatsis

The WTO and International Investment Law: Converging Systems
Jürgen Kurtz

Export Restrictions on Critical Minerals and Metals: Testing the Adequacy of WTO Disciplines
Ilaria Espa

Optimal Regulation and the Law of International Trade: The Interface between the Right to Regulate and WTO Law
Boris Rigod

The Social Foundations of World Trade: Norms, Community, and Constitution
Sungjoon Cho

Public Participation and Legitimacy in the WTO
Yves Bonzon

The Challenge of Safeguards in the WTO
Fernando Piérola

General Interests of Host States in International Investment Law
Edited by Giorgio Sacerdoti, with Pia Acconci, Mara Valenti and Anna De Luca

The Law of Development Cooperation: A Comparative Analysis of the World Bank, the EU and Germany
Philipp Dann

WTO Disciplines on Subsidies and Countervailing Measures: Balancing Policy Space and Legal Constraints
Dominic Coppens

Domestic Judicial Review of Trade Remedies: Experiences of the Most Active WTO Members
Edited by Müslüm Yilmaz

The Relevant Market in International Economic Law: A Comparative Antitrust and GATT Analysis
Christian A. Melischek

International Organizations in WTO Dispute Settlement: How Much Institutional Sensitivity?
Marina Foltea

Public Services and International Trade Liberalization: Human Rights and Gender Implications
Barnali Choudhury

The Law and Politics of WTO Waivers: Stability and Flexibility in Public International Law
Isabel Feichtner

African Regional Trade Agreements as Legal Regimes
James Thuo Gathii

Liberalizing International Trade after Doha: Multilateral, Plurilateral, Regional, and Unilateral Initiatives
David A. Gantz

Processes and Production Methods (PPMs) in WTO Law: Interfacing Trade and Social Goals
Christiane R. Conrad

Non-Discrimination in International Trade in Services: "Likeness" in WTO/GATS
Nicolas F. Diebold

The Law, Economics and Politics of Retaliation in WTO Dispute Settlement
Edited by Chad P. Bown and Joost Pauwelyn

The Multilateralization of International Investment Law
Stephan W. Schill

Trade Policy Flexibility and Enforcement in the WTO: A Law and Economics Analysis
Simon A. B. Schropp

Law and Politics on Export Restrictions: WTO and Beyond
Chien-Huei Wu

NEW ASIAN REGIONALISM IN INTERNATIONAL ECONOMIC LAW

PASHA L. HSIEH
Singapore Management University

CAMBRIDGE
UNIVERSITY PRESS

CAMBRIDGE
UNIVERSITY PRESS

University Printing House, Cambridge CB2 8BS, United Kingdom

One Liberty Plaza, 20th Floor, New York, NY 10006, USA

477 Williamstown Road, Port Melbourne, VIC 3207, Australia

314–321, 3rd Floor, Plot 3, Splendor Forum, Jasola District Centre, New Delhi – 110025, India

103 Penang Road, #05–06/07, Visioncrest Commercial, Singapore 238467

Cambridge University Press is part of the University of Cambridge.

It furthers the University's mission by disseminating knowledge in the pursuit of education, learning, and research at the highest international levels of excellence.

www.cambridge.org
Information on this title: www.cambridge.org/9781108845601
DOI: 10.1017/9781108980210

© Pasha L. Hsieh 2022

This publication is in copyright. Subject to statutory exception and to the provisions of relevant collective licensing agreements, no reproduction of any part may take place without the written permission of Cambridge University Press.

First published 2022

A catalogue record for this publication is available from the British Library.

ISBN 978-1-108-84560-1 Hardback

DAMAGED

Cambridge University Press has no responsibility for the persistence or accuracy of URLs for external or third-party internet websites referred to in this publication and does not guarantee that any content on such websites is, or will remain, accurate or appropriate.

CONTENTS

FIGURES

TABLES

PREFACE

The impasse of the World Trade Organization (WTO) Doha Round has galvanized trade and investment agreements in the Asia-Pacific region to proliferate at an unprecedented rate. This book provides the first systematic analysis of new Asian regionalism as a paradigm shift in international economic law. It represents the culmination of my observations and research in the past decade, taking into account the impact of recent mega-regional trade pacts, US-China trade tensions and the COVID-19 pandemic. The main contribution of the book is to fill a major gap in the literature on the evolving legal regimes of Asian regionalism. By introducing theoretical lenses and explaining business implications, I hope to facilitate interdisciplinary dialogues between regionalism studies in law and international relations and to bridge academia and practice in global economic governance.

I coined the terms the "Third Regionalism" and the "New Regional Economic Order (NREO)" to contextualize Asian regionalism and its implications for North-South relations in the multilateral trading system. To substantiate my claims, the methodology of the book is intentionally eclectic. The Association of Southeast Asian Nations (ASEAN) centrality has emerged as a well-recognized operational concept in the regional architecture. Therefore, I focus on the broader implications of the legalization of the ASEAN Economic Community rather than the conventional country-centered approach. In particular, I illuminate the origin and change of the ASEAN Plus Six framework, which led to the Regional Comprehensive Economic Partnership (RCEP) as the world's largest free trade agreement by economic scale.

In today's multipolar world, new Asian regionalism is of global significance. I do not parochially perceive Asia's new normative integration process as a pure intra-regional evolution. To shed light on endogenous and exogenous influences, I examine the strengths and weaknesses of EU and US initiatives with ASEAN and key Asian economies. Moreover, I evaluate the soft-law development of the Asia-Pacific Economic

Cooperation (APEC) and its nexus with ASEAN, the RCEP and the Comprehensive and Progressive Agreement for Trans-Pacific Partnership (CPTPP).

These collective analyses reinforce what I have attempted to convey. With the arrival of the Asian century, the region's regulatory influences enrich global rulemaking and require a more in-depth, on-the-ground study. I define new Asian regionalism as a new normative integration process that has evolved with the ASEAN Plus Six framework, which underpins Asia's ascending economic power. More fundamentally, I argue that new Asian regionalism has emerged amid the Third Regionalism and contributed to the NREO, which reinvigorates the role of developing countries in shaping international trade norms. The argument that I advance challenges the West-centric understanding of Asian trade and investment pacts as improper or low quality. As empirical findings demonstrate, multifaceted cultural and political factors resulted in the pragmatic incrementalism model that has crystalized legal structures of Asian integration.

This book has had a long gestation period since I first embarked on international economic law research. I am indebted to my mentors of international law and political science, including Chun-i Chen, Bruno Coppieters, Jacques deLisle and Ma Ying-jeou. They exposed me to the new world of theoretical debates and firsthand legal challenges that confront China, Taiwan and the Asia-Pacific. My experience as a junior lawyer at the WTO Appellate Body Secretariat expanded my horizon of the multilateral trade regime and negotiations. Working with and learning from Georges Abi-Saab and Werner Zdouc tremendously enhanced my practical understanding of the intersection between trade rules and public international law.

I am fortunate to develop my academic career in Singapore, a cosmopolitan city-state and hub of Asia's trade, investment and digital agreements. At Singapore Management University (SMU), I am grateful to Dean Goh Yihan of the Yong Pung How School of Law and Director Yip Man of the Centre for Commercial Law in Asia for their encouragement and support. I also thank my colleagues, Locknie Hsu, Lee Pey Woan, Liu Kung-Chung, Low Kee Yang, Tang Hang Wu and Yeo Tiong Min, for their insightful advice.

I had the opportunity to present papers that underpin core ideas of the book at various conferences and faculty workshops organized by the American Society of International Law, the Asian Society of International Law, the European Parliament, the Institute for Global

Law and Policy of Harvard Law School, Seoul National University, the Society of International Economic Law, National Taiwan University and the US-Asia Law Institute of New York University Law School. I benefited from the feedback of organizers and participants, including particularly Dukgeun Ahn, Antony Anghie, Jerome A. Cohen, Yuka Fukunaga, Jaemin Lee, Tsai-yu Lin, Chang-fa Lo, Shin-yi Peng, Sonia E. Rolland and Peter Van den Bossche. These papers have been published in journals such as the *Journal of International Economic Law*, the *Journal of World Investment & Trade* and the *Leiden Journal of International Law*. The comments from editors and reviewers enabled me to explore fundamental issues at fuller length in this book.

Throughout the writing process, I benefited from deep and rich conversations with a group of outstanding experts: William Burke-White, Julien Chaisse, Christopher Chen, Manjiao Chi, Sungjoon Cho, Matthew Erie, Ilaria Espa, Yoshifumi Fukunaga, Weixia Gu, Shintaro Hamanaka, Benjamin Hartmann, Jean Ho, Meredith Kolsky Lewis, Julian Ku, Carlos A. Kuriyama, Inu Manak, Bryan Mercurio, Fabio Morosini, Krista Nadakavukaren Schefer, Thomas Streinz, Marcus Wagner, Heng Wang, Timothy Webster, Müslüm Yilmaz and David Zaring. They provided me with insights into APEC, the CPTPP, the RCEP and the WTO, as well as trade policies of China, the European Union and the United States.

Special thanks to Joe Ng and the staff of Cambridge University Press for their guidance. I also appreciate Chai Yee Xin of the SMU Kwa Geok Choo Law Library and my research assistants, Rachel Chang, Chen Sicong, Nicholas Kuek, Terrence Lerh, Lim Wei Ming, Mei-Yi Lin, Liu Jiayi, Victoria Liu, Soh Kian Peng and Tan Yoong San, for their dedicated work. I acknowledge with gratitude the funding provided by the SMU Lee Kong Chian Fellowship, the Center of International Legal Studies of National Chengchi University and the Sumitomo Foundation of Japan. Finally, I profoundly thank my family and friends, including Kuei-Lan Chiu, Christine Y. Chang, Melisma Cox and Scott Y. Lin, for their long-standing support.

ABBREVIATIONS

AANZFTA	ASEAN-Australia-New Zealand Free Trade Agreement
ABAC	ASEAN Business Advisory Council
ABIF	ASEAN Banking Integration Framework
ABMI	Asian Bond Market Initiative
ACFTA	ASEAN-China Free Trade Agreement
ACIA	ASEAN Comprehensive Investment Agreement
ACMF	ASEAN Capital Markets Forum
ACPE	ASEAN Chartered Professional Engineer
ADMM+	ASEAN Defense Ministers' Meeting Plus
ADR	Alternative Dispute Resolution
AEC	ASEAN Economic Community
AEC Blueprint 2015	ASEAN Economic Community Blueprint 2015
AEC Blueprint 2025	ASEAN Economic Community Blueprint 2025
AEM	ASEAN Economic Ministers
AFAS	ASEAN Framework Agreement on Services
AfCFTA	African Continental Free Trade Area
AFIF	ASEAN Financial Integration Framework
AFTA	ASEAN Free Trade Area
AHKFTA	ASEAN-Hong Kong Free Trade Agreement
AIA	ASEAN Investment Area Agreement
AIIB	Asian Infrastructure Investment Bank
AIPO	ASEAN Inter-Parliamentary Organization
AMS	ASEAN Member State
AOIP	ASEAN Outlook on the Indo-Pacific
APEC	Asia-Pacific Economic Cooperation
AQRF	ASEAN Qualifications Reference Framework
ARF	ASEAN Regional Forum
ARIA	Asia Reassurance Initiative Act of 2018
ARISE	ASEAN Regional Integration Support from the EU
ASEAN	Association of Southeast Asian Nations
ASEAN MNP Agreement	ASEAN Agreement on the Movement of Natural Persons

ASEM	Asia-Europe Meeting
ATIGA	ASEAN Trade in Goods Agreement
ATISA	ASEAN Trade in Services Agreement
AWGIPC	ASEAN Working Group on Intellectual Property Cooperation
BIT	Bilateral Investment Treaty
BRI	Belt and Road Initiative
CAFTA-DR	Dominican Republic-Central America FTA
CEPT	Common Effective Preferential Tariff Scheme
CETA	Comprehensive Economic and Trade Agreement
ChAFTA	China-Australia Free Trade Agreement
CJEU	Court of Justice of the European Union
CLMV	Cambodia, Lao PDR, Myanmar and Vietnam
COVID-19	Coronavirus Disease 2019
CPTPP	Progressive Agreement for Trans-Pacific Partnership
CTC	Change in Tariff Classification
DEA	Digital Economy Agreement
DSM	Dispute Settlement Mechanism
DSU	Dispute Settlement Understanding
EAEG	East Asia Economic Group
EAFTA	East Asian Free Trade Area
EAI	Enterprise of ASEAN Initiative
EAS	East Asia Summit
ECOTECH	APEC Economic and Technical Cooperation
EDSM	ASEAN Protocol on Enhanced Dispute Settlement Mechanism
EEA	European Economic Area
EEC	European Economic Community
E3	US-ASEAN Expanded Economic Engagement
EHP	Early Harvest Program
EPPD	Economic Prosperity Partnership Dialogue
E-READI	Enhanced Regional EU-ASEAN Dialogue Instrument
EU	European Union
EUSFTA	EU-Singapore Free Trade Agreement
EVFTA	EU-Vietnam Free Trade Agreement
EVSL	Early Voluntary Sectoral Liberalization
FDI	Foreign Direct Investment
FET	Fair and Equitable Trade
FTA	Free Trade Agreements
FTAAP	Free Trade Area of the Asia Pacific
GATS	General Agreement on Trade in Services
GATT	General Agreement on Tariffs and Trade

GDP	Gross Domestic Product
GDPR	General Data Protection Regulation
GI	Geographical Indication
GPA	Agreement on Government Procurement
GSP	Generalized Scheme of Preferences
GVC	Global Value Chain
HS	Harmonized System
IAI	Initiative for ASEAN Integration
ICJ	International Court of Justice
ICS	Investment Court System
ICSID	International Centre for Settlement of Investment Disputes
ICSID Convention	Convention on the Settlement of Investment Disputes between States and Nationals of Other States
IGA	ASEAN Investment Guarantee Agreement
IIA	International Investment Agreement
IP	Intellectual Property
IPA	Investment Protection Agreement
ISDS	Investor-State Dispute Settlement
ISI	Integrated Sourcing Initiative
ITA	Information Technology Agreement
LCC	Low-Cost Carriers
MAAS	Multilateral Agreement on Air Services
MAFLAFS	Multilateral Agreement for the Full Liberalization of Air Freight Services
MAFLPAS	Multilateral Agreement for the Full Liberalization of Passenger Air Services
MFN	Most-Favored-Nation
MLEC	UNCITRAL Model Law on Electronic Commerce
MNP	Movement of Natural Persons
MRA	Mutual Recognition Agreement
MSME	Micro, Small, and Medium Enterprise
NAFTA	North American Free Trade Area
NIEO	New International Regional Economic Order
NLD	National League for Democracy
NREO	New Regional Economic Order
NT	National Treatment
NTB	Non-Tariff Barrier
NTM	Non-Tariff Measure
OECD	Organisation for Economic Co-operation and Development
OPTAD	Organization for Pacific Trade and Development

PCA	Partnership and Cooperation Agreements
PECC	Pacific Economic Cooperation Conference
PNTR	Permanent Normal Trade Relations
PRC	People's Republic of China
PSU	Policy Support Unit
PTA	Preferential Trade Agreement
QAB	Qualified ASEAN Bank
QFB	Qualifying Full Bank
RCEP	Regional Comprehensive Economic Partnership
RFPE	Registered Foreign Professional Engineer
RIATS	Roadmap for Integration of the Air Travel Sector
ROC	Republic of China (Taiwan)
ROO	Rules of Origin
RVC	Regional Value Content
SDT	Special and Differential Treatment
SMBD	Senior Management and Board of Directors
SME	Small and Medium Enterprise
SOE	State-Owned Enterprise
SPS	Sanitary and Phytosanitary
TAC	Treaty of Amity and Cooperation in Southeast Asia
TBT	Technical Barriers to Trade
TFA	Trade Facilitation Agreement
TIFA	Trade and Investment Framework Arrangement
TPP	Trans-Pacific Partnership
TREATI	Trans-Regional EU-ASEAN Trade Initiative
TRIMs	Trade-Related Investment Measures
TRIPs	Agreement on Trade-Related Aspects of Intellectual Property Rights
TTIP	Transatlantic Trade and Investment Partnership
UN	United Nations
UNCITRAL	United Nations Commission on International Trade Law
UNCTAD	United Nations Conference on Trade and Development
UNECE	UN Economic Commission for Europe
USMCA	United States-Mexico-Canada Agreement
USTR	United States Trade Representative
VCLT	Vienna Convention on the Law of Treaties
WTO	World Trade Organization

1

Introduction: New Asian Regionalism As a Global Paradigm Shift

I Introduction

This book offers a panoramic account of new Asian regionalism in international economic law. It explores interrelated theoretical and substantive claims on proliferating trade and investment agreements in the Asia-Pacific. More specifically, it argues that new Asian regionalism has emerged amid the third wave of global regionalism and contributed to the New Regional Economic Order (NREO), which reinvigorates the role of developing countries in shaping international trade norms. The research therefore serves as a timely response to the rival of the Asian century.[1]

New Asian regionalism is of global significance and has attracted the attention of governments and businesses for several reasons. First, Asian countries have become the locomotives of international commerce and have energized the shift of the world's economic center of gravity to the region. In terms of global gross domestic product (GDP), Asia is poised to exceed the rest of the world in the 2020s.[2] In particular, China will replace the United States as the world's largest economy.[3] India will overtake the United Kingdom (UK), Germany and Japan and become the third largest economy.[4] As a ten-country bloc, the Association of

[1] Valentina Romei & John Reed, *The Asian century Is Set to Begin*, Mar. 26, 2019, Financial Times, www.ft.com/content/520cb6f6-2958-11e9-a5ab-ff8ef2b976c7 (last visited Feb. 16, 2021); Asian Development Bank (ADB), *Asia 2050: Realizing the Asian Century: Executive Summary* (2011), at 5.

[2] ADB, *supra* note 1, at 3–4.

[3] Centre for Economics and Business Research (CEBR), *World Economic League Table 2021* (2020), at 70–71.

[4] *Id.* at 113–14; PWC, *The Long View: How Will the Global Economic Order Change by 2050* (2017), at 7.

Southeast Asian Nations (ASEAN) will rise to the equivalent of the fourth largest economy in the world.[5] Given the rising power of Asian economies, their legal and geopolitical strategies to trade policy have become critical areas of study.

Second, Asia has integrated at an unprecedented rate. In the past twenty years, Asian regionalism has witnessed a tenfold increase of free trade agreements (FTAs), which represent almost half of global trade pacts.[6] The "ASEAN Plus Six" framework based on the bloc's external agreements with Asia-Pacific economies has underlined the legal regimes of new Asian regionalism.[7] This structure has enriched the NREO that is reconstructing a new hub-and-spoke system in the multipolar world.

Asian states have also played a leadership role in ushering in mega-FTAs, including the Comprehensive and the Progressive Agreement for Trans-Pacific Partnership (CPTPP) and the Regional Comprehensive Economic Partnership (RCEP).[8] Given the stalled World Trade Organization (WTO) negotiations, these unprecedented pacts will shape global rulemaking. As the COVID-19 pandemic caused the decline of global trade by 32 percent and foreign direct investment by 42 percent, Asia's new trade, investment and digital economy agreements manifest the region's normative response to the economic recovery.[9]

Lastly, soaring populist nationalism in the West, as evidenced by Brexit and the Donald Trump administration's "America First" policy, led to the US-China trade war and disrupted the global supply chain. Despite

[5] Australian Government, *ASEAN's Economic Growth*, www.austrade.gov.au/asean-now/why-asean-matters-to-australia/asean-economic-growth/ (last visited Feb. 16, 2021). At present, the Association of Southeast Asian Nations (ASEAN) is the world's fifth largest economy. ASEAN, *ASEAN Key Figures 2020* (2020), at 39.

[6] World Trade Organization (WTO), Regional Trade Agreements Database, https://rtais.wto.org/UI/PublicMaintainRTAHome.aspx (last visited Feb. 16, 2021); ADB, Table 2. FTAs by WTO Notification and Status (Cumulative), https://aric.adb.org/fta (last visited Feb. 16, 2021).

[7] From 2002 to 2017, ASEAN concluded "ASEAN Plus One" free trade agreements (FTAs) sequentially with seven economies, including China, Japan, India, Korea, Australia and New Zealand, and Hong Kong. Vinod K. Aggarwal & Jonathan T. Chow, *The Perils of Consensus: How ASEAN's Meta-regime Undermines Economic and Environmental Cooperation*, 17 (2) Rev. Int'l Pol. Econ. 262, 267–71 (2010); ASEAN, *ASEAN Integration Report 2019* (2019), at 131–32.

[8] For the analysis of plurilaterlism, see Meredith Kolsky Lewis, *The Origin of Plurilateralism in International Trade Law*, 20 J. World Invest. & Trade 633, 637–40 (2019).

[9] WTO, Trade Shows Signs of Rebound from COVID-19, Recovery Still Uncertain, Oct. 6, 2020, www.wto.org/english/news_e/pres20_e/pr862_e.htm (last visited Feb. 17, 2021); United Nations Conference on Trade and Development (UNCTAD), *Investment Trends Monitor* (2021), Issue 38, at 1.

the signing of the European Union (EU)-UK Trade and Cooperation Agreement and US President Joe Biden's pledge to regain America's credibility and alliances, isolationist approaches have crippled the hegemony of neoliberalism.[10] Developing countries, particularly those in Asia, are in search of an alternative model of economic integration. Neither the Washington Consensus nor the Brussels Effect provide holistic answers to new Asian regionalism.[11]

The intended objective of Asian countries is to devise a new trade-development approach for the South (developing nations) and subsequently transform its dependent relationship with the North (developed nations). Nevertheless, I caution that it is inappropriate to ignore the impact of the US Indo-Pacific strategy and the EU's "strategic engagement" with Asia on interregional trade agreements.[12] As Asian regionalism should not be perceived as a pure intra-regional process, the book will evaluate both endogenous and exogenous influences.[13]

It is now urgent and necessary to have a comprehensive and coherent understanding of new Asian regionalism, especially from a legal perspective that has not been fully explored before. By focusing on Asian trade and investment initiatives as legal regimes, this book seeks to fill a major gap in the literature on regionalism, which commentators have criticized as Euro-centric.[14] As Asian regionalism has been in the conventional domain of international relations (IR), most books are authored by political scientists and explain regionalism theories from political and economic perspectives.[15] Legal books on pertinent topics are primarily edited collections that focus on either single agreements or countries and

[10] European Commission, *EU-UK Trade and Cooperation Agreement: A New Relationship, with Big Changes* (2020), at 1–2; White House, *Remarks by President Biden on America's Place in the World*, Feb. 4, 2021, www.whitehouse.gov/briefing-room/speeches-remarks/2021/02/04/remarks-by-president-biden-on-americas-place-in-the-world/ (last visited Feb. 8, 2021).

[11] For these two terms, see Sonia E. Rolland, *Development at the WTO* 51–52 (2012); Anu Bradford, *The Brussels Effect: How the European Union Rules the World* 26–36 (2020).

[12] Department of State, *A Free and Open Indo-Pacific Advancing a Shared Vision* (2019), at 5–21; European Commission, *Trade for All: Towards a More Responsible Trade and Investment Policy* (2015), at 31–32.

[13] Björn Hettne, *The New Regionalism Revisited, in* Theories of New Regionalism 22, 26–27 (Fredrik Söderbaum & Timothy M. Shaw eds. 2003).

[14] *E.g.*, Amitav Acharya, *Regionalism beyond EU-Centrism, in* The Oxford Handbook of Comparative Regionalism 109, 109–19 (Tanja A. Börzel & Thomas Risse 2016); Fredrik Söderbaum, *Rethinking Regionalism* 7–8 & 174–75 (2016).

[15] *E.g.*, Christopher M. Dent, *East Asian Regionalism* (2d ed. 2016); Ellen L. Frost, *Asia's New Asian Regionalism* (2008); Edward J. Lincoln, *East Asian Economic Regionalism* (2004); *Network Power: Japan and Asia* (Peter J. Katzenstein & Takashi Shiraishi eds. 1997).

mostly predate the entry into force of the CPTPP and the conclusion of the RCEP.[16]

While there are legal monographs on economic integration in the EU, North America and Africa, this is the first book-length analysis of the legal frameworks of new Asian regionalism.[17] There are extremely few legal texts prepared for teaching and researching international economic law that systematically explores evolving legal regimes of Asian agreements and their impact on the multilateral trading system. I hope that this book not only advances new legal and theoretical arguments, but also serves as the most up-to-date reference book that bridges academia and practice.

II New Asian Regionalism in the Global Context

New Asian regionalism is a paradigm shift in international economic law. In my view, new Asian regionalism can be defined as a new normative integration process that has evolved with the ASEAN Plus Six framework, which underpins Asia's ascending economic power. The scope of "Asia" as a region has been subject to debate because Asia and its relevant geographic terms such as the Asia-Pacific, East Asia and the Indo-Pacific are by their nature heterogeneous and lack a consensus on their definitions.[18] National governments and international institutions, including the Asia-Pacific Economic Cooperation (APEC), the Asia-Europe Meeting (ASEM) and the WTO, adopted their own interpretations delineating the region.[19] Instead of exhausting definitions or

[16] *E.g., Megaregulation Contested: Global Economic Ordering after TPP* (Benedict Kingsbury et al. 2019); *The China-Australia Free Trade Agreement: A 21st Century Model* (Colin B. Picker et al. 2018); *Paradigm Shift in International Economic Law Rule-Making: TPP as a New Model for Trade Arrangements?* (Julien Chaisse et al. eds. 2017); *China in the International Economic Order: New Directions and Changing Paradigms* (Lisa Toohey et al. eds. 2015).

[17] A rare legal monograph on "non-Western" regionalism is James Thuo Gathii, *African Regional Trade Agreements as Legal Regimes* (2011).

[18] Anja Jetschke et al., *Asia, in* The Oxford Handbook of Comparative Regionalism 225, 226–27 (Tanja A. Börzel & Thomas Risse 2016); Shaun Breslin et al., *Regions in Comparative Perspective, in* New Regionalism in the Global Political Economy: Theories and Cases 1, 5–6 (Shaun Breslin et al. eds. 2002).

[19] Department of State, *supra* note 12, at 8–15; *Asia-Pacific Economic Cooperation, Member Economies*, www.apec.org/about-us/about-apec/member-economies (last visited Feb.19, 2021); *Asia-Europe Meeting, Fostering Dialogue & Cooperation between Asia & Europe*, www.aseminfoboard.org/about/overview (last visited Feb. 19, 2021); WTO, *World Trade Statistics Review 2020* (2020), at 63.

demarcating the boundaries of Asia, I focus on countries that have energized major normative changes to new trade dynamics.

A *Early Waves of Global Regionalism*

Legal scholars have conventionally analyzed regional integration from the lens of WTO law. Debates have centered on Article XXIV of the General Agreement on Tariffs and Trade (GATT), Article V of the General Agreement on Trade in Services (GATS) and the Enabling Clause.[20] Trade agreements' compatibility with these legal bases, as well as WTO-plus and extra provisions and commitments, provide key indications for "deep" or "high-level" regionalism.

Unlike the narrow lens of the legal discourse, political scientists have developed operational definitions of regionalism. To them, regionalization and regionalism are different concepts. Regionalization denotes informal integration or soft regionalism that enhances economic, political and cultural interactions, which are often propelled by non-state actors.[21] Regionalism is nonetheless "a primarily state-led process of building and sustaining formal regional institutions and organizations" and can encompass mandates for economic and security cooperation.[22] While regionalization usually indicates bottom-up efforts, it can energize states to pursue regionalism based on a top-down approach.[23] Empirically, Asian integration includes both regionalization and regionalism as the IR literature has defined. Furthermore, legal schemes such as ASEAN and other FTAs signify "a solid form of" Asian regionalism, but consultative forums without binding instruments including APEC and the ASEM also promote integration.[24]

It is essential to contextualize new Asian regionalism in the international context. In the post–World War II era, there have been three waves of global regionalism.[25] Jagdish Bhagwati coined the term "First

[20] WTO, *The WTO's Rules*, www.wto.org/english/tratop_e/region_e/regrul_e.htm (last visited Feb. 19, 2021).

[21] Tanja A. Börzel & Thomas Risse, *Introduction: Framework of the Handbook and Conceptual Clarifications, in* The Oxford Handbook of Comparative Regionalism 3, 8 (Tanja A. Börzel & Thomas Risse 2016); Andrew Hurrell, *Regionalism in Theoretical Perspective, in* Regionalism in World Politics: Regional Organization and International Order 37, 39–40 (Louise Fawcett & Andrew Hurrell eds. 1995).

[22] Dent, *supra* note 15, at 8–10; Börzel & Risse, *supra* note 21, at 7–8.

[23] Edward D. Mansfield & Etel Solingen, *Regionalism*, 13 Ann. Rev. Pol. Sci. 145, 147.

[24] *Id.*

[25] Most scholars addressed either the first two waves of global regionalism or the early stage of third wave of global regionalism. Jagdish Bhagwati, *Termites in the Trading System:*

Regionalism" in reference to the proliferation of FTAs in the 1950s and 1960s.[26] During this first wave of global regionalism, political considerations principally drove the process of regionalism. The United States hesitated to pursue trade pacts under Article XXIV of the GATT because it "remained wedded to multilateralism and nondiscrimination in trade liberalization through the Kennedy Round."[27] However, Washington actively supported the founding of the European Economic Community (EEC) in 1957, as it could prevent the war between France and Germany and counterbalance Soviet influences in Central and Eastern Europe.[28]

Perceived as a model, the EEC triggered developing countries to form trade blocs in regions such as East Africa and Central America.[29] In Asia, the founding of ASEAN in 1967 marked the inception of Asian regionalism.[30] Akin to Bhagwati's observation, the formation of ASEAN was politically oriented, as Southeast Asian countries aimed to create a loose security alliance against communist expansion.[31] He considered most trade initiatives in the First Regionalism "failures," given that developing countries often centered on industrialization policies of import substitution, which sought to remedy the weakness of their small-scale economies.[32] Absent serious trade liberalization, the policy yielded the marginal trade-creation effect.[33]

How Preferential Agreements Undermine Free Trade 29–32 (2008); Fredrik Söderbaum & Luk van Langenhove, *Introduction: The EU as a Global Actor and the Role of Interregionalism*, 27(3) Eur. Integration 249, 255 (2005); Sungjoon Cho, *Breaking the Barrier between Regionalism and Multilateralism: A New Perspective on Trade Regionalism*, 42(2) Harv. Int'l L. J. 419, 427 (2001); Edward D. Mansfield & Helen V. Milner, *The New Wave of Regionalism*, 53(3) Int'l Organ. 589, 600–01 (1999).

26 Bhagwati, *supra* note 25, at 29–31.

27 *Id.* at 31; Jagdish Bhagwati, *Regionalism versus Multilateralism*, 15 World Econ. 535, 539 (1992).

28 WTO, *World Trade Report 2011* (2011), at 52l; Bhagwati, *supra* note 25, at 31; Cho, *supra* note 25, at 427; Söderbaum & Van Langenhove, *supra* note 25, 255.

29 WTO, *supra* note 28, at 52; Bhagwati, *supra* note 25, at 29.

30 Amita Acharya, *Foundations of Collective Action in Asia: Theory and Practice of Regional Cooperation*, ADBI Working Paper Series, No. 344 (2012), at 5–10.

31 The founding members of ASEAN include Indonesia, Malaysia, the Philippines, Singapore and Thailand. Rodolfo C. Severino, *Southeast Asia in Search of an ASEAN Community: Insights from the Former ASEAN Secretary-General* 1–11 (2006).

32 Bhagwati, *supra* note 27, at 538–39; Bhagwati, *supra* note 25, at 29.

33 Bhagwati, *supra* note 27, at 538–39; Cho, *supra* note 25, at 427–28. For discussion on Jacob Viner's trade creation and trade diversion effects of customs unions, see Aaditya Mattoo et al., *Trade Creation and Trade Diversion in Deep Agreements*, Policy Research Working Paper, No. 8206 (2017), at 2–10.

The second wave of global regionalism developed during the Uruguay Round in the 1980s and 1990s. In the "Second Regionalism," Bhagwati highlighted the limited success evidenced by the EU and the North American Free Trade Agreement (NAFTA), the precursor to the United States-Mexico-Canada Agreement (USMCA).[34] Tellingly, the NAFTA signified the changing stance of the United States on FTAs.[35] Based on these empirical cases, Richard Baldwin proffered the "domino theory" as the driving force for regionalism because non-FTA members would be prompted to pursue FTAs to maintain export advantages.[36] According to political scientists, this era was also characterized as post-hegemonic regionalism.[37] FTAs that evolved in the new multipolar world were due to declining US hegemony relative to powers of the EU, China and other emerging economies.[38] As a prominent example, Mercosur was established as a customs unions built on South-South FTAs that promote economic and political integration.[39]

Asia rose to be an academic focus because of the economic miracles of selected countries. Kaname Akamatsu's "flying geese" model depicts Japan-led development patterns in post-war Asia.[40] As exemplifications of such patterns of remarkable growth rates, newly industrialized economies (Hong Kong, South Korea, Singapore and Taiwan) become known as Four Asian Tigers or Little Dragons.[41] Since the 1990s, Deng

[34] Bhagwati, *supra* note 25, at 31–35.

[35] *Id.* at 32–34.

[36] Richard Baldwin, *A Domino Theory of Regionalism*, NBER Working Paper Series, No. 4465 (1993), at 2–5.

[37] Jorge F. Garzón, *Multipolarity and the Future of Economic Regionalism*, 9 (1) Int'l Theory 101, 104–15 (2016); Mario Telò, *Introduction: Globalization, New Regionalism and the Role of the European Union, in* European Union and New Regionalism: Competing Regionalism and Global Governance in a Post-Hegemonic Era 1, 5–10 (Mario Telò ed. 2014).

[38] Garzón, *supra* note 37; Mario Telò, *supra* note 37, at 5–10; Hettne, *supra* note 13, at 23–24; Björn Hettne, *The New Regionalism: Implications for Development and Peace, in* Björn Hettne & András Inotai, *The New Regionalism: Implications for Global Development and International Security*, UNU/WIDER World Institute for Development Economics Research 1, 1–2 (1994).

[39] WTO, *supra* note 28, at 52–53.

[40] Kiyoshi Kojima, *The "Flying Geese" Model of Asian Economic Development: Origin, Theoretical Extensions, and Regional Policy Implications*, 11 J. Asian Econ. 375, 377 (2000); T. J. Pempel, *Transpacific Torri: Japan and the Emerging Asian Regionalism, in* Network Power: Japan and Asia 47, 52–53 (Peter J. Katzenstein & Takashi Shiraishi eds. 1997).

[41] *Id.*; Debayan Pakrashi & Paul Frijters, *Takeoffs, Landing, and Economic Growth*, ADBI Working Paper Series, Nov. 641 (2017), at 6–7.

Xiaoping's economic reforms and Open Door Policy revolutionized China as a "leading dragon."[42] Modeled after Asian Tigers, the Tiger Cub Economies in Southeast Asia also became noteworthy for their export-oriented development.[43] During this period, Asian enterprises galvanized regionalization, whereas most governments still prioritized WTO-premised multilateralism over FTA-centered regionalism.

ASEAN and APEC represented significant developments in Asia. As the domino theory suggested, the EU, NAFTA and Mercosur motivated ASEAN to expedite internal integration by creating the ASEAN Free Trade Area.[44] Unlike the EU that transformed the Westphalian system, ASEAN's integration has been depicted as "sovereignty-reinforcing regionalism," which has enhanced rather than weakened state capacity and building.[45] APEC also indicates a different normative approach. Based on soft-law, APEC has operated on nonbinding rules and decisions. Its Bogor Declaration aimed to realize "free and open trade and investment in the Asia-Pacific" for developed and developing economies by 2010 and 2020, respectively.[46] These Bogor Goals represent the "open regionalism" principle, which encourages twenty-one members to accord liberalization benefits to other nations and arguably contracts inherently discriminatory regionalism.[47] Notwithstanding distinct structures of ASEAN and APEC, the two institutions have functioned as twin engines for Asian regionalism.

B Third Regionalism with Unique Characteristics

I refer to the third wave of global regionalism as the "Third Regionalism" that has developed in tandem with the WTO Doha Round since the 2000s. The "new" aspects of new Asian regionalism are intertwined with fundamental economic and geopolitical changes in the Third Regionalism, which lays the normative foundation for the NREO. Since

[42] Justin Yifu Lin, *From Flying Geese to Leading Dragons New Opportunities and Strategies for Structural Transformation in Developing Countries*, Policy Research Working Paper, No. 5702 (2011), at 4– 5.

[43] These economies include Indonesia, Malaysia, the Philippines, Thailand and Vietnam. Pakrashi & Frijters, *supra* note 41, at 4–5.

[44] Severino, *supra* note 31, at 222–23; WTO, *supra* note 28, at 96–97.

[45] Söderbaum & Van Langenhove, *supra* note 25, 256; Tom Ginsburg, *Authoritarian International Law*, 114(2) Am. J. Int'l L. 221, 243–44 (2020); Tom Ginsburg, *Eastphalia Asian Regionalism*, 44 UC Davis L: Rev. 859, 870–71 (2010–11).

[46] 1994 Leaders' Declaration (1994) (Bogor Declaration).

[47] John Ravenhill, *APEC and the Construction of Pacific Rim Regionalism* 140–42 (2001); Ippei Yamazawa, *APEC: New Agenda in Its Third Decade* 11–14 (2012).

2008, the WTO impasse resulting from unreconciled issues on agricultural market access and subsidies has invigorated states to turn from multilateralism to bilateralism and plurilateralism.[48] Trade agreements have thus proliferated.[49]

Growing populist nationalism has vastly weakened the hegemonic stability premised on dominant US power and the embedded liberalism that guided the post-war international order.[50] Under Xi Jinping's leadership, China's mercantilist-Leninist policy pursuing an assertive position on global rulemaking through platforms such as the Belt and Road Initiative has posed unprecedented challenges.[51] In Washington, the "China Reckoning" that recognized the failures of past US policy became a rare bipartisan consensus.[52] Multifaceted US-China tensions that Trump intensified will continue, as the Biden administration deems a more "authoritarian China" to be the "most serious competitor."[53]

On the EU side, protectionism similarly escalated amid the European debt crisis and the Brexit saga. Brussels' decreasing share of global trade "for two decades" and its limited security forces outside the EU's neighborhood have endangered its normative power.[54] The COVID-19 crisis has devastated nations across the Atlantic. Compared with the successful handling of the pandemic by Asia-Pacific countries such as Singapore,

[48] For the WTO's agricultural issues, see Randy Schnepf, *WTO Doha Round: Implications for U.S. Agriculture*, Congressional Research Services (CRS) Report (2014), at 1–11.

[49] From 2008 to 2021, the number of FTAs in force increased from 181 to 341. WTO, *supra* note 6.

[50] Anthea Roberts et al., *Toward a Geoeconomic Order in International Trade and Investment*, 22 *J.* Int'l Econ. *L.*655, 656–61 (2019); John Gerard Ruggie, *International Regimes, Transactions, and Change: Embedded Liberalism in the Postwar Economic Order*, 36 (2) Int'l Organ. 379, 392–98 (1982); Michael C. Webb & Stephen D. Krasner, *Hegemonic Stability Theory: An Empirical Assessment*, 15(2) Rev. Int'l Stud. 183, 183–86 (1989).

[51] Office of the Secretary of State, *The Elements of the China Challenge* (2020), at 4–36; Charles W. Boustany Jr. & Aaron L. Freidberg, *Answering China's Economic Challenge: Preserving Power, Enhancing Prosperity*, NBR Report, No. 76 (2019), at 25–27.

[52] Kurt M. Campbell & Ely Ratner, *The China Reckoning: How Beijing Defied American Expectation*, 97(2) Foreign Aff. 60, 60–68 (2018).

[53] White House, Interim National Security Strategic Guidance (2021), at 19–20; White House, *Remarks by President Biden on America's Place in the World*, Feb. 4, 2021, www.whitehouse.gov/briefing-room/speeches-remarks/2021/02/04/remarks-by-president-biden-on-americas-place-in-the-world/ (last visited Feb. 8, 2021).

[54] WTO, Trade Policy Review: Report by the Secretariat: European Union, WT/TPR/S/395 (2019), at 25. For the normative power concept, see Ian Manners, *Normative Power Europe: A Contradiction in Terms?* 40(2) J. Common Market Stud.235, 236–52 (2002).

Taiwan and New Zealand, sluggish US and EU responses have exacerbated doubts about Western governance models.[55]

In response to the WTO deadlock and hegemonic instability, countries have expedited trade pacts in the Third Regionalism. I identity four unique characteristics of FTAs that distinguish them from their counterparts in the first two waves of global regionalism. First, South-South FTAs that outpaced North-North FTAs in the 1990s now represent two-thirds of global trade pacts.[56] North-South FTAs and North-North FTAs, which had dominated the FTA landscape in the post-war era, account for 25 percent and 10 percent of current FTAs, respectively.[57] These trends symbolize developing countries' policy change from FTA conservatism to activism and their preferences over South-South FTAs.

Second, the Third Regionalism witnesses the emergence of mega-FTAs. As the CPTPP, the RCEP and the African Continental Free Trade Area (AfCFTA) evidence, these mega-pacts involve a significant number of countries with enormous collective economies of scale.[58] Based on their GDP, the RCEP, the USMCA, the post-Brexit EU and the CPTPP are the world's top four trading blocs.[59] As an ASEAN-led process, the RCEP alone accounts for 30 percent of global GDP.[60] Moreover, the AfCFTA, Mercosur and the Pacific Alliance are typical

[55] Lowy Institute, *Covid Performance Index: Deconstructing Pandemic Reponses*, https://interactives.lowyinstitute.org/features/covid-performance/ (last visited Feb. 23, 2021); Jinshan Hong, *The Covid Resilience Ranking: The Best and Worst Places to Be in Covid: U.S. Stages a Recovery*, Feb. 25, 2021, Bloomberg, www.bloomberg.com/graphics/covid-resilience-ranking/ (last visited Mar. 1, 2021).

[56] WTO, *supra* note 28, at 55–56.

[57] *Id.* Asia-Pacific FTAs follow similar trends, United Nations Economic and Social Commission for Asia and the Pacific, *Asia-Pacific Trade and Investment Report: Recent Trends and Development 2016* (2016), at 90.

[58] The African Continental Free Trade Area (AfCFTA) is the largest FTA by the number of participants. As Eritrea that has not signed the agreement, the AfCFTA includes fifty-four parties. Brock R. Williams & Nicolas Cook, *The African Continental Free Trade Area (AfCFTA)*, CRS: In Focus (2020), at 1.

[59] Their shares of global gross domestic product are 30 percent, 27.8 percent, 17.8 percent and 13.5 percent, respectively. Joint Leaders' Statement on the Regional Comprehensive Economic Partnership (RCEP) (Joint Leaders' Statement on the RCEP) (2020); ASEAN, *supra* note 7, at 127; Government of Canada, *About the Comprehensive and Progressive Agreement for Trans-Pacific Partnership*, July 16, 2019, www.international.gc.ca/trade-commerce/trade-agreements-accords-commerciaux/agr-acc/cptpp-ptpgp/back grounder-document_information.aspx?lang=eng (last visited Dec. 31, 2020); World Bank, *GDP (current US $;)*, https://data.worldbank.org/indicator/NY.GDP.MKTP.CD (Jan. 1, 2021).

[60] Joint Leaders' Statement on the RCEP, *supra* note 59; ASEAN Framework for Regional Comprehensive Economic Partnership (2011).

South-South FTAs because their membership includes only developing countries. Parties to these mega-FTAs will increase their agenda-setting and rule-making influence over global trade governance.

Third, interregional FTAs represent a new feature of economic agreements. Political scientists have developed detailed typologies of interregionalism.[61] "ASEAN Plus One" FTAs, the CPTPP and the RCEP are arguably interregional, as they connect East and South Asian and Pacific nations. Pursuant to Heiner Hänggi's definitions, prospective EU trade agreements with Mercosur and ASEAN constitute doctrinal cases of interregionalism.[62] Markedly, the new ASEAN-EU strategic partnership reiterated the bilateral FTA objective, which is to be implemented through the building-block approach based on EU trade and investment pacts with Singapore and Vietnam.[63] These agreements illustrate that interregionalism forms a key component of the Third Regionalism.

Finally, comprehensive FTAs became a norm. Trade agreements no longer focus merely on tariff and services liberalization. The comprehensiveness of FTAs can be judged by their WTO-plus and extra provisions, which refer to rules and commitments that exceed current WTO standards and that fall outside WTO obligations.[64] In comparison with South-South FTAs, North-North and North-South FTAs cover more WTO-plus and extra components, including those that can be legally enforced.[65]

The dichotomy between FTAs and bilateral investment treaties (BITs) became blurred, as modern FTAs often incorporate investment chapters. Investor-state dispute settlement (ISDS) reforms such as the EU-proposed Investment Court System are a hotly debated topic for both

[61] Heiner Hänggi, *Interregionalism as a Multifaceted Phenomenon: In Search of a Typology*, *in* Interregionalism and International Relations: A Stepping Stone to Global Governance? 31, 40–41 (Jürgen Ruland et al. 2005); Jürgen Ruland, *Interregionalism: An Unfinished Agenda*, *in* Interregionalism and International Relations: A Stepping Stone to Global Governance? 295, 295–97 (Jürgen Ruland et al. 2005); Vinod K. Aggarwal & Edward A. Fogarty, *Between Regionalism and Globalism: European Union Interregional Trade Strategies*, *in* EU Trade Strategies: Between Regionalism and Globalism 1, 5 (Vinod K. Aggarwal & Edward A. Fogarty eds. 2004).

[62] European Commission, *EU-Mercosur Trade Agreement: Building Bridges for Trade and Sustainable Development (2019)*; Co-Chairs' Press Release: 23rd ASEAN-EU Ministerial Meeting (2020) (23rd ASEAN-EU Ministerial Meeting), paras. 4–16.

[63] *Id.* para. 8; European Commission, *Trade for All: Towards a More Responsible Trade and Investment Policy* (2015), at 31–32.

[64] Claudia Hofmann et al., *Horizontal Depth: A New Database on the Content of Preferential Trade Agreements*, Policy Research Working Paper, No. 7981 (2017), at 4; Richard Baldwin, *Multilateralizing Asian Regionalism*, ADBI Working Paper Series, No. 431 (2013), at 8–9.

[65] Hofmann et al., *supra* note 64, at 22.

FTAs and BITs.[66] Governments have also underscored provisions on the disciplines of state-owned enterprises (SOEs) and sustainable development that mandates environmental and labor protection. In addition, as lockdowns and safe-distancing measures dramatically drove electronic commerce (e-commerce), rules on data flow and localization are a "new normal" for trade pacts.[67]

C ASEAN-Centered Regime in Asia

These unique FTA characteristics have enriched Asian integration. As a normative integration process, new Asian regionalism has developed with the ASEAN Plus Six framework. Distinct from the EU that has been premised on cooperation between France and Germany, the China-Japan rivalry has enabled ASEAN to propel Asian integration. Institutional interactions such as summits among ASEAN Plus Three countries that include China, South Korea and Japan commenced in the 1990s.[68]

The 1997 Asian financial crisis was the watershed occurrence. Asian countries' disappointment about US-led monetary institutions led to the signing of the 2000 Chiang Mai Initiative, which is a currency swap arrangement among ASEAN Plus Three nations.[69] This framework further expanded to the ASEAN Plus Six framework, including Australia, India and New Zealand as additional members. In the Third Regionalism, this sixteen-party framework has been at the core of the Asia-Pacific's economic and security cooperation.

ASEAN's constitutional moment occurred when it adopted the ASEAN Charter, which codified established practice and conferred legal personality on the bloc "as an inter-governmental" organization.[70] In 2015, the next milestone that converted an "association" to a "community" was the launching of the three-pillared ASEAN Community, which comprises the ASEAN Security Community, the ASEAN Socio-Cultural Community and the ASEAN Economic

[66] United Nations Commission on International Trade Law, https://uncitral.un.org/en/working_groups/3/investor-state (last visited Sept. 30, 2020); European Commission, *Consultation Strategy: Impact Assessment on the Establishment of a Multilateral Investment Court for Investment Dispute Resolution* (2016), at 1.

[67] *See generally* WTO, E-commerce, Trade and the COVID-19 Pandemic (2020), at 1–5.

[68] Severino, *supra* note 31, at 265–67.

[69] *Id.* This Initiative transformed to the Chiang Mai Initiative Multilateralization in 2010.

[70] Charter of the Association of Southeast Asian Nations (2007) (ASEAN Charter), art. 2(2)(m).

Community (AEC).[71] Based on the "Global ASEAN" objective of the AEC Economic Blueprint 2025, upgrading and consolidating ASEAN Plus One FTAs will integrate "the AEC into the global economy" and solidify ASEAN's centrality in regional frameworks.[72] These ASEAN Plus One FTAs were concluded between ASEAN as a bloc and six Dialogue Partners (China, Japan, India, South Korea, Australia and New Zealand).[73] The AEC and these FTAs form the ASEAN Plus Six framework and constitute the ASEAN-centered regime in the economic arena.

As Figure 1.1 below demonstrates, mega-FTAs including the CPTPP and the RCEP have further enriched legal regimes of new Asian regionalism. The Trans-Pacific Partnership (TPP) was the key instrument that advanced President Barack Obama's pivot to Asia strategy. Trump's decision to withdraw the United States from the TPP frustrated Asian allies. In 2018, Australia, Canada and Japan led the remaining parties to conclude the CPTPP, which is based on the TPP except for twenty-two suspended provisions.[74] The CPTPP covers four ASEAN countries, as well as seven CPTPP parties that are also APEC and RCEP members. While the eleven-party CPTPP does not technically form ASEAN's mega regime, the CPTPP has influenced ASEAN's internal and external pacts. Other ASEAN countries may also become new parties to the CPTPP.

Concluded in 2020, the fifteen-country RCEP became the latest mega-FTA. RCEP negotiations were conducted under the ASEAN Plus Six framework. Nevertheless, India decided to withdraw from the talks due to its concerns about trade deficits and limited access to external services markets.[75] As Figure 1.1 shows, India currently stands outside major regional trade initiatives. Notably, the inception of RCEP negotiations "ended the debate" between the China-preferred ASEAN Plus Three

[71] Tang Siew Mun, *Is ASEAN Due for a Makeover*, 39 (2) Contem. Southeast Asia 239, 243 (2017); ASEAN Secretariat, *ASEAN 2025: Forging Ahead Together* (2015).

[72] ASEAN, *supra* note 7, at 131–32; ASEAN Economic Community Economic Blueprint 2025 (2015), paras. 79–80.

[73] The ASEAN-Hong Kong FTA and Investment Agreements were concluded in 2017, but Hong Kong is not ASEAN's Dialogue Partner. For information on ASEAN's Dialogue Partners, see Severino, *supra* note 31, at 264–336.

[74] *See generally* Department of Foreign Affairs and Trade (DFAT), CPTPP Suspensions Explained (2019).

[75] ISEAS Yusof Ishak Institute, *Webinar on "Trade Implication of RCEP for ASEAN and India,"* Dec. 15, 2020, www.iseas.edu.sg/media/event-highlights/webinar-on-trade-implication-of-rcep-for-asean-and-india/ (last visited Jan. 8, 2021); Gaurav Choudhury, *India Decides Not to Join RCEP: Decoding the Reasons behind Its Decision*, Nov. 4, 2019, www.moneycontrol.com/news/economy/policy/india-decides-not-to-join-rcep-decoding-the-reasons-behind-its-decision-4602701.html (last visited Jan. 8, 2021).

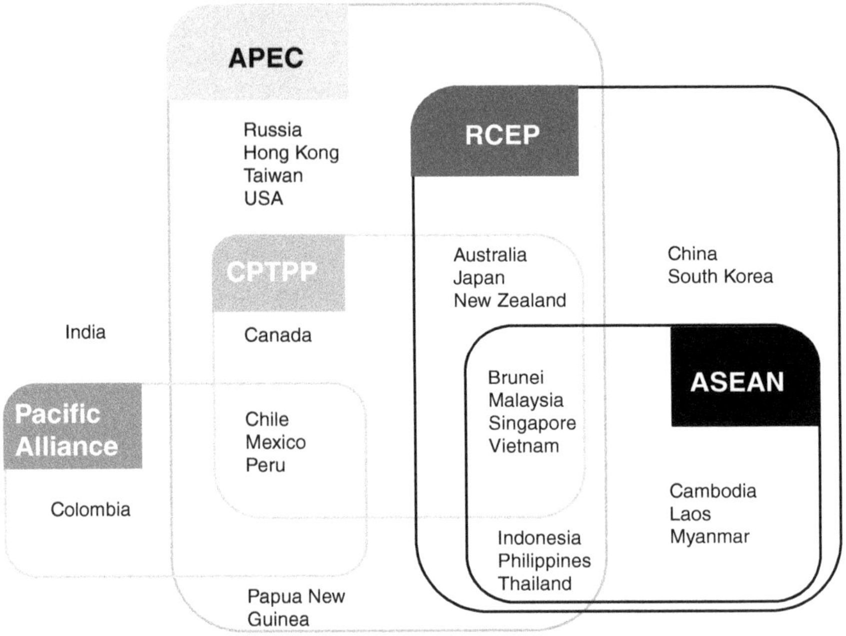

Figure 1.1 Major Asia-Pacific trade initiatives (2021)

model and Japan-supported ASEAN Plus Six approach.[76] Recognized by its members, the RCEP was initiated and led by ASEAN and will fortify ASEAN centrality in Asia-Pacific agreements.[77]

The CPTPP and the RCEP are both competing and complementary. Building upon the Bogor Goals, the APEC Putrajaya Vision 2040 reinstates APEC's incubator role for a prospective Free Trade Area of the Asia-Pacific (FTAAP) that consists of 21 APEC economies.[78] As pathways to the FTAAP, the two mega-FTAs will alleviate the "noodle bowl" syndrome

[76] DFAT, *Background to the Regional Comprehensive Economic Partnership (RCEP) Initiative*, www.dfat.gov.au/trade/agreements/negotiations/rcep/Pages/background-to-the-regional-comprehensive-economic-partnership-rcep-initiative (last visited Jan. 5, 2020). China and Japan proposed the East Asian Free Trade Area (EAFTA) and the Comprehensive Economic Partnership for East Asia (CEPEA), respectively, in the 2000s. Compared with the EAFTA, the CEPEA includes three more countries (Australia, India and New Zealand). Rodolfo C. Severino, *Japan's Relations with ASEAN*, *in* ASEAN-Japan Relations 17, 26–28 (Takashi Shiraishi & Takaaki Kojima eds. 2014).

[77] Joint Leaders' Statement on the RCEP, *supra* note 59; ASEAN Framework for Regional Comprehensive Economic Partnership (2011).

[78] 2020 Leaders' Declaration (2020).

caused by rules of origin under overlapping agreements.[79] Furthermore, the CPTPP and the RCEP highlight Asia's normative responses to populist nationalism and the post-pandemic recovery. Both pacts adopted open accession clauses that enable states and separate customs territories to join the pacts.[80] London's application for CPTPP membership and Hong Kong's intention to join the RCEP exemplify the magnifying global impact of new Asian regionalism.[81]

III Theoretical Dimensions and Normative Explanations

Based on empirical analyses, I contend that new Asian regionalism contributed to the NREO, which invigorates the role of developing countries in shaping international trade norms in the Third Regionalism. To bridge the gap between IR and legal studies on regionalism, I also introduce pertinent theoretical discussions with new dimensions and articulate the NREO as the normative framework that helps understand the changing paradigms of North-South relations.

A Regionalism Theories: Challenges and Limitations

Understanding new Asian regionalism in international economic law from an interdisciplinary perspective requires introducing regionalism theories, which rapidly evolved in the First Regionalism.[82] As one of the oldest political science theories, realism has been applied to analyze regionalism since European integration in the 1950s.[83] Classical realism or a more recent variant, neo-realism, considers the state-centric international system as an anarchy, which makes self-help essential for the

[79] 2010 Leaders' Declaration (2010); Richard Baldwin & Masahiro Kawai, *Multilateralizing Asian Regionalism*, ADBI Working Paper Series, No. 431 (2013), at 11–12.

[80] Progressive Agreement for Trans-Pacific Partnership (2018), art. 5; Regional Comprehensive Economic Partnership (2020), art. 20.9.

[81] Department for International Trade & The Rt Hon Elizabeth Truss MP, *UK Applies to Join Huge Pacific Free Trade Area CPTPP*, Jan. 30, 2021, www.gov.uk/government/news/uk-applies-to-join-huge-pacific-free-trade-area-cptpp (last visited Feb. 10, 2021); Natalie Wong, *Mainland Chinese Commerce Official Backs Hong Kong Joining RCEP Trade Bloc, with City Leader Carrie Lam Hoping to Start Talks "at Earliest Opportunity,"* Nov. 30, 2020, S. China Morning Post, www.scmp.com/news/hong-kong/hong-kong-economy/article/3111913/mainland-commerce-official-backs-hong-kong-joining (last visited Jan. 26, 2021).

[82] Breslin et al., *supra* note 18, at 2–3.

[83] Hurrell, *supra* note 21, at 45–46.

survival of nations.[84] As rational actors, countries pursue their power according to their national interests in the hegemonic world.

Realism has influenced the research area of international political economy by perceiving trade relations as a zero-sum game that compels states to maximize economic benefits.[85] Economic regionalism is understood "as a strategy in the game of neo-mercantilist competition."[86] Although realist studies have centered on great powers, scholars have also explored regionalism as an alliance formation against or restricting the exercise of hegemonic power.[87] As the ASEAN-centered regime illustrates, developing countries have utilized various balancing, bandwagoning and hedging strategies to buttress their collective power in Asia.[88]

Parallel to realism, discussions based on other mainstream IR theories flourished. Functionalism posits that rising interdependence between countries promotes integration.[89] Super-national institutions invigorate the "spillover" effect, which transforms cooperation of constituent states from technical matters of low politics into arenas of high politics.[90] Pursuant to institutionalism, regional structures create a set of rules and practices that increase efficiency and make state behavior predictable.[91] While sharing realism's premise on the anarchic, state-centric international system, institutionalism proffers a different conclusion for regional cooperation.[92]

[84] Realism and neorealism are primarily based on Hans Morgenthau, *Politics among Nations* (1954) and Kenneth Waltz's *Theory of International Politics* (1979). William C. Wohlforth, *Realism*, *in* The Oxford Handbook of International Relations 131, 132–37 (Christian Reus-Smit & Duncan Snidal eds. 2008).

[85] Jonathan Kirshner, *Realist Political Economy: Traditional Themes and Contemporary Challenges*, *in* Routledge Handbook of International Political Economy (IPE): IPE as a Global Conversation 36, 37–39 (Mark Blyth ed. 2009).

[86] Hurrell, *supra* note 21, at 48.

[87] *Id.* at 50; Fredrik Söderbaum, *supra* note 14, at 37–39; Stephan M. Walt, *Alliance Formation and the Balance of Power*, 9 (4) Int'l Sec.3, 4–8 (1985).

[88] Walt, *supra* note 87, at 5–8; Darren J. Lim & Zack Cooper, *Reassessing Hedging: The Logic of Alignment in East Asia*, 24 (4) Sec. Stud. 696, 697–99 (2015).

[89] Hurrell, *supra* note 21, at 59–61; Fredrik Söderbaum, *Old, New, and Comparative Regionalism: The History and Scholarly Development of the Field*, *in* The Oxford Handbook of Comparative Regionalism 16, 21–23 (Tanja A. Börzel & Thomas Risse eds. 2016).

[90] Hurrell, *supra* note 21, at 59.

[91] *Id.* at 61–63; Tobias Lenz & Gary Marks, *Regional Institutional Design*, *in* The Oxford Handbook of Comparative Regionalism 513, 518–20 (Tanja A. Börzel & Thomas Risse eds. 2016).

[92] Anne-Marie Slaughter & Thomas Hale, *International Relations, Principal Theories*, Oxford Public International Law (2013), https://opil.ouplaw.com/view/10.1093/law:epil/9780199231690/law-9780199231690-e722?prd=EPIL (last visited Feb. 3, 2021).

As political scientists concede, an inherent weakness of the theoretical discourse lies in an Euro-centric bias because of the methodology that universalizes European experiences without exploring other integration cases.[93] In the Second Regionalism, scholars began to challenge existing theoretical hypotheses and findings. They contended that theories based on European developments were "of little use in" understanding Asian regionalism, as its evolution contradicts theoretical predictions.[94] According to them, it would be an unwarranted assumption to perceive EU-style institutionalization as the standards by which to measure Asian regionalism to then reach the conclusion that Asian initiatives are improper and of low quality.[95] Notably, their stance is to strengthen theoretical and empirical investigations in other regions rather than utterly ignore European experiences.

These reflections gave rise to the constructivist understanding of regionalism in the 1990s.[96] Constructivism subscribes to ontology under which regional identity or awareness motivates regionalism.[97] Constructivists averred that inter-state relations are intersubjective and the struggles for the recognition of identities instead of material power provoke state actions.[98] In theorizing Asian regionalism, ASEAN became a salient case in comparison with the EU.[99]

To highlight challenges to theoretical weaknesses, Björn Hettne and Federick Söderbaum proposed the "new regionalism approach."[100] The objective of the approach is to remedy the overreliance on a single theory and to seek to broaden the ambit of empirical scrutiny. Thus, this approach denotes "a multidimensional process of regional integration" and encompasses "economic, political, social and cultural

[93] Söderbaum, *supra* note 14, at 7–9; Hurrell, *supra* note 21, at 60–63.

[94] Amitav Acharya, *Whose Ideas Matter? Agency and Power in Asian Regionalism* 27 (2009); Peter J. Katzenstein, *Introduction: Asian Regionalism in Comparative Perspective, in* Network Power: Japan and Asia 1, 5 (Peter J. Katzenstein & Takashi Shiraishi eds. 1997).

[95] Katzenstein, *supra* note 94, at 3; Breslin et al., *supra* note 18, at 13; Alice Ba, *Institutional Divergence and Convergence in the Asia-Pacific? ASEAN in Practice and in Theory*, 27 (2) Cam. Rev. Int'l Aff.295, 300 (2014).

[96] Söderbaum, *supra* note 89, at 27.

[97] Hurrell, *supra* note 21, at 64–65; Slaughter & Hale, *supra* note 92.

[98] Alexander Wendt, *Collective Identity Formation and the International State*, 88 (2) Am. Pol. Sci. Rev. 384, 384–85 (1994); Lenz & Marks, *supra* note 91, at 520–22.

[99] Amitav Acharya, *Constructing a Security Community in Southeast Asia: ASEAN and the Problem of Regional Order* 3–5 (3rd ed. 2014); Acharya, *supra* note 14, at 123–26; Lenz & Marks, *supra* note 91, at 521; Ba, *supra* note 95, at 304–06.

[100] Hettne, *supra* note 13, 22–23; Söderbaum, *supra* note 14, at 29–30; Acharya, *supra* note 14, at 119; Söderbaum, *supra* note 88, at 28.

aspects."[101] Although the new regionalism approach became influential, it was also criticized for encompassing "an eclectic body of literature" that does not amount to a theory.[102] Furthermore, the approach remains "somewhat EU-centric" because of its emphasis on Europe as "the most advanced" regionalism that propels the new regionalism.[103]

B Normative Framework of the NREO

In the Third Regionalism, political scientists urged the research to go even beyond the new regionalism approach and to buttress the attention to comparative regionalism that reflects the multipolar reality in the post-hegemonic world.[104] As the first book that systematically deciphers the legal regimes of new Asian regionalism, this research promotes interdisciplinary interactions by responding to theoretical challenges of IR research. The empirical discussions also fill the literature gaps by analyzing legal developments, which political scientists have been unable to do due to the disciplinary divide.

I propose the NREO as the normative framework through which to understand the contemporary dynamics of Asia-Pacific trade and investment agreements that have shaped new Asian regionalism. The NREO is distinct from the New International Economic Order (NIEO) movement in the 1970s. The NIEO crystalized developing countries' call for nonreciprocal preferences essential for development under the United Nations (UN) and the GATT.[105] In contrast with failed NIEO attempts, the NREO fortifies the collective power of developing countries and devises a South-based trade-development roadmap. New Asian regionalism symbolizes and reinforces the NREO in the multilateral trading system.

Conventional theoretical debates have been preoccupied with states' request for power or identity with less focus on the role of development in regionalism and its impact on North-South relations. To offer insight into the global context of new Asian regionalism, I employ the new dependency theory as the theoretical basis for the NREO. This new

[101] Hettne, *supra* note 38, at 11.

[102] Acharya, *supra* note 14, at 119. Scholars have used the new regionalism "approach" and the new regionalism "theory" interchangeably. *E.g.*, Dent, *supra* note 15, at 12.

[103] Acharya, *supra* note 14, at 119; Björn Hettne & Federick Söderbaum, *Theorising the Rise of Regionness*, 5 (3) New Pol. Eco. 457, 458 (2000).

[104] Björn Hettne, *Beyond the "New" Regionalism*, 10 (4) New Pol. Eco 543, 543–46 (2005); Söderbaum, *supra* note 14, 30–31; Söderbaum, *supra* note 89, at 29–32.

[105] Nils Gilman, *The New International Economic Order: A Reintroduction*, 6 (1) Humanity 1, 2–3 (2015); Rolland, *supra* note 11, at 45 & 69 (2012).

theoretical lens helps remedy the theoretical and empirical blind spots that IR scholars previously cautioned. Significantly, the dependency school shares the realist angle of national interests, but interprets the international system from a South-based standpoint.[106] Pursuant to Theotonio Dos Santos and Raúl Prebisch who advocated the NIEO, the unequal neocolonial trade relationship between dominant and subordinate economies resulted in the "underdevelopment" dilemma.[107]

Taking into account Latin American developments, classical dependency theorists asserted that external unfairness subordinated the development of the South to the self-interests of the North.[108] Global trade has accelerated the North-bound trade surplus from the South and has substantially worsened the dependency of the latter.[109] This inherent structure caused the unequal relationship between the "central" and "peripheral" countries.[110] Getting out of the structure of dependency would require the South to sever economic ties with the North and focus on South-South trade to implement the self-reliance model of import substitution.[111] Nonetheless, their neo-Marxist stance contravenes the economic trajectory of many developing countries in Asia.

In response to the shortfall of the classical dependency theory, the new dependency theory argued for the possible coexistence of dependency and development.[112] Academics observed that the nature of dependency can be dynamic because developing countries could transform dependent capitalism into export-driven economies.[113] Instead of becoming "trapped" in

[106] Alan Gilbert, *Must Global Politics Constrain Democracy? Great-Power Realism, Democratic Peace, and Democratic Internationalism* 32–33 (1999); Alvin Y. So, *Social Change and Development: Modernization, Dependency, and World-System Theories* 91–98 (1990).

[107] Fernando Henrique Cardoso & Enzo Faletto, *Dependency and Development in Latin America* 16–19 (Marjory Mattingly Urquidi trans. 1979); Theotonio Dos Santos, *The Structure of Dependence*, 60 (2) Am. Econ. Rev. 231, 231–34 (1970); Rolland, *supra* note 11, at 20–21.

[108] Cardoso & Faletto, *supra* note 107, at 16–17; Richard Peet & Elaine Hartwick, *Theories of Development: Contentions, Arguments, Alternatives* 188–89 (3d ed. 2015).

[109] So, *supra* note 106, at 95–102.

[110] Cardoso & Faletto, *supra* note 108, at 16–17; Peet & Hartwick, *supra* note 108, 188.

[111] So, *supra* note 106, at 98–106.

[112] *Id.* at 157–65.

[113] For example, South Korea and Taiwan have had dependent relations with US and Japan markets. *Id.*; James Mahoney et al., *Dependency Theory*, *in* The Oxford Handbook of the Politics of Development 22, 28–29 (Carol Lancaster & Nicolas van de Walle 2018); Thomas Baron Gold, *State and Society in the Taiwan Miracle* 21–90 (1986); David Kang, *South Korean and Taiwanese Development and the New Institutional Economics*, 49 (3) Int'l Organ.555, 586 (1995).

the unequal external relationship, the new dependency theory highlights the impact of the South's internal structures on reforming neocolonial ties with the North.[114] Development experiences of Asian Tigers verify the hypothesis of the theory. As ASEAN and the RCEP exemplify, modern South-South FTAs that streamline the regional supply chain enhance the cost-effectiveness and enable developing nations to alter the North-South structure that was once perceived as unfair. Consequently, the new dependency theory underlines the theoretical basis for the NREO.

The shift from the NIEO to the NREO has fundamentally influenced global and Asian trade orders. Even prior to the birth of ASEAN, the idea for Asian regionalism surfaced at the Indonesia-hosted Bandung Conference in which anticolonial nationalism of Asian-African states elevated the Non-Aligned Movement.[115] Similar to what classical dependency theorists suggested, these countries' main focus was political solidarity. The economic aspect of South-South cooperation was confined to the nationalistic concept of self-help that sought to minimize reliance on the North.[116]

In the 1970s, Non-Aligned Movement members joined the Group of 77 in passing the UN Declaration that calls for NIEO principles, which demanded absolute sovereignty and affirmative action in international trade norms.[117] Their endeavors through the UN Conference on Trade and Development (UNCTAD) shaped trade-development rules under the Part IV of the GATT.[118] In particular, the UNCTAD pushed for the GATT to incorporate core provisions on special and differential treatment. These provisions included the nonreciprocity exception to the most-favored-nation principle and the 1979 Enabling Clause, which granted the South preferential market access to the North and facilitated trading schemes between developing countries.[119]

[114] So, *supra* note 106, at 137–65.

[115] Amita Acharya, *Foundations of Collective Action in Asia: Theory and Practice of Regional Cooperation*, ADBI Working Paper Series, No. 344 (2012), at 5–16.

[116] *Id.*

[117] 3201 (S-VI). Declaration on the Establishment of a New International Economic Order, A/RES/S-6/3201 (1974); Karl P. Sauvant, *The Early Days of the Group of 77*, www.un.org/en/chronicle/article/early-days-group-77 (last visited Mar. 1, 2021); Gilman, *supra* note 105, at 2.

[118] Rolland, *supra* note 11, at 20–21.

[119] General Agreement on Tariffs and Trade (GATT) (1994), art. XXXVI:8; Differential and More Favorable Treatment of Reciprocity and Fuller Participation of Developing Countries, GATT Doc. L/4903 (1979). GATT contracting parties adopted the permanent Enabling Clause after the 1971 decision, which granted a ten-year waiver permitting generalized system of preferences to depart from GATT norms. Generalized System of Preferences, Decision of 25 June 1971, L/3545 (1971); Rolland, *supra* note 11, at 72.

Nevertheless, the NIEO movement quickly waned during the Uruguay Round, as debt crises caused developing countries to diverge on their positions on the North and the Thatcher-Reagan alliance rejected additional demands from the South.[120] The creation of Bretton Woods institutions empowered the "Washington Consensus" to become golden rules for economic reforms and compelled the South to engage in North-defined free trade.[121] Notwithstanding the inclusion of more special and differential treatment requirements such as technical assistance and transition periods, the WTO has been criticized for ignoring countries' development needs.[122]

Ironically, the neoliberal Washington Consensus is by no means a panacea for development. In fact, policy reforms including trade and investment liberalization, privatization and deregulation sustained "underdevelopment" of Latin America, thus exacerbating their dependency on the North.[123] In comparison, the developmental state model that centered on state-controlled industrial policy, utilized export subsidies and gradually liberalized import regimes led to the rapid growth of East Asian countries.[124]

C *Asia's Quest for a New Consensus*

In the Third Regionalism, the WTO Doha Development Agenda and the UN Sustainable Development Goals prompted developing countries to rethink their trade strategies for development.[125] The NREO reflects developing countries' frustrations about the NIEO and the Washington Consensus and manifests their efforts to reconstruct a development-friendly economic order. Importantly, there are three intertwined levels of legal norms that underpin new Asian regionalism. APEC continues to be a key forum that yields soft-law instruments that form "common law" in the Asia-Pacific.[126] Bilateral FTAs that include particularly those

[120] Chantal Thomas & Joel P. Trachtman, *Editors' Introduction*, *in* Developing Countries in the WTO Legal System 1, 9 (Chantal Thomas & Joel P. Trachtman eds. 2009).

[121] *Id.* at 9–10; Rolland, *supra* note 11, at 51. John Williamson coined the term "Washington Consensus." John Williamson, *The Strange History of the Washington Consensus*, 27 (2) J. Post Keynesian Eco. 195, 195–97 (2004).

[122] Thomas & Trachtman, *supra* note 120, at 10–11.

[123] Peet & Hartwick, *supra* note 108, 98–99; Dani Rodrik, *Straight Talk on Trade: Ideas for a Sane World Economy* 36 (2018).

[124] Stephan Haggard, *Developmental States* 1–30 (2018); Rodrik, *supra* note 123, at 36.

[125] *See generally* Ministerial Declaration, WT/MIN(01)/DEC/1 (2001); Resolution adopted by the General Assembly on 25 September 2015, A/RES/70/1 (2015).

[126] For soft law theories, see Andrew T. Guzman & Timothy L. Meyer, *International Soft Law*, 2 (1) J. Legal Analysis 171, 187–202 (2010).

concluded with the North such as the US-Korea FTA and the EU-Vietnam FTA invigorate hard-law requirements in politically sensitive areas including sustainable development and human rights. The ASEAN's mega-regime built on the ASEAN Plus Six framework situates in between the two levels and constitutes the core driving force for the NREO.

In essence, the NREO is a process through which Asian countries request a trade-development model other than the Washington Consensus. Unlike the NIEO, the NREO seeks to transform rather than cut trade ties with the North. The rise of China triggered interest in the "Beijing Consensus."[127] This Chinese model relies heavily on the role of SOEs in advancing economic objectives of authoritarian governments and features vast infrastructure-focused investment.[128] Arguably, increasing concerns about China's "debt-trap diplomacy" under the Belt and Road Initiative and its cover-up on the coronavirus have undermined the Beijing Consensus.[129]

Distinct from China's party-state system, some Asian democracies offer different lessons. With the technological evolution, they have gradually altered the center-periphery relationship beyond what new dependency theorists had depicted. For instance, the global shortage of semiconductor chips has severely impacted technology industries that produce 5G mobile phones and laptops essential to the "work from home" mode amid the COVID-19 pandemic. The shortage also halted the production of German and US-made automobiles particularly because self-driving and electric cars require additional chips.[130] Remarkably, Taiwan and South Korea dominate the market by producing almost 80 percent of the world's chips.[131] The advancement of their high-tech industry thus makes the North dependent on them in critical

[127] Joshua Copper Ramo created the term "Beijing Consensus." Michael W. Dowdle et al., *Dialogus de Beijing Consensus, in* The Beijing Consensus? How China Has Changed Western Ideas of Law and Economic Development 15, 15–26 (Weitseng Chen ed. 2017).

[128] Gregory Shaffer & Henry Gao, *A New Chinese Economic Order*? 23 (3) J. Int'l Econ. L. 607, 610–11 (2020).

[129] Pradumna B Rana & Ji Xianbai, *BRI's "Debt Trap Diplomacy,"* RISI Commentary, No. 191 (2020), at 1–2.

[130] Hiroyuki Koizumi, *Global Chip Shortage Threatens Automakers Worldwide*, Jan. 9, 2021, Nikkei Asia, https://asia.nikkei.com/Business/Automobiles/Global-chip-shortage-threatens-automakers-worldwide (last visited Mar. 5, 2021).

[131] TSMC (Taiwan), Samsung (South Korea) and UMC (Taiwan) are the world's top three semiconductor chips manufacturers. *Total Revenue of Top 10 Foundries Expected to Increase by 18% YoY in 4Q20 While UMC Overtakes GlobalFoundries for Third Place, Says TrendForce*, Dec. 7, 2020, www.trendforce.com/presscenter/news/20201207-10587.html (last visited Mar. 5, 2021).

sectors. Biden's 2021 executive order to secure critical supply chains that include semiconductor chips as "essential products" best illustrate the new change to the neocolonial dependency ties.[132]

More fundamental to the NREO, the ASEAN Plus Six framework resulted in a new "ASEAN Consensus" in Asia. The Washington or Beijing Consensus attempted to create an international order that bolsters the realist power of hegemonies. However, the ASEAN Consensus helps forge an Asian identity from a constructivist view and formulates interdependent, predictable regional structures that functionalism and institutionalism posit. The approach to legal and economic reforms follows pragmatic incrementalism and seeks a policy balance between the Washington and Beijing Consensuses. While taking into account Asian Tigers' experiences, the ASEAN Consensus relies more on a regional alliance scheme that keeps the bloc in commend of new trade dynamics.[133] The consensus has converged on the positions of ASEAN Plus Six countries such as China and Japan. It is also recognized by the United States and the EU, which pledged "to support ASEAN Centrality and ASEAN-led mechanisms in the evolving regional architecture."[134]

The ASEAN Consensus represents the multilateralization of the "ASEAN way" under the ASEAN Plus Six framework. The ASEAN way embodied the Indonesian notions of *musyawarah* and *mufakat* (consultations and consensus) and built the foundation for ASEAN's formative years and consequent operations.[135] Emphasizing principles of consensus, sovereign equality and noninterference in internal affairs, the ASEAN way denotes both a code of conduct and a decision-making process.[136] The unique approach of reaching consensus following informal consultations departs from the majority-vote system and does not equate with unanimity.[137]

I do not claim that the ASEAN approach is "the perfect model." It is nonetheless "a feasible model" for the Global South. It cannot be denied that

132 White House, *Fact Sheet: Securing America's Critical Supply Chains*, Feb. 24, 2021, www.whitehouse.gov/briefing-room/statements-releases/2021/02/24/fact-sheet-securing-americas-critical-supply-chains/ (last visited Mar. 1, 2021).

133 Walter Woon, *The ASEAN Chapter: A Commentary* 71–72 (2016).

134 Co-chairs' Press Release of the 23rd ASEAN-EU Ministerial Meeting (2020); Chairman's Statement of the 8th ASEAN-United States Summit (2020), para. 5.

135 Severino, *supra* note 31, at 1–23; Acharya, *supra* note 99, at 62–66.

136 UNCTAD, ASEAN at 50: Achievements and Challenges in Regional Integration 6–7 (2017); Amitav Archarya, *Ideas, Identity, and Institution-Building: From the "ASEAN Way" to the "Asia-Pacific Way"?* 10 (3) Pac. Rev. 319, 328 (1997); Acharya, *supra* note 99, at 62–66.

137 Acharya, *supra* note 99, at 65; Acharya, *supra* note 136, at 331.

the ASEAN way has created a level of comfort that enables the bloc to move slowly but steadily make notable progress since the founding of ASEAN.[138] It is no longer correct to characterize the ASEAN way as a pure political or soft-law concept. The legalization of the ASEAN way through the ASEAN Charter and the AEC extends the application to treaty implementation and demonstrates hard-law obligations with structured flexibility.[139]

The ASEAN way emerged as a consensus for new Asian regionalism also because its core values correspond to Confucianism-based legal cultures in East Asia. Confucius' emphasis of *li* (virtues) over *fa* (law) has led to the public aversion to the use of the formal dispute settlement system.[140] This feature was not only prominent in ancient China, but also incorporated in the Qing Dynasty's nineteenth-century treaties with Britain and America mandating officials' duty to amicably solve disputes.[141] The preference over non-ligation approaches resulted in the proliferation of arbitral institutions in Asia and strong support for mediation provisions in FTAs, BITs and other pacts such as the Singapore Convention on Mediation.[142]

Also comparable to the ASEAN way, Confucian values based on interpersonal trust have influenced contractual and treaty negotiations. An agreement is often regarded as a relationship or confidence-building process. The legal practice evidenced in Asian states such as China and Korea is to first have generic rather than detailed agreements and reserve

138 Marty Natalegawa, *Does ASEAN Matter? A View from Within* 28–29 (2018); Kishore Mahbubani & Jeffery Sng, *The ASEAN Miracle: A Catalyst for Peace* 2–3 (2017).

139 *E.g.*, ASEAN Charter, arts. 20 & 21; Sungjoon Cho & Jurgen Kurtz, *Legalizing the ASEAN Way: Adopting and Reimagining the ASEAN Investment Regime*, 66 Am. J. Com. L. 233, 253–55 (2018); David Chin Soon Siong, *ASEAN's Journey towards Free Trade, in* Economic Diplomacy: Essays and Reflections by Singapore's Negotiations 209, 216 (C. L. Lim & Margaret Liang eds. 2011).

140 According to the Analects of Confucius, he stated that "[i]n hearing lawsuits, I am no different from other people. What we need for there to be no lawsuits!" (聽訟, 吾猶人也, 必也使無訟乎!); Joshua Karton, *Beyond the "Harmonious Confucian": International Commercial Arbitration and the Impact of Chinese Cultural Values, in* Legal Thoughts between the East and the West in the Multilevel Legal Order: Liber Amicorum in Honor of Professor Herbert Han-pao Ma 519, 525–26 (Chang-fa Lo et al. eds. 2016).

141 *E.g.*, China-United Kingdom Treaty of Bogue (1843), art. XIII; China-United States Treaty of Tientsin (1858), art. I.

142 *E.g.*, Weixia Gu, *China's Arbitration Modernisation under Judicial Efforts and Marketisation Waves, in* The Developing World of Arbitration: A Comparative Study of Arbitration Reform in the Asia Pacific 17, 19–29 (Anselmo Reyes & Weixia Gu eds. 2018). The Singapore Convention on Mediation entered into force in 2020. *Entry into Force Celebration*, www.singaporeconvention.org/events/scm2020 (last visited Aug. 3, 2020).

flexibility for implementation.[143] This practice facilitates these countries' reception of the ASEAN integration approach that commences with a framework agreement, followed by specific pacts on tariffs, services, investment and dispute settlement.[144] These agreements collectively form integral parts of FTAs. This pragmatic incrementalism manifests the landmark feature of most ASEAN Plus One agreements and has influenced trade agreements between China and Taiwan.[145] Although these normative features are different from the Western notion of legalization, they have immensely refined legal frameworks of new Asian regionalism.[146]

IV Structure and Objectives of the Book

This book makes the case for new Asian regionalism as a paradigm shift in international economic law. By systematically examining legal regimes, the book substantiates the contention that new Asian regionalism has surfaced in the Third Regionalism and contributed to the NREO, which enhances the role of developing countries in shaping global trade norms. The methodology to achieve the goal is eclectic. It focuses on unique structures and principles of the ASEAN Plus Six framework and Asia's major economic institutions and agreements. To underscore the international significance of the research, the book also provides a comprehensive understanding of the endogenous and exogenous impact on Asia-Pacific agreements. Legal analyses and findings of new Asian regionalism will therefore energize theoretical and empirical debates of global regionalism.

Following Chapter 1 that introduces theoretical and normative concepts, Chapter 2 investigates the origin of the ASEAN framework and the legalization of the ASEAN way that has influenced ASEAN's internal and external FTAs. It details the evolution of ASEAN's economic integration under the AEC Blueprint 2025. By challenging the assumption of viewing ASEAN as an incomplete EU, the chapter identities key differences between the two blocs in the legal status of regional treaties and treaty-making power. It also discusses how pragmatic incrementalism has been applied to AEC agreements, such as tariff liberalization flexibility for Cambodia, Laos, Myanmar and Vietnam and the "package" structure of

143 *E.g.*, Dong-Young Kim, *Adapting the MGA for Negotiating with South Korean Counterparts*, Asialink Bus. (2015), at 3.

144 Chin, *supra* note 139, 217–30.

145 Pasha L. Hsieh, *The China-Taiwan ECFA, Geopolitical Dimensions and WTO Law*, 14 (1) J. Int'l Econ. L. 121, 140–47 (2011).

146 Cho & Kurtz, *supra* note 139, at 245–49; Woon, *supra* note 133, at 157–58.

services liberalization. ASEAN's implementation of US-style ISDS and state-to-state dispute settlement mechanisms modelled after the WTO, as well as e-commerce and development schemes, offer critical lessons for developing nations. Collectively, AEC agreements and commitments have shaped the ASEAN-centered regime in Asia-Pacific FTAs.

The conclusion of the RCEP that was negotiated under the ASEAN Plus Six structure signifies a milestone in new Asian regionalism. To echo the analysis in Chapter 2, Chapter 3 explains the multilateralization of the ASEAN way under the RCEP. The chapter first clarifies the common misconception that RCEP talks were dominated by China. Instead, the RCEP is recognized to be initiated and led by ASEAN. In addition, the argument against the RCEP's quality and ambition often ignores the Asian approach of pragmatic incrementalism. Although the RCEP will coexist with current trade and investment pacts, the de facto consolidation of rules of origin under the AEC and ASEAN Plus One FTAs will result in immediate and substantial benefits to businesses.

The chapter further evaluates the impact of the RCEP on the ASEAN centrality and China's trade strategy, as well as India's concerns that led to its withdrawal from RCEP negotiations. In terms of substantive contents, the chapter compares the RCEP with the CPTPP and other ASEAN agreements. It focuses on the RCEP's tariff liberalization, hybrid services schedules, and the omission of ISDS and SOE rules. Moreover, it deciphers the RCEP's implications for regional and global trading systems such as the forum shopping problem and the institutionalization of the prospective RCEP Secretariat.

Chapter 4 turns to underexplored dimensions of the EU's influences on new Asian regionalism. While Brussels' agreements with Japan, Korea and Comprehensive Agreement on Investment with China have attracted much academic attention, trade and investment pacts with Singapore and Vietnam constitute building-blocks for the ASEAN-EU FTA. The structure of agreements in line with the Court of Justice of the EU's Opinion 2/15 is of significance to both the EU and Asian states. Parallel to my claim for the Third Regionalism, the new development of ASEAN-EU ties led to the "Third Interregionalism" that elevated bilateral ties to the new strategic partnership in 2020.[147]

The chapter scrutinizes the comparison between EU agreements with Singapore and Vietnam as pathfinders to the ASEAN-EU FTA. In particular, it explores the legal concept of "ASEAN cumulation" and special

[147] Co-Chairs' Press Release: 23rd ASEAN-EU Ministerial Meeting (2020), para. 4.

rules for Asian good products in EU FTAs with two ASEAN countries. It also identifies potential weaknesses of FTAs in areas of services liberalization and digital trade and analyzes salient provisions on non-tariff barriers and geographical indications. As for Investment Protection Agreements, the chapter explains the two-tiered Investment Court System and mediation rules for investor-state disputes. It also considers how Partnership and Cooperation Agreements may suspend FTAs in cases of violations of human rights and sustainable development requirements, which mandate enforceable environmental and labor standards. EU sanctions in response to present situations in Cambodia and Myanmar including the Rohingya crisis and the military coup may have led to a deterioration of ASEAN-EU relations. Nevertheless, the bilateral legal frameworks have substantially enriched the normative development of interregionalism.

Supplemental to Chapter 4's analysis of the exogenous impact, Chapter 5 illuminates US influences on Asian trade and investment pacts in line with the changing trade strategies of the Obama, Trump and Biden administrations. More specifically, it explains legal challenges to the US-China trade war including the national security exception under Article XXI of the GATT and the implementation of the Phase One deal. To situate the ASEAN-US strategic partnership in the wider context of the Indo-Pacific strategy, the chapter examines negotiations of US FTAs and Trade and Investment Framework Arrangements with ASEAN countries. To advance Biden's agenda to restore US credibility and reunite Asian allies, I urge the White House to rethink its potential accession to the CPTPP and a strategy for the ASEAN-US FTA. To strengthen the claims, the chapter evaluates the suspended provisions of the TPP and side letters that involve ISDS and intellectual property, as well as ASEAN and EU models for the prospective ASEAN-US FTA.

Notwithstanding proliferating economic agreements, Chapter 6 contends that APEC's role in rejuvenating new Asian regionalism should not be underestimated. The chapter details APEC's decision-making process and its three-phased evolution since the 1980s. Legal and political strategies of critical stakeholders such as ASEAN, Australia, China, Japan and the United States have influenced the direction and operation of APEC. As a trans-Pacific forum, APEC has converged the consensus on trade and investment matters that led to model rules, nonbinding principles and trade facilitation cooperation. Contrary to the conventional understanding, minimizing concerns for "sovereign costs" has galvanized economies to make extra and innovative commitments.[148]

More fundamentally, APEC demonstrates the transformation from soft-law commitments to hard-law obligations by facilitating the passage of the Information Techonomic Agreement and supporting negotiations for the Environmental Goods Agreement at the WTO. To realize the APEC Putrajaya Vision 2040, I suggest that APEC professionalize its secretariat and fortify the peer-review process. Looking forward, APEC's constructive incubator role in advancing the expansion of agreements such as the CPTPP and RCEP will contribute to the FTAAP.

Chapter 7 concludes the book. Asia has transformed and progressed dramatically in the post-war era. A sound legal architecture is critical for buttressing economic institutions and implementing new agreements. Based on empirical findings of the book, I hope the recommendations for enterprises and governments will reinforce the legal regimes of new Asian regionalism and provide valuable lessons for the multilateral trading system.

[148] The concept of sovereign costs, see Chris Brummer, *Why Soft Law Dominates International Finance – and Not Trade*, 13 (3) J. Int'l Econ. L. 623, 623–24 (2010); Harmut Hillgenberg, *A Fresh Look at Soft Law*, 10 (3) Eur. J. Int'l L. 500, 509.

2

The Legalization of the ASEAN Economic Community

I Introduction

The rise of Asia has resulted in salient implications for regionalism theories and international economic law. As the first institutionalized bloc in Asia, the Association of Southeast Asian Nations (ASEAN) has prompted political scientists to reevaluate Eurocentric theories in the context of global regionalism. Premised on constructivism, some scholars argue for understanding ASEAN's regionalism via the lens of the emerging regional identity.[1] Looking beyond the realist view of the balance of power, other commentators aver that ASEAN created a regime that has channeled competing powers into a norm-based regional structure.[2]

It is now widely acknowledged that the ASEAN framework constitutes the origin and indispensable pillar of new Asian regionalism.[3] From a legal perspective, it is imperative to decipher the structure of ASEAN based on South-based regionalism and its implications for the normative framework of the New Regional Economic Order (NREO). Amid rising protectionism

1 Amitav Acharya, *The Quest for Identity: International Relations of Southeast Asia* 1–3 (2000); Alice Ba, *Institutional Divergence and Convergence in the Asia-Pacific? ASEAN in Practice and in Theory*, 27(2) *Cam. Rev. Int'l Aff.* 295, 304–06 (2014).

2 Evelyn Goh, *Great Powers and Hierarchical Order in Southeast Asia: Analyzing Regional Securities Strategies*, 32(3) Int'l Security 113, 139–40 (2007/08); Vinod K. Aggarwal & Jonathan T. Chow, *The Perils of Consensus: How ASEAN's Meta-regime Undermines Economic and Environmental Cooperation*, 17(2) Rev. Int'l Pol. Econ. 262, 267–69 (2010).

3 *E.g.*, Tran Van Hoa, *Globalisation,* Crises and the Emergence of New Asian Regionalism: Genesis and Current Development, *in* New Asian Regionalism: Responses to Globalisation and Crises 9, 9–15 (Tran Van Hoa & Charles Harve eds. 2003); Ellen L. Frost, *Asia's New Regionalism* 132–35 (2008); Amitav Acharya, *Foundations of Collective Action in Asia: Theory and Practice of Regional Cooperation*, ADBI Working Paper Series, No. 344 (2012), at 5–14.

and sluggish World Trade Organization (WTO) negotiations, ASEAN's evolving structure from 1967 to 2021 provides valuable lessons for revitalizing the trade-development nexus and global production networks.

Markedly, the founding of ASEAN was driven by political rather than economic considerations. Pursuant to the Bangkok Declaration, Indonesia, Malaysia, the Philippines, Singapore and Thailand established the bloc in 1967 as a loose security alliance to contain widespread communism.[4] Given Cold War hostilities and sustained armed conflicts that made the region known as the Balkans of Asia, ASEAN was deemed to be "born to fail, not to succeed."[5] ASEAN subsequently expanded to a ten-member organization in 1999, following the accession of Brunei and the addition of four least-development members, Cambodia, Laos, Myanmar and Vietnam (known as CLMV countries). The vast development gap between the six earlier members and CLMV countries gave rise to a two-tiered ASEAN that has posed hurdles to effective integration.

Despite multifaceted "birth defects," ASEAN grew into a rising trade power and illustrates the collective power of the Global South in a multipolar world. As Asia's third largest economy next to China and India, the ten-country bloc is poised to become the fourth largest economy by 2030.[6] The establishment of the ASEAN Economic Community (AEC) in 2015 is a milestone amid the global wave of the Third Regionalism since the inception of the Doha Round. Transforming from an "association" to a "community" signifies a higher degree of integration and reinforces the concept of ASEAN law based on internal and external agreements of the bloc.[7] Divergent from the European path, the legalization of the AEC and emerging ASEAN law enriches the normative construction of the NREO and provides an alternative model for developing countries.

Facing populist nationalism in the Global North, ASEAN has transformed into a hub that solidifies Asia-Pacific economies to pursue liberalization through free trade agreements (FTAs). From 2002 to 2017, ASEAN signed "ASEAN Plus One" FTAs sequentially with China, Japan, India, Korea, Australia and New Zealand and Hong Kong. The ASEAN-centered regime also includes the Regional Comprehensive

[4] *ASEAN Historical Timeline, in* 50 Years of ASEAN and Singapore xiii–xvi (Tommy Koh et al. eds. 2017).

[5] Kishore Mahbubani & Jeffery Sng, *The ASEAN Miracle: A Catalyst for Peace* 3–5 (2017).

[6] The Association of Southeast Asian Nations (ASEAN): 12 Things to Know, Nov. 8, 2017, www.adb.org/features/asean-12-things-know (last visited Nov. 15, 2019).

[7] Tang Siew Mun, *Is ASEAN Due for a Makeover*, 39(2) Contem. Southeast Asia 239, 243 (2017).

Economic Partnership (RCEP), for which ten ASEAN states and five partners "concluded text-based negotiations" in 2019 and signed the agreement in 2020.[8] Albeit India's pending decision to join the RCEP, this mega-FTA will be the world's largest trade pact in economic scale and will augment ASEAN's influence. Comparable to ASEAN-initiated security arrangements such as the ASEAN Regional Forum, these FTAs buttress ASEAN centrality, a notion that the ASEAN Chapter mandated to maintain the "driver's seat" status of the bloc for new Asian regionalism.[9]

The chapter will provide the most up-to-date examination of the legalization of the AEC. In particular, it will offer insight into the major characteristics of the new AEC Blueprint 2025 and the changing nature of the "ASEAN way" that have collectively shaped Asian integration. Furthermore, it will analyze ASEAN's evolving legal framework that governs trade in goods, trade in services, investment protection and liberalization and dispute settlement. Emerging areas such as banking services, electronic commerce (e-commerce) and development assistance will also be discussed. Importantly, ASEAN's economic integration trajectory is distinct from the neoliberal approach premised on the Washington Consensus. The chapter will explain why and how the ASEAN approach guided by the pragmatic incrementalism could benefit the development of the Global South. Finally, the chapter will examine the externalization of the ASEAN way under ASEAN's external agreements that underpin the regional economic architecture.

II Building the AEC under the Evolving ASEAN Way

As ASEAN's founding document, the Bangkok Declaration reveals that member states were preoccupied only with economic cooperation instead of economic integration in the 1960s. They merely committed to promoting "the greater utilization of their agriculture and industries, including the study of the problems of international commodity trade."[10] The rationale was due to the postcolonial mindset of nationalism and

[8] ASEAN Framework for Regional Comprehensive Economic Partnership (2011); Joint Leaders' Statement on the Regional Comprehensive Economic Partnership (RCEP) (2019); Joint Leaders' Statement on the Regional Comprehensive Economic Partnership (RCEP) (2020).

[9] Charter of the Association of Southeast Asian Nations (2007) (ASEAN Charter), art. 2(2)(m); Walter Woon, *The ASEAN Charter: A Commentary* 71–72 (2016).

[10] *See generally* The Association of Southeast Asian Nations (ASEAN) Declaration (Bangkok Declaration) (1967), aims & purposes 1, 3 and 5.

protectionism, as well as the development strategy of import substitution rather than the export-led growth (with the exception of Singapore).[11] To ensure a commercially viable market for large industrial projects and to efficiently allocate regional resources, ASEAN countries signed the first economic agreement in 1977.[12] Although the agreement called for preferential trading arrangements, it failed to increase intra-ASEAN trade because of high tariff rates and lengthy exclusion lists. The product-by-product negotiations generated meaningless items for liberalization such as snow ploughs that are hardly used in the tropical region.[13]

Confronting global regionalism and the economic rise of China and India, ASEAN states shifted their focus to trade liberalization and decided to form the ASEAN Free Trade Area (AFTA) in 1992.[14] The results remained unsatisfactory, as insignificant margins of preferences and complex procedures for meeting the rules of origin necessary for preferential tariffs led to a low utilization of the scheme by businesses.[15] In response to the 1997 Asian financial crisis and the urgent need to deepen cooperation beyond tariff reductions, Singapore Prime Minister Goh Chok Tong proposed the AEC concept in 2002.[16] The following year, ASEAN leaders endorsed the plan of the Bali Concord II to establish an ASEAN Community "comprising three pillars."[17] These intertwined pillars encompass the AEC, the ASEAN Security Community and the ASEAN Socio-Cultural Community.

In 2007, ASEAN states decided to bring forward the 2020 deadline to 2015 and approved the AEC Blueprint 2015 that detailed the agenda for

[11] Alice Ba, *(Re)Negotiating East and Southeast Asia: Region, Regionalism, and the Association of Southeast Asian Nations* 88–89 (2009).

[12] Rodolfo C. Severino, *Southeast Asia in Search of an ASEAN Community: Insights from the Former ASEAN Secretary-General* 214–16 (2006). For major programs that focused on industrial complementation and cooperation in the 1970s and 80s, see Amitav Acharya, *The Making of Southeast Asia: International Relations of a Region* 178–79 (2000).

[13] Severino, *supra* note 12, at 216.

[14] The ASEAN Free Trade Area was proposed by Thai Prime Minister Anand Panyarachun, with the support of Malaysia and Singapore. *Id.* at 28–29 & 222–25; Tham Siew Yean & Sanchita Basu Das, Introduction: The ASEAN Economic Community and Conflicting Domestic Interests, *in* Moving the AEC Beyond 2015: Managing Domestic Consensus for Community-Building 1, 3–4 (Tham Siew Yean & Sanchita Basu Das eds. 2016).

[15] See generally Bryan Mercurio, *Trade Liberalisation in Asia: Why Intra-Asian Free Trade Agreements Are Not Utilised By the Business Community*, 6(1) Asian J. WTO & Int'l Health L. & Pol. 109, 110–36 (2011).

[16] Interview with Goh Chok Tong, The Story of the ASEAN Economic Community, 1/2017) ASEAN Focus 22, 22–23 (2017).

[17] Declaration of ASEAN Concord II (Bali Concord II) (2003). The creation of the ASEAN Community is guided by the ASEAN Vision 2020 adopted in 1997.

"a single market and production base."[18] The AEC plan ambitiously envisioned the free flow of goods, services, investment, skilled labor and freer flow of capital.[19] ASEAN's pivotal constitutional comment also occurred in 2007. The ten countries adopted the ASEAN Charter that reiterates AEC principles and confers legal personality on the association "as an inter-governmental" organization.[20] The ASEAN Charter goes beyond codifying the established practice and constructs institutional mechanisms for implementing ASEAN agreements and dispute settlement.

A Post-2015 Vision under the AEC Blueprint 2025

In December 2015, ASEAN officially launched the AEC and adopted the AEC Blueprint 2025 for the post-2015 vision. The new Blueprint 2025 that succeeded the AEC Blueprint 2015 is incorporated into the guiding document of "ASEAN 2025: Forging Ahead Together," which charts the prospective roadmap of the ASEAN Community.[21] Remarkably, the AEC Blueprint 2025 includes five key characteristics.

The first and most important characteristic is "A Highly Integrated and Cohesive Economy."[22] The main goal is "to enhance ASEAN's trade and production networks" and "establish a more unified market" by facilitating "the seamless movement of goods, services, investment, capital and, skilled labour."[23] The term "a more unified market" reflects ASEAN's indigenous approach. It replaces the AEC Blueprint 2015's objective to form "a single market and production base," which resembles the European Single Market. The new clauses on the seamless movement arguably manifest a higher degree of liberalization than the previous Blueprint to further the "free" flow of goods, services, investment and skilled labor and the "freer" flow of capital.

The second characteristic of the AEC Blueprint 2025 is "A Competitive, Innovative and Dynamic ASEAN." It centers on the convergence and cooperation of competition laws and policies, consumer protection and intellectual property regimes.[24] The focus on sustainable economic

18 A Historic Milestone for FDI and MNEs in ASEAN 9 (2017); ASEAN Economic Community Blueprint (2007) (AEC Blueprint 2015), paras. 9–40.
19 AEC Blueprint 2015, paras. 4 & 9.
20 ASEAN Charter, arts. 1(1) & 3.
21 Kuala Lumpur Declaration on ASEAN 2025: Forging Ahead Together (2015).
22 ASEAN Economic Community Blueprint 2025 (2015) (AEC Blueprint 2025), paras. 7–24.
23 *Id.* para. 7.
24 *Id.* paras. 25–44.

development at regional and national levels also reinforces the commitments of ASEAN countries to the United Nations (UN) 2030 Agenda for Sustainable Development.[25] The third characteristic, "Enhanced Connectivity and Sectoral Cooperation," aims to support the infrastructure-based Master Plan on ASEAN Connectivity.[26] Critical to digital trade, this characteristic pledges to promote e-commerce transactions by harmonizing legal frameworks for consumer rights and data protection.[27]

"A Resilient, Inclusive, People-Oriented and People-Centred ASEAN" represents the fourth characteristic.[28] Different from the previous Blueprint that focused on the development of small and medium enterprises, the AEC Blueprint 2025 extends its ambit to cover micro enterprises. Concrete steps include efforts to increase exporters' utilization of rules of origin under FTAs and the ASEAN self-certification scheme. In addition, a new initiative will further narrow ASEAN's development gap and intensify capacity building assistance to CLMV countries.

The objective of the fifth characteristic, "A Global ASEAN," is to buttress ASEAN centrality by orienting the bloc as the center in new Asian regionalism.[29] ASEAN met the intended goals of concluding negotiations for the RCEP and agreements with Hong Kong. As ASEAN's economic success hinges on an effective implementation mechanism, the new Blueprint mandates that the AEC Council "monitor and enforce compliance of all measures."[30] The ASEAN Secretariat is also required to develop an enhanced monitoring framework.

B Legalizing the ASEAN Way and ASEAN Law

The integration of ASEAN is conventionally analyzed from economic and political perspectives. Discussion on the role of law in the process of regionalism remains limited. A key example is the ASEAN way, which commentators often discuss but have yet to reach a consensus on its nature. I observe that the legalization of the AEC has transformed the ASEAN way to a hybrid political and legal concept. It is no longer accurate

25 *Id.* paras. 40–41; *see generally* Complementarities between the ASEAN Community Vision 2025 and the United Nations 2030 Agenda for Sustainable Development: A Framework for Action (2017).

26 AEC Blueprint 2025, paras. 45–66.

27 *Id.* paras. 52–53.

28 *Id.* paras. 67–78.

29 AEC Blueprint 2025, paras. 79–80.

30 *Id.* paras. 81–82.

to interpret the ASEAN way simply as nonbinding soft law. The ASEAN way in the Third Regionalism has demonstrated its hard-law obligations with structured flexibility. This change is guided by the pragmatic incrementalism and has made ASEAN law distinguishable from EU law.[31]

In fact, the ASEAN way predates the founding of ASEAN and can trace its origin back to the 1955 Bandung Conference, where anticolonial nationalism prompted the gathering of Asian-African states.[32] Resting upon the Indonesian concepts of *musyawarah* and *mufakat* (consultations and consensus), the ASEAN way denotes the collective principles of sovereignty, noninterference and consensus decision-making.[33] The ASEAN way can be therefore understood as the code of conduct in interstate interactions, as well as the decision-making process for reaching consensus by consultations.[34] The ASEAN way invigorated ASEAN's birth in 1967 and enabled ASEAN members to build trust after Indonesia abandoned its *Konfrontasi* (confrontation) campaign targeted at the Malaysian Federation, which President Sukarno viewed as the influence of British imperialism.[35] The ASEAN Charter reinforces the legalization of the ASEAN way. It stresses the operating principles of the ASEAN way and requires economic commitments to be implemented under "a formula for flexible participation" grounded on consensus.[36]

The ASEAN way has provided a normative basis for countries to cooperate in sensitive areas with less concern about the "sovereignty costs" that would undermine regulatory authority.[37] Based on the Western understanding of legalization, lawyers and regionalism theorists may instantly consider the ASEAN way as a nonlegal or soft-law

[31] In my view, the "pragmatic incrementalism" is more elaborate than "pragmatic integration," which previous commentators loosely defined. United Nations Conference on Trade and Development (UNCTAD), *ASEAN at 50: Achievements and Challenges in Regional Integration* 7 (2017).

[32] History and Evolution of Non-Aligned Movement, Aug. 22, 2–12, http://mea.gov.in/in-focus-article.htm?20349/History+and+Evolution+of+NonAligned+Movement (last visited Nov. 18, 2019).

[33] Severino, *supra* note 12, at 1–11; Ingo Venzke and Li-Ann Thio, *The Internal Effects of ASEAN External Relations* 9–17 (2016); UNCTAD, *supra* note 31, at 6; Amitav Acharya, *Constructing a Security Community in Southeast Asia: ASEAN and the Problem of Regional Order* 3–5 (3rd ed. 2014).

[34] Amitav Archarya, *Ideas, Identity, and Institution-building: From the "ASEAN Way" to the "Asia-Pacific Way"?* 10(3)Pac. Rev. 319, 328–30 (1997). It should be noted that consensus is not tantamount to every member's explicit agreement. *Id.* at 331.

[35] Aggarwal & Chow, *supra* note 2, at 268; Severino, *supra* note 12, at 2–3.

[36] ASEAN Charter, preamble & art. 21(2).

[37] For the concept of sovereignty costs, see Oona A. Hathaway, *International Delegation and State Sovereignty*, 71(1) L. & Contemp. Problems 115, 119–20 (2008).

approach.[38] They have undervalued the outcome of ASEAN in comparison with what they considered the "real" integration in Europe and North America. As seasoned diplomats have observed, ASEAN has never progressed in a linear fashion, but has often moved "like a crab."[39] Although progress is not clear in the short term, it is significant in the long term. ASEAN's evolution into the center in Asia's hub-and-spoke structure since 1967 has substantiated this observation.

Concededly, I do not argue for ASEAN to be the perfect model of regionalism. What I emphasize is the legal value of ASEAN experiences for developing countries, particularly given embedded problems of the European Union (EU) that have caused the Euro crisis and the Brexit saga. Legal scholars and political scientists have frequently compared ASEAN with the EU. Yet, it is an oversimplification to characterize the AEC as an incomplete or halfway version of the EU. While European integration offers reference, ASEAN has never sought to replicate the EU model. The goal of the AEC is to intensify FTA-plus arrangements rather than pursue a common market or customs union. The ASEAN way, which has influenced the AEC and ASEAN law from structural and operational perspectives, gave rise to an alternative model to the EU. I offer the following comparative analysis.

First, ASEAN is inherently distinct from the EU in its legal status. The EU functions as a supranational institution, whereas ASEAN is an intergovernmental organization. As for law enforcement and implementation, the EU's top-down approach is best evidenced by the "direct effect" of EU treaties and regulations that preempt national legislation. Nevertheless, ASEAN's regionalism is based on horizontal integration. The ASEAN Charter only mandates that members "take all necessary measures" to implement ASEAN agreements.[40] National constitutions of ASEAN states are unlikely to be interpreted as conferring regional agreements self-executing power.[41] Although ASEAN agreements have no direct effect, it does not mean ASEAN law has no impact on domestic law. ASEAN judges may exercise their discretionary power by resorting to a national law concept akin to the US

[38] *See generally* Sungjoon Cho & Jurgen Kurtz, *Legalizing the ASEAN Way: Adopting and Reimagining the ASEAN Investment Regime*, 66 Am. J. Com. L. 233, 238–53 (2018).

[39] Mahbubani & Sng, *supra* note 5, at 3.

[40] ASEAN Charter, art. 5(2).

[41] Diane A. Desierto, *ASEAN's Constitutionalization of International Law: Challenges to Evolution under the New ASEAN Charter*, 49 Colum. J. Transnat'l L. 268, 300–03 (2010–11).

Charming Betsy principle, which allows statutes to be interpreted in consistence with states' obligations under ASEAN agreements.[42] Consequently, the authority of ASEAN law at the regional level could extend to the domestic legal realm.

Second, the ASEAN way has been applied as the "ASEAN Minus X" formula, which can be traced back to the 1992 Framework Agreement on Enhancing ASEAN Economic Cooperation.[43] This formula is not only enshrined in the legal framework that governs services liberalization, but is also reinforced in the ASEAN Charter as a primary mechanism for flexible participation.[44] The ASEAN Minus X formula is a fast-track solution, under which a specific agreement "agreed" upon by ten states can be "implemented" without all of them. Two or more states could initiate negotiations and liberalize selected sectors, allowing the subsequent accession of other states.[45] To avoid the free rider problem, the concessions would only be granted on a reciprocal basis. Thus, ASEAN integration would not be dragged down to the pace of countries unwilling to cooperate and trade liberalization benefits could incentivize these states to make additional commitments. Entry into force provisions under selected ASEAN Plus One FTAs similarly incorporate the ASEAN Minus X formula.[46] An example is the ASEAN-Australia-New Zealand FTA (AANZTA), which only requires the ratification and notification by "Australia, New Zealand and at least four ASEAN Member States," instead of by all parties, to enable the agreement to become effective.[47]

Lastly, the ASEAN Charter's treaty-making power provisions do not equal the European concept of "competences" that member states conferred under EU law. For matters that fall with the exclusive competences of the EU, it alone can negotiate and conclude international treaties that bind individual members. Nonetheless, ASEAN's power is severely confined

[42] J. H. H. Weiler, *ASEAN Law, the ASEAN Way and the Role of Domestic Courts, in* The ASEAN Law Conference 2018: A Compendium of Speeches, Papers, Presentations and Reports 43, 49–50 (2019).

[43] Severino, *supra* note 12, at 31–32 & 352–53.

[44] Based on the Protocol to Amend the ASEAN Framework Agreement on Services (2003), Article IV bis (ASEAN Minus X modality) was added to the Framework Agreement on Services (AFAS); ASEAN Charter, art. 21(2).

[45] Framework Agreement on Enhancing ASEAN Economic Cooperation (2012), art. I:3.

[46] Peter Jan Kuijper et al., *From Treaty-Making to Treaty-Breaking: Models for ASEAN External Trade Agreements* 97–98 (2015).

[47] For example, "Australia, New Zealand and at least four ASEAN Member States" could enable the pact to enter into force. Agreement Establishing the ASEAN-Australia-New Zealand Free Trade Area (2009) (AANZFTA), ch. 18, art. 7.2.

because it does not extend to the conclusion of agreements that would create obligations on individual states.[48] The legal obligation of ASEAN members is limited to the "endeavor to develop common positions and pursue joint actions" under the ASEAN Charter.[49] The practice of concluding external agreements by ten states collectively remains unchanged. Their representatives often convene the ASEAN Caucus meetings to align their stances prior to negotiations of trade agreements with external partners.

III Legal Framework of the ASEAN Economic Community

The creation of the AEC has invigorated ASEAN's legalization process in new Asian regionalism and reinforced the normative foundation for the NREO. Under the AEC Blueprint 2025, three interrelated agreements identified in Figure 2.1 below underpin the new economic community's framework for "the seamless movement of" trade.[50] The ASEAN Trade in Goods Agreement (ATIGA) facilitates the free flow of goods, the ASEAN Trade in Services Agreement (ATISA) governs trade in services and the ASEAN Comprehensive Investment Agreement (ACIA) enhances investment liberalization and protection. Their evolution and unique structures reflect the evolving process of South-based regionalism. The legal challenges and prospective reforms for AEC-related agreements will be further detailed in the remainder of this section

A Trade in Goods

On one hand, tariffs are the obvious barriers to trade in goods and hence tariff eliminations are perceived as direct benefits of economic integration. On the other hand, as tariff cuts involve "Grand Bargains" that harm selected domestic industries, tariff concessions often become the deal breaker in trade negotiations.[51] In ASEAN, the 1992 Common Effective Preferential Tariff scheme enabled the AFTA, the precursor to today's AEC. To remedy the low utilization of the AFTA, the 2009 ASEAN Trade

48 ASEAN Charter, art. 41(7); Rules of Procedure for Conclusion of International Agreements by ASEAN (2011), rule 1.

49 ASEAN Charter, art. 41(4).

50 AEC Blueprint 2025, paras. 7–15.

51 *See* Sylvia Ostry, *The Uruguay Round North-South Grand Bargain: Implications for Future Negotiations*, *in* The Political Economy of International Trade Law: Essays in Honor of Robert E. Hudec 285, 285–89 (Daniel L. M. Kennedy & James D. Southwick eds. 2002) (explaining the "Grand Bargain" negotiations).

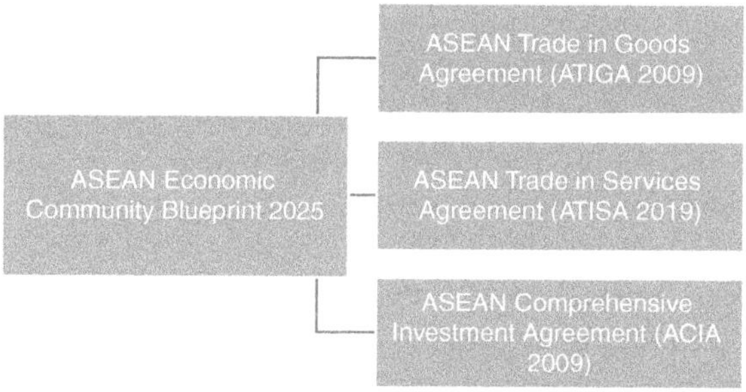

Figure 2.1 Legal framework for intra-ASEAN trade liberalization

in Goods Agreement (ATIGA) consolidated and streamlined previous agreements on goods and trade facilitation.[52] The legal framework has increased ASEAN's intra-regional trade from 15 percent in the 1970 to 24 percent in the 2010s, only below that of intra-EU and intra-North America trade.[53]

1 Tariff Eliminations and Rules of Origin

The AFTA started the initial step of integration between ASEAN's developing nations and least developed countries. The tariff eliminations under the AFTA did not radically mandate zero tariff rates. Instead, the AFTA included exceptions that permitted CLMV countries and sensitive goods, such as agricultural products, to achieve 0–5 percent tariff rates for a longer period.[54] This incremental consolidation approach provided a level of comfort where member states could minimize domestic opposition and stimulate enhanced integration.

The ATIGA inherited the AFTA's features that highlight the "country-specific, product-specific" tariff elimination schedule. A lengthier transition period represents special and differential treatment for CLMV countries. Products are divided in different categories and subject to different schedules of tariff reductions. The categories include

[52] Kanya Satyani Sasradipoera, *ASEAN Trade in Goods Agreement (ATIGA), in* ASEAN: Life after the Charter 89, 90–92 (S. Tiwari ed. 2010); ASEAN Trade in Goods Agreement (2009) (ATIGA), art. 91(2).

[53] In 2017, intra-regional trade in the European Union (EU 28 countries) and North America is 64 percent and 50 percent, respectively. World Trade Organization (WTO), *World Trade Statistical Review 2019* (2019), at 55.

[54] Masahiro Kawai & Kanda Naknoi, *ASEAN Economic Integration through Trade and Foreign Direct Investment: Long-Term Challenges*, ADBI Working Paper Series, No. 545 (2015), at 12.

information and communications technology products, priority sectors products (such as automotive and textiles) and unprocessed agricultural products.[55] In the current ATIGA tariff schedule, 99.3 percent of tariffs have been eliminated by six more developed ASEAN countries and 97.7 percent by CLMV countries.[56] ASEAN's tariff eliminations demonstrate an obvious result of South-South regionalism.

From a business perspective, tariff liberalization will yield substantive results only if it can be utilized. Rules of origin are designed to prevent free riders by limiting beneficiaries to manufacturers from FTA partners. Since complex and divergent rules of origin in Asian FTAs caused the "noodle bowl" syndrome and inhibited the FTA usage, a main objective of the AEC Blueprint 2025 is to simplify and enhance the implementation of these rules.[57] Most common rules of origin include the Change in Tariff Classification (CTC) and Regional Value Content (RVC) rules. The CTC rule qualitatively assesses whether products are classified under tariff schedules different from those of their original materials. The RVC rule quantitatively examines whether the products meet the FTA value-added thresholds.

Arguably based on the requirement under the 1977 Agreement on ASEAN Preferential Trading Arrangements, subsequent agreements have applied the RVC 40 percent rule as the main rules of origin.[58] Preferential tariff treatment depends on proof that 40 percent of the product's value comes from ASEAN countries. However, companies have found it cumbersome and costly to procure documents to meet the benchmark. The AFTA Council therefore changed ASEAN's rules of origin to also allow for CTC. The ATIGA adopted this more flexible coequal rule.[59] The ATIGA also incorporated the rule of "accumulation," which takes into account goods from any ASEAN country for the RVC calculation.[60] This rule facilitates the allocation of manufacturing bases across the region. ASEAN integration will be strengthened because external agreements, such as the EU-Singapore FTA, have followed a similar rule.

[55] ATIGA, art. 19; ASEAN Framework Agreement for the Integration of Priority Sectors (2004), art. 2(1)(a).

[56] *See* ASEAN, *ASEAN Integration Report* 2019 (2019), at 19–20 ("ASEAN has eliminated 98.6% of the total number of tariff lines in 2019.").

[57] Richard Baldwin & Masahiro Kawai, *Multilateralizing Asian Regionalism*, ADBI Working Paper Series, No. 431 (2013), at 11–12; AEC Blueprint 2025, para. 10(ii).

[58] Stefano Inama & Edmund W. Sim, *Rules of Origin in ASEAN: A Way Forward* 27, fn. 2 (2015).

[59] Joint Media Statement of the 17th AFTA Council Meeting (2013), paras. 11–12.

[60] ATIGA, art. 30.

2 Non-Tariff and Trade Facilitation Measures

Although tariff cuts have significantly increased intra-ASEAN trade, the rapid increase of non-tariff measures have impeded regional integration. Non-tariff "measures" are not tantamount to non-tariff "barriers." Non-tariff measures refer to "policy measures . . . that can potentially have an economic effect on international trade in goods, changing quantities traded, or prices or both."[61] Non-tariff measures such as labeling or hygienic requirements may be adopted for legitimate purposes, but can become non-tariff barriers when measures are applied discriminatorily or to enforce protectionism.[62]

Non-tariff measures have affected 58 percent of trade in the Asia-Pacific region.[63] Recent statistics show that in the past twenty years, intra-ASEAN tariffs have fallen from 8.9 percent to 4.2 percent, but the number of non-tariff measures has proliferated by 360 percent.[64] Sanitary and phytosanitary (SPS) measures and technical barriers to trade (TBT) alone account for 75 percent of non-tariff measures.[65] While Thailand, the Philippines and Malaysia are the most frequent users of non-tariff measures, CLMV countries have exhibited a low usage of these measures.[66]

Pursuant to the AEC Blueprint 2025, the ATIGA aims to minimize the application of non-tariff measures.[67] The policy challenge is that the blanket abolition of these measures will incur backlash, as regulatory authority of states will be impaired. Notably, the ATIGA has combined hard-law and soft-law requirements. It first mandates transparency by requiring ASEAN countries to include non-tariff measures in the ASEAN Trade Repository.[68] Launched as a key trade facilitation mechanism in

61 UNCTAD, *Non-tariff Measures: Evidence from Selected Developing Countries and Future Research Agenda: Developing Countries in International Trade Studies* (2010), at 99.

62 UNCTAD, *International Classification on Non-Tariff Measures* (2019), at 1–4; ASEAN Business Advisory Council & EU-ASEAN Business Council, *Non-Tariff Barriers (NTBs) in ASEAN and Their Elimination from a Business Perspective* (2019), at 36.

63 United Nations Economic and Social Commission for Asia and the Pacific (UNESCAP) & UNCTAD, *Asia-Pacific Trade and Investment Report 2019: Navigating Non-tariff Measures towards Sustainable Development* (2019), at 39.

64 The number of non-tariff measures increased from 1,634 to 5,886 from 2000 to 2019. Lili Yang Ing et al., *NTMs in ASEAN: Ways toward Regulatory Convergence*, *in* Regional Integration and Non-Tariff Measures in ASEAN 90, 91 (Lili Yan Ing et al. eds. 2019); ASEAN, *supra* note 56, 20–21.

65 ASEAN, *supra* note 56, 21.

66 UNESCAP, *Asia-Pacific Trade and Investment Report 2016: Recent Trends and Development* (2016), at 79.

67 AEC Blueprint 2025, para. 10(g).

68 ATIGA, art. 40.

2016, this web-based repository is linked to national repositories and provides a single point of access to customs and other trade-related information.[69]

The ATIGA also requires inter-regional bodies to identity non-tariff barriers, which are subject to different periods of elimination depending on countries.[70] In addition, the chapters on TBT and SPS measures provide guidelines that encourage cooperation and reference to international standards.[71] Unlike the European Commission, the ASEAN Secretariat's lack of capacity has severely undermined its role in monitoring non-tariff measures and enforcing the rules. The effect of the ATIGA in this area remains to be seen.

Along with the ASEAN Trade Repository, the implementation of other trade facilitation measures also provides important lessons. In 2019, ASEAN states amended the ATIGA to enable the self-certification scheme.[72] Under the past framework, enterprises had to submit required paperwork to customs officials and apply for certificates of origin (known as Form D) in order to utilize ATIGA preferential tariffs. The procedure can be costly and time-consuming. The new scheme releases the administrative burden by allowing certified exporters to self-declare the origin of their products on commercial invoices. The cost savings are significant to small and medium-sized enterprises.

Furthermore, the creation of the ASEAN Single Window has expedited the customs clearance procedure to enable the electronic exchange of necessary information. With the accession of Brunei and Cambodia in 2019, seven ASEAN countries have participated in the live exchange of the e-Form D and, moreover, six members implemented the ASEAN Customs Transit System in 2020.[73] The ASEAN Minus X approach for joining the scheme has allowed more advanced members to pilot new trade facilitation initiatives and contribute to the capacity building of remaining members at a later stage.

[69] ASEAN, *supra* note 56, at xiv & 25.

[70] *Id.* art. 42.

[71] *Id.* chs. 7 & 8.

[72] First Protocol to Amend the ATIGA (2019) (amending Article 38 of the ATIGA).

[73] See ASEAN, *supra* note 56, at 27 (indicating that other countries include Indonesia, Malaysia, Singapore, Thailand and Viet Nam); Ministry of Trade and Industry Singapore, *Soother Cross-Border Transit Movement of Goods within Southeast Asia with the ASEAN Customs Transit System* (2020) (explaining that participating members include Cambodia, Laos, Malaysia, Thailand and Singapore).

B Trade in Services

The importance of trade in services is no less than that of tariff reductions. Services liberalization is essential to ASEAN's commitments to UN Sustainable Development Goals. Development policies have traditionally centered on manufacturing. Contrary to the conventional understanding that services should only be prioritized at an advanced development stage, inclusive development and economic modernization actually rely on services.[74] The fact that a 10 percent increase in trade in services leads to a 6 percent growth in trade in goods is evidence of the intimate correlation between the two major modes of trade.[75] With digital technology, services trade will also enable countries to escape the "middle-income trap," which often occurs in middle-income developing countries such as Malaysia and Thailand.[76]

Remarkably, services trade has outgrown agriculture and mining and buttressed the welfare of the underprivileged community.[77] To illustrate, the liberalization of health services maximizes the delivery of health care to the needy and tourism services allow up to 25 percent of tourism expenditures to directly reach the poor in least developed countries.[78] Comparable to other developing nations, 60.7 percent of ASEAN foreign direct investment (FDI) inflows are now associated with the service sector and thus benefit poverty reduction through job creation.[79] Moreover, the development of services trade is pivotal to gender equality. This is evidenced by the fact that 90.5 percent and 88 percent of female

[74] Zakariah Rashid et al., *Regional Market for Goods, Services, and Skilled Labor*, *in* Realizing the ASEAN Economic Community: A Comprehensive Assessment 20, 44 (Michael G. Plummer & Chia Siow Yue eds. 2009); ASEAN 2030: Toward a Borderless Economic Community 120 (2014).

[75] Juan Blyde & Natalia Sinyavskaya, *The Impact of Liberalizing Trade in Services on Trade in Goods: An Empirical Investigation*, 11:3 *Rev. Dev. Econ.* 566, 573 (2007).

[76] Tran Van Tho, *The Middle-Income Trap: Issues for Members of the Association of Southeast Asian Nations*, ADBI Working Paper Series, No. 421 (2013), at 22–29.

[77] ASEAN Secretariat & World Bank, *ASEAN Integration Monitoring Report* 93 (2013); Joy Abrenica et al., *The Future of Trade in Services for Developing Countries*, *in* Trade and Poverty Reduction in the Asia-Pacific Region: Case Studies and Lessons from Low-Income Communities 341, 347–48 (Andrew L. Stoler et al. eds. 2009).

[78] Aaditya Mattoo & Gianni Zanini, *Services Trade Agreements and Negotiations: An Overview*, *in* Handbook of Trade Policy for Development 661, 665 (Arvid Lukauskas et al. eds. 2013); Jonathan Mitchell, *An Unconventional but Essential Marriage: Pro-Poor Tourism and the Mainstream Industry*, Private Sector & Dev., No. 7 (2010), at 5.

[79] ASEAN, *supra* note 56, at 39; WTO, Mode 3 – Commercial Presence, S/C/W/314, Apr. 7, 2010, at 9.

employment in Brunei and Singapore, respectively, concentrate on the services sector.[80]

1 Successive Packages of Services Commitments

Recognizing the preeminence of services liberalization, the AEC Blueprint 2025 aims to "further broaden and deepen services integration within ASEAN" and facilitates its "integration into the global supply chain."[81] Like the ATISA approach, ASEAN's legal framework for trade in services is based on the pragmatic incrementalism. The 2019 ATISA consolidates ten successive "packages" of services commitments negotiated under the Framework Agreement on Services (AFAS).[82]

ASEAN states commenced services negotiations since the signing of the AFAS in 1995. The goal was to achieve "a free trade area in services" that exceeds the level of the WTO General Agreement on Trade in Services (GATS).[83] The unique structure of successive packages under the AFAS was designed to allow for gradual domestic reforms and to prevent the political backlash that would hamper liberalization. Schedules of services commitments finalized under multiple rounds of negotiations cumulatively "form an integral part of" the AFAS.[84] Because of the AFAS's non-self-executing nature, each country ought to sign the protocol that embodies specific commitments. Each package of commitments will take effect after the completion of domestic ratification procedures. In 2018, ASEAN states signed the most recent protocol to implement the tenth package of commitments.

A common inquiry is whether ASEAN's approach has actually led to GATS-plus commitments or even enabled AFAS services commitments to exceed those of ASEAN Plus One FTAs. The answer is positive. The ASEAN-Australia-New Zealand FTA is perceived to have the highest level of services liberalization among ASEAN FTAs. Empirical study demonstrates that the commitments in the seventh package of AFAS commitments, for the first time, outpaced those of the ASEAN-Australia-New Zealand FTA.[85] This reinforces the previous observation that

[80] ASEAN, *supra* note 56, at 30.
[81] AEC Blueprint 2025, para. 11.
[82] ASEAN, *supra* note 56, at 30.
[83] ASEAN Framework Agreement on Services (1995) (AFAS), art. I(c).
[84] *Id.* art. VIII.
[85] Yoshifumi Fukunaga & Ikumo Isono, *Taking ASEAN+1 FTAs towards the RCEP: A Mapping Study*, ERIA Discussion Paper Series (2013), at 16.

ASEAN has progressed as a "crab" and its development has become obvious in the longer period.

The evolution of services negotiation modalities under the AFAS provides legal and policy options for developing countries in new Asian regionalism. Modeled after the GATS, the AFAS covers four modes of the services trade: Mode 1 (cross-border supply), Mode 2 (consumption abroad), Mode 3 (commercial presence) and Mode 4 (movement of natural persons).[86] WTO members made the fewest commitments to Modes 3 and 4 and these modes are generally subject to more restrictions.[87] With various revisions, AFAS negotiations have largely followed a more conservative GATS-like positive list formula.[88] The request-and-offer bargain obliged member states to list the sectors and modes of supply that they planned to liberalize in binding schedules. The ASEAN Minus X formula that provides for more flexible participation was incorporated in the third round of AFAS negotiations concluded in 2003.[89] Moreover, given the significance and sensitivity of professional mobility, the 2012 ASEAN Agreement on the Movement of Natural Persons (ASEAN MNP Agreement) became effective in 2016 and will guide Mode 4 negotiations.[90]

While most AFAS negotiations are conducted by ASEAN economic ministers, financial services and air transport services are negotiated by finance and transport ministers, respectively. Their commitments are listed as separate AFAS packages. During financial services negotiations, an important development is the implementation of the 2015 ASEAN Banking Integration Framework.[91] An ASEAN bank that attains Qualified ASEAN Bank (QAB) status will be accorded equal treatment in other ASEAN states. However, the ASEAN framework is different from the EU's "single passport" scheme for cross-border banking services.[92] The ASEAN framework provides a platform for participating countries to enter into reciprocal bilateral agreements. It also allows national authorities

86 General Agreement on Trade in Services (1994) (GATS), art. I:2.

87 WTO, *World Trade Report 2019: The Future of Services Trade* (2019), at 170–71.

88 ASEAN, *ASEAN Services Report 2017: The Evolving Landscape* (2017), at 26–27.

89 *Id.* at 27.

90 ASEAN, *supra* note 56, at 36.

91 ASEAN Central Bank Governors agreed on the framework in 2014. ASEAN, *supra* note 56, at 50; Protocol to Implement the Sixth Packages of Commitments on Financial Services under the ASEAN Framework Agreement on Services (2015), art. 5.

92 Christopher Chen, *ASEAN Financial Integration and the Belt and Road Initiative: Legal Challenges and Opportunities for China in Southeast Asia*, *in* International Governance and the Rule of Law in China under the Belt and Road Initiative 163, 169–70 (Yun Zhao ed. 2018).

to retain control over QAB criteria. For instance, following the conclusion of the Indonesia-Malaysia agreement, Indonesia's Bank Mandiri is expected to become the first QAB in Malaysia and will be entitled to the same treatment as local lenders.[93] According to ASEAN experiences, incremental and parallel sector-based negotiations may increase the risk of fragmentation, but can prevent highly regulated sectors from blocking entire negotiations.

According to the AEC Blueprint 2025, a key benefit of the ATISA is to consolidate AFAS commitments under different tracks.[94] More fundamentally, it will shift the negotiation modality from the positive list approach to the more progressive negative list approach, which requires all services sectors to be liberalized unless otherwise specified in the schedules. Currently utilized in 60 percent of global FTAs, the negative list modality was also adopted in the Comprehensive and Progressive Agreement for Trans-Pacific Partnership (CPTPP) including four ASEAN members.[95] The ATISA's built-in agenda to convert AFAS commitments to the negative list approach will eliminate the current practice of scheduling "water" commitments.[96] An example is a country's commitment to permit 70 percent foreign equity in a particular sector, while in reality the country has implemented the commitment prior to the trade agreement. These "commitments" thus deteriorate the value of the AFAS.

ASEAN's FTA-plus path is distinct from the EU's top-down approach and provides an alternative model for the South. I recommend the following critical steps for ASEAN to intensify its services integration in line with the AEC Blueprint 2025. First, the AEC Blueprint 2015 continued to apply the ASEAN Minus X formula and "overall flexibilities" up to 15 percent.[97] These two politically oriented principles, which resemble special and differential treatment, were designed to abate domestic protectionism and stimulate the initial liberalization.

[93] ASEAN, *supra* note 56, at 50; Ng Min Shen, *Bank Mandiri – 1st Indonesian Bank to Operate in Malaysia, Malaysian Reserve*, July 7, 2017, https://themalaysianreserve.com/2017/07/07/bank-mandiri-1st-indonesian-bank-operate-malaysia/ (last visited Nov. 22, 2019).

[94] It includes "the 10th AFAS package, the 9th AFAS Finance Package and the 11th AFAS Air Transport Package." P. D. Djuarno, *ASEAN Economic Ministers Sign ASEAN Trade in Services Agreement*, Apr. 24, 2019, https://en.netralnews.com/news/business/read/26604/asean.economic.ministers.sign.asean.trade.in.services.agreement (last visited Nov. 22, 2019).

[95] WTO, *supra* note 87, at 174; Tham Siew Yean, *ASEAN Trade in Services Agreement (ATISA): Advancing Services Liberalization for ASEAN?* 54 Persp. 1, 3 (2019).

[96] Tham, *supra* note 95, 3–4; Ministry of Trade and Industry, Minister Chan Chun Sing at the 25th ASEAN Economic Ministers' Retreat in Phuket, Thailand, Apr. 23, 2019, at 3.

[97] ASEAN, ASEAN Economic Community (2008) (AEC Blueprint 2015), para. 21 & fn. 2.

Singapore concluded ASEAN Minus Agreements with Laos on education services and with Brunei on telecommunication services.

As these agreements illustrate, the ASEAN Minus X formula contributed to fragmented commitments at different speeds. It also became ambiguous whether a state can opt out of the commitments to which it initially agreed if it cannot meet the commitments at the implementation stage.[98] Moreover, the 15 percent flexibility proviso enabled states to exclude sensitive services industries from commitments. Nonetheless, neither ASEAN agreements nor the AEC Blueprint 2025 elaborated on the definition of "overall flexibilities," thus making it difficult to comprehend whether and how countries should schedule their services commitments based on the rule. Construing these exceptions narrowly and basing them on objective criteria is necessary to effectively implement the ATISA.

Second, the highly integrated AEC hinges on the further liberalization of Modes 3 and 4. Although the original Blueprint set foreign equity participation at 70 percent, most states have unilaterally increased the foreign equity threshold.[99] To illustrate, seven ASEAN countries committed to permitting 100 percent foreign ownership in the sector of hospital services, but Indonesia, Myanmar and Thailand maintained the 70 percent benchmark.[100] A detailed review of domestic corporate and investment laws further demonstrates that foreign equity restrictions are imposed on various services sectors related to agriculture, mining, telecommunications and news media.[101] Consequently, ATISA negotiations should minimize limitations of market access and national treatment for Mode 3, so that domestic regulation will not cripple the effectiveness of equity commitments.

Lastly, the Mode 4 liberalization that promotes cross-border labor mobility has great potential for development owing to the effect of remittances and skill transfer. At the WTO, most Mode 4 horizontal commitments are related to intra-corporate transferees and business visitors.[102] ASEAN states follow the same trend. Intra-ASEAN labor mobility is closely intertwined with commercial presence. Markedly, the CPTPP mandates that the cross-border supply of a service not be conditioned

[98] Severino, *supra* note 12, at 352–53.
[99] AEC Blueprint 2015, para. 21
[100] ASEAN & UNCTAD, *ASEAN Investment Report 2019: FDI in Services: Focus on Health Care* (2019), at xxv.
[101] Locknie Hsu et al., *Improving Connectivity between ASEAN's Legal Systems to Address Commercial Issues* (2018), at 24–28.
[102] Presence of Natural Persons (Mode 4), S/C/W/301, Sept. 15, 2009, at 21.

on "a representative office or any form of enterprise."[103] The AEC should adopt this rule to delink commitments of Mode 4 with those of Mode 3, thus creating more opportunities for independent professionals.

2 Professional Mobility and Mutual Recognition Arrangements

The aim of the AEC Blueprint 2025 to facilitate the movement of "skilled labor" also highlights the difference with the European concept of freedom of movement. More specifically, while EU law grants all "workers" fundamental rights of intra-region movement and residence, ASEAN law limits the scope of liberalization to professionals.[104] The ASEAN MNP Agreement is the primary AEC instrument for professional mobility. The agreement, which superseded AFAS Mode 4 commitments, applies to skilled labor rather than all "natural persons."[105] It expedites the movement of intra-corporate transferees, business visitors, contractual service suppliers and other professionals as defined in ASEAN countries' schedules of commitments.[106]

Markedly, the ASEAN MNP Agreement extends merely to the service sector.[107] For example, the intra-ASEAN transfer of a Singapore-based sales manager of an agricultural or manufacturing plant in Vietnam falls outside the ambit of the ASEAN MNP Agreement. It is because neither agriculture nor manufacturing belongs to the service sector. However, the Singapore manager's entry to Vietnam and other ASEAN states for business trips is guaranteed under the ACIA, which encompasses "services incidental to" nonservice sectors.[108]

Comparable to the GATS, the ASEAN MNP Agreement covers the provision of services on a nonpermanent basis, so that intra-regional labor mobility will not become a political immigration issue like the one

[103] Comprehensive and Progressive Agreement for Trans-Pacific Partnership (2018) (CPTPP), art. 10.6.

[104] *See generally* Susanne Kraatz, *Free Movement of Workers*, May 2019, www.europarl.europa.eu/factsheets/en/sheet/41/free-movement-of-workers (last visited Nov. 25, 2019).

[105] ASEAN Agreement on the Movement of Natural Persons (2012) (ASEAN MNP Agreement), preamble.

[106] *Id.* art. 2:1. Intra-corporate transferees include executives, managers and specialists employed by companies.

[107] The ASEAN MNP Agreement stipulates that it covers persons engaged in trade in services, goods and investments, but none of the ASEAN countries made commitments in nonservices sectors. *Id.* preamble & art. 1(b).

[108] ASEAN Comprehensive Investment Agreement (2009) (ACIA), art. 3.3(f).

in the EU that contributed to Brexit. The ASEAN MNP Agreement aims to facilitate the "temporary" entry or stay of service providers.[109] It does not hinder a government's "measures affecting natural persons seeking access to the employment market" and "measures regarding citizenship, residence or employment on a permanent basis."[110] Thus, ASEAN governments are permitted to maintain visa requirements for public purposes, provided that the benefits under the agreement are not nullified or impaired.

Other than the schedule of Mode 4 commitments under the ASEAN MNP Agreement, ASEAN's Mutual Recognition Arrangements (MRAs) promote the recognition of qualifications and professional mobility. As MRAs require significant changes in national legislation that allows for foreign professionals, they are only subject to loose requirements under Article VII of the GATS and are rarely regulated in FTAs. While the EU Qualifications Directive forms the legal basis for automatic recognition of licenses and certifications for over 800 professions, ASEAN MRAs do not accord such direct recognition.[111] Instead, ASEAN MRAs provide a scheme of regional cooperation that harmonizes domestic laws regulating various professions.[112] The ASEAN way has resulted in profession-specific or "à la carte" harmonization schemes, which enable national authorities to exercise discretion under a regional structure.

Since the first MRA on engineering services was concluded in 2005, ASEAN has finalized MRAs for eight professions.[113] The implementation approaches vary across MRAs. To build consensus for fully fledged MRAs, the framework arrangements on accountancy services and surveying services focus on facilitating information exchanges and identifying assessment standards. For example, the 2009 Framework Arrangement on Accountancy Services has led to the 2014 MRA on Accounting Services. At first glance, health care-related MRAs that govern dentists, doctors and nurses seem to require a simple process. Following certification by his or

[109] ASEAN MNP Agreement, art. 2.1. Yet, due to the ambiguity as to what length of time "temporary" entails, ASEAN members' commitments vary across different categories of natural persons.

[110] ASEAN MNP Agreement, art. 2.2.

[111] Shintaro Hamanaka & Sufian Jusoh, *Understanding the ASEAN Way of Regional Qualification Governance: The Case of Mutual Recognition Agreements in the Professional Service Sector*, 12(4) Reg. & Governance 486, 490–98 (2018).

[112] AFAS, art. V.

[113] ASEAN Mutual recognition arrangements (MRAs) cover (1) engineering services; (2) nursing services; (3) architectural services; (4) surveyors; (5) medical practitioners; (6) dental practitioners; (7) tourism professionals; and (8) accountancy services. ASEAN, *supra* note 56, at 36.

her country of origin, a medical doctor with sufficient qualification and without ethics violations may register as a foreign medical practitioner in the host country.[114] However, the actual outcome has been largely limited by MRAs' "right to regulate" provisions that keep the national authorities' regulatory power over these highly regulated practitioners.[115]

Different from the schemes above, MRAs on accounting, architectural and engineering services have created regional bodies.[116] The ASEAN-level professional institutions and national regulatory bodies have established a three-step registration process. For example, an engineer who meets the MRA's educational and experience requirements should first be certified by the domestic regulatory body, which submits the application to the ASEAN committee.[117] After being approved as an ASEAN Chartered Professional Engineer, the engineer is eligible to apply to be a foreign engineer in another ASEAN state. As the most visible arrangement, the MRA on Engineering Services has enabled more than 3,700 engineers on the ASEAN register.[118]

For ASEAN countries, the MRA on Tourism Professionals has great impact on development. A notable example is the Philippines where the tourism sector contributes to 12.8 percent of employment.[119] Unique to other arrangements, this MRA governs "unregulated" professions because there is no international standard for tourism services providers.[120] The MRA will advance the regional tourism industry by developing a common curriculum and competency standards for thirty-two job titles such as

114 *E.g.*, ASEAN MRA on Medical Practitioners (2009), art. 3.1.

115 *Id.* art. 5.

116 These MRAs created the ASEAN Chartered Professional Engineer Coordinating Committee, the ASEAN Architecture Council, and the ASEAN Charted Professional Account Coordinating Committee, respectively. ASEAN MRA on Engineering Services (2005), art. 3.1; ASEAN MRA on Architectural Services (2007), art. 3.1; ASEAN MRA on Accounting Services (2014), art. 4.2.

117 ASEAN MRA on Engineering Services (2005), art. 3; Deunden Nikomborirak & Supunnavadee Jitdumrong, *ASEAN Trade in Services*, *in* The ASEAN Economic Community: A Work in Progress 95, 104–05 (Sanchita Basu Das ed. 2013).

118 *See* ASEAN, *supra* note 56, at 35 ("As of June 2019, there were 3,733 engineers on the ASEAN Chartered Professional Engineers Register, 545 architects registered as ASEAN Architects, and 3,205 accountants registered as ASEAN Chartered Professional Accountant.").

119 Trade Policy Review, Report by the Secretariat: the Philippines, WT/TPR/S/368 (2018), at 81.

120 Tour guides in some ASEAN states are subject to regulatory requirements, so that they are not covered under the MRA. Yoshifumi Fukunaga, *Assessing the Progress of ASEAM MRAs on Professional Services*, ERIA Discussion Paper Series (2015), at 26.

laundry manager and travel consultant.[121] A Web-based database will also be created to facilitate registered tourism professionals seeking employment in other ASEAN countries.[122]

As I explained previously, ASEAN's skilled labor-centered policy has been implemented through Mode 4 commitments and MRAs. Nevertheless, there remains significant room for improving the movement of natural persons. The reality is that current MRAs cover only 1.5 percent of ASEAN's work force and 87 percent of intra-ASEAN workers are unskilled and thus do not benefit from the MRAs.[123] De jure and de facto obstacles to utilize the MRAs cannot be ignored. To illustrate, the MRA provisions that mandate minimum years of experience from three to ten years have restricted the number of eligible professionals.[124]

Given extra national requirements, satisfying the MRA criteria does not guarantee employment. The labor market test is a common hurdle. A Malaysian company attempting to recruit a foreign engineer bears the burden of proving the absence of local engineers for the specific project.[125] Additional obstacles include restrictions on nationality, residency and language requirements. In domestic law, a more fundamental "loophole" is the lack of additional benefits accorded to ASEAN nationals by MRAs in comparison with those extended to foreign professionals. Without going through the MRA process, an engineer from any country may register as a temporary engineer in Malaysia and a foreign nurse may work as a consultant in Indonesia.[126] In other words, domestic rules have diminished the actual value of MRAs for ASEAN professionals.

121 A person who possesses a tourism certificate issued by a national agency in compliance with MRA requirements can be recognized as a "Foreign Tourism Professional" in another ASEAN state. ASEAN MRA on Tourism Professionals, arts. II–III; ASEAN, *ASEAN Mutual Recognition Arrangement on Tourism Professionals (MRA): Handbook* (2013), at 18.

122 *Id.* at 45–46.

123 Alexander Chipman Koty, *Labor Mobility in ASEAN: Current Commitments and Future Limitations*, ASEAN Briefing, May 13, 2006, www.aseanbriefing.com/news/2016/05/13/asean-labor-mobility.html (last visited Nov. 25, 2019).

124 Guntur Sugiyarto & Dovelyn Rannveig Agunias, *A "Freer" Flow of Skilled Labour within ASEAN: Aspirations, Opportunities and Challenges in 2015 and Beyond*, IOM-MPI Issues in Brief, No. 11 (2014), at 3.

125 Nikomborirak & Jitdumrong, *supra* note 117, at 130.

126 Yoshifumi Fukunaga, *Challenges of ASEAN MRAs on Professional Services*, *in* ASEAN Law in the New Regional Economic Order: Global Trends and Shifting Paradigms 111, 115–19 (Pasha L. Hsieh & Bryan Mercurio eds. 2019) (ASEAN Law in the New Regional Economic Order).

ASEAN ought to further harmonize national laws and regulations in order to remedy the current weaknesses. Based on common criteria, ASEAN countries should narrowly apply the MRAs' "subject to domestic laws and regulations" provisions and enlarge the right of independent practice for professionals.[127] States should also increase the distinction between ASEAN and other foreign professionals by according the former more preferential treatment. Although ASEAN's labor mobility is limited to skilled labor, the leaders should bear in mind that facilitating the movement of semi-skilled or unskilled workers will yield poverty-related gains and reduce the bloc's two-tiered development gap. An interim step can be modeled on the MRA on Tourism Professionals and to include MRAs on additional unregulated professions.

C *Investment Liberalization and Investor-State Disputes*

Sound investment law and policy are critical to FDI inflows that catalyze development for the Global South. ASEAN has become an appealing investment magnet because of its rapid growth and emerging markets ranging from Indonesia to Myanmar. In the past two decades, ASEAN's FDI inflows have ascended more than sixfold and the value of FDIs now accounts for 21 percent of FDI stock in all developing countries.[128] Significantly, given China's economic slowdown, ASEAN overtook China in attracting FDI for the first time in 2013.[129] Other than intra-ASEAN FDIs, the top five investors in ASEAN are Japan, China, Hong Kong, the United States and the Netherlands.[130] FDI expedites the consolidation of foreign investors' production network and led to over 450 cross-border sales of mergers and acquisitions in ASEAN.[131]

The AEC Blueprint 2025 mandates that the ACIA achieve the "progressive liberalization" of current restrictions, enhance investment protection and improve transparency of investment rules.[132] Concluded in 2009, the ACIA integrates the 1987 Agreement for the Promotion and Protection of Investments and the 1998 Framework Agreement on the

[127] *E.g.*, ASEAN MRA on Nursing Services (2006), art. 3.2; ASEAN MRA on Engineering Services (2005), art. 3.3.

[128] ASEAN, ASEAN at 50: A Historic Milestone for FDI and MNEs in ASEAN (2017), at xiii & 6–7.

[129] Justin Wood, *Re-drawing the ASEAN Map: How Companies Are Crafting New Strategies in South-east Asia* (2017), at 4.

[130] ASEAN & UNCTAD, *supra* note 100, at 22.

[131] *Id.* at 23–30.

[132] AEC Blueprint 2025, para. 14.

ASEAN Investment Area. The pre-ACIA pacts and their amending protocols failed to generate the expected impact. The 1987 Agreement was similar to conventional bilateral investment treaties (BITs) and did not include investment liberalization.[133] The 1998 Framework Agreement was not sufficiently progressive to enable ASEAN states to recover from the Asian financial crisis because of the temporary and sensitive exclusion lists.[134]

1 Reforming the Investment Regime: Beyond a BIT

The ACIA improves previous agreements by incorporating investment liberalization, protection, promotion and facilitation. Although the ACIA does not create direct effect in domestic law, it provides best practices for newer ASEAN countries. The recent enactment of Laos and Myanmar's investment laws evidences the ACIA's impact on shaping the substance of domestic laws.[135] Looking ahead, it is vital to streamline the linkage between the ACIA and other AEC agreements. The commercial presence of enterprises under the ACIA's commitments can be obstructed by Mode 4 restrictions under the ASEAN MNP Agreement.

There are notable features of the ACIA. The scope of its application extends only to ASEAN investors and investments. As "investors" can be natural and juridical persons, a non-ASEAN company is entitled to the benefits and protection under the ACIA if the company is incorporated under the law of an ASEAN country and has "substantive business operations" in the country.[136] Akin to the US Model BIT, the ACIA adopted a broad, non-exhaustive and asset-based definition of investments, which denote "every kind of asset" ranging from movable and immovable property to intellectual property rights.[137] To avoid ambiguity that could result in proliferating claims, the ACIA excludes assets that do not have "the characteristics of an investment."[138]

Critical to investors, the ACIA's liberalization of cross-border investment extends to five main sectors (agriculture, fishery, forestry,

133 Julien Chaisse & Sufian Jusoh, *The ASEAN Comprehensive Investment Agreement: The Regionalisation of Laws and Policy on Foreign Investment* 67–68 (2016).

134 Julien Chaisse, *The ACIA: Much More Than a BIT of Protection for Foreign Investors, in* ASEAN Law in the New Regional Economic Order 232, 237 (2019).

135 Sufian Jusoh, *Investment Liberalization in ASEAN: Moving Myths to Reality, in* ASEAN Law in the New Regional Economic Order 209, 218–25 (2019).

136 ACIA, arts. 3(1), 4(d) & 19; Julien Chaisse & Sufian Jusoh, *supra* note 133, at 76–78.

137 ACIA, art. 4(c).

138 *See id.* art. 4(c) & fn. 2 ("The characteristics of an investment include the commitment of capital, the expectation of gain or profit, or the assumption of risk.").

manufacturing and mining and quarrying), as well as sectors that cover services incidental to these main sectors.[139] In 2019, the Fourth Protocol to Amend the ACIA further enhanced the liberalization efforts. The original ACIA included a single, negative-list annex that covers states' existing and future nonconforming measures in the liberalized sectors.[140] Following the international trend, the Fourth Protocol transformed a single annex to two-annex negative lists.[141] ASEAN countries would indicate their existing nonconforming measures in the first index and schedule reservations for policy discretion allowing for future measures in the second index.[142] This new modality accords additional transparency for potential investors.

In addition to provisions on national treatment and most-favored-nation treatment, the ACIA prohibits performance requirements. Tellingly, the Fourth Protocol amended the original provision that applied the WTO Agreement on Trade-Related Investment Measures (TRIMs).[143] The new TRIMs-plus requirement, which extends to pre-establishment and post-establishment stages of investment, makes the level of the ACIA's performance requirement even higher than that of ASEAN Plus One agreements.[144]

As for the standards of investment protection, controversies have often resulted from the interpretation of fair and equitable treatment. ACIA provisions prevent the host country's arbitrary decisions and accord investors due process such as rights to legal representation and appeal in legal proceedings.[145] Investors are likely to resort to BITs to seek compensation in cases of expropriation. Importantly, the ACIA clarifies the disputed concept of indirect expropriation by defining it as a public action that "has an effect equivalent to direct expropriation without formal transfer of title or outright seizure."[146] This type of determination

139 *Id.* art. 3(3).

140 *Id.* art. 9; ASEAN, ASEAN Comprehensive Investment Agreement: A Guidebook for Businesses & Investors (2d 2015), at 10–11.

141 Ministry of Trade and Industry, *supra* note 96, at 4.

142 *Id.* at 4 fn. 6.

143 ACIA, art. 7; Ministry of Trade and Industry, *supra* note 96, at 5.

144 Ministry of Trade and Industry, *supra* note 96, at 5. For Agreement on Trade-Related Investment Measures-plus provisions in Asian free trade agreements, see United Nations, *South-South Trade in Asia: The Role of Regional Trade Agreements* (2008), at 90–91.

145 ACIA, art. 11; ASEAN, *supra* note 140, at 15.

146 ACIA, art. 14; ACIA Annex 2: Expropriation and Compensation, art. 2(b).

will entail "a case-by-case, fact-based inquiry" and consider several factors such as the economic impact of public measures.[147]

2 New Challenges to the ISDS Mechanism

In new Asian regionalism, a significant development is the backlash against the investor-state dispute settlement (ISDS) mechanism, which has become contentious in trade negotiations. Initially designed to overcome the local court bias and the hurdle for an investor's home state to exercise diplomatic protection, ISDS entitles foreign investors to sue host states in international judicial bodies. The Convention on the Settlement of Investment Disputes between States and Nationals of Other States (ICSID Convention) culminated multilateral efforts to create a mechanism to adjudicate investor-state disputes under the auspices of the World Bank.[148] As three ASEAN states (Laos, Myanmar and Vietnam) are yet to join the ICSID Convention, the ACIA is of significance to resolve investor-state disputes in the region.

Under the influence of the US Model BIT and the North American Free Trade Agreement, the ACIA went beyond conventional BITs by incorporating more detailed arbitration procedures than those of the ICSID Convention.[149] The ACIA stipulates that an ASEAN investor may bring the claim against the host state according to the procedures of regional arbitral centers or the ICSID Convention.[150] Subject to their jurisdiction, domestic courts such as the Singapore International Commercial Court may also hear ISDS cases arising from the ACIA.[151]

The ACIA aims to balance rights between states and investors. For instance, the clarification of fair and equitable treatment and the exclusion of most-favored-nation treatment in ISDS procedures prevent proliferating claims that undermine states' regulatory sovereignty.[152] Undeniably, as an investment pact enacted to invigorate South-based regionalism, the ACIA is required to include additional procedural rules. A loophole arguably exists in Article 41, which stipulates that an arbitral tribunal shall "request a joint interpretation of" the disputing ACIA provision.[153]

147 ACIA Annex 2: Expropriation and Compensation, art. 3.

148 163 states signed the Convention. List of Contracting States and Other Signatories of the Convention (as of Apr. 12, 2019), ICSID/3.

149 *See generally* Zewei Zhong, *The ASEAN Comprehensive Investment Agreement: Realizing a Regional Community*, 6(1) Asian J. Comp. L. 1, 4–5 (2011).

150 ACIA, arts. 32 & 33. The procedure, refer to ASEAN, *supra* note 140, at 22.

151 Singapore International Commercial Court Users Guide (2019), at 1–2.

152 ACIA, art. 6 fn. 4(1) & art. 11(2).

153 ACIA, art . 41(2).

Nevertheless, the ACIA explains neither the required format of the request nor to which agency the tribunal should make the request.[154]

At the global level, there have been more than 3,200 international investment agreements and 1,000 ISDS disputes.[155] However, none of the investors and countries have resorted to the ACIA since it came into effect in 2012. The only ISDS case that arose from ASEAN agreements is *Yaung Chi Oo v. Myanmar*, in which a Singaporean company challenged Myanmar's expropriation of a joint venture brewery.[156] Based on the interpretation of pre-ACIA agreements, the tribunal dismissed the case on jurisdictional grounds without examining its merit.[157] Arguably, the rare utilization of the ACIA is due to the ASEAN way of settling disputes via nonlitigation mechanisms and investors' concerns about undermining long-term relations with governments.

The case of *Philip Morris* v. *Australia* incurred recent public outcry about ISDS provisions. Relying on the Australia-Hong Kong BIT, the tobacco company, Philip Morris, challenged Australia's plain cigarette packaging legislation intended to reduce smoking.[158] Although the tribunal held in favor of Australia, ISDS is widely criticized for creating a "regulatory chill" that makes public policy measures vulnerable to foreign investors' legal challenges. ISDS is also perceived to be undemocratic for enabling foreign corporations to bypass domestic courts' jurisdiction. *Philip Morris* v. *Australia* led to the tobacco carveout clause of the Trans-Pacific Partnership and the Australia-Singapore FTA.[159] The CPTPP further limits the scope of ISDS by suspending selected provisions in the original agreement.[160]

Among ASEAN countries, Indonesia is at the forefront against ISDS because of the cases filed against the country under various BITs. The government has terminated 17 BITs since it unilaterally abrogated the BIT

[154] Cavinder Bull, *Enhancing the Rule of Law in Investor-State Dispute Settlement, in* The ASEAN Law Conference 2018: A Compendium of Speeches, Papers, Presentations and Reports 167, 173–74 (2019).

[155] UNCTAD, *World Investment Report 2020* (2020), at 106–10; UNCTAD, *World Investment Report 2019* (2019), at 18–19.

[156] Yaung Chi Oo Trading Pte Ltd. v. Government of the Union of Myanmar, 42 I.L.M. 404 (2003), paras. 4–8.

[157] *Id.* 76–86.

[158] Philip Morris Asia Ltd. v. Commonwealth of Australia, PCA Case No. 2012–12 (2015), paras. 7–8 & 89.

[159] CPTPP, art. 29.5; Agreement to Amend the Singapore-Australia Free Trade Agreement (2016), art. 22.

[160] CPTPP Suspensions Explained (2019), at 1–2.

with the Netherlands in 2014.[161] This means that the ACIA and ASEAN Plus Ones agreements will be the primary avenues by which foreign investors bring complaints against Jakarta. Since 2017, ISDS reforms have been discussed under the auspices of the UN and now 75 percent of investment agreements include reform elements.[162] In particular, the EU investment agreements with Singapore and Vietnam incorporate Brussels' proposal for the Investment Court System, which includes a two-tiered tribunal system to deal with investor-state disputes.[163] Nonetheless, this concept is unlikely to influence the ACIA because none of the ASEAN countries have considered the system in non-EU agreements.

D *State-to-State Disputes and Emerging Areas*

The ATIGA, the ATISA and the ACIA formed the three pillars for the AEC's legal framework. How do ASEAN countries resolve disputes concerning the interpretation and application of these agreements? A functional dispute settlement mechanism (DSM) would certainly benefit regional integration. The ASEAN Charter signifies a milestone of ASEAN's legalization process because it reinforces three mechanisms for ASEAN disputes of different nature. The mechanisms are respectively governed by the 1976 Treaty of Amity and Cooperation in Southeast Asia (TAC), the 2004 ASEAN Protocol on Enhanced Dispute Settlement Mechanism (EDSM), and the 2010 Protocol to the ASEAN Charter on DSMs.[164] For example, while the ACIA incorporates rules for investor-state disputes, state-to-state disputes arising from the application of the ACIA should rely on the EDSM.

1 Resolving Economic and Noneconomic Disputes

The TAC includes all ASEAN members and completing powers such as China, the United States and the EU. The TAC reflects parties' preference for the nonconfrontational ASEAN way. Although the High Council comprising foreign ministers is tasked with handling disputes, a TAC

161 Stephen L. Magiera, *International Investment Agreements and Investor-State Disputes: A Review and Evaluation for Indonesia*, ERIA Discussion Series (2017), at 4–16; Possible reform of Investor-State dispute settlement (ISDS): Comments by the Government of Indonesia: Note by the Secretariat, A/CN.9/WG.III/WP.156, Nov. 9, 2018, at 2–3.

162 UNCTAD, *IIA Issues Note: International Investment Agreements*, Issue 3 (2019), at 3; *see generally* Working Group III: Investor-State Dispute Settlement Reform, https://uncitral.un.org/en/working_groups/3/investor-state (last visited Nov. 28, 2019).

163 EU-Singapore Investment Protection Agreement (2018), arts. 3.9 & 3.10; EU-Singapore Investment Protection Agreement (2019), arts. 3.38 & 3.39.

164 ASEAN Charter, art. 24.

provision requires members to "have the determination and good faith to prevent disputes from arising."[165] For matters unrelated to the TAC, the EDSM deals with disputes arising from all economic agreements and the Protocol to the ASEAN Charter on DSMs covers noneconomic agreements such as the ASEAN Charter.

Notwithstanding the three ASEAN mechanisms for state-to-state disputes, none of them have been invoked by parties. ASEAN states have submitted territorial and trade disputes to the International Court of Justice (ICJ) and the WTO, respectively, rather than to the High Council of the TAC and the EDSM.[166] This practice shows that ASEAN states prefer international tribunals when ASEAN systems have overlapping jurisdiction. The inherent weakness of the TAC is obvious. TAC-related matters are exceptionally political and the agreement lacks compulsory jurisdiction and detailed procedures.[167] Presumably the only instance where a disputing ASEAN state ever considered utilizing an ASEAN mechanism occurred when Indonesia planned to submit the dispute involving the islands of Sipadan and Ligitan to the TAC.[168] Yet, Malaysia declined because of its territorial disputes with other neighboring states and concerns about the impartiality of ASEAN members.[169] Both Indonesia and Malaysia subsequently agreed to submit the case to the ICJ.

Distinct from the political nature of the TAC, the EDSM provides a scheme for dealing with intra-ASEAN economic disputes arising from AEC agreements. The EDSM includes detailed procedural rules. In fact, the EDSM is closely modeled after the WTO system and provides for the establishment of a panel and the Appellate Body.[170] Moreover, the ESDM follows the WTO's negative consensus rule. Similar to the WTO Dispute Settlement Body, the Senior Economic Officials Meeting will adopt ASEAN panel and Appellate Body reports.[171] The main procedural

[165] Treaty of Amity and Cooperation in Southeast Asia (1976) (TAC), arts. 13–15; Rules of Procedure of the High Council of the TAC (2001), rule 3.

[166] *E.g.*, International Court of Justice cases concerning the Temple Preah Vihear (Cambodia v. Thailand), Palau Sipadan and Pulau Litigan (Indonesia v. Malaysia), Pedra Branca, Middle Rocks and South Ledge (Malaysia v. Singapore) and a WTO case (DS371, the Philippines v. Thailand). Michael Ewing-Chow & Ranyta Yusran, *The ASEAN Trade Dispute Settlement Mechanism*, *in* The Legitimacy of International Trade Courts and Tribunals 365, 385–86 (Robert Howse et al. eds. 2018).

[167] Walter Woon, *Resolving Territorial Disputes in ASEAN*, 30 Chinese (Taiwan) YB Int'l L. & Aff. 1, 4 (2012).

[168] Severino, *supra* note 12, at 12.

[169] *Id.* at 13.

[170] ASEAN Protocol on Enhanced Dispute Settlement Mechanism (2004), arts. 5–14.

[171] *Id.* arts. 9(1) & 12(13).

differences between the WTO and EDSM proceedings lie in different timeframes for the adjudication process.[172]

In 2019, ASEAN states agreed to exclude non-violation claims from the EDSM to ensure the predictability of the system.[173] This change made the EDSM consistent with ASEAN Plus One agreements, but created a substantive difference from WTO proceedings.[174] Non-violation claims, currently allowed under WTO agreements, enable members to bring a complaint to challenge a measure that does not violate the rules, so long as the complainant can show that its benefits are nullified or impaired.[175]

Although the EDSM may be less costly and more locationally convenient than the WTO, ASEAN states have preferred the latter. The first-ever WTO complaint was filed by Singapore against Malaysia and was settled at the consultation stage.[176] The later case on cigarettes between the Philippines and Thailand reached the WTO Appellate Body.[177] A potential explanation for the trend is ASEAN states' confidence in the WTO's institutional framework and established jurisprudence. Commentators may suggest that the trend reveals the weakness in ASEAN's legalization of regionalism. I hold a different view. The fact that the EDSM is considered always as a "backup plan" has reinforced the de facto consolidation of DSMs at multiple levels and fortified the stability of international economic law.

More significantly, populist isolationism is endangering the WTO system. Given the ongoing WTO Appellate Body crisis, the EDSM will be a more feasible option for ASEAN states. The Trump administration's blocking of appointments of Appellate Body Members led to the departure of the "last judge" in 2020.[178] This essentially froze the function of the

[172] *See generally* Ewing-Chow & Yusran, *supra* note 166, at 371–75.

[173] Yashinta Difa Pramuyani, *Indonesia Signs ASEAN Protocol on Dispute Settlement*, Antara News, Nov. 1, 2019, https://en.antaranews.com/news/135715/indonesia-signs-asean-protocol-on-dispute-settlement (Dec. 2, 2019).

[174] *E.g.*, AANZFTA, ch. 17, art. 2(b) fn. 2; ASEAN-Hong Kong Free Trade Agreement (2017), ch. 13, art. 1(b) fn. 18.

[175] General Agreement on Tariffs and Trade (1994) (GATT), art. XXIII:1(b); GATS, art. XXIII:3. In December 2019, WTO members decided to extend the moratorium concerning the initiation of non-violation complaints under the Agreement on Trade-Related Aspects of Intellectual Property Rights (TRIPS 1994). TRIPS, art. 64(2); General Council Decision, TRIPS Non-Violation and Situation Complaints Moratorium, WT/L/1080, 1 Dec. 2019, at 1.

[176] DS1: Malaysia-Prohibition of Imports of Polyethylene and Polypropylene.

[177] DS371: Thailand-Customs and Fiscal Measures on Cigarettes from the Philippines.

[178] Hong Zhao from China was the "last" Appellate Body Member. Appellate Body Members, www.wto.org/english/tratop_e/dispu_e/ab_members_descrp_e.htm (last visited Feb. 2, 2021); *United States Continues to Block New Appellate Body Members for the World Trade Organization, Risking the Collapse of the Appellate Process*, 113(4) Am. J. Int'l L. 822, 822–23 (2019).

tribunal because at least three members are required to form a division to process appeals. A WTO member can now simply "block" the unfavorable panel decision by appealing it to the Appellate Body. Hence, under the AEC Blueprint 2025, the EDSM retains its value as a system "to promote a rule-based community."[179]

2 Digital Trade and E-Commerce

In new Asian regionalism, digital trade has become essential to multinational enterprises, as well as micro, small and medium-sized enterprises. For developing countries, industrialization can no longer rely on the manufacturing sector to absorb labor because technological progress in advanced economies has made their products much more cost-competitive.[180] E-commerce is now a key factor to the economic growth. It involves multifaceted requirements on cross-border data flows and protection. The EU General Data Protection Regulation and the CPTPP well illustrate the significance of regulatory requirements.[181] In 2019, WTO members including six ASEAN states also jointly supported the beginning of "WTO negotiations on trade-related aspects of" e-commerce.[182]

As the home to 360 million internet users, ASEAN's internet economy has reached USD$100 billion in 2019 and is expected to triple by 2025.[183] The AEC centers its enhanced connectivity on e-commerce and deems digital integration to be a top priority for the Fourth Industrial Revolution at the global level.[184] Also following the approach of incremental consolidation, the ASEAN regime on e-commerce creates a policy space of least developed countries in a structured way. As the first regional attempt, the 2020 e-ASEAN Framework Agreement urged the enactment of pertinent domestic laws that facilitate e-commerce transactions.[185]

Based on the Framework Agreement and strategic measures of the AEC Blueprint 2025, ASEAN leaders concluded the 2018 ASEAN Agreement on Electronic Commerce. In particular, states are required to expand paperless trading, recognize the validity of e-signatures, and provide consumer protection for e-commerce and personal data.[186] As for controversial rules to enable

179 AEC Blueprint 2025, para. 82(iv).
180 Dani Rodrik, *Straight Talk on Trade: Ideas for a Sane World Economy* 89–91 (2018).
181 *E.g.*, General Data Protection Regulation (2016), ch. 3; CPTPP, art. 14.13.
182 The ASEAN countries include Brunei, Laos, Malaysia, Myanmar, Singapore and Thailand. Joint Statement on Electronic Commerce, WT/L/1056, Jan. 25, 2019.
183 Google et al., *SEA Internet Economy Report 2019* (2019), at 10–14.
184 AEC Blueprint 2025, paras. 45–53; ASEAN, *supra* note 56, at 145–51.
185 *E.g.*, e-ASEAN Framework Agreement (2000), art. 5.
186 ASEAN Agreement on Electronic Commerce (2018), art. 7.

the electronic transfer of information and to restrict the localization of computer facilities, the requirements are not absolute. The agreement allows for exceptions under "legitimate public policy" and is "subject to [states'] respective laws and regulations."[187] Financial services are also excluded from the requirements.[188]

All ASEAN countries now have legislation on e-commerce after Cambodia enacted its e-commerce law in November 2019.[189] Considering divergent degrees of protection in domestic laws, ASEAN members should further harmonize domestic rules in line with their obligations under different trade agreements.[190] From a structural perspective, it is also vital to note that the agreement accords a longer period of implementation only to Cambodia, Laos and Myanmar.[191] Under the agreement, Vietnam is now considered to have "graduated" from special and differential treatment accorded to least developed countries.

3 Narrowing the Development Gap

While e-commerce is critical to development, ASEAN's structured approach to addressing its two-tiered development gap will provide valuable lessons for South-based regionalism. The economic divergence between the six more developed members and CLMV countries has consistently posed challenges to the AEC as a united market. The AEC Blueprint 2025 stresses the significance of narrowing the development gap via the Initiative for ASEAN Integration (IAI).[192] Built on previous IAI projects, the IAI Work Plan III covers actions from 2016 to 2020 and includes strategic areas, among which trade facilitation is critical to enforce AEC pacts.[193]

As ASEAN's most advanced economy, Singapore has implemented IAI projects by operating English training courses and trade facilitation

[187] *Id.* arts. 7(4) & (6).

[188] *Id.* arts. 7(4)(c) & (6)(c).

[189] *Cambodia Enacts a New E-commerce Law and a Consumer Protection Law*, Nov. 14, 2019, www.tilleke.com/resources/cambodia-enacts-new-e-commerce-law-and-consumer-protection-law (last visited Dec. 12, 2019); ASEAN, supra note 56, at 92.

[190] *E.g.*, Han-Wei Liu, *Data Localization and Digital Trade Barriers: ASEAN in Megaregionalism, in* ASEAN Law in the New Regional Economic Order 371, 379–83 (2019); Jane Kelsey, *The Risks for ASEAN of New Mega-Agreements that Promote the Wrong Model of e-Commerce*, ERIA Discussion Paper Series (2017), at 31–34.

[191] *E.g.*, ASEAN Agreement on Electronic Commerce (2018), art 7(2)(a) & 7(3)(b).

[192] AEC Blueprint 2025, paras. 74–75.

[193] The Initiative for ASEAN Integration (IAI) includes Work Plan I (2000–08), Work Plan II (2009–15) and the current Work Plan (2016–20). Initiative for ASEAN Integration (IAI) Work Plan III (2016), at 9–11.

in CLMV countries.[194] Other capacity building initiatives include the EU's assistance with the ASEAN Trade Repository, the US project on the ASEAN Single Window and Japan's financial support for CLMV officials to gain experience in the ASEAN Secretariat.[195] The involvement of multiple countries signifies their commitments to ASEAN. However, the effectiveness of fragmented IAI programs has been questionable. A main issue is foreign countries' unilateral adoption of IAI initiatives. In practice, project leaders from donor countries have only conducted informal meetings for information exchange without substantive coordination to reduce overlapping programs.[196]

To address the shortcoming and offer WTO-plus development assistance, I propose to consolidate IAI projects according to the Paris Declaration on Aid Effectiveness. Minimizing the transaction costs of the programs and offering need-based advisory assistance will benefit the operation of the AEC. It is imperative to incorporate the principle of ASEAN centrality by aligning development aids rendered by ASEAN and other countries. The ASEAN Secretariat should coordinate and monitor IAI projects. The integrated measures will help achieve the objective of the UN Sustainable Development Goals to revitalize the global partnership by fortifying "North-South, South-South and triangular cooperation."[197] Enhancing the trade-development nexus in the AEC framework will shape the legal development of the NREO.

IV External Agreements in the Global ASEAN Agenda

The legalization of the AEC and the evolution of ASEAN law comprises the bloc's internal agreements and external agreements. These agreements collectively underpin the legal foundation for new Asian regionalism. The AEC Blueprint 2025 aims to achieve ASEAN's global economic agenda by intensifying ASEAN Plus One agreements and the RCEP, thus ensuring its centrality in new Asian regionalism.[198] These pacts share common regulatory and structural features that reinforce global production networks and could provide a model for other FTAs.

194 *See generally* IAI Work Plan III (2016–20): Activities (2017).
195 *Id.*
196 Evaluation Unit et al., *Evaluation of EC Co-Cooperation with ASEAN: Final Report*, vol. 2 (2009), at 96–97.
197 Sustainable Development Goals (2015), Goal 17.
198 AEC Blueprint 2025, paras. 79–80; ASEAN, *supra* note 56, at 131–32.

As Table 2.1 below indicates, ASEAN as a bloc has concluded six sets of ASEAN Plus One agreements with seven Asia-Pacific economies. Except

Table 2.1 *ASEAN's external economic agreements*[199]

External Parties	Components/Agreements
China	- Framework Agreement (2002) - Trade in Goods Agreement (2004) - Dispute Settlement Mechanism Agreement (2004) - Trade in Services Agreement (2007) - Investment Agreement (2009)
Japan	- Framework Agreement (2003) - Agreement on Comprehensive Economic Partnership (2009) - First Protocol to amend the agreement to include the Chapters on Trade in Services, Movement of Natural Persons and Investment (2019)
India	- Framework Agreement (2003) - Trade in Goods Agreement (2009) - Dispute Settlement Mechanism Agreement (2009) - Trade in Services Agreement (2014) - Investment Agreement (2014)
Korea	- Framework Agreement (2005) - Dispute Settlement Mechanism Agreement (2005) - Trade in Goods Agreement (2006) - Trade in Services Agreement (2007) - Investment Agreement (2009)
Australia and New Zealand	- Free Trade Agreement (2009)
Hong Kong	- Free Trade Agreement (2017) - Investment Agreement (2017)
China, Japan, Korea, Australia and New Zealand	- Regional Comprehensive Economic Partnership (RCEP, 2020)

199 Free Trade Agreements with Dialogue Partners, https://asean.org/asean-economic-community/free-trade-agreements-with-dialogue-partners/ (last visited Feb. 2, 2021); ASEAN, *supra* note 56, at 132.

for ASEAN's agreements with Australia, New Zealand and Hong Kong, other ASEAN Plus One FTAs reflect the pragmatic incrementalism, which led to the gradual consolidation approach. Distinct from the North's neoliberal approach that incorporates key components in one comprehensive pact, most ASEAN Plus One agreements follow a "building block" structure. This approach energizes consensus building and provides a model for politically sensitive trade agreements such as the ones across the Taiwan Strait.[200]

Although Australia and New Zealand first approached ASEAN for an FTA, China concluded the first ASEAN Plus One agreement in 2002.[201] ASEAN's agreements with China, Japan, India and Korea follow a common approach based on the bilateral framework agreements. Under WTO law, a framework agreement can be understood as an "interim agreement" that denotes the lowest level of economic integration leading to a full FTA.[202] Article XXIV of the General Agreement on Tariffs and Trade (GATT) requires the interim agreement to "include a plan and schedule for the formation of [the FTA] within a reasonable length of time."[203] As for the timeframe, WTO law stipulates that it "should exceed 10 years only in exceptional cases."[204] However, WTO jurisprudence has neither defined what constitutes "exceptional cases" nor mandated the degree of comprehensiveness of an FTA.

The ASEAN-China FTA is Asia's most significant South-South agreement. The volume of bilateral trade has tripled in the past decade and ASEAN, for the first time, replaced the United States as China's second largest trade partner in 2019.[205] As evidenced by this ASEAN Plus One agreement, the framework agreement not only requires the full FTA to be established "within 10 years," but also incorporates specific agendas for

200 Pasha L. Hsieh, *China-Taiwan Free Trade Agreement*, *in* Bilateral and Regional Trade Agreements: Case Studies 97, 102–09 (Simon Lester et al. eds. 2d ed. 2015).

201 David Chin Soon Siong, *ASEAN's Journey towards Free Trade*, *in* Economic Diplomacy: Essays and Reflections by Singapore's Negotiations 209, 218–19 (C. L. Lim & Margaret Liang eds. 2011).

202 GATT, chapeau to art. XXIV:5, XXIV:5(a) & (b), and XXIV:7(a).

203 *Id.* XXIV:5(c).

204 Understanding on the Interpretation of Article XXIV of the GATT, para. 3.

205 Huang Xilian, *Building Stronger ASEAN-China Relations in New Era*, Jakarta Post, Nov. 2, 2019, www.thejakartapost.com/academia/2019/11/02/building-stronger-asean-china-relations-in-new-era.html (last visited Dec. 3, 2019); Rajiv Biswas, *ASEAN-China Trade Boosting Growth*, China Daily, Nov. 19, 2018, https://global.chinadaily.com.cn/a/201811/19/WS5bf1f6a6a310eff303289619.html (last visited Dec. 3, 2019).

completing other pacts.[206] The framework agreement also includes an "early harvest program" that immediately liberalizes trade in goods, so that parties will be entitled to trade benefits before finalizing additional agreements.[207] With the conclusion of subsequent agreements on trade in goods, DSM, trade in services and investment, the comprehensive ASEAN-China FTA became effective in 2010.

Comparable to AEC agreements, the liberalization process under ASEAN Plus One agreements take into account the development needs of CLMV countries. Goods placed under normative and sensitive tracks are subject to tariff reductions and elimination under different timeframes.[208] For instance, the tariff elimination schedules of ASEAN Plus One FTAs accord transitional periods to CLMV countries from ten to eighteen years from the signing of the agreements.[209] The rules of origin of ASEAN's external FTAs have developed in line with those of the ATIGA. The ASEAN-China FTA Upgrading Protocol that amended the rules of origin came into effect in 2016.[210] Except for the most restrictive rules of origin under the ASEAN-India FTA, all of ASEAN Plus One agreements now follow the ATIGA. The coequal rule under these agreements extends to exporters the flexibility to choose CTC or RVC 40 percent.[211] The harmonization of the rules of origin significantly negates the noodle bowl syndrome and promotes business friendly FTAs in new Asian regionalism.

The AEC agreements have followed the gradual consolidation approach. Commentators preoccupied with the Western notion of legalization and the neoliberal approach of comprehensive trade agreements may suggest that the ASEAN way merely leads to incomplete, fragmented agreements

206 Framework Agreement on Comprehensive Economic Co-operation between the Association of South East Asian Nations and the People's Republic of China (2002), arts. 2 & 8.

207 *Id.* art. 6.

208 Chin, *supra* note 201, at 221–40.

209 Shujiro Urata, Constructing and Multilateralizing the Regional Comprehensive Economic Partnership: An Asian Perspective, ADBI Working Paper Series, No. 449 (2013), at 15.

210 Previously, the rules of origin under the ASEAN-China FTA allowed primarily the Regional Value Content (RVC) 40 percent rule. The 2015 Updating Protocol includes the Change in Tariff Classification (CTC) option. Ministry of Trade and Industry Singapore, *A Guide to Understanding the ASEAN-China Free Trade Area Update* (2016), at 2.

211 The ASEAN-India FTA follows Change in Tariff Subheading (the equivalent of CTC at the Harmonized System at six-digit level) and RVC 35 percent rules, while other ASEAN Plus One FTAs allow CTC or RVC 40 percent. Urata, *supra* note 209, at 15; Sanchita Basu Das et al., *Can ASEAN+1 FTAs Be a Pathway towards Negotiating and Designing the Regional Comprehensive Economic Partnership (RCEP) Agreement?*, 50(2) J. World Trade 253, 266–67 (2016).

with low-level liberalization commitments. The evolution of both ASEAN's internal and external agreement collectively rebuts the assumption. The legal framework for services liberalization is a conspicuous example.

Like the AFAS, ASEAN agreements with China and Korea adopted the successive package structure for services commitments. Although the first package under the ASEAN-China FTA contained rare GATS-minus commitments, the second package remedied the situation by elevating the commitments to GATS-plus.[212] The framework agreements facilitate consensus building and make ASEAN Plus One FTAs "living" agreements. After the 2019 Protocol to amend the ASEAN-Japan FTA by incorporating services and investment provisions, all of ASEAN's agreements with external partners have become "comprehensive" in their coverage. The detailed analysis in Chapter 3 will demonstrate that the evolution of ASEAN agreements has facilitated the formation of the RCEP.

V Conclusion

The founding of ASEAN in 1967 heralded an era of Asian integration. The creation of the AEC in 2015 further signifies a landmark in new Asian regionalism that has evolved since the inception of the Doha Round. This chapter provided the most up-to-date examination of the legal framework for the AEC. It offered insight into how the legalization of the ASEAN way based on the pragmatic incrementalism has contributed to the normative structure of the NREO distinct from the European path.

Significantly, the chapter explained the integrated scheme premised on the gradual evolution of ASEAN agreements including the ATIGA, the ATISA, the ATISA and ASEAN Plus One agreements. These pacts collectively transformed the politically-oriented ASEAN way into a legal concept that imposes soft-law and hard-law obligations. Furthermore, the evolution of these agreements demonstrates incremental consolidation of commitments based on horizontal cooperation. Consequently, the AEC has provided an alternative model of integration to the Global South and the ASEAN-centered regime has formed an essential legal foundation for new Asian regionalism.

[212] Yoshifumi Fukunaga & Hikari Ishido, *Assessing the Progress of Services Liberalization in the ASEAN-China Free Trade Area (ACFTA)*, ERIA Discussion Paper Series (2013), at 3–17; ASEAN, *supra* note 56, 134–36.

3

Signing the RCEP As a Milestone

I Introduction

Fifteen Asia-Pacific countries concluded the Regional Comprehensive Economic Partnership (RCEP) at the virtual summit in November 2020, making the RCEP the world's largest free trade agreement (FTA).[1] As Figure 3.1 below demonstrates, the RCEP's share of global gross domestic product (GDP) amounts to 30 percent, which exceeds that of any existing trade bloc ranging from the United States-Mexico-Canada Agreement (USMCA) to the Pacific Alliance.[2] As a market that covers a population of 2.2 billion and 40 percent of the world's mergers and acquisitions, the economic scale of the RCEP is comparable to that of the European Union (EU) and the Comprehensive and Progressive Agreement for Trans-Pacific Partnership (CPTPP) combined.[3] More fundamentally, the RCEP highlights the pivotal role of Global South powers in world trade governance. This mega-FTA represents a historic milestone of new Asian regionalism that manifests Asia's collective response to populist protectionism and the recovery of the economic effects of the COVID-19 pandemic.

From a normative perspective, the RCEP contributes to the shaping of the New Regional Economic Order (NREO) in the Third Regionalism. The NREO departs from the South's approach of the New International Economic Order (NIEO) in the 1970s. The NREO is overtaking the North-dominated Washington Consensus that underpinned postwar economic

[1] Joint Leaders' Statement on the Regional Comprehensive Economic Partnership (RCEP) (Joint Leaders' Statement on the RCEP) (2020).

[2] *Id.*

[3] *Id.*; United Nations Conference on Trade and Development (UNCTAD), *RCEP Agreement as a Potential Boost for Investment in Sustainable Post-COVID Recovery, Investment Trends Monitor* (2020), at 8.

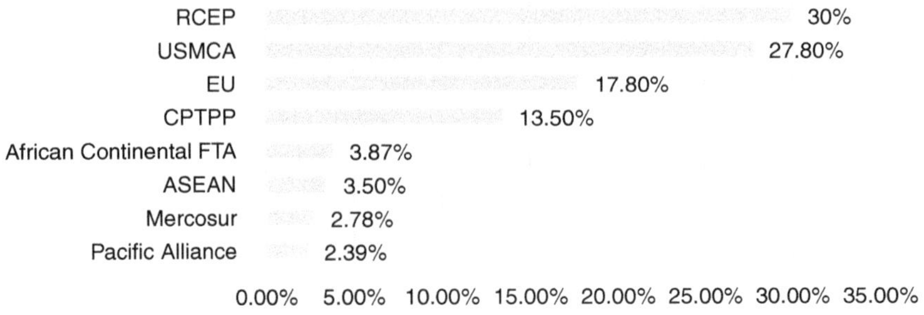

Figure 3.1 Trade blocs: shares of global GDP[4]

order. The new dependency theory expounds the implications of the RCEP. The original, classical dependency theory that influenced the NIEO presupposed the underdevelopment of developing countries to be the result of the neocolonial relationship between the North and the South.[5] The theory predicted the perpetual underdevelopment of the South because international trade only exacerbated dependency on the North.[6] Nevertheless, the economic development of four Asian tigers and the People's Republic of China (PRC) disapproved the prediction.

To remedy the theoretical weakness, the new dependency theorists contended that dependency and development can co-exist.[7] Specifically, dependency is dynamic because certain developing countries have utilized dependent capitalism to pursue export-driven growth and altered neo-colonial ties with the North.[8] While the new dependency theory

4 Joint Leaders' Statement on the RCEP, *supra* note 1; Association of Southeast Asian Nations (ASEAN) Secretariat, *ASEAN Integration Report 2019* (2019), at 127; Government of Canada, *About the Comprehensive and Progressive Agreement for Trans-Pacific Partnership*, July 16, 2019, www.international.gc.ca/trade-commerce/trade-agreements-accords-commerciaux/agr-acc/cptpp-ptpgp/backgrounder-document_information.aspx?lang=eng (last visited Dec. 31, 2020). Gross domestic product of the United States-Mexico-Canada Agreement (three countries), the European Union (twenty-seven countries, after Brexit), African Continental Free Trade Area (fifty-five countries), Mercosur (five countries), the Pacific Alliance (four countries) are based on statistics of the World Bank at https://data.worldbank.org/indicator/NY.GDP.MKTP.CD and the International Monetary Fund at www.imf.org/external/datamapper/PPPSH@WEO/OEMDC/ADVEC/WEOWORLD/VUT (last visited Dec. 31, 2020).

5 *E.g.*, Theotonio Dos Santos, *The Structure of Dependence*, 60 Am. Econ. Rev. 231, 232–34 (1970); Fernando Henrique Cardoso & Enzo Faletto, *Dependency and Development in Latin America* 16–17 (Marjory Mattingly Urquidi trans., 1979).

6 Alvin Y. So, *Social Change and Development: Modernization, Dependency, and World-System Theories* 95–102 (1990).

7 *Id.* at 164–65.

8 *Id.* at 157–64; Thomas Baron Gold, *State and Society in the Taiwan Miracle* 21–90 (1986).

relies on the cases of Taiwan and South Korea in the Second Regionalism, it can be applied to the Third Regionalism in which the Association of Southeast Asian Nations (ASEAN) played a pivotal role. The "ASEAN Plus Six" structure provides new empirical insight into the theory. In particular, the signing of the RCEP augments the economic and normative capacities of Asian developing countries. The collective power of these nations has enabled them to escape from the underdevelopment dilemma. Amid the World Trade Organization (WTO) impasse and eroding US influence, the RCEP further empowers these countries to fill the leadership vacuum left by America and to guide the emerging NREO.

The RCEP should be understood objectively without subscribing to the EU or US-centric standpoint of regionalism.[9] I will clarify the three main myths associated with this mega-FTA. First, the RCEP has been inaccurately portrayed as a China-led trade pact.[10] This understanding is parochial in situating the RCEP in the context of the US-China rivalry. It misses the larger picture of the RCEP's impact on regional and multilateral trading systems. In fact, the RCEP was initiated and led by the ten-country ASEAN.[11] Although the role of China cannot be ignored, RCEP parties including Beijing recognize that the RCEP reinforces the "ASEAN centrality in regional frameworks."[12] While the normative power of the EU has been coined as the "Brussels Effect," what drove new Asia regionalism is the ASEAN Effect premised on the ASEAN Plus Six framework.[13] The RCEP will enhance the transformation of the "ASEAN way" from soft-law obligations into hard-law rules with structured flexibility.

9 *E.g.*, Amitav Acharya, *Whose Ideas Matter? Agency and Power in Asian Regionalism* 27 (2009); Fredrik Söderbaum, *Rethinking Regionalism* 7–8 & 175 (2016).

10 *E.g.*, Keith Bradsher & Ana Swanson, *China-Led Trade Pact Is Signed, in Challenge to U.S.*, Nov. 15, 2020, N.Y. Times, www.nytimes.com/2020/11/15/business/china-trade-rcep.html (last visited Jan. 1, 2021).

11 Joint Leaders' Statement on the RCEP, *supra* note 1; Grace Ho, *RCEP Negotiators Recount Twists and Turns in 8-Year Journey to World's Biggest Trade Pact*, Nov. 28, 2020, Straits Times, www.straitstimes.com/business/economy/rcep-negotiators-recount-twists-and-turns-in-8-year-journey-to-worlds-biggest-trade (last visited Jan. 1, 2020).

12 Joint Leaders' Statement on the RCEP, *supra* note 1; Deng Xijun, *RCEP: Historic Milestone for ASEAN Centrality*, Nov. 20, 2020, Jakarta Post, www.thejakartapost.com/academia/2020/11/20/rcep-historic-milestone-for-asean-centrality.html (last visited Jan. 1, 2021).

13 For information on the Brussels Effect, see Anu Bradford, *The Brussels Effect: How the European Union Rules the World* 26–36 (2020).

Second, since the inception of its negotiations, the RCEP has been dubbed an FTA of low quality and ambition.[14] Even after its conclusion, RCEP leaders' proclamation of the RCEP "as a modern, comprehensive, high-quality and mutually beneficial agreement" is regarded as political rhetoric.[15] Criticism against the RCEP is often based on comparisons to the Trans-Pacific Partnership (TPP) or the CPTPP that incorporates higher-standard provisions and value-based commitments on labor and environmental protection. This position ignores two complementary approaches of regionalism. The vertical approach pursues innovative and high-standard norms but is accepted by a smaller number of countries. The horizontal approach stresses the multilateralization of WTO-plus and extra rules to which more developing countries are willing to adhere. While the CPTPP follows the former, the RCEP represents the latter. By 2030, the CPTPP and the RCEP are projected to increase annual global incomes by $147 and $186 billion, respectively.[16] Neither regionalism approach should be taken lightly.

I concede that the RCEP is a rule-taker. It does not seek to "invent" rules that are absent in US or EU FTAs. However, the membership and economic scale of the RCEP indicate that the "Western" rules it adopts became "Asian" rules of global significance. For instance, the RCEP's consolidation of rules of origins alone will yield immediate and substantial benefits to Asian businesses. The pragmatic incrementalism of ASEAN's internal and external FTAs also suggests that various review clauses of the RCEP will make it a "living agreement."

Finally, while the RCEP cements the FTA network among RCEP members, it may worsen trade fragmentation. From the FTA linkage perspective, the RCEP makes Japan a clear "winner," as Tokyo presently lacks bilateral FTAs with China, Korea and New Zealand.[17] The RCEP fills the void and serves as the benchmark for sequent negotiations of agreements such as the China-Japan-Korea FTA. Notwithstanding these benefits, commentators averred that Asian integration has been hindered by the "noodle bowl" syndrome, as complex and divergent rules of origin

[14] Jeffery D. Wilson, *Mega-Regional Trade Deals in the Asia-Pacific: Choosing Between the TPP and RCEP?* 45(2) J. Contemp. Asia 343, 349 (2015); Tim McDonald, What Is the Regional Comprehensive Economic Partnership (RCEP)? Nov. 16, 2020, BBC, www.bbc.com/news/business-54899254 (last visited Jan. 1, 2020).

[15] Joint Leaders' Statement on the RCEP, *supra* note 1.

[16] Peter A. Petri & Michael G. Plummer, *East Asia Decouples from the United States: Trade War, COVID-19, and East Asia's New Trade Blocs*, Peterson Institute for International Economics Working Paper (2020), at 4–5.

[17] *RCEP: A Guide to the World's Largest Trade Agreement*, Asia House Advisory Briefing (2020), at 5.

under different FTAs limit their actual usage.[18] In reality, the syndrome has influenced other areas ranging from services and investment regulations to dispute settlement mechanisms.

An ideal solution is to enable the RCEP to replace internal FTAs and bilateral investment agreements (BITs). This clean-slate model was what Australia, New Zealand and Singapore advocated during TPP negotiations.[19] Nevertheless, neither the CPTPP nor the RCEP will supersede existing agreement between members. In particular, the RCEP reiterates the parties' intention for the RCEP to coexist with other agreements already in place.[20] While the RCEP will not eliminate the noodle bowl syndrome on a de jure basis, it will alleviate the trade fragmentation problem on a de facto basis, galvanizing businesses to utilize the RCEP over existing pacts.

The chapter offers insight into the evolution of the RCEP and argues that this mega-FTA serves as a milestone for new Asian regionalism. It will examine how the RCEP converges the legal and political agendas of ASEAN and China. It will also explain India's decision to withdraw from RCEP negotiations in 2019.[21] The chapter will shed light on the RCEP's role in consolidating rules of origin, regulations services, as well as arguably weaker provisions on investment protection, government procurement and electronic commerce (e-commerce). A comparative analysis will be based on contemporary agreements such as ASEAN Plus One FTAs and the CPTPP. Lastly, the chapter will assess the systemic impact of the RCEP on regional and global trading systems. Prospective normative conflicts due to overlapping agreements and the institutionalization of the RCEP Secretariat will be of significance to world trade law.

II Legal and Political Agendas of Asian Powers

The shift of economic gravity to Asia marks the most salient feature of the Third Regionalism. By 2050, 52 percent of global GDP will arise from Asia, enabling the region to attain a dominant economic status that it once possessed before the eighteenth-century Industrial

[18] Richard Baldwin & Masahiro Kawai, *Multilateralizing Asian Regionalism*, ADBI Working Paper Series, No. 431 (2013), at 11–12; AEC Blueprint 2025, para. 10(ii).

[19] Deborah K. Elms & C. L. Lim, *An Overview and Snapshot of the TPP Negotiations, in* The Trans-Pacific Partnership: A Quest for a Twenty-first-Century Trade Agreement 21, 35–37 (C. L. Lim et al. eds. 2012).

[20] Regional Comprehensive Economic Partnership (2020) (RCEP), art. 20.2.

[21] *E.g.*, Surendar Singh & Ram Singh, *Domestic Sources of India's Trade Policy References in RCEP Negotiations*, 54(4) J. World Trade 503, 503–13 (2020).

Revolution.[22] China, Japan, ASEAN and India are among the world's top six largest economies.[23] China's rapid recovery from the COVID-19 pandemic is expected to allow the country to overtake America as the number one economy in 2028.[24] India and ASEAN will also become the world's third and fourth largest economies, respectively.[25]

In the 1990s, the evolution of the Asia-Pacific Economic Cooperation (APEC) escalated aspirations for Asian regionalism. Due to its institutional weakness, APEC itself has achieved no major breakthroughs from the Bogor Goals, which had targeted "free and open trade and investment in the Asia-Pacific" by 2020.[26] The Asian financial crisis exacerbated Asian leaders' frustrations over US-dominated global financial institutions and prompted the creation of the "ASEAN Plus Three" framework for currency stability.[27] The subsequent global financial crisis further accelerated Asian integration. The ASEAN-based framework evolved into the ASEAN Plus Six structure that forms the normative basis for the Asian FTA network.

A ASEAN Centrality

ASEAN is not regarded as a conventional power. European integration has been premised on French-German cooperation, whereas ASEAN centrality became a consensus for new Asian regionalism because of the China-Japan rivalry. Beijing and Tokyo have been Asia's strongest regional powers since the Meiji Restoration. At the inception of the Third Regionalism, they vigorously competed for Asia's economic leadership. In 2001, the East Asian Vision Group proposed the East Asian Free Trade Area (EAFTA).[28] China preferred the EAFTA proposal, which was based on the ASEAN Plus Three framework.

[22] Asian Development Bank, *Asia 2050: Realizing the Asian Century: Executive Summary* (2011), at 3–5.

[23] ASEAN Secretariat, *ASEAN Key Figures 2020* (2020), at 39.

[24] Centre for Economics and Business Research (CEBR), *World Economic League Table 2021* (2020), at 70–71.

[25] *Id.* at 113–14; Australian Government, *ASEAN's Economic Growth*, www.austrade.gov.au/asean-now/why-asean-matters-to-australia/asean-economic-growth/ (last visited Jan. 4, 2021).

[26] 1994 Leaders' Declaration (1994), para. 6.

[27] ASEAN Plus Three countries (China, Korea and Japan) created the currency swap arrangement, the Chiang Mai Initiative, which was the predecessor to the Chiang Mai Initiative Multilateralisation Agreement.

[28] *Report of the East Asian Vision Group II (EAVGII)* (2012), at 43–46; Rodolfo C. Severino, *Japan's Relations with ASEAN*, *in* ASEAN-Japan Relations 17, 26–28 (Takashi Shiraishi & Takaaki Kojima eds. 2014).

In 2006, Japan proposed the alternative Comprehensive Economic Partnership for East Asia (CEPEA), which extended membership of the EAFTA to ASEAN Plus Six parties.[29] Tokyo favored the CEPEA because India, Australia and New Zealand would counterbalance Chinese influence and the CEPEA would help implement the Fukuda Doctrine by enhancing ties with ASEAN.[30] In the meantime, APEC's Free Trade Area of the Asia Pacific (FTAAP) proposal and the Obama administration's plan to join TPP negotiations made roadmaps to Asian regionalism increasingly complex.[31]

In 2009, leaders of the East Asia Summit began to task their officials with evaluating EAFTA and CEPEA proposals, which were later incorporated into a joint Chinese and Japanese initiative.[32] In 2011, to avoid being marginalized and to buttress the ASEAN centrality, the bloc "ended the debate by proposing its own model for" the FTA, known as the RCEP, which would serve as an alternative pathway to the FTAAP.[33] The ASEAN Framework for the RCEP highlighted this mega-FTA as "an ASEAN-led process."[34] ASEAN also outlined key principles, including the inclusion of "an open accession clause" and "special and differential treatment" accorded to Cambodia, Laos, Myanmar and Vietnam (CLMV countries).[35]

Pursuant to the subsequent Guiding Principles and Objectives for the RCEP, ASEAN Plus Six leaders essentially agreed to merge EAFTA and CEPEA initiatives and to utilize the RCEP to improve existing ASEAN Plus One FTAs.[36] After sixteen leaders announced the RCEP at the East

29 Severino, *supra* note 28, at 27–28; Tamura Akihiko, *"Extrovert Regionalism" – CEPEA Portends Direction of Japan's New Trade Policy*, Japan Spotlight, Jul./Aug. 2017, at 38.

30 Seungjoo Lee, *Institutional Balancing and the Politics of Mega-FTAs in East Asia*, 56 Asian Survey 1055, 1069 (2016); Sueo Sudo, Japan's ASEAN Policy: In Search of Proactive Multilateralism 69–75 (2015).

31 Asia-Pacific Economic Cooperation (APEC), *ABAC Recommendations to APEC Leaders*, Nov. 11, 2004, www.apec.org/Press/News-Releases/2004/1111_abacrecmdleaders (last visited Jan. 4, 2021); Ian F. Fergusson & Brock R. Williams, *The Trans-Pacific Partnership (TPP): Key Provisions and Issues for Congress*, Congressional Research Service (2016), at 1–3.

32 Department of Foreign Affairs and Trade (DFAT), *Background to the Regional Comprehensive Economic Partnership (RCEP) Initiative*, www.dfat.gov.au/trade/agreements/negotiations/rcep/Pages/background-to-the-regional-comprehensive-economic-partnership-rcep-initiative (last visited Jan. 5, 2020).

33 *Id.*

34 *See generally* ASEAN Framework for Regional Comprehensive Economic Partnership (2011).

35 *Id.*

36 *See generally* Guiding Principles and Objectives for Negotiating the Regional Comprehensive Economic Partnership (2012) (RCEP Guiding Principles and Objectives).

Asia Summit, negotiations commenced in 2013.[37] In 2015, the original deadline for completing the RCEP became unachievable because of divergent development levels and conflicting priorities among members.[38] The rapid development of the TPP under US leadership overshadowed the RCEP. When the TPP was concluded in 2016, RCEP parties were still working on market access commitments without producing the text of the agreement.[39]

President Donald Trump's "America first" policy changed the game. His decision to withdraw the United States from the TPP in 2017 shifted Asia-Pacific countries' focus back to the RCEP. The new CPTPP talks and the US-China trade war expedited RCEP negotiations. Following thirty rounds of negotiations and various ministerial and leaders' meetings, RCEP parties finally concluded the mega-FTA with twenty chapters and associated annexes in 2020.[40] Amid the recession caused by COVID-19, the RCEP also represents Asian countries' normative response to trade revitalization.

For ASEAN, the RCEP helps accomplish the "Global ASEAN" objective of the ASEAN Economic Community (AEC) Blueprint 2025 by "integrating the AEC into the global economy."[41] From 2002 to 2017, ASEAN concluded six ASEAN Plus One FTAs with China, Japan, India, South Korea, Hong Kong, Australia and New Zealand.[42] To address the criticism against the RCEP, I contend that the amendments and upgraded negotiations of ASEAN Plus One FTAs demonstrate the pragmatic incrementalism of the ASEAN way.[43] These FTA experiences suggest that the RCEP will evolve and should not be overlooked based on its current form.

[37] DFAT, *supra* note 32; Joint Declaration on the Launch of Negotiations for the Regional Comprehensive Economic Partnership (2012); DFTA, *RCEP News*, www.dfat.gov.au/trade/agreements/not-yet-in-force/rcep/news (last visited Jan. 5, 2021).

[38] RCEP Guiding Principles and Objectives, sec. VIII.

[39] DFAT, *Eleventh Round of Negotiations – 15–19 February 2016, Bander Seri Begawan, Brunei Darussalam*, www.dfat.gov.au/trade/agreements/negotiations/rcep/news/Pages/eleventh-round-of-negotiations-15-19-february-2016-bander-seri-begawan-brunei-darussalam (last visited Jan. 5, 2021).

[40] DFAT, *supra* note 37.

[41] ASEAN Economic Community Blueprint 2025 (2015), para. E.

[42] *See generally* ASEAN, *Free Trade Agreements with Dialogue Partners*, https://asean.org/asean-economic-community/free-trade-agreements-with-dialogue-partners/ (last visited Jan. 5, 2021).

[43] ASEAN Secretariat, *supra* note 4, at 132. For the analysis of the pragmatic incrementalism in domestic law, see Shyamkrishna Balganesh, *The Pragmatic Incrementalism of Common Law Intellectual Property*, 63(6) Vanderbilt L. Rev. 1543, 1564–67 (2010); Arie Freiber, *Therapeutic Jurisprudence in Australia: Paradigm Shift or Pragmatic Incrementalism?* 20 (2) L. in Context 6, 11 (2003).

The RCEP provides a legal foundation for consolidating Asia-Pacific FTAs and advancing the ASEAN centrality in regional frameworks. The RCEP evidences that new Asian regionalism is operated on the "ASEAN consensus" rather than the Washington or Beijing consensus. As the new dependency theory posits, the RCEP will enable the collective power of the South to play a leadership role in shaping the trade-development nexus and new relations with the North.

B China As the Largest RCEP Economy

Since Deng Xiaoping's economic reform in the 1970s, China has ascended to a "new great power" at the global stage.[44] The United States and the EU now perceive China as a "serious competitor" or "systemic rival" not simply because of China's economic and industrial preeminence, but also because it advocates for a mercantilist Leninist model of development.[45] The Beijing model challenges Western dominance in the developing world. Departing from neoliberal private enterprise-based market economies, the PRC's approach combines authoritarian governance with large-scale infrastructure investment by state-owned enterprises (SOEs).[46] As the RCEP and Chinese FTAs illustrate, values-based considerations such as human rights and sustainable development are "delinked" from China's trade agreements and foreign economic policy.

As the largest RCEP economy, China's evolving legal and political agenda underlies its motivation for pursuing the mega-FTA. First, as "legitimacy concerns first and foremost the right to govern," the authority of the Chinese Communist Party has been premised on China's economic performance rather than democratic authorization of political power.[47] Similar to the rationale for China to enter the WTO, Chinese leaders have pursued the "two-level game" for utilizing FTAs to internalize international commitments, hence locking in and accelerating domestic

[44] Congyan Cai, *New Great Powers and International Law in the 21st Century*, 24(3) Eur. J. Int'l L. 755, 775–90 (2013).

[45] Lia Eustachewich, *Joe Biden Calls Russia an "Opponent," China a "Competitor" during Town Hall*, Sept. 18, 2020, N.Y. Post, https://nypost.com/2020/09/18/joe-biden-calls-russia-an-opponent-and-china-a-competitor/ (last visited Nov. 26, 2020); European Commission & High Representative of the Union for Foreign Affairs and Security Policy, *EU-China – Strategic Outlook*, Joint (2019) 5 final (2019), at 1.

[46] Gregory Shaffer & Henry Gao, *A New Chinese Economic Order?* 23(3) J. Int'l Econ. L. 607, 610–11 (2020).

[47] Jean Marc Coicaud, *Legitimacy and Politics: A Contribution to the Study of Political Right and Political Responsibility* 10 (2002).

economic reform.[48] The RCEP allows the central government to incrementally intensify external pressure on the domestic industry. Regardless of criticism against the RCEP, it cannot be ignored that China, for the first time, agreed on the more liberal negative list of investment and on the transfer of cross-border data and the prohibition of data localization.[49]

China's 14th five-year plan (2021–25) and 2035 version call for a "dual circulation" development strategy.[50] In President Xi Jinping's words, China will use its "super-large market scale and the potential of domestic demand to establish a new development pattern featuring domestic and international dual circulations that complement each other."[51] The dual circulation strategy responds to the economic recession caused by the US-China trade war and the COVID-19 pandemic. It aims to stimulate domestic consumption and demand to remedy the weakness of the current export-oriented economy. The RCEP will provide the impetus for the domestic restructuring that is essential to bolster domestic productivity and consumption.

Second, China has shifted from a passive participant to an assertive stakeholder in global rulemaking. As the most powerful PRC leader in the post-Mao Zedong era, Xi brought Deng's concept of "socialism with Chinese characteristics" to an unprecedented level. According to Xi's "Chinese dream of national rejuvenation," China will construct "a socialism that is superior to capitalism" and seek "the dominant position" in

48 Jacques deLisle, *China's Rise, the U.S., and the WTO: Perspectives from International Relations Theory*, 2018 Univ. Ill. L. Rev. 57, 64 (2018); Jappe Eckhardt & Hongyu Wang, *China's New Generation Trade Agreements: Importing Rules to Lock in Domestic Reform*, Reg. & Governance (2019), https://onlinelibrary.wiley.com/doi/abs/10.1111/rego.12258 (last visited Jan. 6, 2021).

49 Wang Fan, *China Vows to Expand Global Free Trade Area Network*, Nov. 25, 2020, ECNS, www.ecns.cn/news/economy/2020-11-25/detail-ihaeatyh1835100.shtml (last visited Jan. 6, 2021); Ines Willemyns, *The EU, China and the Free Flow of Data – How Domestic Concerns Might Prevent Agreement at the Multilateral Level*, Nov. 15, 2019, www.qmul.ac.uk/euplant/blog/items/the-eu-china-and-the-free-flow-of-data–how-domestic-concerns-might-prevent-agreement-at-the-multilateral-level.html (last visited Jan. 6, 2021); Regional Comprehensive Economic Partnership (2020) (RCEP), arts. 12.14 & 12.15.

50 中共中央关于制定国民经济和社会发展第十四个五年规划和二〇三五年远景目标的建议 [The Central Committee of the Chinese Community Party's Proposals for Formulating the 14th Five-Year Plan (2021–25) for National Economic and Social Development and the Long-Range Objectives through the Year 2035] (2020) (14th Five-Year Plan), www.gov.cn/zhengce/2020-11/03/content_5556991.htm (last visited Dec. 10, 2020).

51 Denise Jia, *"Dual Circulation": 5 Things to Know about China's New Economic Development Strategy*, Sept. 8, 2020, Straits Times, www.straitstimes.com/asia/east-asia/chinas-new-economic-development-pattern-of-dual-circulation-5-things-to-know-about-it (last visited Jan. 6, 2020); CEBR, *supra* note 24, at 70.

the world.[52] Launched in 2013, the Belt and Road Initiative (BRI) is recognized as Xi's noteworthy initiative to realize his "Chinese dream."[53] The BRI is also commonly known as One Belt One Road, which denotes Beijing's Silk Road Economic Belt and the twenty-first-century Maritime Silk Road. Absent a treaty-based framework, the BRI is primarily a soft law-based scheme.[54]

Enforcing the BRI requires institutional support and hard-law agreements. The China-led Asian Infrastructure Investment Bank (AIIB) represents the BRI-centered institution. The AIIB provides concessional loans for infrastructure building to facilitate the export of Chinese production, capital and labor, thus filling Asian countries' needs, which US-dominated financial institutions cannot fulfill. As AIIB membership includes all RCEP countries except Japan, the bank will be the financial cornerstone of the BRI and the RCEP.[55]

In 2015, China's State Council adopted the BRI as the guiding principle for Chinese FTAs.[56] The 14th five-year plan also pledges to pursue the BRI-based development plan and a "high-standard FTA network."[57] In addition to FTAs, China's recent BITs have included more comprehensive rules such as investment protection provisions.[58] The finalization of the RCEP and the EU-China Comprehensive Agreement on Investment in 2020 represents the most recent, concrete results of the BRI. In particular, the RCEP strengthens China's power of discourse in international lawmaking and refutes US protectionism by "showing that multilateralism and free trade is the right way."[59]

52 Office of the Secretary of State, *The Elements of the China Challenge* (2020), at 4–36.

53 Julien Chaisse & Mitsuo Matshshita, *China's "Belt and Road" Initiative: Mapping the World Trade Normative and Strategic Implications*, 52(1) J. World Trade 163, 165–70 (2018).

54 Heng Wang, *China's Approach to the Belt and Road Initiative: Scope, Character and Sustainability*, 22(1) J. Int'l Econ. L. 29, 35–41 (2019).

55 Asian Infrastructure Investment Bank, *Members and Prospective Members of the Bank*, Jan. 6, 2021, www.aiib.org/en/about-aiib/governance/members-of-bank/index.html (last visited Jan. 7, 2021).

56 State Council, 国务院关于加快实施自由贸易区战略的若干意见 [Several Opinions of the State Council on Accelerating the Implementation of the Strategies for Free Trade Areas] (2015).

57 14th Five-Year Plan, *supra* note 50.

58 Wendy Leutert & Zachary Haver, *From Cautious Interaction to Mature Influence: China's Evolving Engagement with the International Investment Regime*, 93(1) Pac. Aff. 59, 70–73 (2020); Julien Chaisse & Jamieson Kirkwood, *Chinese Puzzle: Anatomy of the (Invisible) Belt and Road Investment Treaty*, 23(1) J. Int'l Econ. L. 245, 251–52 (2020).

59 Ministry of Foreign Affairs of the People's Republic of China, *Li Keqiang Attends the 4th RCEP Summit*, Nov. 15, 2020, www.fmprc.gov.cn/mfa_eng/zxxx_662805/t1832894.shtml (last visited Jan. 7, 2021).

Finally, the RCEP buttresses China's efforts to deepen ties with ASEAN and undermine US hegemony in Asia. In essence, the RCEP implements the Chinese version of the Monroe Doctrine and enables Beijing to garner support from ASEAN countries, which Obama and Trump administrations sought to lure under their TPP and Indo-Pacific strategies. Notably, China was the first ASEAN Dialogue Partner that concluded an ASEAN Plus One FTA and their subsequent Upgrade Protocol was implemented in 2019.[60] As locomotives for the Asian economy, ASEAN and China have become each other's largest trading partner.[61] As the world's most crucial South-South FTA, the evolving ASEAN-China FTA provides valuable lessons for the RCEP to be a "living agreement." The ASEAN-China FTA and the RCEP collectively fortify China's economic and political leverage in US-China conflicts, which will likely continue during the presidency of Joe Biden.

C *India's Withdrawal*

India was a RCEP negotiating party. Its decision to opt out of RCEP talks in 2019 "was a political call at the highest level."[62] According to Indian Prime Minster Narendra Modi, "neither Gandhi's policy of self-reliance nor [his] wisdom" supports India's participation in the RCEP.[63] India's positions on the WTO, ASEAN and China have influenced its policy on the RCEP. Since 2017, India's annual merchandise trade deficit has exceeded $160 billion.[64] The robust services sector contributes to India's services surplus, which only covers 53.9 percent of its deficit in merchandise trade.[65]

To protect farmers, India included high bound tariff rates on agricultural products in its WTO commitments and currently applies average tariff rates of 32.7 percent on agricultural imports in order to protect the

[60] ASEAN, *supra* note 42; ASEAN Secretariat, *supra* note 4, at 132.

[61] ASEAN Secretariat, *supra* note 4, at 127; *The State Council of the People's Republic of China, Full Text: Speech by Premier Li Keqiang at 23rd China-ASEAN Summit*, Nov. 13, 2020, http://english.www.gov.cn/premier/speeches/202011/13/content_WS5fade6dbc6d0f7257693f972.html

[62] Nirmala Ganapathy, *Indian Official Says Delhi's Thinking Over Pact Has Not Changed*, Nov. 16, 2020, Straits Times, at A9.

[63] Prachi Priya & Aniruddha Ghosh, *India's Out of RCEP: What's Next for the Country and Free Trade?* Nov. 15, 2020, Diplomat, https://thediplomat.com/2020/12/indias-out-of-rcep-whats-next-for-the-country-and-free-trade/ (last visited Jan. 7, 2020).

[64] World Trade Organization (WTO), Trade Policy Review, Report by India, WT/TPR/G403 (2020), at 6.

[65] *Id.* at 8–9.

domestic industry.[66] At the WTO, India has advocated for the liberalization of liberalizing labor mobility, known as Mode 4 within the definition of the General Agreement on Trade in Services (GATS).[67] This strategy facilitates the exportation of India's information technology (IT)-related professional services. India's withdrawal from RCEP talks should not be construed as a policy against ASEAN. In fact, India has supported the ASEAN centrality and acknowledged the significance of bilateral economic relations, making India the sixth largest trading partner of ASEAN.[68] The ASEAN Outlook on the Indo-Pacific also signifies ASEAN's intention to further engage India.[69]

In the 1990s, India's "Look East Policy," which sought to forge neglected economic links to East Asia, led to the 2003 ASEAN-India Framework Agreement, as well as FTAs with Thailand, Singapore and Malaysia.[70] Nevertheless, in the ASEAN-India trade pact, Indian agricultural products are largely immune to liberalization, as they are either excluded or scheduled under the sensitive track.[71] The fact that bilateral services and investment agreements were only concluded in 2014, eleven years after the Framework Agreement, demonstrates India's conservative stance.[72] The services commitments are barely GATS-plus and mutual recognition arrangements have limited progress.[73] At present, India only

[66] Dutch Ministry of Agriculture, *Nature and Food Quality, Tariff Changes on Import of Agricultural Products in India*, Mar. 13, 2020, www.agroberichtenbuitenland.nl/actueel/nieuws/2020/03/13/tariff-changes-agricultural-products-in-india (last visited Jan. 7, 2021).

[67] *See generally* Special Session of the Council for Trade in Services, Communication from India: Proposed Liberalisation of Movement of Professionals Under General Agreement on Trade in Services (GATS), WTO Doc. S/CSS/W/12 (2000); Special Session of the Council for Trade in Services, Communication from Brazil, Colombia, Dominican Republic, El Salvador, India, Indonesia, Nicaragua, The Philippines and Thailand: Review of Progress in Negotiations, Including Pursuant to Paragraph 15 of the Guidelines for Negotiations, WTO Doc. TN/S/W/23 (2004).

[68] Chairman's Statement of the 17th ASEAN-Indian Summit (2020), paras. 4 & 7.

[69] *Id.* para. 6.

[70] WTO, *supra* note 64, at 18; Rodolfo C. Severino, *Southeast Asia in Search of an ASEAN Community: Insights from the Former ASEAN Secretary-General* 290–94 (2006).

[71] Razeen Sally, *ASEAN FTAs: State of Play and Outlook for ASEAN's Regional and Global Integration*, *in* The ASEAN Economic Community: A Work in Progress 320, 356–57 (Sanchita Basu Das et al. eds. 2013).

[72] ASEAN, *supra* note 42.

[73] *See* ISEAS Yusof Ishak Institute, *Webinar on "Trade Implication of RCEP for ASEAN and India,"* Dec. 15, 2020, www.iseas.edu.sg/media/event-highlights/webinar-on-trade-implication-of-rcep-for-asean-and-india/ (last visited Jan. 8, 2021) (referring to Pralok Gupta's observations).

accounts for 2.9 percent of ASEAN's total trade.[74] As the FTA has exacerbated deficits and failed to generate much services exports, the Modi administration pledged not to "repeat the mistake" in RCEP negotiations.[75]

Arguably, the RCEP could benefit Modi's "Act East Policy," which he announced in 2014 with the aim of adopting more action-based strategies to revitalize economic relations with Asian partners.[76] In particular, the RCEP could advance the "Make in India" campaign to transform the country into a global manufacturing hub.[77] Contrary to Indian leaders' pessimistic view, empirical studies suggest that the RCEP will have an enormous income effect on India. Joining the RCEP can help India gain $60 billion, whereas withdrawing from the pact will result in a $6 billion loss.[78]

Notwithstanding potential positive effects, India had specific reasons for its opposition to the RCEP. India had trade deficits of more than $100 billion with all RCEP parties except Cambodia, Laos, Myanmar and the Philippines.[79] Lower-cost dairy products from Australia and New Zealand and industrial goods from China were main concerns.[80] In particular, India runs a trade deficit of $53 billion with China and border disputes that caused the death of Indian solders made the RCEP with Beijing politically unacceptable.[81]

Based on its WTO and ASEAN-India FTA experiences, India intended to tie its tariff concessions to access to other services markets, but RCEP members' services commitments disappointed New Delhi. During negotiations, India proposed to grant RCEP countries 42.5 percent to 80 percent tariff reductions, depending on three categories of

[74] ASEAN Secretariat, *supra* note 4, at 127.

[75] Amiti Sen, *India Pushes for Easy Visa for Professionals under RCEP*, Nov. 23, 2018, Hindu Bus. Line, www.thehindubusinessline.com/economy/india-pushes-for-easy-visa-for-professionals-under-rcep/article7792816.ece (last visited Jan. 8, 2021).

[76] Ashok Sajjanhar, *Taking Stock of India's "Act East Policy,"* ORF Issue Brief, No. 142 (2016), at 1– 4.

[77] WTO, *supra* note 64, at 11.

[78] Petri & Plummer, *supra* note 16, at 24.

[79] Gaurav Choudhury, *India Decides Not to Join RCEP: Decoding the Reasons behind Its Decision*, Nov. 4, 2019, www.moneycontrol.com/news/economy/policy/india-decides-not-to-join-rcep-decoding-the-reasons-behind-its-decision-4602701.html (last visited Jan. 8, 2021); Sachin Kumar Sharma et al., *A Quantitative Assessment of India's Withdrawal from RCEP: Issues and Concerns* (2020), at 6–7.

[80] ISEAS Yusof Ishak Institute, *supra* note 73; Sharma et al., *supra* note 79, at 7.

[81] Choudhury, *supra* note 79; Prachi Priya & Aniruddha Ghosh, *India's Out of RCEP: What's Next for the Country and Free Trade?* Dec. 15, 2020, Diplomat, https://thediplomat.com/2020/12/indias-out-of-rcep-whats-next-for-the-country-and-free-trade/ (last visited Jan. 8, 2021).

countries.[82] RCEP parties turned down this proposal. They also rejected India's demand to be excluded from most-favored-nation (MFN) requirements for investment and to include "an auto-trigger mechanism" that could be invoked against unexpected flows of imports.[83]

For Australia, China and New Zealand, Modi's decision means a loss of an exceptional opportunity to forge the FTA link with India. When the RCEP was concluded in 2020, RCEP ministers included a declaration that indicated "their strong will to re-engage India in the RCEP" and authorized India to participate in RCEP meetings as an observer prior to its accession.[84] Despite these efforts, it is unlikely that New Delhi will soon change its cautious position on the RCEP.

III Strengths and Weaknesses of the RCEP

There are currently thirty FTAs that cover 83 percent of international trade among RCEP members.[85] A common approach to assessing the RCEP's extra benefits to Asian integration is to compare the RCEP with the "high-standard" TPP or the CPTPP. Commentators following this approach often reached a conclusion that dismissed the meaningful impact of the RCEP. This viewpoint does not stand. It ignores the impact of the RCEP's economic scale on FTA developments. For instance, the RCEP improved ASEAN Plus One FTAs in four areas, including competition, e-commerce, government procurement and intellectual property rights.[86]

Given the diverse economic stages of fifteen parties, the RCEP pursues pragmatism instead of perfectionism. As Table 3.1 below demonstrates, the RCEP does not include key CPTPP rules on SOEs, labor and environmental protection, anti-corruption and investor-state dispute settlement (ISDS). Unlike modern US and EU FTAs, the RCEP's omission of

[82] Singh & Singh, *supra* note 21, at 511; *see also* Asit Ranjan Mishra, India's New Stance at RCEP May Benefit China, Aug. 9 2016, Livemint, www.livemint.com/Politics/qGEPZqVoHO4U4YYvfBgCNP/Indias-new-stance-at-RCEP-may-benefit-China.html ("[India] proposed 80% tariff cuts to [ASEAN] countries, 65% to South Korea and Japan and finally 42.5% tariff liberalization to China, Australia and New Zealand with which it does not have free-trade agreements.").

[83] Choudhury, *supra* note 79; ISEAS Yusof Ishak Institute, *supra* note 73.

[84] Ministers' Declaration on India's Participation in the Regional Comprehensive Economic Partnership (RCEP) (2020) (Ministers' Declaration on India's Participation).

[85] United Nations Economic and Social Commission for Asia and the Pacific (UN ESCAP), *Preferential Trade Agreements in Asia and the Pacific: Trends and Development, Asia-Pacific Trade and Investment Trends 2020/2021* (2020), at 7 & fn. 8.

[86] *See* ISEAS Yusof Ishak Institute, *supra* note 73 (referring to Sulaimah Mahmood's discussion).

Table 3.1 *Comparison between the RCEP and the CPTPP*[87]

	RCEP	CPTPP	Notes
Status	Signed in 2020	Signed and entered into force in 2018	12-member TPP was signed in 2016
Members	15 India withdrew in 2019	11 United States withdrew in 2017	7 common members: Australia, Brunei, Japan, Malaysia, New Zealand, Singapore, Vietnam
Global trade	28%	15%	
Global population	30%	7%	
Contents	20 Chapters	30 Chapters	Main CPTPP areas not covered in the RCEP: SOEs, Labor, Environment, Anti-corruption, ISDS
Countries/economies that intend to join	Hong Kong	China, Columbia, Indonesia, Philippines, Korea, Thailand, Taiwan, United Kingdom	

87 Petri & Plummer, *supra* note 16, at 7–9; *RCEP: A Guide to the World's Largest Trade Agreement*, *supra* note 17, at 1–3; Fung Business Intelligence, *RCEP: A Game Changer for Trade in Asia – Textile and Apparel Supply Chains Are Key Beneficiaries* (2020), at 5; DFAT, *CPTPP News*, www.dfat.gov.au/trade/agreements/in-force/cptpp/news/Pages/cptpp-news (last visited Jan. 8, 2020); Comprehensive and Progressive Agreement for Trans-Pacific Partnership (2018) (CPTPP).

these sensitive areas reflects the need to balance comprehensiveness with regulatory sovereignty. Presumably, the RCEP's strategy of "having the deal first and establishing details later" is embedded in Asia's legal practice, which is distinct from that of Western legalist culture.

A *Incremental Tariff Liberalization and Trade Facilitation*

The level of tariff cuts provides a key reference for the RCEP's quality. While the CPTPP will eventually lead to 99 percent of tariff elimination rate, the RCEP aims to make 92 percent of goods traded among members duty free.[88] The RCEP's tariff concessions are not significant compared to those of ASEAN's external FTAs. The average tariff elimination of the ASEAN-Japan FTA, the ASEAN-Korea FTA, the ASEAN-China FTA and the ASEAN-Australia-New Zealand FTA ranges from 92.8 percent to 95.7 percent.[89]

1 Exclusions and Extended Phase-In Periods

During negotiations, agricultural and automotive products emerged as challenging issues.[90] A compromise was achieved by excluding or extending the phase-in periods for these sensitive goods. Duties will remain in place for 39 percent of ASEAN's food exports, and Japan will keep its current tariffs on beef, dairy, sugar, pork, rice and wheat, all of which were eliminated under the CPTPP.[91] The phase-in periods in tariff schedules make it easier for domestic industries to make the necessary adjustments and upgrades. The four ASEAN Plus One FTAs above grant extra flexibility to CLMV countries, allowing tariff elimination for selected products in ten to eighteen years from the date of ratification.[92] The RCEP is even

88 Government of Canada, About Tariff Elimination under the CPTPP, Feb. 11, 2019, www.international.gc.ca/trade-commerce/trade-agreements-accords-commerciaux/agr-acc/cptpp-ptpgp/tariff-elimination-droits_de_douane.aspx?lang=eng (last visited Jan. 11, 2021); Ministry of Trade Industry Singapore (MTI), *Regional Comprehensive Economic Partnership Agreement Signed* (2020), at 4.

89 Yoshifumi Fukunaga & Ikumo Isono, *Taking ASEAN+1 FTAs towards the RCEP: A Mapping Study*, ERIA Discussion Paper Series, ERIA-DP-2013–2 (2013), at 8.

90 Ho, *supra* note 11.

91 Stephen Olson, *Keep RCEP in Perspective*, Nov. 17, 2020, *Hinrich Foundation*, www.hinrichfoundation.com/research/article/ftas/keep-rcep-in-perspective/ (last visited Jan. 11, 2021); *The Meaning of RCEP, the World's Biggest Trade Agreement*, Nov. 15, 2020, Economist, www.economist.com/finance-and-economics/2020/11/15/the-meaning-of-rcep-the-worlds-biggest-trade-agreement (last visited Jan. 11, 2021).

92 Shujiro Urata, *Constructing and Multilateralizing the Regional Comprehensive Economic Partnership: An Asian Perspective*, ADBI Working Paper Series, No. 449 (2013), at 14–15.

more flexible. The phase-in periods can extend to twenty years or more and apply to parties other than CLMV countries.[93]

From the business perspective, RCEP members' tariff commitments and time frames for duty-free treatment for imports are vital. To illustrate, the Chinese market is of significance to Japanese and Korean automakers. However, China entered "U," denoting no commitments on its current 25 percent tariff, for most imported vehicles and Chinese tariffs for automotive parts will only gradually decrease from the first year to reach zero in the sixteenth year.[94] This example suggests that the RCEP's trade diversion effect, which will negatively impact nonparties, may only occur in the long run. For instance, Taiwan may lose up to $3 billion because of its exclusion from the RCEP.[95] Yet, the immediate impact on Taiwanese exports to ASEAN is limited because 70 percent of them are IT products that have been made without tariffs under the WTO Information Technology Agreement.[96]

Notwithstanding exclusions and phase-in periods, the RCEP will likely alter the regional supply chain, making the RCEP a sourcing hub for key industries and "decouple" countries outside the region. When the RCEP is fully implemented, the tariff elimination rate for Japanese goods to China will rise from 8 percent to 87 percent and the pact will eliminate $50 billion worth of tariffs from China-bound automotive parts.[97] The removal of tariffs will also enable ASEAN to become the largest overseas market of used cards for Chinese automakers.[98]

2 Harmonizing Rules of Origin of ASEAN Plus One FTAs

As a key trade facilitation effort, the RCEP will facilitate the consolidation of rules of origin between the AEC and the four ASEAN Plus One FTAs.

[93] *See e.g.*, RCEP, Annex 1, Schedule of Tariff Commitments: Cambodia, at 2–3 (indicating that tariffs on certain products will only be eliminated in Year 20).

[94] *See* RCEP, Annex 1: Schedule of Tariff Commitments of China: Section C: For Japan, at 1069–72 (referring to categories of HS Codes 8703 and 8708).

[95] Petri & Plummer, *supra* note 16, at 11.

[96] Pan Tzu-yu et al., *Taiwan Not Expected to Be Hard Hit by New Regional Trade Pact: Experts*, Nov. 15, 2020, Focus Taiwan: CAN English News, https://focustaiwan.tw/business/202011150013 (last visited Jan. 12, 2021).

[97] Jon Emont & Alastair Gale, *Asia-Pacific Countries Sign Major Trade Pact in Test for Biden*, Nov. 15, 2020, Wall St. J., www.wsj.com/articles/asia-pacific-nations-sign-major-china-backed-trade-deal-11605434779 (last visited Jan. 12, 2021).

[98] Kentaro Iwamoto, *Five RCEP Takeaways: Asia Cements Grip as Free Trade Torchbearer*, Nov. 16, 2020, Nikkei Asia, https://asia.nikkei.com/Politics/International-relations/Five-RCEP-takeaways-Asia-cements-grip-as-free-trade-torchbearer (last visited Jan. 12, 2021).

Harmonizing rules of origin will yield a salient, immediate impact on value chains and alleviate the noodle bowl syndrome. Among ASEAN FTAs, Change in Tariff Classification (CTC) and Regional Value Contents (RVC) constitute the most common rules of origin that enable non-originating goods to benefit from FTAs.

Following the implementation of the Upgrade Protocol to the ASEAN-China FTA, all of ASEAN's internal and external FTAs follow the flexible co-equal rule, which allows rules of origins to be satisfied by either the CTC or the RVC.[99] It is therefore not a surprise that the RCEP adopted the same approach and set the RVC benchmark at 40 percent.[100] In other words, to meet the RCEP's product-specific rules, the use of materials from non-RCEP parties in the production of final products is permitted to go up to 60 percent of the value of these products.[101] The RCEP's RVC of 40 percent rule is "generous," particularly compared with the more "protectionist" USMCA that set the RVC benchmark at 60 percent.[102]

In practice, the RCEP's "cumulation" provision will enable materials from fifteen members to count toward the RVC's 40 percent benchmark, thus entitling them to RCEP tariff benefits.[103] The RCEP will therefore bridge ASEAN's internal and external FTAs that are presently "delinked." To illustrate, Chinese automotive companies may commence their operations in Bangkok by importing and assembling completely knocked down units that are manufactured in China. Finished vehicles can serve ASEAN and Australian markets.

The ASEAN Trade in Goods Agreement (ATIGA) and ASEAN FTAs with China and Australia encompass the RVC 40 percent rule for automotive parts and vehicles.[104] Nonetheless, preferential tariffs for

[99] ASEAN Secretariat, *supra* note 4, at 132; 266–67; Sanchita Basu Das et al., *Can ASEAN+1 FTAs Be a Pathway towards Negotiating and Designing the Regional Comprehensive Economic Partnership (RCEP) Agreement?* 50 J. World Trade 253, 266–67 (2016); *see also* MTI, *A Guide to Understanding the ASEAN-China Free Trade Area Upgrade* (2016), at 2 ("Previously, the majority of ACFTA exports would only qualify as originating when at least 40% of the value of a finished good originates from ACFTA Parties (RVC40).").

[100] *See generally* RCEP, ch. 3, Annex 3A: Product-Specific Rules; ASEAN, Summary of the Regional Comprehensive Economic Partnership Agreement (2020), at 3.

[101] Asian Development Bank (ADB), *Regional Comprehensive Economic Partnership Agreement: Overview and Economic Impact*, ADB Brief, No. 164 (2020), at 3.

[102] Gegory Spak et al., *Overview of* Chapter 4 *(Rules of Origin) of the US-Mexico-Canada Trade Agreement* (2018), at 2&6 fn. 16.

[103] RCEP, art. 3.4.

[104] Erlinda M. Medalla & M. Supperamaniam, *Suggested Rules of Origin Regime for EAFTA*, Philippine Inst. for Dev. Stud. Discussion Paper Series, No. 2008–22 (Rev.) (2009), at 15–16.

completed cars that are exported to Australia will likely be denied because the cumulative provision under the ASEAN-Australia-New Zealand FTA does not recognize the value of the Chinese components for the RVC calculation. The RCEP's cumulative rules will facilitate business operations by filling the FTA gap.

The RCEP will similarly reduce business and legal costs for preparing different certificates of origin, depending on export destinations and the selection of FTAs. For instance, intra-ASEAN exports that utilize the ATIGA require "Form D," whereas the same products exported to Australia and Japan require "Form AANZ" and "Form AJ" under respective ASEAN Plus One FTAs.[105] The time and resources needed for compiling rules of origin documents, which certificates of origin require, often hinder the actual usage of FTAs. Shockingly, the utilization rate of Asian FTA is only 28 percent and the rate of exporters' use of Forms AANZ and AJ that entitle products to FTA tariff preferences is even lower than 5.5 percent.[106] With its uniform rules of origin and certificate of origin, the RCEP can remedy the weakness of fragmented ASEAN FTAs.

Compared with contemporary FTAs, the RCEP parties' tariff schedules are rather complex. Some countries including Australia and Brunei have single schedules for all members, but countries such as Indonesia and Vietnam have six schedules applying to different parties.[107] The governments' dissemination and analysis of the use of tariff benefits will be vital. Other trade facilitation provisions such as permitting exporters to self-declare the origin of imported products and customs procedures that enable the release of perishable goods in six hours will further enhance the utilization rate of the RCEP.[108] These provisions will also accelerate RCEP members' commitments under the WTO Trade Facilitation Agreement with country-specific special and differential treatment (SDT) for implementing requirements, including the release of goods and the application of IT.[109]

[105] Singapore Customs, *Application Procedures for a Certificate of Origin via TradeNet and Related Administrative Matters* (2020), at 4.

[106] Masahiro Kawai & Ganeshan Wignaraja, *Main Findings and Policy Implications*, *in* Asia's Free Trade Agreements: How is Business Responding? 33, 34 (2011); Lili Yan Ing et al., *How Do Exports and Imports Affect the Use of Free Trade Agreements? Firm-level Survey Evidence from Southeast Asia*, ERIA Discussion Paper Series (2016), at 7.

[107] *See generally* RCEP, Annex I – Schedules of Tariff Commitments.

[108] RCEP, arts. 3.16.1(b) & 4.11.6(a).

[109] *See e.g.*, ch. 4, Annex 4A: Periods of Time to Implement the Commitments.

B Hybrid Services Schedules and Commitments

Liberalizing trade in services is pivotal to realize the WTO's Doha Development Agenda and the United Nations (UN) Sustainable Development Goals. For developing countries, services trade accounts for 65 percent of their inward foreign direct investment (FDI) and helps them escape from the "middle income traps."[110] Prime RCEP examples include income contributions of tourism services to Cambodia and Thailand, as well as remittances by overseas workers to Indonesia and the Philippines. Transport, financial and digital services also constitute the backbone of trade in goods and became even more critical amid the COVID-19 crisis.

In terms of the modality of services commitments, the ASEAN Framework Agreement on Services and ASEAN Plus One FTAs adopt a GATS-like positive list approach, whereas the CPTPP follows the negative list approach. The positive list modality enables countries to retain regulatory sovereignty because they liberalize only the sectors indicated in their services schedules. The negative list approach is considered more aggressive and automatically covers newly developed areas because all sectors are to be liberalized unless otherwise specified. The RCEP employs a hybrid approach. Eight members used positive list scheduling under Annex II and seven parties adopted the negative list approach by including their reservations and nonconforming measures in Annex III.[111]

A scrutiny of schedules is necessary for understanding the actual degree of services liberalization. The fact that the negative list schedules of Korea and Malaysia exceed 100 pages exemplifies the complexity of services commitments.[112] Moreover, constitutional limitations can compromise RCEP members' services liberalization. For example, constitutions of the Philippines and Myanmar stipulate that natural resources are owned by the state.[113] These constitutional provisions resulted in reservations on the

110 WTO, *Background Note by Secretariat, Council for Trade in Services: Mode 3 – Commercial Presence*, S/C/W/314 (2010), para. 24; Pasha L. Hsieh, *Reassessing the Trade-Development Nexus in International Economic Law: The Paradigm Shift in Asia-Pacific Regionalism*, 37(2) NW. J. Int'l L. & Bus. 321, 346–47 (2017).

111 RCEP, Annex II – Schedules of Specific Commitments for Services & Annex III – Schedules of Reservations and Non-Conforming Measures for Services and Investment.

112 Korea's and Malaysia's schedules include 112 and 137 pages, respectively. RCEP, Annex III – Schedules of Reservations and Non-Conforming Measures for Services and Investment.

113 Constitution of the Republic of the Union of Myanmar (2008), art. 37(a); Constitution of the Republic of the Philippines (1987), art. XII, secs. 2 & 10.

part of these RCEP members about the national treatment requirement of investment for "mining and quarrying" and their related services.[114]

The RCEP's provisions on services trade reinforce my argument for the ASEAN way-based pragmatic incrementalism. The RCEP contains the ratchet mechanism for services and investment, under which members "commit to automatically extend the benefits of any future" agreements to all other RCEP countries.[115] This mechanism thus enables the RCEP to always be "the best deal" for enterprises. Furthermore, according to Article 8.12, RCEP parties that initially adopted the positive list approach are required to transition to negative list scheduling in six years after the RCEP enters into force.[116] The same provision exhibits the RCEP's development-oriented nature by permitting Cambodia, Laos and Myanmar to have a fifteen-year transition period instead.[117]

Based on current services commitments, RCEP members will increase foreign ownership restrictions for 65 percent of sectors such as computer and logistics services industries.[118] The ASEAN-Australia-New Zealand FTA is the ASEAN Plus One FTA with the highest level of services liberalization.[119] New and extra services commitments of the RCEP that exceed those of the ASEAN-Australia-New Zealand FTA and other intra-RCEP FTAs will result in de facto consolidation of agreements.[120] In addition, the annexes on financial, telecommunication and professional services will form the basis for regulatory harmonization and mutual recognition involving these services.[121] Comparable to the ASEAN-Australia-New Zealand FTA, the RCEP includes a separate Annex for specific Mode 4 (movement of natural persons) commitments.[122] The extended periods of stay accorded to business visitors and intra-corporate transferees will energize Asia-Pacific operations of multinational enterprises.

[114] RCEP, Annex III: Schedules of Reservations and Non-Conforming Measures for Services and Investment: Myanmar, at 19 & Annex III: Schedules of Reservations and Non-Conforming Measures for Services and Investment: The Philippines, at 10.

[115] RCEP, Arts. 8.7.3, 8.7.4 and 10.8.1; New Zealand Foreign Affairs & Trade, *Regional Comprehensive Economic Partnership: National Interest Analysis* (2020), at 36.

[116] RCEP, art. 8.12.7.

[117] *Id.*

[118] MTI, *supra* note 88, at 4.

[119] Fukunaga & Isono, *supra* note 89, at 16.

[120] DFAT, *Regional Comprehensive Economic Partnership: Outcomes: Services and Investment* (2020), at 4–6.

[121] RCEP, Annex 8A: Financial Services; Annex 8B: Telecommunication Services; and Annex 8C: Professional Services; New Zealand Foreign Affairs & Trade, *supra* note 115, at 37–40.

[122] RCEP, Annex IV – Schedules of Specific Commitments on Temporary Movement of Natural Persons.

C Investment Issues and the Absence of ISDS

36 percent of global FDI outflows amounting to $6.5 trillion come from fifteen RCEP countries.[123] Both chapters on services and investment of the RCEP include provisions on national treatment and MFN, thus harmonizing ASEAN Plus One FTAs and improving the investment environment.[124] The rules on expropriation and the prohibition of performance requirements, including the imposition of conditions for acquisitions or a certain percentage of domestic content, are vital to foreign investors.[125] Much academic attention on trade agreements focuses on ISDS reforms such as the EU-proposed Investment Court System. ASEAN's internal and external agreements mostly adopted US-style ISDS schemes with detailed rules on arbitration. While the ASEAN-Hong Kong Investment Agreement contains no ISDS, it articulates that investor-state dispute rules will form part of its work program.[126] The RCEP follows the same approach. It leaves the ISDS mechanism for negotiations within two years after the RCEP becomes effective.[127]

Undoubtedly, ISDS enforces investment protection, which the RCEP's Guiding Principles and Objectives identified as a pillar of investment.[128] In 2015, RCEP parties agreed to include ISDS provisions.[129] Why did the final text of the RCEP depart from the consensus? Although Japan and Korea pushed for detailed ISDS rules during RCEP negotiations, the changing stances of other countries and the CPTPP prompted the RCEP to omit ISDS.[130] In particular, New Zealand's new government declared its refusal to include ISDS in any FTAs in 2017.[131] In addition to

123 UNCTAD, *supra* note 3, at 6

124 RCEP, arts. 8.4, 8.6, 10.3 and 10.4; Das et al., *supra* note 99, at 271–72.

125 RCEP, art. 10.6; Annex 10B: Expropriation, art. 2.

126 Agreement on Investment among the Governments of the Hong Kong Special Administrative Region of the People's Republic of China and the Member States of the Association of Southeast Asian Nations (2017) (ASEAN-Hong Kong Investment Agreement), at art. 22.1(e).

127 RCEP, art. 10.18.1.

128 RCEP Guiding Principles and Objectives, sec. III.

129 DFAT, *Regional Comprehensive Economic Partnership (RCEP): Discussion Paper on Investment* (2017), at 4.

130 Belinda Townsend, *Update on the Regional Comprehensive Economic Partnership Agreement – NGO Briefing* (2015), at 2.

131 Post-Cabinet Press Conference: Monday, Oct. 31, 2017 (2017), at 1; *Deborah Elms on the Absence of ISDS, Prospects for a Secretariat, and Dispute Settlement in RCEP*, Nov. 18, 2020, Int'l Econ. L. & Policy Blog, https://ielp.worldtradelaw.net/2020/11/the-absence-of-isds-in-rcep.html (last visited Jan. 18, 2021).

the CPTPP's suspended provisions that narrow the ISDS scope of the original TPP, New Zealand's side letters with five countries exclude ISDS entirely.[132]

To prevent a "loophole" for utilizing ISDS under other pacts, the RCEP's nonapplication of MFN to "any international dispute resolution procedures or mechanisms" makes it impossible for investors to resort to agreements with ISDS provisions. However, an investor's home state may still exercise diplomatic protection by using the RCEP's state-to-state dispute settlement mechanism, except for disputes involving pre-establishment rights.[133] In response, the host state may rely on general exceptions that incorporate Article XX of the General Agreement on Tariffs and Trade (GATT) and Article XIV of the GATS.[134] In terms of security exceptions, the scope of RCEP is broader than that of Article XXI of the GATT. Article 17.13 of the RCEP extends to measures protecting "critical public infrastructures," which may be "publicly or privately owned," and to actions "taken in time of national emergency."[135] According to the WTO panel in *Russia – Traffic in Transit*, "emergency" refers to unexpected and urgent dangers, conflicts or disasters.[136]

Markedly, the RCEP accords SDT to "Least Developed Country Parties" when they involve dispute settlement procedures.[137] ASEAN's external FTAs, such as the ASEAN-Australia-New Zealand FTA and the ASEAN-Hong Kong Investment Agreement, extend SDT to "newer ASEAN Member States" that denote CLMV countries.[138] Given that the UN does not consider Vietnam as a least developed country, the RCEP departs from the ASEAN practice and confines SDT to Cambodia, Laos and Myanmar.[139] The RCEP mandates that the

[132] DFAT, *CPTPP Suspensions Explained* (2019), at 1–2; New Zealand's CPTPP Investor-State Dispute Settlement Side Letters with Australia, Brunei, Malaysia, Peru and Vietnam (2018).

[133] RCEP, art. 17.11; Michael Ewing-Chow & Junianto James Losari, *The RCEP Investment Chapter: A State-to-State WTO Style System for Now*, Dec. 8, 2020, Kluwer Arb. Blog, http://arbitrationblog.kluwerarbitration.com/2020/12/08/the-rcep-investment-chapter-a-state-to-state-wto-style-system-for-now/ (last visited Jan. 19, 2021).

[134] RCEP, art. 17.12.

[135] RCEP, art. 17.13(b)(iii) & (iv).

[136] Panel Report, *Russia – Measures Concerning Traffic in Transit*, WT/DS512/R (2019), para. 7.72.

[137] RCEP, art. 19.18.

[138] Agreement Establishing the ASEAN-Australia-New Zealand Free Trade Area (2009) (AANZFTA), ch. 17, art. 18; ASEAN-Hong Kong Investment Agreement, at art. 18

[139] *E.g.*, RCEP, arts. 15.6 & 19.18.

parties bringing complaints against these three countries "exercise due restraint" and that the panel explicitly identify how SDT is considered in procedures.[140]

D Soft-Law Rules on Government Procurement and E-Commerce

As I previously identified, four chapters of the CPTPP that are absent in the RCEP include the chapters on SOEs, labor and environmental protection, and anti-corruption.[141] Article 17.10, which is the only RCEP provision on environmental obligations, requires parties to comply with the Convention on Biological Diversity.[142] The lack of these CPTPP chapters increases criticism against the quality and standards of the RCEP. Yet, the fact that selected RCEP countries have incorporated these areas in their new agreements suggests that such areas may be included in the RCEP in the future. To illustrate, four ASEAN countries accepted commitments under the CPTPP. The recent EU-China Comprehensive Agreement on Investment also covers SOE disciplines.[143] Considering domestic opposition in least developed country members, the RCEP's omission of more sensitive CPTPP chapters can be construed as a necessary compromise to finalize the world's largest FTA.

As government procurement and e-commerce provisions exemplify, some notable commitments of the RCEP cannot be enforced by the dispute settlement mechanism under Chapter 19.[144] These soft-law requirements serve as the foundation for subsequent hard-law obligations rather than loopholes. The public procurement market is vital to enterprises in RCEP countries. As of 2021, only five RCEP members are parties to the WTO Agreement on Government Procurement.[145] As no ASEAN Plus One FTAs include chapters on government procurement, the RCEP helps enhance transparency and cooperation for public

[140] RCEP, art. 19.18; Diane Desierto, *The Regional Comprehensive Economic Partnership (RCEP)'s Chapter 19 Dispute Settlement Procedures*, Nov. 16, 2020, EJIL: Talk! www.ejiltalk.org/the-regional-comprehensive-economic-partnership-rceps-chapter-19-dispute-settlement/ (last visited Jan. 19, 2021).

[141] CPTPP, chs. 17, 19, 20 and 26.

[142] RCEP, art. 17.10.

[143] *E.g.*, European Commission, EU-China Comprehensive Agreement on Investment (2020), at 1.

[144] *E.g.*, RCEP, arts. 12.17.3 and 16.8.

[145] These five countries include Australia, Japan, Korea, New Zealand, Singapore. WTO, Parties, Observers and Accessions, www.wto.org/english/tratop_e/gproc_e/memobs_e.htm (last visited Jan. 19, 2021).

procurement rules.[146] The RCEP excludes pertinent provisions from the dispute settlement mechanism and does not include specific government procurement commitments, which the parties may include pursuant to later negotiations based on the review clause.[147]

Enterprises also pay particular attention to e-commerce provisions of the RCEP. Digitalization is now a necessity in contemporary economic agreements, as e-commerce facilitates 12 percent of global trade in goods via digital platforms such as Amazon or Alibaba.[148] In the Asia-Pacific, lockdown and safe distancing measures in response to COVID-19 drove a 70 percent increase in e-commerce orders and benefited small and medium-sized enterprises.[149] Also, digitalization enables developing countries to be service economies without going through manufacture-based industrialization, thus helping them pursue an accelerated development path different from the experiences of Asian tigers and China.[150] Hence, the RCEP's consolidation of rules on e-commerce and data protection strengthens the trade-development nexus in the NREO.

The RCEP's e-commerce provisions are of the soft-law nature because various members such as Cambodia, Indonesia and Vietnam adopted protectionist data policies.[151] In addition, these provisions do not apply to government procurement and financial service suppliers.[152] Tellingly, the RCEP obliges parties to "maintain" the current practice of not imposing custom duties on electronic transmissions in line with the WTO decision.[153] In other words, the practice may change if WTO members decide not to extend the e-commerce moratorium. The RCEP also prohibits data localization and barriers to the cross-border transfer of data.[154] Under SDT provisions, Vietnam is given an additional period of five years to implement these rules and an eight-year transition period applies to Cambodia, Laos and Myanmar.[155]

[146] ASEAN, *supra* note 100, at 7; ADB, *supra* note 101, at 4; RCEP, arts. 16.4, 16.5 & 16.8.
[147] RCEP, arts. 16.6, 16.8 & 20.8.
[148] Mckinsey Global Institute, *Digital Globalization: The New Era of Global Flows* (2016), at 7.
[149] Organisation for Economic Co-operation and Development, *Leveraging Digital Trade to Fight the Consequences of COVID-19* (2020), at 10–11.
[150] Dani Rodrik, *Straight Talk on Trade: Ideas for a Sane World Economy* 89–91 (2018).
[151] Jeff Paine, *Asean's Digital Economy Offers Potential in Post-Covid World*, Bus. Time, Nov. 17, 2020, at A19.
[152] RCEP, arts. 12.1(b)(iii) & 12.3.2.
[153] RCEP, art. 12.11.
[154] RCEP, arts. 12.14–12.15.
[155] RCEP, fns. 11 & 13.

All RCEP countries may rely on other exceptions to e-commerce rules. Contradictory data-related measures "necessary to achieve a legitimate public policy objective" and "for the protection of its essential security interests" can be justified.[156] The implementing party can decide "the necessity behind the implementation of such legitimate public policy" and other parties cannot dispute measures that protect essential security interests.[157] On the one hand, these self-judging and exclusion of dispute clauses create vast policy space. On the other hand, the RCEP is an "improvement" to the ASEAN Agreement on E-commerce, as the RCEP no longer includes the vague "subject to their respective laws and regulations" clause.[158]

IV Implications for Regional and Multilateral Trading Systems

Pragmatism rather than perfectionism drove the finalization of the mega-FTA. ASEAN FTA experiences will guide the RCEP's evolving process. Arguably, the RCEP is a rule-taker instead of a rulemaker. Nevertheless, the rules that the RCEP adopted became default standards for new Asian regionalism. The RCEP will therefore result in systemic implications for regional and multilateral trading systems.

A Normative Fragmentation of Multilayered FTAs and BITs

According to the Guiding Principles and Objectives for the RCEP, the four ASEAN Plus One FTAs and other pacts between RCEP members "will continue to exist and no provision in the RCEP agreement will detract from the terms and conditions in these" pacts.[159] Article 20.2 of the RCEP confirms the intention of fifteen parties to have the RCEP "coexist with their existing international agreements."[160] Thus, the RCEP does not envision de jure consolidation of intra-RCEP FTAs and BITs.

Normative conflicts may arise from overlapping FTAs. To illustrate, forum shopping can occur under multilayered FTAs between China and Singapore. This is because dispute settlement mechanisms of the RCEP, the ASEAN-China FTA and the China-Singapore FTA may apply to the

156 RCEP, arts. 12.14 & 12.15.
157 RCEP, arts. 12.14.3(b) & 12.15.3(b) & fns. 12 & 14.
158 ASEAN Agreement on Electronic Commerce (2019), arts. 4(a) & 6(b).
159 RCEP Guiding Principles and Objectives, principle 5.
160 RCEP, art. 20.2.1.

same dispute. Conflicting situations worsen if RCEP parties decide to include ISDS provisions because investors will be entitled to resort to the RCEP, ASEAN-Plus One FTAs and BITs.[161] Based on WTO jurisprudence and the Vienna Convention on the Law of Treaties (VCLT), the analysis of the RCEP vis-à-vis other pacts could shed light on the noodle bowl syndrome in the Third Regionalism.

1 WTO-RCEP Conflicts

Trade law scholars and practitioners are no strangers to jurisdictional clashes between the WTO and FTAs. WTO tribunals made it clear that FTAs can barely exclude the WTO's jurisdiction. In *Mexico–Soft Drinks*, Mexico's defense relied on the forum exclusion clause of the USMCA's predecessor, the North American Free Trade Agreement (NAFTA), when the United States challenged Mexico's tax measures at the WTO.[162] Mexico averred that the WTO complaint constituted part of "a broader dispute" it had brought against America in NAFTA proceedings and hence the forum exclusion clause mandates that the NAFTA be the sole forum.[163] The Appellate Body rejected this argument. It ruled that a panel's declining its own jurisdiction would "diminish" a complaining party's right under the WTO Dispute Settlement Understanding (DSU).[164] Although "legal impediments" may exclude the WTO's jurisdiction, the Appellate Body found that no such impediments exist in the case.[165]

Peru–Agricultural Products is the subsequent case where Guatemala challenged the consistency of Peru's Price Range System with the Agreement on Agriculture and the GATT.[166] Peru argued that Guatemala contravened "good faith" obligations under the DSU because Guatemala waived the right to bring the WTO complaint under their bilateral FTA.[167] The Appellate Body examined paragraph 9 of Annex 2.3 of the FTA and found that a waiver to relinquish DSU rights "must be made clearly" and "cannot be lightly assumed."[168] Such provisions

[161] RCEP, art. 10.18.1(a).

[162] Appellate Body Report, *Mexico – Tax Measures on Soft Drinks and Other Beverages*, WT/DS308/AB/R (2006), para. 42.

[163] *Id.* paras. 42 & 54; North American Free Trade Agreement (1993), art. 2005.6.

[164] Appellate Body Report, *supra* note 162, paras. 46 & 48–53.

[165] *Id.* para. 54.

[166] Appellate Body Report, *Peru – Additional Duty on Imports of Certain Agricultural Products*, WT/DS457/AB/R (2015), para. 4.1.

[167] *See id.* para. 5.19 ("Peru alleges that Guatemala … acted contrary to good faith … obligations under Articles 3.7 and 3.10 of the DSU.").

[168] *Id.* para. 5.25.

therefore do not amount to "legal impediments," which the Appellate Body articulated in *Mexico–Soft Drinks*.[169]

According to the RCEP, it is "without prejudice to the rights of a Party to have recourse to dispute settlement procedures" under the WTO or other applicable FTAs.[170] The choice of forum clause of the RCEP stipulates that once the complaining party selects the forum by requesting the establishment of a panel, the forum "shall be used to the exclusion of other fora."[171] WTO jurisprudence indicates that this forum exclusion provision neither diminishes WTO members' rights under the DSU nor excludes WTO jurisdiction. The RCEP's lack of a "supremacy clause," which prioritizes WTO agreements when they are consistent with the FTA, will have no impact on WTO tribunals' jurisdictional decision.[172]

2 RCEP-FTA/BIT Conflicts

The RCEP coexists with four ASEAN Plus One FTAs and bilateral FTAs and BITs between RCEP parties.[173] How do parties reconcile the differences between rules of multilayered agreements? RCEP provisions reflect a common approach adopted by ASEAN's external FTAs such as ASEAN-Australia-New Zealand FTA and the ASEAN-Japan FTA.[174] The RCEP first affirms "existing rights and obligations" arising from other FTAs.[175] Following a request, relevant parties are obliged to engage in consultations and reach "a mutually satisfactory solution."[176] The RCEP also clarifies that favorable treatment provided by an agreement "does not mean there is an inconsistency."[177]

The ASEAN-Japan FTA incorporates "general principles of international law," which the parties should consider when they attempt to reach a solution in cases of inconsistency between agreements.[178] Despite the RCEP's lack of a similar provision, the VCLT as customary international law applies to RCEP parties. Article 30.3 of the VCLT on the

[169] *See id.* at 21, fn. 106 ("[W]e do not consider that Members may relinquish their rights and obligations under the DSU beyond the settlement of specific disputes.").
[170] RCEP, art. 19.3.2.
[171] RCEP, arts. 19.5.1 & 19.5.2.
[172] *E.g.*, Agreement on Comprehensive Economic Partnership among Member States of the Association of Southeast Asian Nations and Japan (2008) (ASEAN-Japan FTA), art. 10.3.
[173] RCEP, art. 20.2.1.
[174] RCEP, art. 20.2; AANZFTA, art. 2; ASEAN-Japan FTA, art. 10.
[175] RCEP, art. 20.2.1(b).
[176] RCEP, art. 20.2.2.
[177] RCEP, art. 20.2.2 & fn. 1.
[178] ASEAN-Japan FTA, art. 10.4.

application of successive treaties provides that "the earlier treaty applies only to the extent that its provisions are compatible with those of the later treaty."[179] According to this later-in-time rule, the applicable scope of the RCEP should subsequently be confined to treaties on the same subject matter. Nevertheless, it can be averred that Article 20.2 of the RCEP constitutes a special law. Such a *lex specialis* interpretation may exclude the application of Article 30.3 of the VCLT, which is a general rule, therefore allowing the RCEP's forum exclusion provision to prevail.[180]

Most of intra-RCEP FTAs and BITs include ISDS mechanisms. The RCEP's prospective inclusion of ISDS provisions can thus lead to forum shopping between applicable agreements. Notably, Singapore and Vietnam's investment agreements with the EU will terminate their bilateral BITs with EU states.[181] This clean-slate approach is nonetheless rare. For instance, the continuous validity of the China-Singapore BIT after the conclusion of the China-Singapore FTA, which incorporates the ASEAN-China Investment Agreement, creates overlapping jurisdiction over investor-state claims.[182] In practice, parties' BITs and their subsequent FTAs usually have distinct scopes and carveouts, making the application of Article 30.3 of VCLT legally difficult.

Contrary to conventional wisdom, parties may even "intentionally" keep parallel agreements with ISDS mechanisms. ASEAN's sole ISDS case, *Yaung Chi Oo v. Myanmar*, is illustrative of regional jurisprudence on successive treaties. This case concerned the 1987 and 1998 intra-ASEAN investment agreements.[183] According to the Tribunal, the two disputed pacts encompassed different scopes of investment and ASEAN countries had no intention to merge them.[184]

179 Vienna Convention on the Law of Treaties (1969), art. 10.3; see also Alexander Orakhelashvili, *Article 30 of the 1969 Vienna Convention on the Law of Treaties: Application of the Successive Treaties Relating to the Same Subject-Matter*, 31 ICSID Rev. 344, 361 (2016) ("[T]o what extent the lex posterior rule stated in Article 30 VCLT would be applied in arbitral practice is not certain . . . .").

180 *E.g.*, Tania Voon & Elizabeth Sheargold, *Australia, China and the Co-Existence of Successive International Investment Agreements*, *in* The China-Australia Free Trade Agreement: A 21st Century Model 215, 228 (Colin B. Picker et al. eds. 2017).

181 EU-Singapore Investment Protection Agreement (IPA) (2018), ch. 4, annex 5; EU-Singapore IPA (2019), ch. 4, annex 6.

182 Free Trade Agreement between the Government of the People's Republic of China and the Government of the Republic of Singapore (2009), art. 84.1.

183 Yaung Chi Oo Trading Pte Ltd. v. Gov't of the Union of Myanmar, ASEAN I.D. Case No. ARB/01/1 (Mar. 31, 2003), 42 I.L.M. 540 (2003), paras. 76–78.

184 *Id.* paras. 77–82.

Article 12 of the 1998 agreements provides that it "shall prevail" if it "provides for better and enhanced provisions."[185] Based on "the general practice of ASEAN with respect to successive agreements," the Tribunal ruled that Article 12 should not be interpreted to amend the 1987 agreement because the two agreements "are clearly intended to operate separately."[186] Article 20.2 of the RCEP can be understood as codifying the ASEAN FTA practice by confirming parties' intention for the co-existence approach.[187] Given complexities associated with the application of the VCLT and overlapping pacts, the RCEP will only promote de facto rather than de jure consolidation of Asia-Pacific agreements.

B *Institutionalization of the RCEP Secretariat and Beyond*

The RCEP is an evolving process. Its evolution will shed light on the institutionalization and expansion of FTAs and energize plurilateral trade approach to implementing Sustainable Development Goals. The RCEP represents the culmination of ASEAN Plus One FTAs. The evolution of the RCEP will build on ASEAN's institutionary memory, which the CPTPP and other agreements do not possess.

It is common for ASEAN Plus One FTAs to authorize parties to form joint committees and require the ASEAN Secretariat to provide administrative and technical support.[188] The RCEP takes a step further. In addition to creating the senior official-level RCEP Joint Committee, the agreement mandates that "a RCEP Secretariat" be established to provide support for the Joint Committee.[189] In comparison, the CPTPP merely creates "a Trans-Pacific Partnership Commission" without planning to establish a secretariat.[190] Moreover, the Secretary-General of ASEAN is designated as the depositary of the RCEP, whereas New Zealand serves as the depositary of the CPTPP.[191]

The development of the ASEAN Secretariat provides valuable lessons for the RCEP Secretariat. ASEAN was founded in 1967, but the

185 *Id.* para. 79.
186 *Id.* paras. 80–82.
187 RCEP, art. 20.2.1.
188 *E.g.*, AANZFTA, ch. 2, art. 11; ASEAN-Japan FTA, art. 11; Framework Agreement on Comprehensive Economic Cooperation Among the Governments of the Member Courtiers of the Association of Southeast Asian Nations and the Republic of Korea (2005), art. 5.4.
189 RCEP, arts. 18.2 & 18.3.1(i).
190 CPTPP, art. 27.1.
191 RCEP, art. 20.5; CPTPP, art. 30.7.

Jakarta-based ASEAN Secretariat was only established in 1976 and its legal capacity was merely recognized under Indonesian law.[192] The ASEAN Charter conferred legal personality on ASEAN as an international organization.[193] Pursuant to the mandate of the ASEAN Charter, a separate agreement details ASEAN's legal capacities, as well as privileges and immunities of ASEAN, its Secretary-General and staff of the ASEAN Secretariat.[194] These instruments are indispensable for the operation of the ASEAN Secretariat and for the future of the RCEP Secretariat.

The institutionalization of the secretariat will empower the RCEP to become a global rule setter. This substantiates my analysis of the new dependency theory, which posits that the collective power of developing countries will alter conventional North-South relations. While US and EU standards remain relevant, the pacts that RCEP parties ratify and the implementing regulations, which the RCEP Secretariat adopts, will become rules for Asia. It is particularly critical for new domains where Asian countries excel, such as artificial intelligence, drones or travel bubble schemes amid the COVID-19 pandemic. Built on the ASEAN FTA framework, the RCEP's normative power will therefore ascend.

To maintain ASEAN centrality and accelerate work efficiency, I recommend that the RCEP Secretariat form close institutional ties with the ASEAN Secretariat. The practice and experience of ASEAN's internal and external pacts are intertwined with the evolution of the RCEP. For example, in the arenas ranging from tariff liberalization to dispute settlement, the RCEP's SDT provisions that apply to least developed countries will follow the approach of ASEAN FTAs.

Implementing the RCEP's economic and technical cooperation activities also requires monitoring and the allocation of resources that RCEP partners, such as Australia and Japan, provided under ASEAN Plus One FTAs.[195] The consolidation of financial and technical support will benefit the implementation of the UN Sustainable Development Goals and the Initiative for ASEAN Integration Work

[192] ASEAN, ASEAN Secretariat, https://asean.org/asean/asean-secretariat/ (last visited Jan. 26, 2021); Agreement between the Government of Indonesia and ASEAN Relating to the Privileges and Immunities of the ASEAN Secretariat (1979), arts. 2 & 3.

[193] Charter of the Association of Southeast Asian Nations (2007) (ASEAN Charter), art. 3.

[194] ASEAN Charter, ch. VI; Agreement on Privileges and Immunities of the Association of Southeast Asian Nations (2009), arts. 2–3.

[195] *E.g.*, RCEP, arts. 15.3 & 15.4; AANZFTA, ch. 12.

Plan IV (2021–25).[196] The role of the RCEP Secretariat in centralizing foreign assistance and setting the trade-development agenda will provide insight to the Global South.

To multilateralize RCEP rules by expanding this mega-FTA, the RCEP Secretariat's implementation of the accession process is essential. Building on the Bogor Goals, the new APEC Putrajaya Vision 2040 reiterates the significance of the FTAAP agenda.[197] As pathways to the FTAAP, both the RCEP and the CPTPP adopted open accession clauses, which allow states and separate customs territories to join these mega-FTAs.[198] The RCEP practice also implies that ASEAN Plus One FTA partners will be accorded priority in the accession process.

In response to India's withdrawal from RCEP negotiations, RCEP ministers emphasized their intention to re-engage India and accorded the country observer status.[199] Other than India, Hong Kong is the remaining ASEAN Plus One FTA partner that has not joined the RCEP. With Beijing's support, Hong Kong will be the most likely candidate for the RCEP.[200] The enlargement of both the RCEP and CPTPP will collectively contribute to the normative development of the NREO.

V Conclusion

Since ASEAN issued its Framework for the RCEP in 2012, fifteen parties completed the mega-FTA in 2020, making it the world's largest FTA by economic scale and population. Contrary to conventional understanding, RCEP negotiations represent an ASEAN-led rather than a China-dominated process. As an instrument that is expected to follow the ASEAN way, the RCEP is a living agreement based on the pragmatic incrementalism. The immediate effect of the RCEP will be the harmonization of rules of origin among ASEAN's internal and external FTAs, thus promoting de facto consolidation of FTAs.

196 UN, *The 17 Goals*, https://sdgs.un.org/goals (last visited Jan. 26, 2021); ASEAN, Initiative for ASEAN Integration (IAI) Work Plan IV (2021–2025) (2020), at 7–9.

197 APEC, *APEC Putrajaya Vision 2040*, www.apec.org/Meeting-Papers/Leaders-Declarations/2020/2020_aelm/Annex-A (last visited Jan. 26, 2021).

198 RCEP, art. 20.9; CPTPP, art. 30.4.

199 Ministers' Declaration on India's Participation, *supra* note 84.

200 Natalie Wong, *Mainland Chinese Commerce Official Backs Hong Kong Joining RCEP Trade Bloc, with City Leader Carrie Lam Hoping to Start Talks "at Earliest Opportunity,"* Nov. 30, 2020, S. China Morning Post, www.scmp.com/news/hong-kong/hong-kong-economy/article/3111913/mainland-commerce-official-backs-hong-kong-joining (last visited Jan. 26, 2021).

This chapter found that the RCEP converges key legal and political agendas of Asian powers, including particularly ASEAN centrality and China's BRI and dual circulation strategy. Although the RCEP's tariff and services liberalization will be a lengthy process, it takes into account the development needs of least developed countries and minimizes the trade diversion effect. The absence of ISDS and the inclusion of soft-law government procurement and e-commerce also reflects the necessary compromise between states at diverse economic stages.

For international economic law, the RCEP's normative conflicts with intra-RCEP trade and investment agreements will provide valuable lessons. The institutionalization of the RCEP Secretariat and its role in facilitating accession procedures and setting the trade-development agenda will enhance the status of the RCEP as a global rulemaker. Consequently, the RCEP will energize the collective power of developing countries and serve as the legal foundation for new Asian regionalism.

4

Constructing Interregionalism: The New EU Strategy to Asia

I Introduction

Asia and Europe have encountered their most turbulent relations since Brussels first formulated its "New Asia Strategy."[1] Rising populist protectionism, stalled World Trade Organization (WTO) negotiations and the COVID-19 crisis have crippled economic ties between the European Union (EU) and Asian economies. In 2020, the European Commission led by President Ursula von der Leyen introduced "a model of open strategic autonomy."[2] Recognizing the essential role of global trade for the post-pandemic recovery, the policy mandates that the EU shape "the new system of global economic governance" and deepen bilateral ties to consolidate global value chains.[3]

The Commission stressed that achieving EU objectives relies on "strategic engagement" with the Asia-Pacific, which "is crucial to European economic interests."[4] In particular, trade negotiations with China, Japan, Korea and the ten-country Association of Southeast Asian Nations (ASEAN) are imperative. For Asian countries, securing the EU as a trade and investment partner is of equal significance, particularly amid US isolationism and the unprecedented recession. Consequently, the rapidly evolving legal framework between Asia and Europe enriches the concept of interregionalism. It also advances exogenous influences to

1 Commission of the European Communities, Towards a New Asia Strategy, COM(94) 314 final (1994), at 3–10.

2 European Commission, Europe's Moment: Repair and Prepare for the Next Generation, COM(2020) 456 final (2020), at 12–13.

3 *Id.*

4 European Commission, Trade for All: Towards a More Responsible Trade and Investment Policy (2015), at 31–32.

new Asian regionalism and shapes the New Regional Economic Order (NREO).

In 2010 and 2018, the EU concluded free trade agreements (FTAs) with Korea and Japan, respectively.[5] The EU and China "concluded in principle the negotiations for a Comprehensive Agreement on Investment" in 2020 and Brussels' other potential trade and investment partners include Australia, New Zealand and Taiwan.[6] The 2015 "Trade for All" strategy of the EU articulates "an ASEAN strategy based on individual agreements" that will lead to "a region-to-region" framework.[7] The entry into force of the EU-Singapore FTA in 2019 and the EU-Vietnam FTA in 2020 reinforces this building-block approach, which guides the roadmap to the ASEAN-EU FTA.[8]

Comprising fast-growing emerging markets, ASEAN has emerged as the priority on the EU's Asia policy agenda. As the pivotal regional integration initiative, ASEAN is deemed to be the EU's natural partner that shares "a common DNA."[9] Economically, ASEAN is Brussels' "third largest trading partner outside Europe" and Asia's third largest trade power, which is poised to be the world's fourth largest economy by 2030.[10] Politically, the EU's recognition of "the arrival of the Asian century" and changing perception of China as "a systemic rival" have invigorated Brussels to cement ties with other Asian countries.[11] For EU

5 Csilla Lakatos & Lars Nilsson, The EU-Korea Free Trade Agreement: Anticipation, Trade Policy Uncertainty and Impact, Chief Economist Note (2015), at 4; Ministry of Foreign Affairs of Japan, The Signing of the Agreement between the European Union and Japan for an Economic Partnership, Jul. 17, 2018, www.mofa.go.jp/press/release/press4e_002107.html (last visited Sept. 1, 2020).

6 European Commission & High Representative of the Union for Foreign Affairs and Security Policy, EU-China – Strategic Outlook, Joint (2019) 5 final (2019), at 6; European Parliament, European Parliament Resolution of 7 October 2020 on the Implementation of the Common Commercial Policy – Annual Report 2018, P9_TA-PROV(2020)0252 (2020), para. 38; European Commission, EU and China Reach Agreement in Principle on Investment, Dec. 30, 2020, https://trade.ec.europa.eu/doclib/press/index.cfm?id=2233 (last visited Feb. 4, 2021).

7 European Commission, *supra* note 4, at 31.

8 European Commission, *Overview of FTA and Other Trade Negotiations* (Updated Aug. 2020), at 2–3

9 European External Action Service (EEAS), EU-ASEAN: Natural Partners (2013), at 1.

10 European Commission, *Association of South East Asian Nations (ASEAN)*, May 5, 2020, https://ec.europa.eu/trade/policy/countries-and-regions/regions/asean/ (last visited Sept. 2, 2020); ASEAN, *Investing in ASEAN: Association of Southeast Asian Nations* (2019/2020), at 5.

11 EEAS, *Annual German Ambassadors' Conference 2020: Opening Remarks by High Representative/Vice President Josep Borrell*, May 25, 2020, https://eeas.europa.eu/headquarters/headquarters-homepage/79817/annual-german-ambassadors%E2%80%99-

leaders, the elevation from the "Dialogue Partnership to a Strategic Partnership" with ASEAN in 2020 will enable the EU to engage Asia "through all ASEAN-led processes" and implement Brussels' new Indo-Pacific strategy for security and economic purposes.[12]

Against this backdrop, the EU's new trade and investment agreements with Singapore and Vietnam are significant, as they enforce Brussels' Asia strategy after the Treaty of Lisbon as "pathfinders" for a region-to-region FTA, these agreements also signify the new phase of ASEAN-EU relations and present legal models for interregionalism.[13] Their structures and commitments provide templates and benchmarks for future trade pacts between the EU or the post-Brexit United Kingdom (UK) and Asian countries. Under the EU-UK Withdrawal Agreement, EU FTAs with Singapore and Vietnam continued to apply to Britain during the transition period through the end of 2020.[14] Based on the EU's experience, London will likely target selected ASEAN countries as priority FTA partners in Asia.

Notwithstanding their vast economic divergences, Singapore and Vietnam are both rational choices for EU agreements because they are Brussels' top two trading partners in ASEAN.[15] Singapore is the most advanced ASEAN country to achieve a per capita gross domestic product (GDP) of more than $64,000, whereas Vietnam's GDP is lower than

conference-2020-opening-remarks-high-representative-vice-president_en (last visited Sept. 2, 2020); European Commission & High Representative of the Union for Foreign Affairs and Security Policy, *supra* note 6, at 1.

12 Co-Chairs' Press Release: 23rd ASEAN-EU Ministerial Meeting (2020) (23rd ASEAN-EU Ministerial Meeting), paras. 4–16; Joint Statement of the 22nd EU-ASEAN Ministerial Meeting (2019), at 1–3; European Commission, Indo-Pacific: Council Adopts Conclusions on EU Strategy for Cooperation, Apr. 19, 2021, www.consilium.europa.eu/en/press/press-releases/2021/04/19/indo-pacific-council-adopts-conclusions-on-eu-strategy-for-cooperation/ (last visited Aug. 1, 2021).

13 European Parliament, European Parliament Resolution on Regional Free Trade Areas and Trade Strategy in the European Union (2002/2044(INI)), P5_TA(2003)0237 (2003), para. D; Foreword by Singapore Minister for Communications & Information and Minister-in-Charge of Trade Relations S. Iswaran, *in* European Commission & Ministry of Trade and Industry Singapore (MTI), *European Union – Singapore Trade and Investment Agreements* (2019), at 5.

14 Agreement on the withdrawal of the United Kingdom of Great Britain and Northern Ireland from the European Union and the European Atomic Energy Community, 2019/C 384 I/01 (2019), arts. 2 & 126–27.

15 Singapore and Vietnam are the European Union (EU's sixteenth and seventeenth trade partners in the world). Other Asian countries among the EU's top fifteen partners include China, Japan, South Korea, India and Taiwan. European Commission, Client and Supplier Countries of the EU 27 in Merchandise Trade (Value %) (2019, Excluding Intra-EU Trade) (2019), at 1.

$2,400.[16] Singapore is a free port and a regional hub for European companies. Its duty-free regime and absence of agricultural exports makes Singapore a popular FTA partner. As of 2020, Singapore possesses the most extensive FTA network among Asian economies.[17] It has also immensely contributed to the creation of the ASEAN Economic Community (AEC) and the Asia-Europe Meeting (ASEM).[18]

Different from Singapore, Vietnam is a socialist republic. Vietnam's remarkable growth since its "Doi Moi" economic reforms in 1986 has led to a 70 percent decrease in poverty rates.[19] The country has also become a key beneficiary of the US-China trade war because manufacturing bases are being relocated to Vietnam to escape US tariffs on "Made in China" products.[20] Both Singapore and Vietnam are parties to two mega-regional trade agreements, the Comprehensive and Progressive Agreement for Trans-Pacific Partnership (CPTPP) and the Regional Comprehensive Economic Partnership (RCEP). The EU's agreements with these two ASEAN countries thus provide gateways for EU exporters into the new regional supply chain.

The distinctions in the EU's trade and investment agreements with Singapore and Vietnam reflect different approaches to accommodating diverse stages of development. From a legal standpoint, EU FTAs with the two ASEAN states should be comprehended in tandem with the Investment Protection Agreements (IPAs) and the Partnership and Cooperation Agreements (PCAs). IPAs govern investment matters such as the mechanism for investor-state disputes. PCAs facilitate cooperation on human rights and other noneconomic issues and function as "a prerequisite" for EU FTAs.[21] The EU-Singapore FTA, which

[16] ASEAN, *ASEAN Key Figures 2019* (2019), at 32.

[17] As of 2020, Singapore concluded twenty-five free trade agreements (FTAs). World Trade Organization (WTO), Regional Trade Agreements Database, http://rtais.wto.org/UI/PublicSearchByMemberResult.aspx?MemberCode=702&lang=1&redirect=1 (last visited Sept. 2, 2020).

[18] The ASEAN Free Trade Area, the predecessor to the ASEAN Economic Community, and the Asia-Europe Meeting were initiated by Singapore Prime Minister Goh Chok Tong. Rodolfo C. Severino, *Southeast Asia in Search of An ASEAN Community: Insights from the Former ASEAN Secretary-General* 29 & 334 (2006).

[19] World Bank, *The World Bank in Vietnam*, Apr. 27, 2020, www.worldbank.org/en/country/vietnam/overview (last visited Sept. 2, 2020).

[20] VOA News, *US-China Trade War Seen as Boosting Vietnam Growth*, Jan. 12, 2020, www.voanews.com/east-asia-pacific/us-china-trade-war-seen-boosting-vietnam-growth (last visited Sept. 2, 2020).

[21] European Parliament, European Parliament Resolution of 8 May 2008 on Trade and Economic Relations with the Association of South East Asian Nations (ASEAN), P6_TA (2008)0195 (2008), para. H.

originally incorporated investment protection provisions, resulted in controversy about the scope of the "common commercial policy" under the Treaty on the Functioning of the EU.[22] In 2017, the Court of Justice of the EU (CJEU) in the Opinion 2/15 ruled that most aspects of the original EU-Singapore FTA are within the EU's exclusive competence.[23] Nevertheless, provisions on nonforeign direct investment (portfolio investment) and investor-state dispute settlement (ISDS) fall outside the common commercial policy and hence involve the shared competence between the EU and its Member States.[24] Their approvals are necessary for these provisions to take effect.

In response to the Opinion 2/15, the EU-Singapore FTA was split into the FTA and the IPA.[25] In 2019, the European Parliament gave consent to the EU-Singapore FTA, IPA and PCA, but the latter two instruments will only become effective after the twenty-seven national parliaments of the EU ratify them.[26] In other words, the amended EU-Singapore FTA can be understood as an "EU-only" agreement, whereas the IPA and the PCA are "mixed" agreements.[27] After the 2012 EU-Vietnam PCA, the EU-Vietnam FTA followed Singapore's approach, dividing into the FTA and IPA, which the European Parliament ratified in 2020.[28] In practice, this bifurcation approach expedites the FTA implementation. It prevents a single EU member's boycott such as Belgium's rejection of the EU-

[22] *See generally* Opinion 2/15 of the Court (2017).

[23] *Id.* The European Union (EU) and Singapore completed negotiations for provisions on goods and services and provisions on investment protection of the original EU-Singapore FTA in 2013 and 2014, respectively. MTI, *EUSFTA*, www.mti.gov.sg/Improving-Trade/Free-Trade-Agreements/EUSFTA (last visited Sept. 2, 2020).

[24] European Parliament, CJEU Opinion on the EU-Singapore Agreement (2017), at 2.

[25] Andrei Suse & Jan Wouters, *Exploring the Boundaries of Provisional Application: The EU's Mixed Trade and Investment Agreements*, 53(3) J. World Trade 395, 399 (2019).

[26] European Commission, *Agreement with Singapore Set to Give a Boost to EU-Asia Trade*, Feb. 13, 2019, http://trade.ec.europa.eu/doclib/press/index.cfm?id=1980 (last visited Sept. 2, 2020).

[27] David Kleimann & Gesa Kübek, *The Signing, Provisional Application, and Conclusion of Trade and Investment Agreements in the EU: The Case of CETA and Opinion 2/15*, 45(1) Legal Issues Eco. Integration 13, 22–24 (2018); Parliament of the United Kingdom, 8 EU – Singapore Partnership and Cooperation Agreement, Jan. 15, 2019, https://publications.parliament.uk/pa/cm201719/cmselect/cmeuleg/301-xlix/30111.htm (last visited Sept. 3, 2020).

[28] European Commission, *EU-Viet Nam Free Trade Agreement – Joint Press Statement by Commissioner Malmström and Minister Tran Tuan Anh*, Jun. 30, 2019, http://trade.ec.europa.eu/doclib/press/index.cfm?id=2041&utm_source=dlvr.it&utm_medium=facebook (last visited Sept. 3, 2020); World Bank, *Vietnam: Deepening International Integration and Implementing the EVFTA* (2020), at 20.

Canada Comprehensive Economic and Trade Agreement (CETA) in 2016 and the Dutch opposition to the EU-Mercosur pact in 2020.[29]

This chapter will provide the most timely and comprehensive account of EU FTAs with Singapore and Vietnam in light of contemporary trade strategies and domestic legal reforms. It argues that the innovative designs of these FTAs in tandem with IPAs and PCAs will shape ASEAN-EU interregionalism in the post-pandemic era. Based on the best practices of other Asian, EU and US agreements, the chapter will further offer insight into the deficiencies of Singapore and Vietnam's pacts and offer legal and policy recommendations for prospective negotiations.

To substantiate these contentions, the chapter will first examine the nexus between the interdisciplinary theories of interregionalism and the latest wave of global regionalism. It will assess unique rules of origin for "ASEAN cumulation" and Asian food products.[30] Comparative rules on services commitments and non-tariff measures that are vital to banking, automotive, pharmaceutical and renewable energy industries will also be analyzed. Finally, the chapter will evaluate key "new-generation" issues on geographical indications (GIs), state-owned enterprises (SOEs), investor-state arbitration and mediation mechanisms under the IPA.[31] Moreover, it will explore the nexus between the FTA and the PCA and focus on human rights and sustainable development clauses that reflect European values. Collectively, these provisions construct the new phase of EU-Asian economic agreements and energize the evolution of new interregionalism.

II New Phase of EU-Asian Relations

In the 1980s, ASEAN and China first constructed their respective legal frameworks with the European Economic Community (EEC) by signing cooperation agreements.[32] The forty-year evolution of EU-Asian relations provides rich lessons for the multifaceted notion of

[29] Maia de la Baume, *Walloon Parliament Rejects CETA Deal*, Oct. 14, 2016, POLITICO, www.politico.eu/article/walloon-parliament-rejects-ceta-deal/ (last visited Sept. 3, 2020); Raoul Leering, *Dutch Rejection of Mercosur Now Threatens Wider EU Trade Deals*, Jun. 3, 2020, ING, https://think.ing.com/snaps/dutch-rejection-of-mercosur-sign-of-the-times/ (last visited Sept. 3, 2020).

[30] European Commission & MTI, *supra* note 13, at 10–11.

[31] European Commission, *supra* note 4, at 20–23; European Parliament, *Free Trade Agreement between the EU and the Republic of Singapore – Analysis* (2018), at 14–15.

[32] These agreements are the 1980 ASEAN-European Economic Community (EEC) Cooperation Agreement and the 1985 EEC-China Cooperation Agreement.

interregionalism in international law and relations. FTAs with Singapore and Vietnam signify the EU's most recent attempts to buttress its influence in Asia and advance the Commission's "global leadership" priority.[33] The focus on ASEAN in this research highlights the converged strategies of both the EU and its key members. Due to past colonial ties, the UK had greatly influenced the EU's Asian policy. After Brexit, Germany has demonstrated its ambition in Asian affairs. Berlin's first-ever policy guidelines on the Indo-Pacific region of 2020 emphasizes EU FTAs and the country's "important aim" to strengthen cooperation with ASEAN.[34]

The findings of this chapter fill the gap in the existing theoretical and empirical literature because the analysis deciphers the latest normative development of bilateralism vis-à-vis interregionalism. The detailed examination of legal and political approaches of ASEAN, Singapore and Vietnam avoids the oft-criticized Eurocentric view of regionalism study and North-South agreements.[35] The balanced understanding of ASEAN-EU ties also explains the transformation of interregionalism from the core-periphery relationship to an equal partnership between the world's "two most advanced regional integration initiatives."[36]

A Conceptualizing Interregionalism: Evolving Forms and Theories

Most legal scholars do not distinguish interregionalism from regionalism, as both concepts concern the compatibility of trade agreements with WTO law. Legal debates have centered on Article XXIV of the General Agreement on Tariffs and Trade (GATT), Article V of the General Agreement on Trade in Services (GATS) and the Enabling Clause.[37] Unlike the narrow lens of the legal discourse, political scientists have developed diverse theoretical angles and typologies of interregionalism beyond conventional discussions on regionalism. To them,

33 EU Mission to ASEAN, *Blue Book 2020: EU-ASEAN Natural Partners* (2020), at 6.

34 Federal Foreign Office, *"Germany – Europe – Asia: Shaping the 21st Century Together": The German Government Adopts Policy Guidelines on the Indo-Pacific Region*, Sept. 1, 2020, www.auswaertiges-amt.de/en/aussenpolitik/regionaleschwerpunkte/asien/german-government-policy-guidelines-indo-pacific/2380510 (last visited Sept. 3, 2020).

35 For criticism on the view of Euro-centrism, *see e.g.*, Amitav Acharya, *Whose Ideas Matter? Agency and Power in Asian Regionalism* 27 (2009); Fredrik Söderbaum, *Rethinking Regionalism* 7–8 & 175 (2016).

36 EU Mission to ASEAN, *supra* note 33, at 11.

37 WTO, The WTO's Rules, www.wto.org/english/tratop_e/region_e/regrul_e.htm (last visited Sept. 4, 2020).

interregionalism is a state-led process and can be "defined as cooperation between the two specific regions composed of *states* within an interregional framework."[38] Interregionalism is not only "the conjoining of two independent regions," but also a mutual process to yield a "double regional project" that will deepen economic and political interactions.[39]

The types of interregionalism vary. The most classical form is pure interregionalism, which refers to a region-to-region framework such as the ASEAN-EU FTA.[40] As the ASEM and Asia-Pacific Economic Cooperation illustrate, transregionalism means "a dialogue process," in which individual states discuss wide-ranging matters under a loose interregional framework.[41] In addition, hybrid or quasi-interregionalism denotes an institutionalized structure between a region and one or more countries that belong to another region.[42] EU agreements with Singapore and Vietnam, as well as the Lomé Convention with African, Caribbean and Pacific (ACP) countries, represent this type of interregionalism.

In reality, various forms of interregionalism are intertwined. The ASEM as a transregional mechanism facilitates Asia-Europe dialogues that pave the way for economic agreements. The EU's building-block approach aims to transform bilateral, quasi-interregional agreements into a pure interregional FTA between the EU and ASEAN. Furthermore, political scientists have utilized international relations theories to interpret interregionalism. The realist school posits that states pursue economic regionalism "as a strategy in the game of neo-

[38] Fredrik Söderbaum & Luk Van Langenhove, *Introduction: The EU as a Global Actor and the Role of Interregionalism*, 27(3) Eur. Integration 249, 258 (2005).

[39] Julie Gilson, *New Interregionalism? The EU and East Asia*, 27(3) Eur. Integration 307, 309–10 (2005); Ralf Roloff, *Interregionalism in Theoretical Perspective: State of the Art, in* Interregionalism and International Relations: A Stepping Stone to Global Governance? 17, 18 (Jürgen Ruland et al. 2005).

[40] Vinod K. Aggarwal & Edward A. Fogarty, *Between Regionalism and Globalism: European Union Interregional Trade Strategies, in* EU Trade Strategies: Between Regionalism and Globalism 1, 5 (Vinod K. Aggarwal & Edward A. Fogarty eds. 2004); Söderbaum, *supra* note 35, at 176–77.

[41] Jürgen Ruland, *Interregionalism: An Unfinished Agenda, in* Interregionalism and International Relations: A Stepping Stone to Global Governance? 295, 296 (Jürgen Ruland et al. 2005); Söderbaum, *supra* note 35, at 177.

[42] Söderbaum, *supra* note 35, at 177; Aggarwal & Fogarty, *supra* note 40, at 5; Heiner Hänggi, *Interregionalism as a Multifaceted Phenomenon: In Search of a Typology, in* Interregionalism and International Relations: A Stepping Stone to Global Governance? 31, 40–41 (Jürgen Ruland et al. 2005).

mercantilist competition."[43] From a large state's perspective, interregionalism is perceived to be a bargaining tool to advance the hegemonic status in trade politics.[44] Ian Manners proposed the influential notion of "Normative Power Europe" by contending that the EU has shaped the international system as a normative power rather than as a civilian or military power.[45]

Realist and legal commentators have criticized Manners' contention for ignoring the EU's coercive statecraft or the so-called "Brussels Effect."[46] In fact, it has become the EU's mandate to promote European values in economic agreements, which contain enforceable dispute settlement mechanisms.[47] The merger of ideological and material powers in EU agreements have galvanized Brussels' hegemonic status in global regulatory standards.[48]

Realism also explains interregionalism from the standpoint of small states. Singapore and Vietnam demonstrate a unique middle way of the realist stance. Rather than jumping on the bandwagon by associating with a great power or balancing by counteracting the power via alliance, they have used EU pacts as their "hedging" strategy to maximize national interests.[49] Vietnam has played the "EU card" strategically because the EU-Vietnam FTA can decrease trade dependence on China and increase leverage on economic and security ties with the United States.

[43] Andrew Hurrell, *Regionalism in Theoretical Perspective, in* Regionalism in World Politics: Regional Organization and International Order 37, 48–49 (Louise Fawcett & Andrew Hurrell eds. 1995).

[44] *Id.* at 46–50; Tobias Lenz & Gary Marks, *Regional Institutional Design, in* The Oxford Handbook of Comparative Regionalism 513, 517–18 (Tanja A. Börzel & Thomas Risse 2016).

[45] Ian Manners, *Normative Power Europe: A Contradiction in Terms?* 40(2) J. Common Market Stud. 235, 236–52 (2002).

[46] Adrian Hyde-Price, *"Normative" Power Europe: A Realist Critique*, 13(2) J. Eur. Pub. Pol'y 217, 218–20 (2006); Anu Bradford, *The Brussels Effect*, 107(1)NW. Univ. L. Rev. 1, 66 (2012); Anu Bradford, *The Brussels Effect: How the European Union Rules the World* 26–36 (2020).

[47] European Commission, *supra* note 4, at 20–23.

[48] Ha Hai Hoang & Daniela Sicurelli, *The EU's Preferential Trade Agreements with Singapore and Vietnam: Market vs. Normative Imperatives*, 23(4) Contemp. Pol. 369, 371–79 (2017); Ha Hau Hoang, *Normative Power Europe through Trade: Vietnamese Perceptions*, 30(2) Int'l Rel. 176, 191–94 (2015).

[49] Darren J. Lim & Zack Cooper, *Reassessing Hedging: The Logic of Alignment in East Asia*, 24 (4) Sec. Stud. 696, 697–99 (2015); Trang (Mae) Nguyen, *International Law as Hedging: Perspectives from Secondary Authoritarian States*, 114 Am. J. Int'l L. Unbound 237, 237–40 (2020).

Other mainstream theories of international relations similarly provide justifications for interregionalism. According to functionalism, supernational institutions created by the interregional framework will enhance the spill-over effect on the arena of high politics between regions.[50] Institutionalism avers that the interregional structure, which establishes new norms and practices, will fortify cooperation and influence the behavior of member states.[51] Importantly, political scientists concede that these theories are inherently EU-centric because they are mostly premised on EU integration experiences and fall short of explaining regionalism or interregionalism involving Asian countries.[52]

To remedy the weaknesses in assessing regionalism from a single theory, Björn Hettne and Federick Söderbaum advocated for the "new regionalism approach" that represents "a multidimensional process of regional integration."[53] In line with this approach, the analysis of ASEAN from the angle of constructivism emerged.[54] Distinct from realism preoccupied with material power, the ontological focus of constructivism understands interregionalism as a process for promoting collective identity-building. For instance, the EU and ASEAN have functioned as the "other" in realizing their respective identities. Intra-state and interregional relations are thus perceived to be intersubjective and recognition of identity by other parties propels state actions.[55]

Pursuant to a constructivist perspective of normative power, Brussels' promotion of "regional replication" by exporting integration experiences to ASEAN enhances the EU's prestige and identity as the model for regionalism.[56] The EU's recognition of the ASEAN as an equal partner

[50] Hurrell, *supra* note 43, at 59–60.

[51] Ruland, *supra* note 41, at 302–03; Lenz & Marks, *supra* note 44, at 518–20.

[52] Ruland, *supra* note 41, at 303; Hurrell, *supra* note 43, at 60; Amitav Acharya, *Regionalism beyond EU-Centrism*, *in* The Oxford Handbook of Comparative Regionalism 109, 110–19 (Tanja A. Börzel & Thomas Risse 2016).

[53] Björn Hettne, *The New Regionalism: Implications for Development and Peace*, *in* Björn Hettne & András Inotai, The New Regionalism: Implications for Global Development and International Security, UNU/WIDER World Institute for Development Economics Research 1, 11 (1994); Fredrik Söderbaum, *Old, New, and Comparative Regionalism: The History and Scholarly Development of the Field*, *in* The Oxford Handbook of Comparative Regionalism 16, 26–28 (Tanja A. Börzel & Thomas Risse 2016).

[54] Amitav Acharya, *The Making of Southeast Asia: International Relations of A Region* 11–12 (2012); Söderbaum *supra* note 53, at 27.

[55] Alexander Wendt, *Collective Identity Formation and the International State*, 88(2) Am. Pol. Sci. Rev. 384, 384–85 (1994); Lenz & Marks, *supra* note 44, at 520–21.

[56] Aggarwal & Fogarty, *supra* note 40, at 18–19; Ian Manners & Richard Whitman, *The "Difference Engine": Constructing and Representing the International Identity of the European Union*, 10(3) J. Eur. Pub. Pol'y 380, 385 (2003).

rather than a rule-taking protégé also magnifies the international status and identity of the ten-country bloc comprising relatively small, less developed countries.[57] It is inaccurate to simply characterize the EU as "the" model for ASEAN because it has never intended to form a European-style single market or customs union. The declining share of the EU's GDP in the world, Brexit and the sluggish handling of the COVID-19 pandemic have made ASEAN and other Asian countries doubtful of EU governance.[58]

In addition, ASEAN's ascendance is evidenced by the prediction that Indonesia alone will be the world's fifth largest economy ahead of Germany and France by 2024.[59] The central status of the "ASEAN Plus Six" structure in new Asian regionalism is shaping ASEAN's identity vis-à-vis interregional relations with the EU. These changing dynamics substantiate the hypothesis of the new dependency theory that explains transforming North-South relations. Based on the theory, the coexistence of ASEAN developing countries' dependency and development has energized them to reconstruct past dominant-subordinate ties with the EU.[60] Despite different foci, these theoretical explanations have collectively enriched academic debates on interregionalism.

B ASEAN-EU Economic Frameworks and Global Regionalism

In tandem with the three waves of global regionalism in the postwar era, interregionalism between ASEAN and the EU has also undergone three corresponding major periods.[61] What I call the "First Interregionalism"

[57] Bernard Ong, *Recognizing Regions: ASEAN' Struggles for Recognition*, 25(4) *Pac. Rev.* 513, 525–26 (2012); Lay Hwee Yeo, *EU-ASEAN Security Cooperation*, *in* EU Security Strategies: Extending the EU System of Security Governance 67, 77 (Spyros Economides & James Sperling eds. 2018).

[58] The EU's share of the world's gross domestic product is expected to fall from 15 percent to 9 percent by 2050. PWC, *The Long View: How Will the Global Economic Order Change by 2050?* (2017), at 4.

[59] By 2024, the five largest economies are expected to be China, the United States, India, Japan and Indonesia. Katharina Buchholz, *Continental Shift: The World's Biggest Economies Over Time*, Jul. 13, 2020, www.statista.com/chart/22256/biggest-economies-in-the-world-timeline/ (last visited Sept. 3, 2020).

[60] Pasha L. Hsieh, *Reassessing the Trade-Development Nexus in International Economic Law: The Paradigm Shift in Asia-Pacific Regionalism*, 37(3) Northwestern J. Int'l L. & Bus. 321, 339–40 (2017).

[61] Jagdish Bhagwati, *Termites in the Trading System: How Preferential Agreements under Free Trade* 29–35 (2008); WTO, *World Trade Report 2011: The WTO and Preferential Trade Agreements: From Co-existence to Coherence* (2011), at 52–55.

encompasses the inceptive evolution of the two blocs and their initial interactions from the 1950s to the 1970s. Six European nations formed the EEC in 1957 and five Southeast Asian states created ASEAN in 1967.[62] Contact between the two blocs began in the 1970s because ASEAN countries (particularly Singapore and Malaysia) became worried about trade deficits and losing their preference to the British market after the UK joined the EEC.[63]

Led by Indonesia, ASEAN trade ministers met their European counterparts in 1972.[64] ASEAN governments established the Special Coordinating Committee of ASEAN Nations comprising trade minsters and ambassadors to the EEC.[65] In 1977, Brussels became ASEAN's dialogue partner and both sides held the very first ministerial meeting comprising foreign ministers in 1978.[66] These dialogues did not yield substantive results during the First Interregionalism. Yet, the EU's recognition of ASEAN as a bargaining power, albeit its loose alliance, was deemed to be a diplomatic success for ASEAN from the constructivist view.[67]

The 1980 ASEAN-EEC Cooperation Agreement marked the inception of the "Second Interregionalism." Although this agreement provided a legal basis for economic and development cooperation, it merely included best-endeavor clauses without agendas or enforcing mechanisms.[68] From ASEAN's perspective, "the EEC's protectionist

[62] ASEAN and the EU Through the Years, *in* 6/2016 ASEAN Focus 12 (2016), at 12–13; European Commission, *European Neighbourhood Policy and Enlargement Negotiations*, Jan. 31, 2020, https://ec.europa.eu/neighbourhood-enlargement/policy/from-6-to-27-members_en#:~:text=Ten%20new%20countries%20join%20the,the%20whole%20of%20western%20Europe (last visited Sept. 2, 2020); *ASEAN Historical Timeline*, *in* 50 Years of ASEAN and Singapore xiii, xiii–xvi (Tommy Koh et al. eds. 2017).

[63] The European Community and ASEAN, *in* Europe Information: External Relations, 16/79 (1979), at 4–5; Paul Joseph Lim, *ASEAN's Relations with the EU: Obstacles and Opportunities*, EU External Aff. Rev. 46, 47 (2012); Commission of the European Communities, Creating a New Dynamic in EU-ASEAN Relations, COM(96) 314 final (1996), at 66.

[64] Commission of the European Communities, *supra* note 63, at 66.

[65] The European Community and ASEAN, *supra* note 63, at 5.

[66] *Id.*; Commission of the European Communities, *supra* note 63, at 66; ASEAN and the EU Through the Years, *supra* note 62, at 13. The EU and ASEAN "entered a relationship in 1972" and the "relationship was formalised in 1977." Tommy Koh & Yeo Lay Hwee, *ASEAN and EU: The Untold Story*, Oct. 14, 2020, Straits Times, at A18.

[67] Severino, *supra* note 18, at 330; Ong, *supra* note 57, at 525–26.

[68] *See generally* Cooperation Agreement between the European Economic Community and Indonesia, Malaysia, the Philippines, Singapore and Thailand – Member Countries of the Association of South-East Asian Nations (1980).

policies with respect to ASEAN's agricultural and commodity exports" caused great concerns.[69] They also found the EEC's generalized scheme of preferences (GSP) inadequate compared with the concessions that ACP countries obtained under the Lomé Convention.[70]

Several resolutions of the ASEAN Inter-Parliamentary Organization (AIPO) criticized the EEC's "extremely slow" implementation of the 1980 agreement and urged Brussels "to refrain from imposing restrictive and unilateral measures."[71] Unlike the European Parliament, the AIPO that later became the ASEAN Inter-Parliamentary Assembly possesses neither legislative power nor the authority to pass legally-binding resolutions.[72] Nonetheless, AIPO resolutions voiced ASEAN's frustrations over the passive position of their European counterpart.

The 1990s witnessed vital transformations of ASEAN-EU frameworks. The 1992 EEC Regulation became the legal basis for providing financial and technical assistance to "developing countries in Asia" including ASEAN states.[73] In the meantime, ASEAN members created the ASEAN Free Trade Area to expedite economic integration. In 1994, Brussels' first "New Asia Strategy" noted the increasing "weight of Asia in the world economy" and called for "proactive economic cooperation" with ASEAN.[74] As the most salient bilateral structure, the ASEM was established in 1996 and now includes the EU, the ASEAN Secretariat, thirty European countries and twenty-one Asian countries such as China, Japan and India.[75] This transcontinental forum was proposed by Singapore Prime Minister Goh Chok Tong, with French President Jacques Chirac's support.[76] Although the ASEM Summit became the highest level meeting between Asia and

69 Severino, *supra* note 18, at 330.

70 Andrew J. Crozier, *The Trade and Aid Policy of the European Union: A Historical Perspective*, *in* EU-ASEAN: Facing Economic Globalisation 57, 69 (Paul J. J. Welfens et al. 2009); Severino, *supra* note 18, at 330.

71 ASEAN Inter-Parliamentary Organization (AIPO), Resolution of the Sixth AIPO General Assembly on ASEAN-EC Economic Cooperation, 6GA/RES.11/83 (1983), at 1; AIPO, Resolution of the Ninth General Assembly of AIPO on the ASEAN-EC Economic Cooperation, WC/GA9/88/KL/29/6 (1988), at 1.

72 Laurence Vandewalle, *The ASEAN Inter-Parliamentary Assembly (AIPA): A Privileged Interlocutor for the European Parliament in South East Asia* (2015), at 1–6.

73 Council Regulation (EEC) No 443/92 of 25 February 1992 on Financial and Technical assistance to, and Economic Cooperation with, the Developing countries in Asia and Latin America (1992).

74 Commission of the European Communities, *supra* note 1, at 3–24.

75 Severino, *supra* note 18, at 334; Asia-Europe Meeting, 30 European Countries, the European Union & 21 Asian Countries, the ASEAN Secretariat, www.aseminfoboard.org/about/partners (last visited Sept. 8. 2020).

76 Severino, *supra* note 18, at 334

Europe, the forum has been challenged for its overly broad topics and the reluctance of Asian countries to respond to Brussels' human rights agenda.[77]

Since the 2000s, the "Third Interregionalism" has coincided with the third wave of global regionalism, which I refer to as the "Third Regionalism."[78] Other than the ASEAN-EU context, the interregional framework between the EU and the ACP countries have also fundamentally been altered. The 1975 Lomé Convention was replaced with the reciprocal, WTO-consistent Cotonou Agreement and its pertinent economic partnership agreements. Unlike the "constructed" ACP region with decentralized power, ASEAN is a defined area and an international organization with legal personality that the ASEAN Charter has conferred.[79] The rise of Asia also made ASEAN-EU interregionalism far more geopolitically and economically important than the EU's interregional relations with other groupings of the "South" such as the African Union or Mercosur.

In essence, the EU's contemporary Asia policy including the Indo-Pacific strategy is premised on the "ASEAN Plus Six" framework. The Commission recognized that the center of gravity in the global economy has shifted to Asia and that ASEAN will likely become the world's largest exporter.[80] To implement "enhanced partnerships" with Asia, the EU sought to forge its "new partnership" with ASEAN and, in 2020, both sides agreed to elevate bilateral ties into a "strategic partnership."[81] Since 2003, the EU has developed a three-pillar economic framework with ASEAN. The Trans-Regional EU-ASEAN Trade Initiative (TREATI), which promotes dialogues on trade and investment issues, has served as a foundation for region-to-region FTA negotiations.[82]

[77] Noel M. Moranda, *Europe and Southeast Asia: ASEAN-EU Interregionalism between Pluralist and Solidarist Societies*, 4(3) Rev. Eur. Stud. 89, 96 (2012); Maria-Gabriela Manea, *Human Rights and the Interregional Dialogue between Asia and Europe: ASEAN-EU Relations and ASEM*, 21(3) Pac. Rev. 369, 379 (2008).

[78] Scholars refer to the new developments as the third-generation or post-hegemonic regionalism. Söderbaum & Van Langenhove, *supra* note 38, at 256–58; Mario Telò, *Introduction: Globalization, New Regionalism and the Role of the European Union, in* European Union and New Regionalism: Competing Regionalism and Global Governance in a Post-Hegemonic Era 1, 5 (Mario Telò ed. 2014).

[79] Charter of the ASEAN (2007), art. 3.

[80] Commissions of the European Communities, Communication from the Commission: A New Partnership with South East Asia, COM (2003) 399 final (2003), at 6.

[81] Commission of the European Communities, Europe and Asia: A Strategic Framework for Enhanced Partnerships, COM(2001) 469 final (2001), at 5–21; *id.* at 3–6; 23rd ASEAN-EU Ministerial Meeting, para. 4.

[82] Commission of the European Communities, A New Partnership with South East Asia, COM(2003) 399 final (2003), at 18–31.

The TREATI created a flexible mechanism that involves "the EU and more than two ASEAN countries."[83] The same mechanism applies to development cooperation, currently known as the Enhanced Regional EU-ASEAN Dialogue Instrument (E-READI).[84] As "a demand-driven instrument," the E-READI provides logistical support for meetings on thematic areas ranging from the digital economy, gender equality and the United Nations (UN) Sustainable Development Goals.[85] For the past forty years, the EU has been the "most significant partner" for ASEAN's development cooperation projects, including the latest ones on sustainable urbanization and timber licensing.[86] Additionally, the ASEAN Regional Integration Support from the EU (ARISE), which was later upgraded to the "ARISE Plus," centers on ASEAN economic integration through the implementation of the AEC Blueprint 2025 such as the new ASEAN Customs Transit System.[87]

These three pillars developed in the Third Interregionalism collectively underpin the new ASEAN-EU Plan of Action and the EU-Asia Connectivity Strategy, which highlights ASEAN as "a central player" in the region.[88] The EU's infrastructure investment-based Connectivity Strategy is perceived to be a response to Beijing's Belt and Road Initiative. The von der Leyen Commission's implementation of the strategy will further counteract China, which became a "systemic rival promoting alternative models of governance," eroding the EU's unity and interests.[89]

83 It is the "EU + x" dialogue mechanism. *Id.* at 31.

84 The initiative was previously known as the Regional EC-ASEAN Dialogue Instrument (READI). Lay Hwee Yeo, *Political Cooperation between the EU and ASEAN: Searching for a Long-Term Agenda and Joint Projects*, *in* EU-ASEAN: Facing Economic Globalisation 45, 53–54 (Paul J. J. Welfens et al. 2009); EEAS, *Enhanced Regional EU-ASEAN Dialogue Instrument (E-READI)*, May 27, 2019, https://eeas.europa.eu/delegations/thailand/49815/enhanced-regional-eu-asean-dialogue-instrument-e-readi_km (last visited Sept. 9. 2020).

85 EU Mission to ASEAN, *supra* note 33, at 17.

86 Mission of the EU to ASEAN, *EU Announces New Development Cooperation Projects with ASEAN to Support Sustainable Urbanisation, Forest Management and Government Accountability*, Aug. 13, 2020, https://eeas.europa.eu/delegations/association-southeast-asian-nations-asean/84050/eu-announces-new-development-cooperation-projects-asean-support-sustainable-urbanisation_en#:~:text=and%20government%20accountability-,Today%20(13%2F8)%2C%20the%20European%20Union%20(EU,and%20ASEAN%20Supreme%20Audit%20Institutions (last visited Sept. 8, 2020).

87 ASEAN Regional Integration Support from the EU, *Background*, https://ariseplus.asean.org/about/ (last visited Sept. 8, 2020); 23rd ASEAN-EU Ministerial Meeting, para. 14.

88 ASEAN-EU Plan of Action (2018–22) (2017); European Commission, Connecting Europe and Asia – Building Blocks for an EU Strategy, JOIN(2018) 31 final (2018), at 8.

89 European Commission & High Representative of the Union for Foreign Affairs and Security Policy, *supra* note 6, at 1–2.

C Roadmap to the Region-to-Region FTA: A Building-Block Approach

Concluding the ASEAN-EU FTA requires a practical roadmap. The EU's building-block approach aims to build the region-to-region FTA on bilateral, pathfinder agreements with individual ASEAN states. Significantly, in the Third Interregionalism, there are fundamental global challenges to the policies of the EU and ASEAN. First, the eclipsing US economic hegemony has eroded the "unipolar moment" of trade governance.[90] A new tripolar economic order based on the agendas of the United States, the EU and China has emerged. However, the unilateralism of the Trump administration fractured the trans-Atlantic alliance, which President Joe Biden seeks to restore. EU relations with China have also been haunted by Beijing's aggressive "wolf warrior" diplomacy, coronavirus cover-up and imposition of National Security Law on Hong Kong.[91] In the past, the US-Singapore FTA and ASEAN FTAs with China and Japan energized trade negotiations with ASEAN.[92] Brussel's changing ties with Washington and Beijing calls for a more "independent" policy on Asia centered on the ASEAN-EU FTA.

Second, emerging mega-regional trade agreements such as the CPTPP and the RCEP mark the most salient feature of the Third Interregionalism. Arguably, these Asia-Pacific pacts fall with the realm of transregionalism rather than interregionalism, as states participate in these FTAs in their individual capacities. However, transregionalism helps construct a normative foundation for interregionalism. As the mega-regionals will result in the trade diversion effect that undermines other interregional trade relations, the EU found it urgent to cement agreements with top ASEAN partners such as Singapore and Vietnam. For ASEAN countries, concluding agreements with the EU diversifies risks owing to China-US trade conflicts and consolidates their central position in global value chains. These factors influence public surveys,

[90] Charles Krauthammer, *The Unipolar Moment*, 70 Foreign Aff. 23 (1990–91).

[91] *E.g.*, Luke Baker & Robin Emmott, *As China Pushes Back on Virus, Europe Wakes to "Wolf Warrior" Diplomacy*, May 14, 2020, Diplomat, www.reuters.com/article/us-health-coronavirus-europe-china-insig/as-china-pushes-back-on-virus-europe-wakes-to-wolf-warrior-diplomacy-idUSKBN22Q2EZ (last visited Sept. 9, 2020).

[92] European Services Forum, Letter to the Commissioner for Trade, Jul. 12, 2020, at 1–2; Alfred C. Robles, Jr., *An EU-ASEAN FTA: The EU's Failure as an International Actor*, 13 Eur. Foreign Aff. Rev. 541, 542 (2008); David Camroux, *Interregionalism or Merely a Fourth-Level Game? An Examination of the EU-ASEAN Relationship*, 27 E. Asia 57, 67 (2010).

which show that 88.7 percent of ASEAN stakeholders support the ASEAN-EU FTA and 81 percent of European enterprises envision that the region-to-region FTA deliver more benefits than bilateral FTAs.[93]

Finally, the COVID-19 pandemic that led to a 32 percent plunge in global trade has posed an imminent threat to ASEAN-EU economic relations.[94] Their GDP decrease by 7–10 percent made the two blocs' recession inevitable.[95] Concluding additional agreements with ASEAN countries and the ASEAN-EU FTA has become an indispensable step for the EU to implement the "open strategic autonomy" policy for economic recovery.[96] Also, the ASEAN-led RCEP and the ASEAN-EU FTA form ASEAN's two-pronged strategy to revitalize trade amid the pandemic. As global investment could plunge by 42 percent, it is critical to attract the ASEAN-bound investment of the EU, which has been the region's largest investor.[97] Moreover, six of the world's top ten exporters of medical and personal protective products are EU members.[98] FTAs that minimize tariffs and non-tariff barriers for these products will help ASEAN governments mitigate the COVID-19 crisis. FTAs' cooperation mechanism will further benefit the continuation of financial and technical support that ASEAN has received from "Team Europe."[99]

These global challenges provide an important context for ASEAN-EU FTA talks. The legal competence and politics of EU and ASEAN institutions have greatly influenced the negotiation and ratification of agreements. Pursuant to the Treaty on the Functioning of the EU, an authorization of the Council of the EU (Council) to launch trade negotiations is based on the Commission's recommendation.[100] The task of the

[93] ISEAS-Yusof Ishal Institute, *The State of Southeast Asia: 2020 Survey Report* (2002), at 3; EU-ASEAN Business Council, *2020 EU-ASEAN Sentiment Survey* (2020), at 7 & 30.

[94] WTO, *Trade Set to Plunge as COVID-19 Pandemic Upends Global Economy*, Apr. 8, 2020, www.wto.org/english/news_e/pres20_e/pr855_e.htm (last visited Sept. 9, 2020).

[95] Iacopo Monterosa et al., *Trade in Time of Corona: What's Next for the EU?* Jun. 2020, ECIPE, https://ecipe.org/blog/trade-in-time-of-corona/ (last visited Sept. 9, 2020); VOA News, *Virus-Fueled Recession Interrupts ASEAN Path to Middle-Income Status*, Apr. 28, 2020, VOA News, www.voanews.com/covid-19-pandemic/virus-fueled-recession-interrupts-asean-path-middle-income-status (last visited Sept. 9, 2020).

[96] European Commission, *supra* note 2, at 12–13.

[97] United Nations Conference on Trade and Investment (UNCTAD), *Investment Trends Monitor* (2021), Issue 38, at 1; European Commission & MTI, *supra* note 13, at 7.

[98] WTO, *Trade in Medical Goods in the Context of Tackling COVID-19* (2020), at 5.

[99] Josep Borrell, *Strengthening EU-ASEAN Partnership, A Urgent Necessity*, Sept. 20, 2020, EEAS, https://eeas.europa.eu/headquarters/headquarters-homepage/85434/strengthening-eu-asean-partnership-urgent-necessity_en (last visited Sept. 25, 2020).

[100] Consolidated Version of the Treaty on the Functioning of the European Union, OJ C 326/47 (TFEU) (2012), arts. 207(3).

Commission is to negotiate an FTA, but its conclusion and effect will be subject to the Council's adoption and the European Parliament's ratification.[101] EU institutions have different foci and considerations. The Council and the Commission are primarily driven by material interests in trade agreements, whereas the Parliament often stresses ideological values such as human rights and sustainable development.[102]

Distinct from the supranational structure of the EU, ASEAN is an international organization and its FTA process remains state-centric. The ASEAN Secretariat possesses a limited role in FTA negotiations because the ASEAN Charter's treaty-making power clause does not apply to agreements that will "create obligations upon individual" members.[103] The entry into force of trade and investment pacts also depends on the ratification of national parliaments rather than the ASEAN Inter-Parliamentary Assembly. These distinctions in institutions' legal capacity have impacted ASEAN-EU trade and investment negotiations.

At the inception of the Third Interregionalism, the European Parliament urged bilateral pathfinder agreements with Singapore and other Asian countries to set benchmarks for trade liberalization.[104] Responding to Singapore Prime Minister Goh's suggestion for Brussels to forge an FTA with ASEAN in 2004, EU Commissioner for Trade Pascal Lamy claimed that a region-to-region FTA was premature.[105] Lamy suggested that the focus be on the TREATI framework, as ASEAN's non-tariff barriers impeded trade and investment.[106] In his view, the EU is "different" because ASEAN countries tend to "launch FTA negotiations first and backload the more contentious regulatory barriers."[107]

The transformation in trade politics prompted the European Commission to alter its stance. The 2006 "Global Europe" report articulated two criteria for FTA partners, including "market potential" and "the

[101] *Id.* arts. 207 & 218; WTO, Trade Policy Review, Report by the Secretariat: European Union, WT/TPR/S/395 (2019), at 33–34.

[102] Lachlan Mckenzie & Katharina L. Meissner, *Human Rights Conditionality in European Union Trade Negotiations: The Case of the EU-Singapore FTA*, 55(4) J. Common Market Stud. *832, 838* (2017).

[103] Charter of the ASEAN (2007), art. 41(7); Rules of Procedure for Conclusion of International Agreements by ASEAN (2011), rule 1.

[104] European Parliament, *supra* note 13, paras. D, X & 23.

[105] Goh Chok Tong, *Asia – Catalyst for Global Economic Integration*, 2 Asia Eur. J. 1, 4 (2004); Pascal Lamy, *Unlocking the Potential of the ASEAN-EU Partnership: The Role of Singapore*, 2 Asia Eur. J 485, 486–87 (2004); Robles, *supra* note 92, at 545.

[106] Lamy, *supra* note 105, 486.

[107] *Id.*

level of protection against EU export interests," and therefore identified ASEAN as an FTA priority.[108] To assess the feasibility of the region-to-region FTA, the EU-ASEAN Vision Group recognized that unlike other regions, "ASEAN is extremely heterogeneous" and includes countries with diverse levels of development. The Vision Group recommended that the agreement achieve the "elimination of tariffs for 90% of trade and tariff lines" within seven years.[109] Unlike most of ASEAN's external pacts that are negotiated under a framework agreement, the ASEAN-EU FTA should be a single-undertaking, comprehensive pact.[110] The FTA should also accord special and differential treatment such as lengthier implementation timeframes for less developed members, which denote Cambodia, Laos, Myanmar and Vietnam.[111]

Following the Council's negotiating mandate, the Commission launched FTA talks with seven ASEAN countries in 2007.[112] Subsequently, the Parliament called for a PCA, which includes "enforceable human rights clauses," to be a prerequisite to "an FTA with any country."[113] As FTA negotiations ran into problems after just two years, the joint committee decided to suspend talks in 2009.[114] The two blocs diverged vastly on sensitive issues ranging from the 90 percent tariff elimination benchmark to public procurement, which Malaysia refused to accept.[115] The EU was further frustrated because including Myanmar in negotiations drew the result toward the "lowest common denominator."[116] Before suspending ASEAN-EU FTA talks, the Commission attempted to salvage the pact by engaging parallel negotiations with a subgroup of "forerunners," including Brunei, Singapore and Thailand.[117] However, this fast-track, complementary approach failed, as only negotiations with Singapore remained constructive.

108 European Commission, *Global Europe: Competing in the World* (2006), at 11.

109 ASEAN-EU Vision Group, *Report of the ASEAN-EU Vision Group: Transregional Partnership for Shared and Sustainable Prosperity* (2006), at 11–12.

110 *Id.*; Commission of the European Communities, Report on the State of Play of the FTA Negotiations with ASEAN, India, the Andean Community and Central America, SEC (2009) 681 final (2009), at 4.

111 ASEAN-EU Vision Group, *supra* note 109, at 11.

112 Commission of the European Communities, *supra* note 110, at 4–5.

113 EU-ASEAN FTA – EC Negotiating Mandate (Draft, 2007), www.bilaterals.org/?draft-eu-asean-fta-negotiating (last visited Sept. 10, 2020), part. 2; European Parliament, *supra* note 21, para. H.

114 Commission of the European Communities, *supra* note 110, at 5.

115 *Id.*; ASEAN-EU Vision Group, *supra* note 109, at 12 fn. 2.

116 Commission of the European Communities, *supra* note 110, at 5.

117 *Id.*

The European Commission's "Trade for All" policy that articulates the ASEAN strategy led to the rebirth of the ASEAN-EU FTA.[118] The Commission proclaimed a building-block approach based on bilateral FTAs, which would start with Singapore and Vietnam and set benchmarks for other ASEAN countries.[119] This approach echoed the European Parliament's previous suggestions for commencing pathfinder agreements to build the foundation for the region-to-region FTA.[120] EU-Singapore FTA negotiations were launched in 2009 and finalized in 2014.[121] In 2012, the EU and Vietnam commenced their FTA talks, which were completed in 2017.[122] These pathfinder agreements have energized the ASEAN-EU FTA. For ASEAN, an FTA with the EU benefits the new "Global ASEAN" objective in the AEC Blueprint 2025 and enhances the bloc's collective power that underpins the NREO.[123] Consequently, both blocs have discussed the resumption of ASEAN-EU FTA negotiations since 2017.[124] The prospective region-to-region FTA and the Comprehensive Air Transport Agreement will represent the most significant interregional agreements.

III EU Agreements with Singapore and Vietnam As Pathfinders

Given the Opinion 2/15 on the EU's competency issues arising from the original EU-Singapore FTA, Brussels and Singapore split the original agreement into the FTA and the IPA in 2017 and signed both instruments in 2018.[125] The EU and Vietnam followed the same approach and signed the new FTA and IPA in 2019.[126] Under Singapore law and practice, the Singapore Parliament's consent is neither sought nor required for a trade pact to become effective.[127] Thus, after the European Parliament ratified the EU-Singapore FTA and IPA in 2019,

118 European Commission, *supra* note 4, at 31–32.

119 *Id.*

120 European Parliament, *supra* note 13, paras. D, X & 23.

121 MTI, *PowerPoint Slides: The EUSFTA: New Opportunities for Our Business* (2020), at 2.

122 World Bank, *supra* note 28, at 20.

123 ASEAN, ASEAN Economic Community 2025 Consolidated Strategic Action Plan (2017), at 46–47.

124 European Commission, *supra* note 8, at 2; ASEAN-EU Plan of Action (2018–22) (2017), para. 2.1(c).

125 MTI, *supra* note 121, at 2.

126 World Bank, *supra* note 28, at 20.

127 C. L. Lim & Mahdev Mohen, *Ch. 05 Singapore and International Law*, Jan. 1, 2015, www.singaporelawwatch.sg/About-Singapore-Law/Overview/ch-05-singapore-and-international-law (last visited Sept. 11, 2020).

the FTA entered into force.[128] In 2020, the EU-Vietnam FTA took effect after the ratification of the European Parliament and the National Assembly of Vietnam.[129] The effect of their IPAs will be subject to the approval of twenty-seven EU members. The legal links between FTAs and PCAs also made these agreements intertwined.

EU FTAs with Singapore and Vietnam crystalize the Third Interregionalism because they exhibit the EU's new-generation agreements and first two FTAs with ASEAN countries. The EU-Singapore FTA is Brussels' third FTA with an Asian country after Korea and Japan. The EU-Vietnam FTA constitutes "the most comprehensive trade agreement the EU has concluded with a developing country."[130] It also accelerates the EU-Vietnam PCA's goal to achieve "the early recognition of Vietnam's market economy status."[131] As for the ASEAN-EU FTA, I concede that persisting obstacles remain. Key challenges include the EU's palm oil disputes with Indonesia and Malaysia and human rights situations in Cambodia and Myanmar such as the Rohingya crisis and the military coup. What I emphasize is that the innovative mechanisms and the trade creation effect of the pathfinder pacts will garner the support of stakeholders and invigorate ASEAN-EU interregionalism. As Table 4.1 below illustrates, the comparison between EU agreements with Singapore and Vietnam enables ASEAN and other Asian governments to better assess the EU's approach.

A Tariff Concessions and ASEAN Cumulative Rules of Origin

Tariff cuts are essential to trade negotiations. EU FTAs with Singapore and Vietnam set benchmarks for the remaining ASEAN countries. Given the divergent developments of Singapore and Vietnam, the levels of tariff liberalization and implementation periods demonstrate two models. Although 99 percent of Singapore's imports enter the country duty free, the EU-Singapore FTA can ensure the predictability for EU enterprises because Singapore's WTO commitments cover only 69.3 percent

[128] MTI, *supra* note 121, at 2.

[129] World Bank, *supra* note 28, at 20; Dezan Shira & Associates, *Vietnam-EU Trade: EVFTA Comes into Effect*, Aug. 3, 2020, www.vietnam-briefing.com/news/vietnam-eu-trade-evfta-comes-into-effect.html/ (last visited Sept. 11, 2020).

[130] European Commission, EU-Vietnam Trade Agreement Enters into Force (2020), at 1.

[131] EU-Vietnam Framework Agreement on Comprehensive Partnership and Cooperation (2012) (PCA), annex: joint declaration on market economy status.

Table 4.1 *Comparison: the EU's trade and investment agreements with Singapore and Vietnam*

FTA	Singapore	Vietnam
Tariff elimination	EU: in 5 years Singapore: eliminated remaining tariffs in 2019	EU: in 7 years Vietnam: in 10 years Commitments on remanufactured/repaired goods
Rules of origin	ASEAN cumulation Quota for Asian food products	Similar; with a narrower scope Including Korea for fabrics
Services, establishment and e-commerce	Specific chapter Positive-list approach	Same Same
Technical barriers to trade	Adopting the UNECE type approval system for vehicles Provisions on renewable energy generation	Same Same
Copyright	70 years after the author's death	50 years after the author's death
Geographical indications	Only EU GIs (190) are protected	Both EU (169) and Vietnamese GIs (39) are protected
State-owned enterprises	No specific chapter; some rules in Chapter on Competition and Related Matters	Specific chapter, separate from Chapter on Competition Policy
Sustainable development	Subject to the chapter-specific dispute settlement mechanism	Same
State-to-state arbitration	150 days, extendable to 180 days	120 days, extendable to 150 days
IPA	Singapore	Vietnam
Definition of investment	Broader	Narrower
Investment Court System (investor-state disputes)	Tribunal of First Instance (6 Members) & Appeal Tribunal (6 Members)	Tribunal (9 Members) & Appeal Tribunal (6 Members)

Table 4.1 (*cont.*)

FTA	Singapore	Vietnam
	Individually & jointly appointed by EU & Singapore 8-year term, may be renewed by the Committee	Appointed by the Committee 4-year term, renewable once
PCA	Singapore	Vietnam
Linkage to the FTA	Forms part of a common institutional framework	Same
Enforcement	Consultations Including a side-letter on the nonexecution mechanism	Same No side letter

of its tariff lines.[132] Specifically, the FTA eliminated Singapore's remaining tariffs on alcoholic beverages such as beer and samsu.[133] On the EU side, tariffs on Singapore exports will be reduced and eliminated in three stages during a five-year period.[134] Political considerations inevitably influenced Brussels' tariff elimination. To illustrate, Italy was concerned that roti pratas, an Indian-influenced flatbread dish, would be substituted for pizzas and therefore tariffs on roti pratas will only be removed by 2025.[135] Selected fish products and vegetables are also immune from the EU's tariff liberalization.[136]

[132] Trade Regulations, Customs and Standards, https://2016.export.gov/singapore/doingbusinessinsingapore/traderegulationscustomsandstandards/index.asp (last visited Sept. 11, 2020); WTO, Trade Policy Review, Report by the Secretariat, Singapore, WT/TPR.S.343 (2016), at 27–28.

[133] WTO, *supra* note 132, at 27; Toh Boon Ho, *PowerPoint Slides: EUSFTA Trade in Goods: Increase Your Products' Price Competitiveness in the EU* (2020), at 15.

[134] EU tariffs on 84 percent of Singapore's exports to the EU were eliminated in the first year, 2019. Singapore International Chamber of Commerce (SICC), *Plain English Guide to the European Union-Singapore Free Trade Agreement* (2020), at 12.

[135] Toh, *supra* note 133, at 16.

[136] *Id.*; European Parliament, *supra* note 31, at 39.

The EU-Vietnam FTA, which exemplifies the focus of "development" in North-South agreements, is key to ASEAN's less developed members. Aiming to eliminate over 99 percent of tariffs, the FTA follows an asymmetric approach that benefits Vietnam.[137] EU tariffs on Vietnam's exports will be cut within seven years, but Vietnam is given a ten-year transitional period to eliminate its tariffs on EU products.[138] As a developing country, Vietnam was entitled to the EU GSP. Vietnam enjoyed lower tariff rates for 75 percent of its exports under the GSP and the EU-Vietnam FTA not only secured but also exceeded existing GSP benefits.[139] For the eight remaining ASEAN GSP beneficiary countries, additional tariff preferences under bilateral and regional FTAs with the EU will be vital.[140]

The provisions on trade in goods under the EU-Vietnam FTA contain unique developing-country friendly features that are not found in the EU-Singapore FTA. Akin to the CPTPP, the EU-Vietnam FTA incorporates rules on "remanufactured goods."[141] These goods are "comprised of parts obtained from" used goods, but include "similar performance and working conditions," life expectancy and warranties comparable to those applicable to new goods.[142] The CPTPP requires "the importation of remanufactured goods" to be subject to the same rules for original goods.[143] The EU-Vietnam FTA also mandates "the same treatment" for remanufactured goods, but allows "specific labelling" to avoid "deception of consumers" and a three-year transitional period for implementation.[144]

[137] European Commission, *EU-Vietnam Trade Agreement – MEMO*, Jul. 31, 2020, https://trade.ec.europa.eu/doclib/press/index.cfm?id=1922 (last visited Sept. 11, 2020).

[138] *Id.*; European Chamber of Commerce in Vietnam (EuroCham), *2019 EVFTA Report: The EU-Vietnam Free Trade Agreement: Perspectives from Vietnam* (2019), at 6.

[139] SICC, *Plain English Guide to the European Union-Vietnam Free Trade Agreement* (2020), at 11.

[140] European Parliament, *The Generalised Scheme of Preferences Regulation (No 978/2012): European Implementation Assessment* (2018), at 93 fn. 32. In the case of Vietnam, the EU will use quotas to limit Vietnam's export of sensitive agricultural products such as rice, eggs and canned tuna. United States Department of Agriculture & Global Agricultural Information Network, *European Union – Vietnam Free Trade Agreement Ratified* (2020), at 6.

[141] Comprehensive and Progressive Agreement for Trans-Pacific Partnership (CPTPP) (2018) (CPTPP), ch.1, sec. B, art. 1.3; EU-Vietnam FTA (2019), art. 2.3(k).

[142] EU-Vietnam FTA, art. 2.3(k).

[143] CPTPP, art. 2.11.1.

[144] EU-Vietnam FTA, art. 2.6.

Current Vietnamese law prohibits the importation of used goods.[145] Under the new rules, European businesses are expected to export more high-value medical devices and car parts that are remanufactured and less costly.[146] Moreover, the EU-Vietnam FTA exempts goods from customs duties on the re-entry to Vietnam after they are repaired in EU states.[147] Hence, provisions on remanufactured and repaired goods enable enterprises in developing countries to save on costs for required equipment.

1 Legal Concept of ASEAN Cumulation

Rules of origin ensure that only goods from FTA partners rather than third parties are entitled to preferential treatment. These rules are significant to global value chains and influence the effectiveness of FTAs. The innovative rules under EU FTAs with Singapore and Vietnam contribute to the objective of the AEC Blueprint 2025 to accomplish "a more united market."[148] In particular, rules of origin that apply the concept of ASEAN cumulation and enable Asian food products to enter the EU duty free should be "regionalized."

As modern trade pacts, EU FTAs with Singapore and Vietnam adopt co-equal rules, which accord exporters the flexibility to choose either the change in tariff classification rule or the regional value content (RVC) rule. Either rule entitles exports to enjoy FTA tariff preferences.[149] Based on the RVC rule, products that do not meet the RVC threshold, 40 percent in most ASEAN FTAs, will be deemed to be non-originating goods ineligible for FTA benefits.[150] ASEAN cumulative rules of origin, under which components produced in other ASEAN countries can count toward an EU FTA's RVC benchmark, reflects the reality of the production chain. For instance, Singapore is not a regional manufacturing base. An RVC rule that considers only "Made in Singapore" products as originating goods would negate FTA benefits.

145 World Bank, *supra* note 28, at 20; EuroCham, *supra* note 138, at 54. Note that Article 2.11.2 of the CPTPP does not apply to Vietnam. CPTPP, art. 2.11.2 fn. 6.

146 Delegation of the European Union to Vietnam, *Guide to the EU-Vietnam Trade and Investment Agreements* (2016), at 28–29.

147 EU-Singapore FTA (2018), art. 2.10.

148 ASEAN Economic Community (AEC) Blueprint 2025 (2015), para. 7.

149 SICC, *supra* note 134, at 13; SICC, *supra* note 139, at 19.

150 Minh Hue Nguyen et al., *The ASEAN Trade in Goods Agreement: Evolution and Regional Implications*, *in* ASEAN Law in the New Regional Economic Order: Global Trends and Shifting Paradigms 22, 39 (Pasha L. Hsieh & Bryan Mercurio eds. 2019).

The legal concept of ASEAN cumulation is by no means new. The EU GSP has granted "regional cumulation" to ASEAN countries except Singapore.[151] Similar rules are also included in "ASEAN Plus One" FTAs. One case is the ASEAN-China FTA, which recognizes components produced in all ASEAN states for the RVC calculation. Japan has concluded bilateral FTAs with seven ASEAN countries and one FTA with ASEAN, but only the latter encompasses ASEAN cumulative rules of origin.[152] EU FTAs with Singapore and Vietnam are unique pathfinders, as they incorporate GSP rules on ASEAN cumulation into bilateral FTAs. However, the scope of ASEAN cumulation under the EU-Vietnam FTA is more limited than that of the EU-Singapore FTA.

First, according to Protocols 1 of the two EU FTAs, processed products from any ASEAN country are entitled to cumulation rules if the country concluded an FTA with the EU.[153] These rules will result in "a domino effect," prompting more ASEAN members to expedite FTAs talks with the EU in order to become a regional export gateway.[154] Presently, the EU-Vietnam FTA's ASEAN cumulative rules of origin are confined to live, fresh or chilled cuttlefish, squid and octopus.[155] The two FTAs envision that after additional agreements are concluded between the EU and ASEAN states, rules of origin will be reviewed and amended "to ensure coherence between" FTAs.[156]

Second, utilizing ASEAN cumulation may not be conditioned on an FTA with the EU. This flexibility exists only in the EU-Singapore FTA. Singapore-based manufacturers are permitted to utilize other ASEAN countries' raw materials and parts for selected products as originating contents under the EU-Singapore FTA.[157] Arguably, the short list of the products listed in Annex D yields a limited impact because these products account for merely "18.8% of Singaporean imports from ASEAN

[151] European Parliament, *supra* note 140, at 93 fn. 32. Even upon the entry into force of the EU-Vietnam FTA, Vietnamese exporters may also continue to enjoy GSP benefits until 2022. EY, *EU-Vietnam Free Trade Agreement Enters into Force as of 1 August 2020* (2020), at 3; Regulation (EU) No 978/2012 of the European Parliament and the Council of 25 October 2012 (2012), art. 5(2)(b).

[152] ASEAN-Japan Agreement on Comprehensive Economic Partnership (2008), art. 24(c). From 2002 to 2008, Japan signed FTAs with Singapore, Malaysia, the Philippines, Thailand, Brunei, Indonesia and Vietnam.

[153] EU-Singapore FTA, protocol 1, art. 3.2; EU-Vietnam FTA, protocol 1, art. 3.2.

[154] Richard Baldwin, *A Domino Theory of Regionalism*, NBER Working Paper Series, No. 4465 (1993), at 2–5.

[155] EU-Vietnam FTA, protocol 1, annex III.

[156] EU-Singapore FTA, protocol 1, art. 34; EU-Vietnam FTA, protocol, art. 37.

[157] EU-Singapore FTA, art. 3(9) & protocol 1, annex D.

countries by value."[158] Nevertheless, the potential expansion of the scope of Annex D will galvanize ASEAN enterprises to restructure their supply chain to benefit from the EU-Singapore FTA.

There are additional features of rules of origin under the EU-Vietnam FTA. Unlike the CPTPP's rigid "yarn-forward" rules that require the use of yarns and fabrics from parties in end products, the EU-Vietnam FTA is "fabric forward," as it extends cumulation to fabrics from Korea.[159] The EU-Singapore FTA lacks this provision. In practice, CPTPP rules pose challenges to the Vietnamese garment and textile sector because of its heavy reliance on yarns and fabrics from non-CPTPP countries including China, Korea and Taiwan.[160] Under the EU-Vietnam FTA, Vietnam can import fabrics from Korea and export finalized products to the EU, thus decreasing dependence on Chinese fabrics. The extension of cumulation will also attract more investment from Korean apparel manufacturing companies.[161] Also, the EU-Vietnam FTA is the first EU FTA that allows the marking of "Made in EU" as the origin for nonagricultural goods.[162] The designation accords EU manufacturers more flexibility in utilizing factories in different EU states without affecting the export of their products to ASEAN.

2 Asian Food Products

Asia is renowned for its diverse food culture. The special rules of origin under the EU-Singapore FTA made it the first trade pact to entitle Asian food exports to zero tariff treatment in the EU. Although such rules are not included in the EU-Vietnam FTA, the Singapore example will provide guidance for the ASEAN-EU FTA. Annex B to Protocol 1 covers food products such as spring rolls, rice noodles and oriental bread.[163] Annex B imposes the limit of "non-originating materials," whereas Annex B(a) constitutes an exception allowing more liberal rules of origin for food products subject to an annual quota of 1,250 tonnes.[164]

[158] EU-Singapore FTA, protocol 1, annex D; European Parliament, *supra* note 31, at 40 fn. 181.

[159] CPTPP, ch. 4 & annex 4-A; EU-Vietnam FTA, protocol 1, art. 7; Tomoo Kikuchi et al., The Effects of Mega-Regional Trade Agreements to Vietnam, 55 J. Asian Eco. 4, 6–7.

[160] Kikuchi et al., *supra* note 159, at 9.

[161] *E.g.*, Choe Nam-suk, *When a New Change Is for a Better Tomorrow, It Has the True Value*, Jun. 27, 2019, Korea Post, www.koreapost.com/news/articleView.html?idxno=9411 (last visited Sept. 15, 2020).

[162] Delegation of the European Union to Vietnam, *supra* note 146, at 29.

[163] EU-Singapore FTA, protocol 1, annex B. In my view, it is unique and useful to include Chinese translations for selected food products.

[164] EU-Singapore FTA, protocol 1, annex B & annex B(a).

Pursuant to Annex B(a), the meat used for popular dim sum dishes such as chicken shaomai may not originate in Singapore, but Annex B mandates that "all the materials" be "wholly obtained" in Singapore.[165] In comparison, the Japan-Singapore FTA requires materials for selected food products to come from "a member country of the ASEAN."[166] The EU-Singapore FTA is more liberal. Annex B(a) simply requires food products to be "made in Singapore" and hence manufacturers are accorded the flexibility to use raw materials from any country rather than ASEAN states.[167] Managed by the European Commission, the Annex B(a) quota is "on a first-come, first served basis."[168] Once the quota is exhausted, exporters will fall back on Annex B rules with more stringent food requirements.

As the EU-Singapore FTA is relatively new, exporters have yet to fully utilize the quota for Asian food products. In my view, this unique mechanism and rules of origin may encounter low utilization rates. The same problem not only exists in ASEAN, but also in the EU. Empirical data demonstrate that only 67 percent of European exporters have used EU FTAs for tariff preferences.[169] A common explanation is that the lack of information due to their capacity constraints impedes enterprises' utilization of the FTAs. To build the ASEAN-EU FTA, governments should enhance the businesses' understanding of FTA mechanisms and simplify the procedures to use them. It is vital for less developed countries such as Vietnam to fully utilize the EU-Vietnam FTA, as the GDP impact of the FTA will be "three times larger than that of the CPTPP."[170]

B Services Trade and Electronic Commerce

EU FTAs with Singapore and Vietnam include rules on trade in services and electronic commerce (e-commerce) in the same chapters.[171] The two areas have become more intertwined during the COVID-19 pandemic, as social distancing and lockdown measures drive the demand for digital

[165] *Id.*; Singapore Customs, PowerPoint Slides: Rules of Origin (2020), at 13.
[166] Japan-Singapore Economic Partnership Agreement (2002), annex II.A.
[167] Annex A: Key Benefits of the EUSFTA & EUSIPA, *in* MTI, European Union and Singapore Sign Free Trade and Investment Protection Agreements (2018), at 3, fn. 2.
[168] EU-Singapore FTA, protocol 1, annex B(a).
[169] UNCTAD, The Use of the EU's Free Trade Agreements: Exporters and Importer Utilization of Preferential Tariffs (2018), at 17.
[170] World Bank, *supra* note 28, at 10 & 36.
[171] Both FTAs have Chapter 8 on "Services, Establishment and Electronic Commerce."

services in diverse sectors including education, finance and telemedicine.[172] Services trade accounts for 70 percent and 40 percent of the GDP of Singapore and Vietnam, respectively.[173] Enhancing services trade will secure Singapore's status as a financial hub and help Vietnam escape from the middle-income trap for the next stage of development.[174] For the EU, as WTO talks are stalled and no ASEAN country is participating in the twenty-three-party Trade in Services Agreement negotiations, FTAs are the only avenue through which Brussels could advance its services-related interests.[175]

The trade in services rules in the two EU FTAs are comparable. Unlike the CPTPP's negative list approach for services commitments, both EU FTAs follow the more conservative GATS-style, positive list approach. A key difference between the agreements lies in the most-favored-nations (MFN) clause. Akin to EU FTAs with Canada and Korea, the EU-Vietnam FTA includes a general MFN clause, but excludes selected sectors such as telecommunication and cultural services.[176] However, the EU-Singapore FTA does not incorporate the clause in the services chapter.[177] In other words, the FTA obliges neither Singapore nor Brussels to extend more favorable services commitments accorded to third countries under their new FTAs. Despite the lack of a general MFN clause, the FTA includes a limited MFN clause in Singapore's commitments for the banking sector.[178]

EU FTAs with Singapore and Vietnam provide enhanced market access under their GATS-plus services commitments, which range from computer and environmental services to air transport services.[179] For example, Singapore allows WTO-plus market access to postal and courier services.[180] In particular, Mode 3 (commercial presence) restrictions

[172] WTO, *Trade in Services in the Context of COVID-19* (2020), at 1–9.

[173] Statista, *Singapore: Distribution of Gross Domestic Product (GDP) across Economic Sectors from 2009 to 2019*, www.statista.com/statistics/378575/singapore-gdp-distribution-across-economic-sectors/ (last visited Sept. 16, 2020); Delegation of the European Union to Vietnam, *supra* note 146, at 51.

[174] *See generally* Aaron Flaaen et al., *How to Avoid Middle-Income Traps? Evidence from Malaysia*, World Bank: Economic Premise, No. 120 (2013), at 1–2.

[175] European Commission, *Trade in Services Agreement (TiSA): Factsheet* (2016), at 2.

[176] EU-Vietnam FTA, art. 8.6; European Parliament, *supra* note 31, at 13–14.

[177] European Parliament, *supra* note 31, at 13–14.

[178] EU-Singapore FTA, annex 8-B.

[179] MTI, *supra* note 121, at 11; Delegation of the European Union to Vietnam, *supra* note 146, at 52.

[180] General Agreement on Trade in Services, Singapore: Schedule of Specific Commitments, GATS/SC/76 (1994); EU-Singapore FTA (2018), ch. 8, annex 8-B.

will be removed for express letter services and relaxed for basic letter services by only requiring service suppliers to be incorporated in Singapore.[181] The EU-Vietnam FTA also benefits the EU distribution sector, as it eliminates the economic needs test incorporated in Vietnam's WTO commitments.[182] For banking services and maritime transport services, the maximum foreign ownership in joint ventures will significantly increase from 30 to 49 percent and from 49 to 70 percent, respectively.[183]

EU FTAs enhance professional mobility, known as Mode 4 (movement of natural persons). Contemporary trade pacts often facilitate intra-corporate transferees and business visitors. To comply with its FTA commitment, Vietnam is still required to extend periods of stay for EU managers, executives and specialists.[184] Remarkably, the EU-Singapore FTA enables entry and stay of "graduate trainees" for one year for "career development" or "training in business techniques or methods."[185] The EU-Vietnam FTA includes comparable provisions for "trainee employees."[186] These rules catering for early-career professionals will magnify the skill-transfer effect critical to development and the people-to-people connectivity under the EU-Asia Connectivity Strategy.[187]

1 Banking and Legal Services

While innovative designs of EU FTAs with Singapore and Vietnam positively shape ASEAN-EU interregionalism and new Asian regionalism, it should be cautioned that the deficiencies of these FTAs require remedy. In terms of selected services commitments and e-commerce rules, other modern agreements provide the best practices for prospective reforms. Compared to its FTAs with Australia and the United States, Singapore's commitments in the banking and legal services sectors under the EU-Singapore FTA exemplify the current weaknesses.

Leading US and European banks such as Citibank and Deutsche Bank have been active in Singapore. The signing of the US-Singapore FTA in 2003 yielded a profound impact on the liberalization of Singapore's financial market. The Monetary Authority of Singapore began to issue

181 EU-Singapore FTA (2018), ch. 8, annex 8-B; European Parliament, *supra* note 31, at 79.
182 EuroCham, *supra* note 138, at 36.
183 *Id.*; Delegation of the European Union to Vietnam, *supra* note 146, at 52.
184 EU-Vietnam FTA, art. 8.14.2; World Bank, *supra* note 28, at 45.
185 EU-Singapore FTA (2018), arts. 8.13 & 8.14.
186 EU-Vietnam FTA (2019), arts. 8.13(i) & 8.14.2(c).
187 ASEAN-EU Plan of Action (2018–22), at 2 & 6.

Qualifying Full Bank (QFB) and wholesale bank licenses, which entitle foreign banks to operate as domestic full banks except for the Singapore dollar retail banking business.[188] The US-Singapore FTA granted preferential treatment to US banks. The QFB privileges include the permission to first have thirty, and then an unlimited number of, business service locations and to participate in local banks' ATM networks.[189] Although the EU-Singapore FTA was concluded fifteen years later, the FTA fails to accord EU banks "better deals." It is true that EU banks are entitled to comparable treatment for the ATM network, but the number of business service locations was only increased from twenty-five to fifty, instead of an unlimited number for US banks.[190]

Unlike the US-Singapore FTA that includes a general MFN clause in the services chapters, the EU-Singapore FTA only includes a limited MFN clause that applies to banking services.[191] Pursuant to the limited MFN clause, EU banks will be accorded more favorable treatment if such treatment is included in Singapore's future FTAs. Nevertheless, for additional banks with QFB privileges, the MFN clause excludes the United States.[192] In other words, if the United States decided to upgrade the US-Singapore FTA, EU banks would not benefit from the MFN clause.

Legal services commitments represent similar weaknesses. International law firms deem Singapore to be a regional hub for commercial disputes. Singapore's FTAs with the United States and Australia eased requirements for their qualified lawyers in joint law ventures and formal law alliances.[193] The EU-Singapore FTA includes the same commitments. Yet, FTAs with Australia and the United States require Singapore to recognize Bachelor of Laws and Juris Doctor degrees from ten Australian schools and four US schools as Singapore law degrees for the purposes of admission to the local bar.[194] No such commitment on

188 *Id.*; Monetary Authority of Singapore, *Types of Deposit-Taking Institutions*, Jun. 23, 2019, www.mas.gov.sg/regulation/Banking/Types-of-Deposit-Taking-Institutions (last visited Sept. 17, 2020).

189 US-Singapore FTA (2003), schedule of Singapore to annex 10B, sec. B.

190 EU-Singapore FTA, annex 8-B.

191 US-Singapore FTA, art. 8(4); EU-Singapore FTA (2018), annex 8-B.

192 EU-Singapore FTA, annex 8-B.

193 Australia-Singapore FTA (2003), annex 4-1(B); US-Singapore FTA, annex 8A.

194 Legal Profession (Qualified Persons) Rules (2002), First, Second, Fourth and Fifth Schedules; Pasha L. Hsieh, *Transnational Legal Services in Asia: Legal Implications of the AEC and the CPTPP*, *in* ASEAN Law in the New Regional Economic Order: Global Trends and Shifting Paradigms 168, 180 (Pasha L. Hsieh & Bryan Mercurio 2019).

the recognition of legal education exists in the EU-Singapore FTA. Arguably, this commitment will be more important to the prospective UK-Singapore FTA because Singapore only recognizes degrees conferred by selected law schools in England rather than those in EU states.[195]

2 Digital Trade Regulations

EU FTAs with Singapore and Vietnam include sections on e-commerce. Modern FTA provisions on e-commerce can accelerate the Fourth Industrial Revolution and the post-pandemic economic recovery. Similar to the deficiencies of services commitments, EU companies may find digital trade regulations in the two EU FTAs disappointing. EU FTAs with Singapore and Vietnam have only five and three articles, respectively, on e-commerce.[196] These rules fail to meet the expected standards for pathfinder agreements. A main reason is that negotiations for the services and e-commerce chapters in the two EU FTAs were completed in 2012 and 2015, respectively.[197] They were unable to incorporate more modern, detailed rules such as those in the CPTPP.

EU FTAs with Singapore and Vietnam include comparable requirements on the following core areas, which facilitate the operation of the EU's multinational enterprises. Both FTAs enable service suppliers' cross-border transfer of information by electronic means and prohibits the imposition of "custom duties on electronic transmissions."[198] Also, both FTAs provide the basis for dialogue for regulatory cooperation.[199] Yet, the EU-Singapore FTA stipulates additional rules for assessing "the feasibility of having a mutual recognition agreement on electronic signatures" and for understanding both sides' legislation on electronic signatures.[200] The CPTPP incorporates a much stronger rule, which mandates that parties "not deny the legal validity of" electronic signatures.[201]

To advance "Europe's Digital Decade" that European Commission President von der Leyen proclaimed in 2020, the roadmap to the

[195] Legal Profession (Qualified Persons) Rules (2002), First & Second Schedules.
[196] EU-Singapore FTA, arts. 8.57–8.61; EU-Vietnam FTA, arts. 8.50–8.52.
[197] MTI, *supra* note 121, at 2; World Bank, *supra* note 28, at 20. I appreciate the insight of Mary Elizabeth Chelliah.
[198] EU-Singapore FTA, arts. 8.26.3 & 8.58; EU-Vietnam FTA, arts. 8.31.3 & 8.51.
[199] EU-Singapore FTA, arts. 8.61; EU-Vietnam FTA, art. 8.52.
[200] EU-Singapore FTA, art. 8.60.
[201] CPTPP, art. 14.6.1.

ASEAN-EU FTA should consider e-commerce provisions of contemporary agreements involving Asian countries.[202] In my view, the CPTPP and Singapore's Digital Economy Agreements (DEAs) provide benchmarks. Unlike inadequate rules of EU FTAs with Singapore and Vietnam, the CPTPP's chapter on e-commerce covers more detailed provisions on online consumer and personal information protection, cybersecurity and source codes.[203] The 2020 Australia-Singapore DEA also provides a valuable example because it not only amends the bilateral FTA, but also extends areas of governance to artificial intelligence, and FinTech and RegTech cooperation.[204]

Vietnam's implementation of e-commerce rules is problematic. A sensitive digital issue is data localization. Subject to legitimate exceptions, both the CPTPP and the ASEAN Agreement on e-Commerce prohibit parties from requiring the location of computing facilities "as a condition for conducting business in" their territories.[205] The CPTPP, which became effective in Vietnam in 2019, reinforces the socialist country's efforts to comply with "Western" standards. However, Vietnam passed Cybersecurity Law, which imposes the data localization requirement and requires foreign companies to submit information to the government upon request.[206] I call the passage of this law the "bad-faith implementation" of the CPTPP.

Precisely speaking, Vietnam does not violate the CPTPP because its dispute settlement provision, as well as Vietnam's side letters with Canada, Japan and New Zealand, provides grace periods for Vietnam.[207] Neither does the CPTPP's rules on personal information protection apply to Vietnam until it "implements its legal framework that

[202] European Commission, State of the Union Address 2020 (2020), at 12.

[203] *E.g.*, CPTPP, arts. 14.7, 14.8, 14.16 & 14.17.

[204] Australia-Singapore Digital Economy Agreement (DEA) (2020), arts. 31–32. Other existing and prospective DEA partners include Chile, New Zealand and Korea. MTI, *Digital Economy Agreements*, www.mti.gov.sg/Improving-Trade/Digital-Economy-Agreements (last visited Sept. 21, 2020).

[205] CPTPP, art. 14.13; ASEAN Agreement on Electronic Commerce (2018), art. 7(6); Benjamin Wong, *Data Localization and ASEAN Economic Community*, 10 Asian J. Int'l L. 158, 177–78 (2020).

[206] EuroCham, *supra* note 138, at 45.

[207] The CPTPP and three side letters accord Vietnam grace periods of two and five years, respectively, after the agreement came into effect for Vietnam in 2019. CPTPP, 14.18.2; Frederick (Fred) R. Burke & Thanh Vinh Nguyen, *Vietnam Has Ratified the CPTPP*, Nov. 14, 2018, www.lexology.com/library/detail.aspx?g=adb9dec6-e374-452f-a65a-873c18517799 (last visited Sept. 21, 2020). I thank Neha Mistra for providing useful information on this issue.

provides" such protection.[208] Yet, adopting Cybersecurity Law that directly contravenes the CPTPP's core requirements constitutes an abuse of the grace period and exceptions premised on the "legitimate public policy."[209] Moreover, the overly vague and broad scope of cybersecurity to protect "national sovereignty" and "social stability" cripples the underlying principles of the EU's General Data Protection Regulation (GDPR).[210] Therefore, for e-commerce provisions in the ASEAN-EU FTA, EU negotiators should consider DEAs, the CPTPP and the GDPR and limiting grace periods to prevent countries' bath-faith implementation.

C *Reducing Non-Tariff Barriers: From Health to Green Industries*

Other than provisions on trade in goods and services, new rules on non-tariff barriers reinforce key initiatives of the Master Plan on ASEAN Connectivity 2025 and the EU-Asia Connectivity Strategy.[211] Markedly, non-tariff "measures" are conceptually and legally different from non-tariff "barriers." While non-tariff measures can be adopted for legitimate purposes, they become non-tariff barriers if those measure are applied in a discriminatory manner and cannot be justified.[212]

As a global issue, non-tariff measures influence 58 percent of trade volume in the Asia-Pacific.[213] ASEAN's reduction of its average tariff rate to 4.2 percent is the most obvious achievement of integration, but the 3.6-time increase of non-tariff measures undermines AEC objectives.[214] Three quarters of these measures are technical barriers to trade (TBT) regulations and sanitary and phytosanitary (SPS) measures.[215] As the AEC Blueprint 2025 imposes merely soft obligations on non-tariff

[208] CPTPP, art. 18.5 fn. 5.

[209] CPTPP, art. 14.11.3 & 14.13.3.

[210] EuroCham, *supra* note 138, at 45–46; General Data Protection Regulation (2016), art. 5.1.

[211] ASEAN, Master Plan on ASEAN Connectivity 2025 (2016), at 19–21; European Commission, *supra* note 88, at 2–3.

[212] ASEAN Business Advisory Council & EU-ASEAN Business Council, *Non-Tariff Barriers (NTBs) in ASEAN and Their Elimination from a Business Perspective* (2019), at 19.

[213] United Nations Economic and Social Commission for Asia and the Pacific (UNESCAP) & UNCTAD, *Asia-Pacific Trade and Development Report 2019* (2019), at 39.

[214] ASEAN, *ASEAN Integration Report* 2019 (2019), at 20; Lili Yan Ing et al., *NTMs in ASEAN: Ways toward Regulatory Convergence*, *in* Regional Integration and Non-Tariff Measures in ASEAN 90, 91–92 (Lili Yan Ing et al. eds. 2019).

[215] Ing et al., *supra* note 214, at 93.

barriers, FTA provisions on TBT, SPS and renewable energy generation have become critical to industries.[216]

A key example of reducing TBT barriers is enhanced flexibility for labeling. Changing labels often requires reshipping back to the export country, thus substantially increasing the exporter's transportation cost and time. EU FTAs with Singapore and Vietnam minimize the problem by allowing "supplementary labelling or corrections to labelling" in the importing country.[217] These business-friendly provisions further decrease the cost by accepting removable stickers or marking the accompanying documentation.[218] SPS chapters also facilitate the export of animal and plant products, including ASEAN countries' coconuts and durians, which are considered low-risk products and do not require phytosanitary certificates.[219]

Imperative to the collective response to the COVID-19 pandemic and the development of the healthcare industry, the reduction of non-tariff barriers under EU FTAs with Singapore and Vietnam applies to pharmaceutical and medical devices.[220] Both FTAs are committed to conforming to "international standards, practices and guidelines" particularly in the area of technical regulations.[221] Moreover, both FTAs impose transparent and nondiscriminatory requirements on rules "that apply to the listing, pricing or reimbursement of pharmaceutical products."[222] Applicants are also accorded "opportunities to provide comments" on authorities' decisions.[223]

Although the two EU FTAs provide benchmarks for health-related TBT rules, I contend that the ASEAN-EU FTA should take into account more elaborate rules in other agreements. To illustrate, the EU-Canada CETA strengthens regulatory coherence for pharmaceutical products by including a protocol on the mutual recognition of certificates of Good

216 ASEAN Business Advisory Council & EU-ASEAN Business Council, *supra* note 212, at 34; EU-Singapore FTA, chs. 4, 5 & 7; EU-Vietnam FTA, chs. 5, 6 & 7.

217 EU-Vietnam FTA, art. 5.9.2(e); EU-Singapore FTA, art. 4.10.2(e).

218 EU-Singapore FTA, art. 4.10.2(f); EU-Vietnam FTA, art. 5.9.2(f).

219 Almudena Minguez Matorras, *PowerPoint Slides: Sanitary and Phytosanitary (SPS) Measures: How the EU SPS Regime Works – Tools to Aid Companies Better Understand the EU SPS Requirements* (2020), at 13.

220 EU-Singapore FTA, annex 2-C, art. 1(a); EU-Vietnam FTA, annex 2-C, art. 1(a); WTO, The Treatment of Medical Products in Regional Trade Agreements (2020), at 7.

221 EU-Singapore FTA, annex 2-C, arts. 1(d) & 2; EU-Vietnam FTA, annex 2-C, art. 1(b) & 3.

222 EU-Singapore FTA, annex 2-C, art. 3.3; EU-Vietnam FTA, annex 2-C, art. 4.4.

223 EU-Singapore FTA, annex 2-C, art. 3.3(c); EU-Vietnam FTA, annex 2-C, art. 4.4(c).

Manufacturing Practices.[224] The Singapore-India FTA lowers technical barriers to the registration of India's generic medicinal products.[225] According to the side letter, products that have been approved by a recognized regulatory authority in selected jurisdictions such as the EU and the UK are subject to a simplified process for obtaining marketing authorization in Singapore.[226] Furthermore, the CPTPP provides more detailed rules than EU FTAs. The CPTPP mandates that the authorities' determination to grant marketing authorization not be based on "sale data or related financial data concerning the marketing of" specific pharmaceutical and medical devices.[227] The determination will also be "subject to an appeal or review process."[228]

As for the EU's automotive industry, the reduction of non-tariff barriers is similarly important because conformity assessment procedures and duplicate certificates constitute costly regulatory burdens. Neither Singapore nor Vietnam is a party to the 1958 Agreement of the UN Economic Commission for Europe (UNECE), which decreases certification requirements for producers and importers of cars and auto parts.[229] EU FTAs oblige Singapore and Vietnam to adopt the UNECE type-approval system under the 1958 Agreement and recognize EU certificates issued pursuant to the system.[230] Despite the relatively limited car markets in Singapore and Vietnam, the two pathfinder agreements provide a template for EU FTAs with ASEAN countries to replicate UNECE-related provisions.[231]

The current markets of Singapore and Vietnam demonstrate the unmet potential for European car manufacturers. Singapore's market

224 Comprehensive Economic and Trade Agreement (2016), protocol on the mutual recognition of the compliance and enforcement programme regarding good manufacturing practices for pharmaceutical products.

225 *See generally* Lim Hng Kiang to Anand Sharma, *Special Scheme for Registration of Generic Medicinal Products from India* (2010).

226 *Id.*

227 CPTPP, annex 8-C, art. 11 & annex 8-E, art. 12(c).

228 CPTPP, annex 8-C, art. 12(c) & annex 8-E, art. 13(c).

229 Iulianna Romanchyshyna, *Tackling Technical Barriers to Trade in EU "New Generation" FTAs: An Example of Open or Conflicting Regionalism?*, *in* Global Politics and EU Trade Policy: Facing the Challenges to a Multilateral Approach, Special Issue: Eur. YB Int'l Econ. L. 41, 58 (Wolfgang Weiß & Cornelia Furculita eds. 2020).

230 EU-Singapore FTA, annex 2-B, arts. 1–3; EU-Vietnam FTA, annex 2-B, arts. 1–3; *id.* at 58.

231 European Commission, *Results of the Industry Consultation from 2010 on a Possible EU Singapore Trade Agreement (2015)*, https://trade.ec.europa.eu/doclib/docs/2015/july/tradoc_153666.pdf (last visited Sept. 22, 2020).

shares of Japanese and EU cars are 58.4 percent and 29.5 percent, respectively.[232] A 25.3 percent of imported vehicles are from Germany, including BMW and Mercedes Benz as the most popular brands.[233] The Vietnamese market reflects a similar Japanese and German car-dominated trend.[234] Unlike Singapore, Vietnam has attempted to cultivate its own automobile industry for the ASEAN market. For instance, Vietnam's car conglomerate, Vingroup, has accelerated the production of "Made in Vietnam" vehicles by incorporating BMW frames and technology.[235] Hence, EU FTAs facilitate the EU automobile industry to expand the export of vehicles and pertinent services to ASEAN.

EU FTAs with Singapore and Vietnam benefit the emerging green industry because these pacts encompass non-tariff barriers chapters on renewable energy generation, separate from chapters on trade and sustainable development.[236] These chapters implement the strategic "European Green Deal" to realize "a climate neutral society" and help both the EU and ASEAN enforce the UN Sustainable Development Goals.[237] Instead of addressing sustainable energy in general, the two EU FTAs identify "the generation of energy from renewable and sustainable sources."[238] Both FTAs also prohibit parties from adopting local contents requirements, partnerships with local companies and discriminatory certification and licensing procedures.[239]

232 Land Transport Authority, *Annual Vehicle Statistics 2019*, www.lta.gov.sg/content/dam/ltagov/who_we_are/statistics_and_publications/statistics/pdf/MVP01-6_Cars_by_make.pdf (last visited Sept. 22, 2020).

233 *Id.*

234 Tomoya Onishi, *Vietnam Car with BMW Tech Takes on Japanese Rivals*, Jun. 15, 2019, Nikki Asian Rev., https://asia.nikkei.com/Business/Companies/Vietnam-car-with-BMW-tech-takes-on-Japanese-rivals#:~:text=HANOI%20%2D%2D%20Leading%20Vietnamese%20conglomerate,factory%20Friday%20against%20all%20expectations.&text=%22I'm%20convinced%20that%20Vingroup,%2C%22%20the%20prime%20minister%20said (last visited Sept. 22, 2020).

235 *Id.*

236 EU-Singapore FTA, ch. 7; EU-Vietnam FTA, ch. 7. Both FTAs also have separate chapters on "Trade and Sustainable Development."

237 European Commission, *2020 Strategic Foresight Report* (2020), at 23–26; European Commission, *supra* note 4, at 20–23; European Commission, *supra* note 88, at 2; ASEAN, *supra* note 211, at 7; UNESCAP, Complementarities between the ASEAN Community Vision 2025 and the United Nations 2030 Agenda for Sustainable Development: A Framework for Action (2017), at 40–41.

238 EU-Singapore FTA, arts. 7.1 & 7.3; EU-Vietnam FTA, arts. 7.1 & 7.3; Anna-Alexandra Marhold, *Externalising Europe's Energy Policy in EU Free Trade Agreements: A Cognitive Dissonance between Promoting Sustainable Development and Ensuing Security of Supply*, 3(1) Eur & World: A L. Rev. 1, 11 (2019).

239 EU-Singapore FTA, art. 7.4; EU-Vietnam FTA, art. 7.4.

Singapore can attract renewable energy-related trade and investment by supporting the ASEAN operations of EU producers of solar, hydroelectric and wind generators. For Vietnam, guaranteeing its energy supply is essential to development. The German government has supported Vietnam's renewable energy plan including the development of wind power.[240] The FTA's cooperation mechanism will further galvanize Vietnam to adopt the best practices from other EU authorities.[241] Currently, Vietnam has fifteen laws that govern non-tariff barriers for trade and investment pertinent to renewable energy generation, but these laws lack a clear definition of "renewable and sustainable sources."[242] ASEAN-EU FTA negotiations should take into account the fact that the ambiguity in domestic law will hamper the FTA implementation.

Notably, a TBT-related dispute concerning the export of palm oil to the EU will likely be a deal-breaker for the ASEAN-EU FTA.[243] Indonesia and Malaysia are the world's largest producers and exporters of palm oil and these issues have prompted Jakarta to file a WTO complaint challenging the EU's Renewable Energy Directive in 2019.[244] The Directive will cause Indonesia's palm oil and oil-palm crop-based biofuels to be phased out by 2030, as their "indirect land use change" effects jeopardize the EU's renewable energy targets.[245] Indonesia contended that the Directive violated various provisions of the TBT Agreement that imposes obligations for adopting nondiscriminatory criteria and conformity assessment procedures.[246] This unresolved dispute will have salient implications for the ASEAN-EU FTA's provisions on renewable energy.

240 *E.g.*, Vietnam Ministry of Industry and Trade, *Vietnamese-German Cooperation Research Projects on Wind Power* (2017).

241 EU-Vietnam FTA, art. 7.7.

242 EU-Vietnam FTA, art. 7.2(d); World Bank, *supra* note 28, at 45.

243 Lin Xueling & Lua Jiamin, *No Huawei Ban, but Relations with China "Complex": EU Foreign Policy Chief*, Jun. 1, 2019, CNA, www.channelnewsasia.com/news/world/no-huawei-ban-but-relations-with-china-complex-eu-foreign-policy-11588102 (last visited Sept. 20, 2020).

244 *Id.*; Michelle Limenta, *Palm Oil for Fuels: WTO Rules and Environmental Protection*, 15 (7) Global Trade & Customs J. 321, 321–22 (2020).

245 Limenta, *supra* note 244, at 322–23; WTO, European Union – Certain Measures concerning Palm Oil and Oil Palm Crop-based Biofuels, WT/DS593/1, G/L/1348, G/TBTB/D/52, G/SCM/D128/1 (2019), at 1–2.

246 WTO, *supra* note 245, at 6–8.

IV Assessing New-Generation Components in Post-Lisbon FTAs

The EU's first-generation FTAs were negotiated prior to 2006 and focused primarily on trade in goods.[247] New-generation FTAs commenced after the "Global Europe" communication and extended the FTA coverage not only to services and investment protection, but also to intellectual property (IP), government procurement and sustainable development.[248] The Treaty of Lisbon, which came into force in 2009, amended and consolidated the Treaty on the EU and the Treaty on the Functioning of the EU.[249] This new constitutional basis accords the EU a more integrated power to enforce its FTA and Asia policies.[250] The EU-Korea FTA is the first new-generation FTA.[251] The EU-Japan FTA adopted the same comprehensive approach. Nevertheless, the lack of investment protection provisions is the key weakness of these FTAs.

EU trade and investment agreements with Singapore and Vietnam brought fundamental legal changes. In response to the CJEU's Opinion 2/15, the EU-Singapore FTA became the first agreement that separated itself into an FTA and an IPA. This bifurcation approach influenced the EU-Vietnam FTA and IPA and ongoing EU-Japan IPA negotiations.[252] The innovative, new-generation components of these FTAs, interlinking to IPAs and PCAs, reiterate my argument that they collectively shape ASEAN-EU interregionalism in the post-pandemic era. From a theoretical standpoint, new EU FTAs with ASEAN countries have strengthened the spillover effect of Brussels' normative power on human and collective identities as "partners in integration."[253] From the policy perspective, these pacts are building blocks for the ASEAN-

[247] European Commission, Report from the Commission to the European Parliament, the Council, the European Economic and Social Committee and the Committee of the Regions on Implementation of Free Trade Agreements: 1 January 2016–31 December 2016, COM(2017) 654 final (2017), at 23–26.

[248] *Id.*, at 7; European Parliament, *supra* note 31, at 17.

[249] European Parliament, *Factsheet on the European Union: The Treaty of Lisbon* (2020), at 1.

[250] Marise Cremona, *Distinguished Essay: A Quiet Revolution – The Changing Nature of the EU's Common Commercial Policy, in* 2017:8 Eur. YB Int'l Econ. L. 3, 5 (Marc Bungenberg et al. eds. 2017).

[251] European Commission, *supra* note 4, at 9; European Commission, *supra* note 247, at 38.

[252] European Commission, *supra* note 8, at 2. The EU and Korea are negotiating a separate FTA chapter on investment instead. I thank Jaemin Lee for his observation on this point.

[253] Council of the EU, *Joint Statement of the 22nd EU-ASEAN Ministerial Meeting*, Jan. 21, 2019, www.consilium.europa.eu/en/press/press-releases/2019/01/21/joint-statement-of-the-22nd-eu-asean-ministerial-meeting/ (last visited Sept. 25, 2020).

EU FTA and partnership, which Brussels deems as "an urgent necessity," particularly given its worsening distrust of Beijing.[254]

A Enhanced Protection of Copyright and Geographical Indications

One major objective of the EU's new-generation FTA is to include Agreement on Trade-Related Aspects of Intellectual Property Rights (TRIPS)-plus provisions. Both EU FTAs with Singapore and Vietnam include IP chapters.[255] Provisions on copyright and GI mechanisms, which represent "the most significant aspect of" the chapters, demonstrate the regulatory framework that consider ASEAN countries' various stages of development.[256]

Given the suspension of selected IP provisions of the original Trans-Pacific Partnership (TPP), the CPTPP does not oblige Singapore and Vietnam to extend the TRIPS Agreement's copyright protection period of fifty years to seventy years following the death of an author.[257] While the EU-Singapore FTA extends the protection period to seventy years, the EU-Vietnam FTAs keeps the fifty-year WTO standard.[258] In reality, the protection period of copyright requires no change to their IP laws. In the case of Singapore, its Copyright Act has incorporated the seventy-year period to comply with the US-Singapore FTA.[259] However, the two EU FTAs do contain additional rules that require IP laws to expand the scope of protection. For example, new provisions will be obliged to cover technological measures and accord specific rights to producers of phonograms.[260]

As a game-changer to ASEAN's IP systems, the strengthened protection of GIs illustrates the exogenous influences of EU FTAs on new Asian regionalism. Although all ASEAN countries are WTO members, the TRIPS Agreement accords limited GI protection.[261] The European Commission has pursued new-generation FTAs to enhance the scope

254 Borrell, *supra* note 99.
255 EU-Singapore FTA, ch. 10; EU-Vietnam FTA, ch. 12.
256 European Parliament, *supra* note 31, at 29.
257 CPTPP (2018), annex: 7.
258 EU-Singapore FTA, art. 10.5; EU-Vietnam FTA, art. 12.11.
259 US-Singapore FTA (2003), art. 16.4; Locknie Hsu, *Ch. 07 Free Trade Agreements: Singapore Legal Developments*, Nov. 17, 2018, www.singaporelawwatch.sg/About-Singapore-Law/Overview/ch-07-free-trade-agreements-singapore-legal-developments (last visited Sept. 25, 2020).
260 EU-Singapore FTA, arts. 10.6 & 10.9; EU-Vietnam FTA, arts. 12.8 & 12.12.
261 Agreement on Trade-Related Aspects of Intellectual Property Rights (1994), arts. 22–24.

of protected GIs and enforcement procedures because of great commercial interests involving European food and drinks such as France's Brie de Meaux and Swedish Vodka.[262]

EU FTAs with Singapore and Vietnam provide a normative basis for ASEAN to harmonize its GI legislation. Although more than 340 GIs are registered in ASEAN, GI regimes vary vastly.[263] Some states including Indonesia, Malaysia, Singapore and Thailand enacted specific GI statutes, whereas GIs are only protected under trademark acts or general IP laws in Brunei and Vietnam.[264] The price increase in Indonesia's Muntok white pepper and other products after their GI registrations is noteworthy.[265] Thus, ASEAN and other Asian governments should note that enhanced GI regimes benefit both local and European producers.

As EU FTAs with Korea and Japan and the 2020 EU-China GI Agreement exemplify, the protection of GI-designated products is mostly reciprocal.[266] The EU-Singapore FTA constitutes an exception because its GI protection is one-sided. While Singapore recognizes 196 European GIs, it listed no item for GI protection in the EU.[267] The policy reason is that Singapore's agricultural exports to Europe are limited and that the Singapore government intended to expedite the finalization of the FTA.[268] As for Vietnam, the FTA protects 169 European GIs in Vietnam and 39 Vietnamese GIs in the EU.[269] The GI recognition of Buon Ma Thuot coffee is particularly important, as the EU is the largest market for Vietnam's coffee exports.[270]

262 WTO, *supra* note 101, at 154; EU-Singapore FTA, annex 10-A; EU-Vietnam FTA, annex 12-A.

263 EU Intellectual Property Office (EUIPO), *Geographical Indications in the ASEAN Region: A Booklet on ASEAN Geographical Indications Procedure and Products* (2019), at 38.

264 *Id.* at 13–33.

265 *Id.* at 9 & 98–100.

266 WTO, *supra* note 101, at 154; William H. Coper, *The EU-South Korea Free Trade Agreement and Its Implications for the United States*, Congressional Research Service (CRS) Report (2011), at 15; European Commission, *EU-China Geographical Indications* (2020), at 1.

267 EU-Singapore FTA, annex 10-A. No item is listed in Section B.

268 Susanna H.S. Leong, *European Union-Singapore Free Trade Agreement: A New Chapter for Geographical Indications in Singapore*, *in* Geographical Indications at the Crossroads of Trade, Development, and Culture: Focus on Asia-Pacific 235, 247–48 (Irene Calboli & Wee Loon Ng-Loy eds. 2017).

269 EU-Vietnam FTA, annex 12-A.

270 EU-Vietnam FTA, annex 12-A, part B; SICC, *supra* note 139, at 5.

Comparable to copyright provisions that recognize Vietnam's development stage, the EU-Vietnam FTA includes more "favorable" GI rules than the EU-Singapore FTA. The EU-Vietnam FTA incorporates exemptions of five GIs, including Champagne and feta cheese, and permits sellers to make "actual commercial use in good faith of" these GIs within certain periods.[271] As Vietnam's GI regime is based on the Civil Code, IP law and various decrees, enforcing these exemptions and protecting homonymous GIs require additional harmonization and clarification of multiple rules.[272]

With respect to enforcement mechanisms, legislative changes to Singapore's GI registration system and border measures provide valuable lessons. To implement its TRIPS obligations, Singapore enacted the Geographical Indications Act 1998 that provides a two-tiered GI protection scheme. Other than basic protection that applies to GIs if they are misleading or result in unfair competition, GIs of wines are entitled to enhanced protection regardless of the misrepresentation result.[273]

Nonetheless, the enforcement of the Act encounters one practical problem. Absent a GI registration system, the party who intends to bring a GI misuse complaint bears a heavy burden "to prove conclusively" to the court that the GI is entitled to be protected in Singapore.[274] To enforce the EU-Singapore FTA, the Geographical Indications Act 2014, which became effective in 2019, remedied this weakness by creating the Registry of GI under the auspices of the IP Office of Singapore.[275] Pursuant to the new Act, a registered GI constitutes prima facie evidence and the Singapore High Court can issue a certificate of validity of the GI registration if it is challenged.[276] Moreover, the enhanced protection for wines under the previous statute now extends to GIs of agricultural products and foodstuffs.[277] The Intellectual Property (Border Enforcement) Act 2018 also provides for new border enforcement measures. Singapore Customs is authorized to seize both imported and exported goods at the request of a GI right holder.[278]

[271] These products include Asiago, Fontina, Gorgonzola, Feta and Champagne. EU-Vietnam FTA, art. 12.28.

[272] EU-Vietnam FTA, arts. 12.27.3 & 12.28; World Bank, *supra* note 28, at 48; EUIPO, *supra* note 263, at 33.

[273] Geographic Indications Act (1998), art. 3.

[274] Leong, *supra* note 268, at 240; Geographical Indications Act (1998), art. 3(1).

[275] Geographical Indications Act (2014), art. 19.

[276] *Id.* arts. 19 & 75–76.

[277] *Id.* art. 4(6)–(9).

[278] Intellectual Property (Border Enforcement) Act (2018), part 2; Audrey Yap, *PowerPoint Slides: The European Union-Singapore Free Trade Agreement (EUSFTA): Intellectual Property Rights* (2020), at 16–17.

Interestingly, the EU-Singapore FTA became a basis for a GI-related decision. In the 2019 case, the applicant applied to register the GI for an Italian cheese, Parmigiano Reggiano, and the opponent requested an extension "to file its notice of opposition and supporting evidence."[279] The IP Office of Singapore rejected the request on the ground that the GI list of the EU-Singapore FTA was made public in 2013 for a public consultation and the opponents failed to oppose the GI in dispute.[280] Hence, the Office decided that granting the opponent's request would delay the FTA's entry into force and undermine the interests of Singapore enterprises.[281] Singapore's two-tiered protection scheme and enforcement measures offers a model for other Asian countries.

B State-Owned Enterprises and Government Procurement

In contrast with IP provisions that accord Vietnam flexibility, the EU-Vietnam FTA contains more stringent rules on SOEs and government procurement than the EU-Singapore FTA. Most ASEAN countries have followed the model of Asian developmental states and their initial economic growth has relied on SOEs in strategic sectors such as public utilities and manufacturing.[282] This trend is noteworthy in Vietnam, as SOEs contribute to almost 30 percent of the state budget and 40 percent of the GDP.[283] Global experiences show that introducing competition and transparency disciplines are essential due to SOEs' inadequate accountability and efficiency. FTAs thus function as an external impetus for SOE reforms.

A significant difference between the EU-Singapore FTA and the EU-Vietnam FTA is that only the latter has a separate chapter on SOEs.[284] The EU-Singapore FTA includes only two pertinent provisions on "public undertakings and undertakings that are entrusted with special or exclusive rights" and "state monopolies" in the competition

[279] Re Application for Extension of Time to file Notice of Opposition and Evidence by U.S. Dairy Export Council and Objection Thereto by Consorzio del Formaggio Parmigiano Reggiano [2019] SGIPOS 12, paras. 2–3.

[280] *Id.* para. 5(a).

[281] *Id.* para. 5(b).

[282] UNCTAD, *The Asian Developmental State and the Flying Geese Paradigm*, No. 213 (2013), at 3–6.

[283] Le Ngoc Dang et al., *State-owned Enterprises Reform in Viet Nam: Progress and Challenges*, ADBI Working Paper Series, No. 1071 (2020), at 2; Delegation of the European Union to Vietnam, *supra* note 146, at 63.

[284] EU-Vietnam FTA, ch. 11.

chapter.[285] Although the EU-Singapore FTA does not define SOEs, the CPTPP determines SOEs on the basis of 50 percent of share capital and voting rights or "the power to appoint a majority of members of the board of directors."[286] The US-Singapore FTA imposes more stringent criteria to categorize an entity as an SOE if the government exercises "effective influence" over the entity.[287]

Like the SOE definitions of the CPTPP and the US-Singapore FTA, the EU-Vietnam FTA adopts the 50 percent benchmark and assesses whether the government "can exercise control over the strategic decisions of the enterprise."[288] The EU-Vietnam FTA also excludes SOEs with small-scale commercial revenues during the five-year grace period.[289] While both EU FTAs encompass principles of nondiscrimination and commercial considerations, the EU-Vietnam FTA imposes additional rules on corporate governance and transparency related to SOEs.[290] In particular, the transparency requirement under the EU-Singapore FTA is confined to "subsidies that relate to trade in goods or to the supply of services" and cannot be enforced.[291] These rules allow the EU-Vietnam FTA to complement the government's SOE reforms including the equitization plans.[292]

In terms of government procurement, both the EU and Singapore are parties to the Agreement on Government Procurement (GPA), but Vietnam and other ASEAN countries have yet to accede to this WTO plurilateral agreement.[293] EU FTAs with Singapore and Vietnam contain provisions on unqualified MFN treatment and national treatment in their government procurement chapters.[294] As a GPA-plus agreement, the EU-Singapore FTA lowers the GPA's value thresholds for covered goods and services and expands the list of government

[285] EU-Singapore FTA, arts. 11.3 & 11.4.

[286] CPTPP, art. 17.1.

[287] US-Singapore FTA (2003), art. 12.8.5; Mark McLaughlin, *Defining a State-Owned Enterprise in International Investment Agreements*, 34(3) ICSID Rev. 595, 617 (2020).

[288] EU-Vietnam FTA, art. 11.1 (g).

[289] EU-Vietnam FTA, art. 11.2.4.

[290] EU-Singapore FTA, art. 11.3; EU-Vietnam FTA, arts. 11.4–11.6.

[291] EU-Singapore FTA, arts. 11.9.1 & 11.14; EU-Vietnam FTA, art. 11.6.2(f).

[292] Dang et al., *supra* note 283, at 5–6; Baker McKenzie, *Vietnam Issues Decision No. 26 on the List of State-Owned Enterprises to Be Equitized by End-2020*, Sept. 9, 2019, www.bakermckenzie.com/en/insight/publications/2019/09/vietnam-issues-decision-no-26 (last visited Sept. 29, 2020).

[293] WTO, *Parties, Observers and Accessions*, www.wto.org/english/tratop_e/gproc_e/memobs_e.htm (last visited Sept. 29, 2020).

[294] EU-Singapore FTA, art. 9.4.1; EU-Vietnam FTA, art. 9.4.1.

entities.[295] The FTA also covers more diverse forms of contracts, such as public-private partnerships that facilitate build-operate-transfer arrangements.[296]

For EU enterprises, Vietnam's public procurement market is lucrative because the country retains a high ratio of almost 40 percent of government investment to GDP.[297] Although Vietnam is not a party to the GPA, the government is committed to opening its market to foreign tenders under the CPTPP and the EU-Vietnam FTA.[298] Compared with the EU-Singapore FTA that applies to central and subcentral government entities, the EU-Vietnam FTA also includes "[o]ther covered entities" such as national hospitals and state-owned railway companies.[299]

By incorporating GPA rules, the EU-Vietnam FTA ensures procedural fairness for awarding public contracts in line with other EU FTAs.[300] The FTA applies more stringent standards for the transparency requirements than the EU-Singapore FTA, which mandates that information be published seventy-two days after the award of each contract.[301] In comparison, the EU-Vietnam FTA stipulates a much shorter timeframe of thirty days.[302] Vietnam's acceptance of these "tougher" rules reinforces the EU's normative power that can shape the Third Interregionalism.

C *Tribunals and Mediation for Investor-State Disputes*

Dispute settlement mechanisms help enforce trade and investment agreements. EU FTAs with Singapore and Vietnam provide that arbitration panels will issue final reports on state-to-state disputes no later than 180 days and 150 days, respectively.[303] A stricter timeframe for panel rulings thus applies to the EU-Vietnam FTA. Other than FTAs' interstate dispute settlement mechanisms, EU IPAs incorporate the Investment Court System (ICS) for investor-state disputes and have received significant academic and professional attention. Following

[295] European Parliament, *supra* note 31, at 26–27.
[296] *Id.* at 27; EU-Singapore FTA, annex 9-I.
[297] Delegation of the European Union to Vietnam, *supra* note 146, at 55.
[298] World Bank, *supra* note 28, at 46.
[299] EU-Vietnam FTA, annex 9-B.
[300] Delegation of the European Union to Vietnam, *supra* note 146, at 55.
[301] EU-Singapore FTA, art. 9.15.2.
[302] EU-Vietnam FTA, art. 9.17.3.
[303] EU-Singapore FTA, art. 14.8.1; EU-Vietnam FTA, art. 15.11.1.

Philip Morris v. *Australia*, conventional ISDS has encountered global criticism because of the lack of independence of arbitrators, legal costs for host states and the "regulatory chill" for public measures.[304] A UN-level working group has discussed ISDS reform since 2017 and modern investment treaties have adopted various reform elements to exclude, limit or improve ISDS procedures.[305] ISDS reform is of significance to Asia, as 80 percent of new ISDS cases "were brought against developing countries and transition economies."[306]

Brussels plans on achieving "the full replacement of the 'old ISDS' mechanism" with the ICS, which includes two-tiered tribunals comparable to the WTO panel and the Appellate Body.[307] As a strong indication of the EU's normative power, the agreements that incorporate the ICS will build the basis for the new Multilateral Investment Court for investor-dispute disputes.[308] Moreover, the two EU IPAs will terminate Singapore and Vietnam's bilateral investment treaties (BITs) with twelve and fifteen EU Member States, respectively.[309] This clean-slate approach aligns with EU countries' post-*Achmea case* agreement that ceased 125 intra-EU BITs and the legal effect of the sunset clauses of 11 already terminated BITs.[310]

304 Nikos Lavranos, *After Philip Morris II: The "Regulatory Chill" Argument Failed – Yet Again*, Kluwer Arbitration Blog, Aug. 18, 2016, http://arbitrationblog.kluwerarbitration.com/2016/08/18/after-philipp-morris-ii-the-regulatory-chill-argument-failed-yet-again/?doing_wp_cron=1595562519.0411059856414794921875 (last visited Sept. 30, 2020); *see generally* Special Issue: UNCITRAL and Investment Arbitration Reform: Matching Concerns and Solutions (Malcolm Langford et al. eds.) *in* 21:2–3 J. World Invest. & Trade (2020).

305 United Nations Commission on International Trade Law (UNCITRAL), https://uncitral.un.org/en/working_groups/3/investor-state (last visited Sept. 30, 2020); UNCTAD, *World Investment Report 2020* (2020), at 115–16.

306 UNCTAD, *supra* note 305, at 111.

307 European Commission, *EU Finalises Proposal for Investment Protection and Court System for TTIP*, Nov. 12, 2015, https://ec.europa.eu/commission/presscorner/detail/en/IP_15_6059 (last visited Oct. 3, 2020); Shai Dothan & Joanna Lam, *A Paradigm Shift? Arbitration and Court-Like Mechanism in Investors' Disputes, in* 2020 Eur. YB Int'l Econ. L. 1, 10–15 (Güneş Ünüvar et al. eds. 2020).

308 European Commission, Report from the Commission to the European Parliament, the Council, the European Economic and Social Committee and the Committee of the Regions: Report on the Implementation of the Trade Policy Strategy Trade for All: Delivering a Progressive Trade Policy to Harness Globalisation, COM (2017) 491 final (2017), at 8.

309 EU-Singapore Investment Protection Agreement (IPA) (2018), ch. 4, annex 5; EU-Singapore IPA (2019), ch. 4, annex 6.

310 UNCTAD, *supra* note 305, at 108.

1 Investment Court System

The EU commenced public consultations on the ICS in 2014.[311] When the investment chapter of the EU-Singapore FTA was finalized in the same year, the original agreement simply indicated a possibility for including an appellate mechanism.[312] Subsequently, the Commission's "Trade for All" communication and the negotiating text of the EU-US Transatlantic Trade and Investment Partnership (TTIP) explicitly articulated the ICS objective and detailed rules.[313] Although the Trump administration suspended TTIP talks, the ICS was incorporated into the EU-Canada CETA and the EU-Vietnam FTA.[314] Categorized as a "mixed" agreement, the CETA was provisionally applied without investment protection provisions including the ICS because controversies arose as to the competence of the EU and its members.[315]

The CJEU's Opinion 2/15 shed light on the interpretation of the "common commercial policy" and resulted in the separation of the IPA from the FTA. It is clear that the EU "shall have exclusive competence" over the common commercial policy under the Treaty on the Functioning of the EU, but the scope of the policy under Article 207 of the Treaty was disputable.[316] According to the CJEU, the ISDS mechanism "removes disputes from the jurisdiction of the courts of the Member States" and thus the mechanism cannot "be established without the Member States' consent."[317] Hence, approval for ISDS falls within the shared competence between the EU and its members.[318] The Opinion 2/15 prompted negotiators to move investment protection provisions from the "already completed" EU FTAs with Singapore and Vietnam to

311 European Commission, *Consultation Strategy: Impact Assessment on the Establishment of a Multilateral Investment Court for Investment Dispute Resolution* (2016), at 1.

312 MTI, *supra* note 121, at 2; Mahdev Mohan, *The European Union's Free Trade Agreement with Singapore – One Step Forward, 28 Steps Back?*, *in* International Investment Treaties and Arbitration Across Asia 180, 198 (Julien Chaisse & Luke Nottage eds. 2018).

313 European Commission, *supra* note 4, at 21; European Commission, *supra* note 311, at 2; Commission Draft Text TTIP – Investment (2015), sec. 3.

314 European Commission, *supra* note 308, at 8; Catherine Titi, *Recent Developments in International Investment Law*, *in* 2018:9 Eur. YB Int'l Econ. L. 383, 392–93 (Marc Bungenberg et al. eds. 2019).

315 David Kleimann & Gesa Kübek, *The Signing, Provisional Application, and Conclusion of Trade and Investment Agreements in the EU: The Case of CETA and Opinion 2/15*, 45(1) Legal Issues Eco. Integration 13, 30–31 (2018).

316 TFEU, arts. 3(1) & 207(1).

317 Opinion 2/15 of the Court (2017), para. 292.

318 *Id.* para. 293; Marise Cremona, *Shaping EU Trade Policy Post-Lisbon: Opinion 2/15 of 16 May 2017*, 14 Eur. Cont'l L. Rev. 231, 255–56 (2018).

separate IPAs. This bifurcation approach will be the model for new EU agreements.

Substantive and procedural contents of EU IPAs with Singapore and Vietnam reflect investment case law and recent agreements.[319] Both IPAs cover national treatment provisions, detailed rules on fair and equitable treatment and indirect expropriation.[320] I identify three major differences between these two IPAs. First, the EU-Singapore IPA encompasses a broader definition of investment, covering more forms of investment such as "other financial assets" and licenses under domestic law.[321] The EU-Vietnam IPA does not include these forms of investment and thus accords less protection to EU investors. Second, the EU-Singapore IPA does not provide MFN treatment, but the EU-Vietnam IPA grants such treatment with certain carveouts.[322] The MFN clause ensures the IPA as a "living" instrument because it guarantees the elevated standards in tandem with either party's prospective investment pacts.

Finally, the two IPAs vary as to their ICS schemes. Under the EU-Singapore IPA, the ICS consists of a Tribunal of First Instance and a permanent Appeal Tribunal.[323] Each tribunal comprises six members who are experienced international law experts from the EU, Singapore and third countries.[324] The ICS under the EU-Vietnam IPA follows a similar structure, including a Tribunal and an Appeal Tribunal.[325] Same as the EU-Singapore FTA, there are six members for an Appeal Tribunal, but a Tribunal encompasses nine rather than six members.[326] In addition, the EU-Singapore IPA allows parties to directly appoint these eight-year term members.[327] Yet, the EU-Vietnam IPA only permits the joint committee to appoint ICS members, presumably diminishing parties' direct control over the composition of the ICS.[328]

[319] *E.g.*, European Parliament, *supra* note 31, at 18–20; Locknie Hsu, *EU-ASEAN Trade and Investment Relations with a Special Focus on Singapore, in* 2015:6 Eur. YB Int'l Econ. L. 233, 243–45 (Christoph Herrmann et al. eds. 2015).

[320] EU-Singapore IPA, ch. 2 & annex 1; EU-Vietnam IPA (2019), ch. 2 & annex 4.

[321] EU-Singapore IPA, art. 1.2.1(d) & (h); EU-Vietnam IPA, art. 1.2(h).

[322] EU-Vietnam IPA, arts. 2.1.2, 2.1.3 & 2.4.

[323] EU-Singapore IPA, arts. 3.9 & 3.10.

[324] EU-Singapore IPA, arts. 3.9.2, 3.9.4, 3.10.2 & 3.10.4.

[325] EU-Vietnam IPA, arts. 3.38 & 3.39.

[326] EU-Vietnam IPA, arts. 3.38.2 & 3.39.2.

[327] EU-Singapore IPA, arts. 3.9.2, 3.9.5, 3.10.2 & 3.10.5.

[328] EU-Vietnam IPA, arts. 3.38.3, 3.38.5, 3.39.3 & 3.39.3.

Appeals are conventionally limited to legal review. For example, as the Dispute Settlement Understanding illustrates, the WTO Appellate Body is authorized to review "issues of law" and "legal interpretation" of the panel.[329] However, other than legal review, both IPAs extend the grounds of appeal to cases where "the Tribunal has manifestly erred in the appreciation of the facts."[330] Comparable to modern investment treaties, both IPAs also incorporate annulment grounds under Article 52 of the International Centre for Settlement of Investment Disputes (ICSID) Convention.[331] The ICSID Secretariat also acts as the secretariats for the ICS and provides necessary support.[332]

As of 2020, Brussels concluded agreements that incorporate the ICS with four countries, Canada, Singapore, Vietnam and Mexico.[333] Commentators may suggest that the ICS will strengthen the EU's normative power by shaping ASEAN-EU interregionalism and new Asian regionalism. I disagree. While the CPTPP considers having "an appellate mechanism," the pact suspended various ISDS provisions of the original TPP.[334] In addition, the recent ASEAN-Hong Kong Investment Agreement, the UK-Japan FTA and the RCEP exclude ISDS entirely.[335] The "new normal" is to limit and exclude ISDS.

The existing ISDS literature, which mostly stresses what the EU "mandates" but rarely articulates what Asian countries prefer, echoes political scientists' challenges to the Eurocentric view of regionalism study. The EU claimed that as a reform, the ICS will replace ISDS mechanisms, but Asian states have viewed the EU proposal as another ISDS-plus scheme. Specifically, they could not appreciate the added value of the ICS in comparison with existing ISDS rules under Asian FTAs such as the ASEAN Comprehensive Investment Agreement and ASEAN Plus One FTAs.

329 Understanding on Rules and Procedures Governing the Settlement of Disputes (1994), art. 17.6.

330 EU-Singapore IPA, art. 3.19; EU-Vietnam IPA, art. 3.54.

331 EU-Singapore IPA, art. 3.19; EU-Vietnam IPA, art. 3.54.

332 EU-Singapore IPA, arts 3.9.16 & 3.10.14.

333 European Parliament, Legislative Train 09.2020 (2020), at 2.

334 CPTPP, art. 9.23.11; CPTPP, annex: 2; AFTINET, *ISDS Victory: RCEP Won't Allow Corporations to Sue Governments*, Oct. 2019, https://isds.bilaterals.org/?isds-victory-rcep-won-t-allow (last visited Oct. 5, 2020).

335 Vivienne Beth & Luke Nottage, *International Investment Agreement and Investor-State Arbitration in Asia*, *in* Handbook of International Investment Law and Policy 1, 8–11 (Julien Chaisse et al. eds. 2020). The UK-Japan FTA and the Regional Comprehensive Economic Partnership (RCEP) have review clauses for prospective discussion on this matter.

Brussels declared that "ISDS is dead" for the EU while negotiating with Japan.[336] However, Tokyo declined to accept the ICS, so that the EU-Japan IPA will be subject to ongoing talks despite the entry into force of the EU-Japan FTA in 2019.[337] Indonesia has opposed ISDS by unilaterally terminating its BITs.[338] Moreover, for least developed countries such as Myanmar, an important financial concern is the cost to sustain two-tiered tribunals including fees to bench members.

2 Mediation Rules 2.0

Although the impact of the ICS on ASEAN-EU interregionalism and new Asian regionalism remains to be seen, mediation mechanisms under the EU IPAs with Singapore and Vietnam may have significant potential for solving investor-state disputes. Mediation reflects Asian culture or the ASEAN Way, but has been ignored in the Western legal discourse that almost equates dispute settlement with proceedings of courts and arbitration. Notably, the Singapore Convention on Mediation (Singapore Convention) that came into force in 2020 includes more than fifty signatories such as five ASEAN countries, China, India and the United States.[339] The Convention is open to accession by the EU and other "regional economic integration organizations."[340] In my view, new EU IPAs and the Convention form "Mediation Rules 2.0" and provide pragmatic alternatives for investor-state disputes.

In the landscape of international dispute settlement, the New York Convention and the Hague Convention enable the recognition of arbitral awards and foreign judgements in domestic courts.[341] As the "missing piece," the Singapore Convention mandates that parties

[336] European Commission, *Factsheet : A New EU Agreement with Japan* (2018), at 6.

[337] European Commission, *supra* note 8, at 2; Clifford Chance, *The EU-Japan Economic Partnership Agreement: A Different Kind of Treaty?* (2018), at 3.

[338] Craig Tevendale & Vanessa Naish, *Indonesia Indicates Intention to Terminate All of Its Bilateral Investment Treaties?* Mar. 20, 2014, https://hsfnotes.com/arbitration/2014/03/20/indonesia-indicates-intention-to-terminate-all-of-its-bilateral-investment-treaties/ (last visited Oct. 5, 2020).

[339] The five ASEAN countries are Brunei, Laos, Malaysia, the Philippines and Singapore. UNCITRAL, *Status: United Nations Convention on International Settlement Agreements Resulting from Mediation*, https://uncitral.un.org/en/texts/mediation/conventions/international_settlement_agreements/status (last visited Oct. 5, 2020).

[340] Singapore Convention on Mediation (2018), art. 12.

[341] United Nations Convention on the Recognition and Enforcement of Foreign Arbitral Awards (1958); Hague Choice of Court Convention (2005).

"enforce a settlement agreement" according to the Convention.[342] Although it is not explicitly stated in the Convention, a broader interpretation of "commercial disputes" in Article 1 suggests that the Convention applies to investor-state mediations.[343] In practice, dispute settlement proceedings under investment treaties often require consultations but provide no procedural rules. The Convention can expedite the dispute settlement process by facilitating mediation at the cooling-off consultation stage.

To complement the Singapore Convention, EU IPAs with Singapore and Vietnam provide more investment-specific mediation rules than the general mediation procedures of the CETA.[344] In particular, annexes of both IPAs stipulate procedural and implementation rules for investor-state mediation and the code of conduct for mediators.[345] IPAs also enable a mediator to "offer advice and propose a solution for consideration of the disputing parties."[346] The expanded role of the mediator exceeds the usual scope of facilitating the self-determination of the parties.[347] Premised on their new rules, the mediation and enforcement mechanisms of the Convention and the two EU IPAs make "Mediation Rules 2.0" ideal for resolving investor-state disputes.

D Human Rights and Sustainable Development

To universalize values that the Treaty of Lisbon proclaimed, the EU has promoted a trade and investment agenda that focuses on human rights

342 Natalie Y. Morris-Sharma, *The Singapore Convention Is Live, and Multilateralism, Alive*, 20(4) Cardozo J. Conflict Resol. 1009, 1014–16 (2019); United Nations Convention on International Settlement Agreements Result from Mediation (2018), art. 3(1).

343 United Nations Convention on International Settlement Agreements Result from Mediation (Singapore Convention on Mediation) (2018), art. 1(1); Mushegh Manukyan, *Singapore Convention Series: A Call for a Broad Interpretation of the Singapore Mediation Convention in the Context of Investor-State Disputes*, Jun. 10, 2019, http://mediationblog.kluwerarbitration.com/2019/06/10/singapore-convention-series-a-call-for-a-broad-interpretation-of-the-singapore-mediation-convention-in-the-context-of-investor-state-disputes/?doing_wp_cron=1595837214.8890540599822998046875 (last visited Oct. 5, 2020).

344 Chester Brown & Phoebe Winch, *The Confidentiality and Transparency Debate in Commercial and Investment Mediation*, *in* Mediation in International Commercial and Investment Disputes 320, 337 (Catherine Titi & Katia Fach Gómez eds. 2019).

345 EU-Singapore IPA, annexes 6, 7 & 11; EU-Vietnam IPA, annexes 8–11.

346 EU-Singapore IPA, annex 6, art. 4.3; EU-Vietnam IPA, annex 10, art. 4.3.

347 Singapore International Dispute Resolution Academy, *SIDRA International Dispute Resolution Survey: 2020 Final Report* (2020), at 24.

and sustainable development.[348] The EU and ASEAN diverge in their approaches to "enforcing" values. ASEAN recognizes the importance of human rights and sustainable development, but focuses on constructive engagement rather than making nontrade issues enforceable via FTAs. Distinctly, the EU's legalist approach has applied to these core values because of the insistence of the European Parliament, which represents ideological interests of European citizens. The EU's "export" of its values to ASEAN may forge a collective identity from a constructivist perspective. A compromise in the EU's approach also reflects the premise of the new dependency theory, which posits that the joint power of developing countries may transform conventional North-South relations.

1 Sanctions under the GSP, PCAs and FTAs

A key enforcement mechanism of the EU is to withdraw tariff preferences under the GSP regulation in order to "penalize" beneficiary countries that violate human rights.[349] In 2020, the European Commission partially suspended Cambodia's privileges under the most favorable GSP scheme of "Everything But Arms."[350] This decision, which would affect 20 percent of Cambodia's exports to the EU, was a response to the Hun Sen government's banning of the opposition party and charging the opposition leader with treason.[351] Worsening human rights situations in Myanmar and the Philippines may also affect their GSP privileges and jeopardize ASEAN-EU FTA talks.[352]

Another oft-ignored linkage between the FTA and the GSP is that once an ASEAN country concludes an FTA with the EU, Cambodia's products can no longer utilize components from that country to meet the GSP cumulation rules.[353] It will severely hurt Cambodia's promising biking industry, as bicycle frames are often imported from ASEAN countries such as Indonesia, Malaysia and Vietnam.[354] This consequence creates

[348] European Commission, *supra* note 4, at 22–23; TFEU, arts. 205 & 207(1); Consolidated versions of the Treaty on European Union, OJ C 326/15 (2012), arts. 3(5) & 21(3).

[349] European Parliament, *supra* note 140, at 13.

[350] European Commission, *Cambodia Loses Duty-Free Access to the EU Market over Human Rights Concerns* (2020), at 1.

[351] Shaun Turton, *Cambodia Loses EU Trade Privileges as It Rushes FTA with China*, Aug. 12, 2020, Nikkei Asian Rev., https://asia.nikkei.com/Economy/Trade/Cambodia-loses-EU-trade-privileges-as-it-rushes-FTA-with-China (last visited Oct. 6, 2020).

[352] European Parliament, *supra* note 140, at 32.

[353] *Id.* at 100–04.

[354] *Id.*; Danielle Keeton-Olsen, *Cambodia's Bicycle Firms Face Bumps in the Road*, Dec. 5, 2019, BBC, www.bbc.com/news/business-50388764#:~:text=Made%20in%20Cambodia

an additional "deterrent" for Cambodia and an incentive for other countries to expedite EU FTAs that require human rights compliance.

To ensure the nexus between trade and human rights, the EU's mandate is to conclude a PCA that contains enforceable human rights provisions as a prerequisite to an FTA.[355] Thus, the EU-Vietnam PCA, which includes a much broader scope than the 1995 Cooperation Agreement, was signed in 2012 and the EU-Singapore PCA was also inked in 2018.[356] The legal linkage between FTAs and PCAs is unambiguous. Both EU FTAs with Singapore and Vietnam provide that PCAs "shall form part of a common institutional framework."[357] Pursuant to PCAs, respecting international human rights is "an essential element" and a party is entitled to take "appropriate measures" in response to any violation of the obligation.[358]

Although both PCAs require consultations to determine these measures, the EU-Singapore PCA's nonexecution mechanism allows "the suspension of" the PCA and the FTA in "exceptional cases of systemic, serious and substantial" violations.[359] The Canada-EU Strategic Partnership Agreement imposes an even more robust conditionality clause that can lead to "the termination of the" CETA.[360] Asian governments should note that EU PCAs with Vietnam, Singapore and Canada illustrate different levels of human rights conditionality that would affect the validity of FTAs at various degrees.

Arguably, the European Parliament prioritized commercial gains and showed "little interest in promoting conditionality in negotiations with Singapore, despite the divergence between European and Singaporean interests on human rights."[361] As for the invocation of the PCA's mechanism that may suspend the FTA, Brussels and Singapore reached

%20is%20a,also%20have%20been%20made%20there.&text=The%20factory%20can%20turn%20out,demand%20is%20there%2C%20he%20adds (last visited Oct. 6, 2020).

355 European Parliament, *supra* note 21, para. H.

356 European Commission, *Human Rights and Sustainable Development in the EU-Vietnam Relations with Specific Regard to the EU-Vietnam Free Trade Agreement* (2016), at 3; Parliament of the United Kingdom, *supra* note 27.

357 EU-Singapore FTA, art. 16.18.1; EU-Vietnam FTA, art. 17.22.2.

358 EU-Singapore Partnership and Cooperation Agreement (PCA) (2018), arts. 1 & 44 and joint declaration on art. 44; EU-Vietnam PCA (2012), arts. 1 & 57.

359 EU-Singapore PCA, arts. 9(2) & 44(4) and joint declaration on art. 44; EU-Vietnam PCA, art. 57(4).

360 European Parliament, *Human Rights in EU Trade Agreements: The Human Rights Clause and its Application* (2019), at 9–10; Canada-EU Strategic Partnership Agreement (2016), art. 28.7.

361 Mckenzie & Messiner, *supra* note 102, at 842–43.

a compromise by including a side letter, which "shall form an integral part of the" PCA.[362] According to the side letter, neither side is aware "of any of each other's domestic laws, or their application, which could lead to the invocation of" the nonexecution mechanism.[363] This commitment essentially denotes the EU's implicit commitment not to challenge human rights-related law and practice of Singapore.

The EU's position seemed to contradict its previous criticism against Singapore's death penalty and detentions as a result of "the continuing misuse of the Internal Security Act" (ISA).[364] In particular, there was no major legislative change and the numbers of capital punishment cases and detainees under ISA orders have not significantly changed.[365] The European Parliament's concern about Singapore's "unenforced" Section 377A of the Penal Code, which criminalizes consensual sex between male adults, also did not become an obstacle to the PCA and the FTA.[366]

Compared with the "low salience of" human rights issues involving the EU-Singapore FTA, EU institutions took a "harsher" stance on Vietnam.[367] In 2014, the European Parliament specifically requested that the European Commission conduct impact studies on human rights for the EU-Vietnam FTA.[368] The Commission declined on the ground that "a sustainability impact assessment had already been carried out in 2009 on the ASEAN-EU FTA."[369] This reason contravenes the

[362] *Id.* at 841; EU-Singapore PCA, art. 50 & side letter; Parliament of the United Kingdom, 6 *EU – Singapore Partnership and Cooperation Agreement*, Mar. 19, 2014, https://publications.parliament.uk/pa/cm201314/cmselect/cmeuleg/83/83xxxv09.htm (last visited Oct. 7, 2020).

[363] EU-Singapore PCA (2018), side letter; *id.* at 841.

[364] *E.g.*, Joint Local Statement on the Death Penalty Case of Moad Fadzir bin Mustaffa in Singapore (2020), at 1; European Parliament, Resolution on the Situation in South-East Asia, A3-0219/91 (1991), para. 28.

[365] Raj Nadarajan, *Number of Radicalised Individuals on ISA Orders at Highest in 7 Years*, Aug. 4, 2019, Today, www.todayonline.com/singapore/number-radicalised-individuals-isa-orders-highest-7-years (last visited Oct. 20, 2020); see Ministry of Home Affairs – Singapore Prison Service, *Judicial Executions*, https://data.gov.sg/dataset/judicial-executions (last visited Oct. 20, 2020).

[366] European Parliament, EU-Singapore Partnership and Cooperation Agreement (Resolution), P8-TA(2019)0093 (2019), para. 6.

[367] Hoang & Sicurelli, *supra* note 48, at 373.

[368] European Parliament, European Parliament Resolution of 17 April 2014 on the State of Play of the EU-Vietnam Free Trade Agreement, P7_TA(2014)0458 (2014), para. 25.

[369] European Parliament, *Driving Trade in the ASEAN Region: Progress of FTA Negotiations* (2016), at 8; European Ombudsman, Decision in Case 1409/2014/MHZ on the European Commission's Failure to Carry Out a Prior Human Rights Impact Assessment of the EU-Vietnam Free Trade Agreement (2016), at 1.

Parliament's previous resolution, which mandates that the Commission carry out separate impact studies on sustainable development and human rights for trade agreements.[370]

The European Ombudsman decided that the Commission's failure to conduct the specific human rights assessment "constituted maladministration."[371] Although the Ombudsman's decision is not legally binding, the Parliament severely criticized the Commission's lack of compliance.[372] The Parliament and its members reiterated their grave concerns about Vietnam's political and religious persecution, Cybersecurity Law and death penalty.[373] According to the Commission, it will only conduct "ex-post evaluations of" human rights after gathering sufficient evidence and data following the entry into force of the EU-Vietnam FTA.[374] Notwithstanding this stance, the European Parliament gave its consent to the FTA in 2020. Based on the practice of the EU FTAs with Singapore and Vietnam, it may be contended that the EU institutions' policies on human rights are inconsistent, thus undermining the values-based trade policy. Yet, it cannot be ignored that the "flexibility" indicated in the EU's enforcement approach is essential to trade talks with Asian countries that hold diverse values of human rights.

2 Enforcing Environmental and Labor Standards

Like human rights, sustainable development constitutes a new-generation component of FTAs and a core value that Brussels wishes to universalize. Compliance with sustainable development provisions also implements commitments of the EU and ASEAN to the UN Sustainable Development Goals. In the Opinion 2/15, the CJEU pointed out that "the objective of sustainable development" constitutes "an integral part of the common commercial policy" within the EU's

[370] European Parliament, European Parliament Resolution of 25 November 2010 on Human Rights and Social and Environmental Standards in International Trade Agreements, P7(2010)0434 (2010), para. 19(b).

[371] European Ombudsman, *supra* note 369, at 1 & 11.

[372] European Parliament, *supra* note 369, at 8. The European Commission explained that the PCA's human rights clauses achieved the same purpose. European Ombudsman, *supra* note 369, at 1.

[373] European Parliament, *supra* note 369, at 8; European Parliament, European Parliament Resolution of 9 June 2016 on Vietnam, P8_TA(2016)0276 (2016), paras. P.1–10; 32 MEPs Send a Joint Letter to Mrs Mogherini and Commissioner Malmström to Ask for More Human Rights Progress in Vietnam, Sept. 17, 2018, http://tremosa.cat/noticies/32-meps-send-joint-letter-mrs-mogherini-and-commissioner-malmstrom-ask-more-human-rights-progress-vietnam (last visited Oct. 7, 2020).

[374] European Commission, *supra* note 356, at 22.

exclusive competence.[375] FTAs and PCAs form the legal framework that promotes sustainable development, which has focused on environmental and labor standards.[376]

Although PCA provisions on renewable energy, natural resources, climate change and employment are not "essential elements," they can still be enforced by "appropriate measures" akin to human rights clauses.[377] The enforcement mechanisms under EU FTAs with Singapore and Vietnam contain more specific rules than PCAs. The FTA chapters on trade and sustainable development require compliance with domestic and international law, such as International Labour Organization (ILO) Conventions and multilateral environmental agreements.[378]

Both EU FTAs with Singapore and Vietnam exclude the chapters on trade and sustainable development from the general dispute settlement and mediation mechanisms.[379] Disputes arising from these chapters will only be subject to chapter-specific mechanisms, which include government consultations and a panel of experts whose final reports will be monitored by a jointly established board.[380] This compromise similarly reflects the EU's pragmatic approach. Contrary to the conventional understanding, it is unlikely that Brussels will bring labor rights complaints against Vietnam. In fact, labor protection clauses under the EU-Vietnam FTA are comparable to those in the CPTPP.[381] Vietnam has revamped its labor legislation to comply with the CPTPP and the EU-Vietnam FTA even before ratifying ILO Conventions on issues such as freedom of association and forced labor.[382]

375 Opinion 2/15 of the Court (2017), paras. 138–47.

376 *Id.* paras. 148–52; European Commission, *supra* note 4, at 22–23.

377 EU-Singapore PCA, arts. 31, 34, 35 & 44; EU-Vietnam PCA, arts. 30, 31, 42, 50 & 57.

378 EU-Singapore FTA, ch. 12; EU-Vietnam FTA, ch. 13.

379 EU-Singapore FTA, art. 12.16.1; EU-Vietnam FTA, art. 13.16.1. The EU's only FTA that applies the general dispute settlement mechanism to sustainable development provisions is the CARIFORUM-EU Economic Partnership Agreement. Gracia Marín Durán, *Sustainable Development Chapters in EU Free Trade Agreements: Emerging Compliance Issues*, 57 Common Market L. Rev. 1, 11 (2020); Kateřina Hradilová & Ondřej Svoboda, *Sustainable Development Chapters in the EU Free Trade Agreements: Searching for Effectiveness*, 52(6) J. World Trade 1019, 1025–29 (2018).

380 EU-Singapore FTA, arts. 12.16–12.17; EU-Vietnam FTA, arts. 12.16–12.17; Hradilová & Svoboda, *supra* note 379, at 1025–26.

381 Kathleen Claussen, *Dispute Settlement under the Next Generation of Free Trade Agreement*, 46(3) Ga. J. Int'l & Com. L. 611, 616 (2018).

382 EuroCham, *supra* note 138, at 56–59; DFDL, *Investment Guide: Vietnam 2020* (7th ed. 2020), at 44–51.

The EU's FTA approach to enforcing sustainable development has been perceived to be "softer" than that the sanction-based model under US FTAs.[383] I argue that recent trends represent an increasing convergence of Brussels and Washington. As the TPP and the United States-Mexico-Canada Agreement exemplify, US-negotiated FTAs apply the general dispute settlement mechanism to labor chapters.[384] However, it does not necessarily result in more efficient enforcement. The US-Guatemala dispute under the labor provisions of the Dominican Republic-Central America FTA (CAFTA-DR) is illustrative.

In 2008, Washington brought the first-ever claim based on FTA labor provisions on the ground that Guatemala violated the CAFTA-DR for failing to effectively enforce labor laws to protect rights of freedom of association and collective bargaining.[385] Nevertheless, the United States did not succeed in the claim. According to the panel, what the US side proved did not "constitute a sustained or recurring course of action or inaction."[386] Moreover, the panel ruled that the evidence on labor law enforcement failed to meet the "in a manner affecting trade" requirement.[387] In essence, the burden of proof and the trade-impact test under the FTA impose limitations on the US model and undermine its perceived "sanctions."

On the European side, EU states reached "a clear consensus" by shifting to a tougher stance on implementing sustainable development in 2018.[388] The Commission's fifteen-point plan pledges "to more assertively enforce the commitments under" FTA chapters on trade and investment by resorting to monitoring and dispute settlement mechanisms.[389] The Commission subsequently filed a claim on labor rights against Korea under the EU-Korea FTA, the very first

383 Billy Melo Araujo, *Labour Provisions in EU and US Mega-regional Trade Agreements: Rhetoric and Reality*, 67 Int'l & Com. L. Q. 233, 240–41 (2018).

384 Cathleen D. Cimino-Isaacs, *Labor Enforcement Issues in U.S. FTAs*, CRS: In Focus (2000), at 2; United States-Mexico-Canada Agreement (2020), art. 31.8.3 & annexes 31-A & 31-B.

385 Cimino-Isaacs, *supra* note 384, at 2; Hradilová & Svoboda, *supra* note 379, at 1036.

386 Dominican Republic-Central America FTA, Arbitral Panel Established Pursuant to Chapter Twenty, In the Matter of Guatemala – Issues Relating to the Obligations Under Article 16.2.1(a) of the CAFTA-DR, Final Report of the Panel (2017), para. 430.

387 *Id.* paras. 498–505.

388 European Commission, *Non-paper of the Commission Services: Feedback and way forward on improving the implementation and enforcement of Trade and Sustainable Development chapters in EU Free Trade Agreements* (2018), at 2.

389 *Id.* at 7–8.

EU FTA that includes a trade and sustainable development chapter.[390] The panel report is expected to evaluate Korea's implementation of ILO conventions and domestic labor legislation.[391] This dispute will influence the trade-sustainable development nexus and the normative features of ASEAN-EU interregionalism.

V Conclusion

The chapter explored the interdisciplinary concept of interregionalism and the roadmap to the ASEAN-EU FTA, which will bring significant exogenous influences to new Asian regionalism in international economic law. As pathfinder agreements following the CJEU's Opinion 2/15, EU FTAs with Singapore and Vietnam aim to achieve the EU's building-block approach and enrich theoretical and empirical debates on the Third Interregionalism. By analyzing and comparing these new agreements, the chapter argued that the innovative designs of the two EU FTAs in tandem with IPAs and PCAs will shape interregionalism. It further contended that the best practices of other modern agreements demonstrate the deficiencies of EU FTAs that require remedies in the post-pandemic era.

Critical global challenges such as the US-China trade war and the COVID-19 crisis have galvanized the EU to focus its new Indo-Pacific strategy on the ASEAN-EU framework. Critical to regional supply chains, EU FTAs with Singapore and Vietnam incorporate new rules on ASEAN cumulation and non-tariff barriers. However, services commitments and provisions on e-commerce under the two EU FTAs should be further improved. As for new-generation components that will shape post-Lisbon agreements, the clauses on GIs, SOEs and government procurement reinforce the EU's normative power and reflect different legal models that accommodate diverse economic development of Singapore and Vietnam.

In the realm of investor-state disputes, Asian states may find it difficult to readily accept the EU's ICS proposal as the ISDS reform. New mediation rules under IPAs and the Singapore Convention nonetheless provide alternatives for solving such disputes. Moreover, FTAs and PCAs collectively enforce EU values of sustainable development

[390] European Commission, *EU-Korea Dispute Settlement over Workers' Rights in Korea Enters Next Stage*, Dec. 18, 2019, https://trade.ec.europa.eu/doclib/press/index.cfm?id=2095 (last visited Oct. 9, 2020); Durán, *supra* note 379, at 25.

[391] European Parliament, *supra* note 6, para. 53.

Table 4.2 *Economic agreements between the EU and ASEAN Plus Six countries (2020)*[392]

	EU FTA	EU IPA	Other EU Agreements	EU GSP
ASEAN (as a bloc)	Negotiations launched in 2007; suspended in 2009; discussing the parameters of an FTA from 2017		Cooperation Agreement (1980)	
Brunei Darussalam				
Cambodia			Cooperation Agreement (1997)	EBA, partially suspended in 2020
Indonesia	Negotiations launched in 2016		PCA (2009)	Standard GSP
Laos			Cooperation Agreement (1997)	EBA

392 *See generally* European Commission, *supra* note 8; European Parliament, *Southeast Asia, Fact Sheets on the European Union* (2020); European Commission, *South Korea*, Apr. 23, 2020, https://ec.europa.eu/trade/policy/countries-and-regions/countries/south-korea/ (last visited Aug. 19, 2020); European Commission, *supra* note 6; European Parliament, *supra* note 140, at 2 fns 5–8; European Commission, *supra* note 350, at 1; European Council & Council of the European Union, *EU-China: Council Authorises Signature of the Agreement on Geographical Indications*, Jul. 20, 2020, https://www.consilium.europa.eu/en/press/press-releases/2020/07/20/eu-china-council-authorises-signature-of-the-agreement-on-geographical-indications/ (last visited Aug. 28, 2020).

Table 4.2 (*cont.*)

Malaysia	Negotiations launched in 2010; put on hold in 2012	Same as FTA	Completed negotiations for the PCA in 2015	
Myanmar		Negotiations launched in 2015		EBA
Philippines	Negotiations launched in 2015	Same as FTA	Framework Agreement on Partnership and Cooperation (2012)	GSP+
Singapore	Signed in 2018; Entered into force in 2019	Signed in 2018	PCA (2018)	
Thailand	Negotiations launched in 2013; no negotiating rounds after 2014		Completed negotiations for the PCA in 2013	
Vietnam	Signed in 2019; Entered into force in 2020	Signed in 2019	Framework Agreement on Comprehensive Partnership and Cooperation (2012)	Standard GSP

Plus Six Countries	EU FTA	EU IPA	Other EU Agreements	EU GSP
Australia	Negotiations launched in 2018	Same as FTA	Framework Agreement (2017)	
China		Concluded in principle the negotiations for a Comprehensive Agreement on Investment in 2020	Agreement on Geographical Indications (2020)	
India	Negotiations launched in 2007; standstill in 2013	Same as FTA		Standard GSP
Japan	Signed in 2018; entered into force in 2019	Under negotiation	Strategic Partnership Agreement (2018)	
Korea	Signed in 2010; provisionally applied from 2011; formally ratified in 2015 (no investment chapter)		Framework Agreement (2010)	
New Zealand	Negotiations launched in 2018	Same as FTA	Partnership Agreement for Relations and Cooperation (2016)	

FTA: Free Trade Agreement; **IPA**: Investment Protection Agreement; **PCA**: Partnership and Cooperation Agreement; **GSP**: Generalized System of Preferences; **EBA**: Everything But Arms

and human rights. The practice of the nonexecution and dispute settlement mechanisms also illustrates the EU's pragmatic approach to ASEAN countries. Hence, the detailed analysis of these EU agreements contributed to the understanding of the EU's trade and investment strategy toward the Asia-Pacific and new Asian regionalism from different perspectives.

5

Revitalizing the US Pivot to Asia

I Introduction

The trade policy of the United States that responds to the rise of Asia is essential to new Asian regionalism in international economic law. In 2010, Asia, for the first time, overtook the European Union (EU) as America's largest export destination.[1] Today, five Asian economies – China, Japan, South Korea, India and Taiwan – are among the top ten trading partners of the United States.[2] The Association of Southeast Asian Nations (ASEAN) is also America's eleventh largest trading partner.[3] The ten-country bloc has received US investment amounting to $329 billion, greater than America's combined total investment in China, India, Japan and South Korea.[4] Despite different approaches, President Barack Obama's "pivot" or "rebalance" to Asia and President Donald Trump's Indo-Pacific strategy both highlighted the priority of Asia in US diplomacy.[5]

1 Kelly Evans, *Sign of the Times: Emerging Asia Surpasses EU as US Export Destination*, May 13, 2010, Wall Street J., https://blogs.wsj.com/economics/2010/05/13/sign-of-the-times-emerging-asia-surpasses-eu-as-us-export-destination/ (last visited Nov. 17, 2010).

2 Ken Roberts, *It's Official: Mexico Is No. 1 US Trade Partner For First Time, Despite Overall US Trade Decline*, Feb. 5, 2020, Forbes, www.forbes.com/sites/kenroberts/2020/02/05/its-official-mexico-is-no-1-us-trade-partner-for-first-time-despite-overall-us-trade-decline/?sh=64baac343eab (last visited Nov. 17, 2020).

3 Office of the United States Trade Representative (USTR), *Association of Southeast Asian Nations (ASEAN)*, https://ustr.gov/countries-regions/southeast-asia-pacific/association-southeast-asian-nations-asean#:~:text=ASEAN%20is%20currently%20our%2011th,was%20%24120.2%20billion%20in%202019 (last visited Nov. 17, 2020).

4 US Mission to ASEAN, *The United States and ASEAN: An Enduring Partnership*, Aug. 2, 2019, https://asean.usmission.gov/the-united-states-and-asean-an-enduring-partnership/ (last visited Nov. 26, 2020).

5 Ian F. Fergusson & Brock R. Williams, *The Trans-Pacific Partnership (TPP): Key Provisions and Issues for Congress*, Congressional Research Service (CRS) Report (2016), at 4–6; Department of State, A Free and Open Indo-Pacific Advancing a Shared Vision (2019), at 5–6.

Inaugurated in 2021, President Joe Biden has pledged to repair alliances and restore US credibility, which reached its nadir due to Trump's unilateral "America first" policy.[6] Biden's imminent challenges include the COVID-19 crisis, political polarization and China's ambition for "extending its global reach."[7] The entry into force of the Comprehensive and Progressive Agreement for Trans-Pacific Partnership (CPTPP) in 2018 and the conclusion of the Regional Comprehensive Economic Partnership (RCEP) in 2020 present further dilemma.[8] Washington's exclusion from the two mega-regional trade agreements accelerates Asia's "decoupling" from America.[9]

The United States was the driving force behind the postwar multilateral trading system, but its declining hegemonic power and rising populist unilateralism made the superpower no longer essential in shaping the New Regional Economic Order (NREO). Embedded liberalism that the United States established to govern the postwar economy is in great peril.[10] The neoliberal Washington Consensus is challenged by the Beijing Consensus that orchestrates "authoritarian international law."[11]

Despite political rhetoric, the United States has lacked a comprehensive legal roadmap to the Asia trade policy. Washington has ignored the positions of Asian leaders that the security alliance should be reinforced by a robust economic backbone. China and ASEAN are both major locomotives for Asian integration. However,

6 Joseph R. Biden, Jr., *Why America Must Lead Again: Rescuing US Foreign Policy after Trump*, 99(2) Foreign Aff. 64, 64–75 (2020); *US President-Elect Joe Biden Claims Victory. Read His Speech in Full*, Nov. 8, 2020, ABC News, www.abc.net.au/news/2020-11-08/us-president-elect-joe-biden-victory-speech-full-transcript/12861698 (last visited Nov. 17, 2020); White House, *Inaugural Address by President Joseph R. Biden, Jr., Jan. 20, 2021*, www.whitehouse.gov/briefing-room/speeches-remarks/2021/01/20/inaugural-address-by-president-joseph-r-biden-jr/ (last visited Feb. 2, 2021).

7 Biden, *supra* note 6, at 65–75.

8 Department of Foreign Affairs and Trade, *Comprehensive and Progressive Agreement for Trans-Pacific Partnership (CPTPP)*, www.dfat.gov.au/trade/agreements/in-force/cptpp/Pages/comprehensive-and-progressive-agreement-for-trans-pacific-partnership (last visited Nov. 17, 2020); Peter A. Petri & Michael G. Plummer, *East Asia Decouples from the United States: Trade War, COVID-19, and East Asia's New Trade Blocs*, Peterson Institute for International Economics (PIIE) Working Paper, No. 20–9 (2020), at 9.

9 Petri & Plummer, *supra* note 8, at 1–5.

10 John Gerard Ruggie, *International Regimes, Transactions, and Change: Embedded Liberalism in the Postwar Economic Order*, 36(2) Int'l Organ. 379, 392–98 (1982); G. John Ikenberry, *The End of International Order?* 94(1) Int'l Aff. 7, 13–17 (2018).

11 Gregory Shaffer & Henry Gao, *A New Chinese Economic Order?* 23(3) J. Int'l Econ. L. 607, 61–13 (2020); Tom Ginsburg, *Authoritarian International Law*, 114(2) Am. J. Int'l L. 221, 231–41 (2020).

the "Asia" policy of both the US government and Congress has been overshadowed by conflicts with China ranging from the South China Sea disputes to the trade war. US leaders have regarded ASEAN as a functional rather than indispensable partner and mostly situated the bloc in the context of the US-China rivalry.

Although ASEAN emerged as the core of the "ASEAN Plus Six" free trade agreements (FTAs) on which new Asian regionalism is premised, Washington has failed to establish meaningful legal frameworks with ASEAN. In fact, America is the only major Pacific power that has yet to conclude an "ASEAN Plus One" FTA. Since 2006, the ASEAN-US Trade and Investment Framework Arrangement (TIFA) has remained primarily a scheme for dialogues without resulting in tangible FTA outcomes.[12]

The White House's "episodic rather than consistent" approach to ASEAN has endangered losing the bloc to Beijing.[13] Built on the pragmatic incrementalism of the ASEAN way, the ASEAN-China FTA materialized under the Framework Agreement and was enhanced by the Upgrade Protocol. In 2020, ASEAN and China became each other's largest trade partner, making the ASEAN-China FTA the most profound South-South agreement in Asia.[14] Even the European Union (EU), a nonresident power, has adopted a more proactive strategy than the United States. As detailed in Chapter 4, Brussels articulated its building-block approach for the ASEAN-EU FTA in the 2015 "Trade for All" strategy.[15] Recent pathfinder agreements with Singapore and Vietnam provide a normative foundation for the prospective region-to-region FTA.

The US-Singapore FTA concluded in 2003 remains the only FTA that Washington signed with an ASEAN country. The US TIFA with ASEAN and the US-Singapore FTA at most constitute transregionalism and

[12] USTR, *Trade Agreements*, https://ustr.gov/trade-agreements (last visited Nov. 17, 2020).

[13] Tommy Koh, *The United States and Southeast Asia, in* America's Role in Asia, Asian and American Views: Recommendations for US Policy from Both Sides of the Pacific 35, 37 (2008); Umair Jamal, *Has the United States lost Southeast Asia to China?* Sept. 18, 2020, ASEAN Today, www.aseantoday.com/2020/09/has-the-united-states-lost-southeast-asia-to-china/ (last visited Nov. 18, 2020).

[14] Association of Southeast Asian Nations (ASEAN), *ASEAN Trade in Goods (IMTS) Dashboard*, https://data.aseanstats.org/dashboard/imts.hs2 (last visited Nov. 18, 2020); Ayman Falak Medina, *ASEAN Overtakes EU to Become China's Top Trading Partner in Q1 2020*, May 15, 2020, ASEAN Briefing, www.aseanbriefing.com/news/asean-overtakes-eu-become-chinas-top-trading-partner-q1-2020/ (last visited Nov. 18, 2020).

[15] European Commission, *Trade for All: Towards a More Responsible Trade and Investment Policy* (2015), at 31–32.

quasi-interregionalism that link America with ASEAN.[16] Lacking a systemic legal approach to ASEAN has handicapped America's realist power and forfeited the opportunity to forge a common identity from the constructive standpoint. The new dependency theory posits that the collective power of developing countries will galvanize the fundamental shift to the North-South relations.[17] In ASEAN-US ties, this hypothesis can be arguably verified in defense collaboration, but remains unproven in bilateral trade and investment relations.

The chapter provides an overview of US agreements with Asia. It argues that revitalizing the US role as a Pacific power requires enhanced legal frameworks with ASEAN and that such frameworks should form an integral part of the US approach to Asia. The chapter will first assess the Asia polices of Presidents Obama, Trump and Biden and their key trade pacts with Asia-Pacific countries. The chapter will also shed light on the China challenge in the new era of President Xi Jinping and US measures that resulted in the US-China trade war. Moreover, the chapter will examine security and economic initiatives that underpin the ASEAN-US strategic partnership, as well as landmark features of the Trans-Pacific Partnership (TPP) and the subsequent CPTPP.[18]

Finally, the chapter proposes a two-pronged roadmap for the Biden administration to reassert US leadership in new Asian regionalism. The roadmap calls for the White House to prioritize accession to the CPTPP and to broaden its liberalization scope and membership for the CPTPP 2.0 as the new US-led Asia-Pacific trade agreement. At the same time, the roadmap urges transforming the TIFA to the ASEAN-US FTA, which allows for flexible participation by ASEAN countries. These proposals will systemically reinvigorate US engagement with Asia.

II Contextualizing US-Asia Legal Frameworks

Beginning with President Woodrow Wilson (1913–21), liberal internationalism emerged as America's national agenda that yielded global

[16] Fredrik Söderbaum, *Rethinking Regionalism* 176–77 (2016); Heiner Hanggi, *Interregionalism as a Multifaceted Phenomenon: In Search of a Typology, in* Interregionalism and International Relations: A Stepping Stone to Global Governance? 31, 40–41 (Jurgen Ruland et al. 2005).

[17] Alvin Y. So, *Social Change and Development: Modernization, Dependency, and World-System Theories* 160–65 (1990).

[18] Trans-Pacific Partnership Leaders Statement (2015).

implications.[19] The legacy of President Franklin Roosevelt (1933–45) galvanized the "US-led liberal hegemonic order" to become the dominant force that led to the Bretton Woods system in the postwar era.[20] What John Gerard Ruggie termed as "embedded liberalism" is the consequence of America's "unipolar moment" premised on its military and economic preeminence.[21] In Asia, Washington crushed Tokyo's East Asian Co-prosperity Sphere that advanced Japan's "quest for Asian hegemony" during World War II.[22] As Henry Kissinger asserted, Asian countries' balance of power strategy affirmed the status of America as a resident power in the Asian order.[23] After the Cold War, Asian regionalism became feasible because of the "hegemonic stability" that the United States provided for the region.[24]

A Post-Asian Financial Crisis Era

During the presidency of Bill Clinton (1993–2001), the Asian financial crisis and the incapacity of US-led monetary institutions in the 1990s constituted a watershed for new Asian regionalism.[25] Asian governments began to consider a "self-help" approach to economic integration without US participation. Known as the Chiang Mai Initiative, the 2000 "ASEAN Plus Three" financial cooperation became the foundation for ASEAN-based economic integration in the Asia-Pacific.[26] Following the September 11 attacks, the George W. Bush government (2001–09) centered US foreign policy on the Middle East and viewed Asia predominantly through the lens of the war on terror. ASEAN leaders' perception that Bush lacked serious commitments to the region crippled the effectiveness of US initiatives to strengthen bilateral relations. Moreover, the global financial crisis from 2007 to 2009 further galvanized the progress of Asian integration.

19 Ikenberry, *supra* note 10, at 13–14.
20 Ikenberry, *supra* note 10, at 14; G. John Ikenberry, *The Next Liberal Order: The Age of Contagion Demands More Internationalism, Not Less*, 99(4) Foreign Affairs 133, 137–38 (2020).
21 Ruggie, *supra* note 10, at 392–98; Charles Krauthammer, *The Unipolar Moment*, 70(1) Foreign Affairs 23, 24–27 (1990).
22 Henry Kissinger, *World Order* 188–209 (2014).
23 *Id.* at 208–11.
24 Michael C. Webb & Stephen D. Krasner, *Hegemonic Stability Theory: An Empirical Assessment*, 15(2) Rev. Int'l Stud. 183, 183–86 (1989).
25 ASEAN +3 Macroeconomic Research Office, *Theme: ASEAN+3 Region 20 Years after the Asian Financial Crisis*, ASEAN+3 Regional Economic Outlook 2017 (2017), at 46.
26 Rodolfo C. Severino, *Southeast Asia in Search of an ASEAN Community: Insights from the Former ASEAN Secretary-General* 264–69 (2006).

To reinforce the US role as "a Pacific nation," Obama (2009–17) shifted the diplomatic focus to Asia and positioned the TPP as the cornerstone of the pivot to Asia strategy.[27] The TPP signified America's return to Asia. It was seen as the most prominent pathway to the Free Trade Area of the Asia-Pacific (FTAAP), which the Asia-Pacific Economic Cooperation (APEC) envisioned.[28] In the meantime, the ASEAN Plus Three framework evolved to the ASEAN Plus Six framework, which became the basis for the RCEP that excludes the United States.

In tandem with the "America first" rhetoric of President Trump (2017–21), the Free and Open Indo-Pacific strategy underscores "[f]ree, fair, and reciprocal trade."[29] To highlight trade deficits and the costs of unemployment as "alarming results," Trump withdrew America from the TPP and negotiated to amend the North American Free Trade Agreement (NAFTA) and the US-Korea FTA.[30] His harsh stance on the World Trade Organization (WTO) further prompted the move to block the appointment of the Appellate Body Members, essentially paralyzing the WTO's "crown jewel" by compelling it to lose the necessary quorum for adjudicating appeals in 2019.[31]

As for Trump's Asia policy, the emphasis on the "Indo-Pacific" rather than the "Asia-Pacific" underscores the ascending status of India. This geographic concept is by no means new, as former Japanese Prime Minister Shinzo Abe first emphasized the strategic role of the Indo-Pacific in his 2007 speech on "The Confluence of the Two Seas."[32] When depicting "America's Pacific Century," Hillary Clinton also proposed to expand the US alliance to forge an Indo-Pacific partnership.[33]

What marked the contrast between Obama's and Trump's Asia policies is that the former is based on the belief that "an engaged America is vital to Asia's future," whereas the latter is preoccupied with "geopolitical

27 *Remarks by President Barack Obama at Suntory Hall*, Nov. 14, 2009, White House, https://obamawhitehouse.archives.gov/the-press-office/remarks-president-barack-obama-suntory-hall (last visited Nov. 19, 2020).

28 *See* 2010 Leaders' Declaration (2010) ("An FTAAP should be . . . building on ongoing regional undertakings, such as ASEAN+3, ASEAN+6, and the Trans-Pacific Partnership, among others.").

29 Department of Defense, *Indo-Pacific Strategy Report: Preparedness, Partnerships, and Promoting a Networked Region* (2019), at 3–4.

30 USTR, *National Trade Policy for 2017* (2017), at 10–13.

31 *Id.* at 4–5; Brandon J. Murrill, *The WTO's Appellate Body Loses Its Quorum: Is This the Beginning of the End for the "Rules-Based Trading System"?*, CRS Legal Sidebar (2019), at 1–2.

32 Tang Siew Mun, *ASEAN's Hard Look at Indo-Pacific*, 3/2018 ASEAN Focus 6, 6–7 (2018).

33 Hillary Clinton, *America's Pacific Century*, 189 Foreign Pol'y 56, 59 (2011).

competition."[34] In the Biden era, an expected policy change is to restore US-led multilateralism. However, given Biden's commitment to curb the coronavirus crisis and to prioritize investment "in Americans" over FTAs, joining the CPTPP is unlikely to be the immediate focus of the new administration.[35]

B *Inherent Bilateralism: US Trade Approach*

What I call "inherent bilateralism" does not equate with unilateralism. As Article XXIV of the General Agreement on Tariffs and Trade (GATT) envisions, multilateralism can be expected to coexist with, and be achieved by, bilateral agreements. Inherent bilateralism exhibits the long-standing feature of US trade policy that has influenced Asian integration. In 1985, to reduce US trade deficits, President Ronald Reagan's Plaza Accord with Japan resulted in the rapid appreciation of the Japanese yen.[36] This accord prompted Japanese investment into ASEAN and led to business-based regionalization between Northeast and Southeast Asia and subsequent state-led regionalism between these two subregions since the 2000s.[37]

The preferred approach to bilateralism is also evidenced in Obama's TPP negotiations. As a dominant economy, the US strategy was to ensure existing FTA partners' market access commitments and to request concessions from other TPP members in bilateral settings before plenary negotiations.[38] Trump's bilateralism was in clinical isolation from the multilateral or plurilateral context. His "new approach" to achieving "much higher standards of fairness" in bilateral trade deals neither reduced US trade deficits nor made fundamental changes to existing FTAs.[39]

[34] *Id.* at 57–58; President of the United States, *National Security Strategy of the United States of America* (2017), at 45.

[35] Biden, *supra* note 6, at 64–75; *US President-Elect Joe Biden Claims Victory. Read His Speech in Full*, *supra* note 6.

[36] Karen Yeung, *China Urged to Avoid Cautionary Tale of Japan and the Plaza Accord in Currency Deal with US*, Feb. 26, 2019, South China Morning Post, www.scmp.com/economy/china-economy/article/2187773/china-urged-avoid-cautionary-tale-japan-and-plaza-accord (last visited Nov. 20, 2020).

[37] Samuel S. Kim, *Regionalization and Regionalism in Asia*, 4(1) J. E Asian Stud. 39, 40–41 (2004); Sueo Sudo, *Japan's ASEAN Policy: In Search of Proactive Multilateralism* 120–41 (2015).

[38] Deborah K. Elms & C. L. Lim, *An Overview and Snapshot of the TPP Negotiations*, *in* The Trans-Pacific Partnership: A Quest for a Twenty-first-Century Trade Agreement 21, 36–37 (C. L. Lim et al. eds. 2012).

[39] USTR, *supra* note 30, at 10–12.

Table 5.1 *Key US economic agreements with Asia-Pacific countries*[40]

ASEAN (as a bloc)	TIFA (2006)
Brunei Darussalam	TIFA (2002)
Cambodia	BTA (1996); TIFA (2006)
Indonesia	TIFA (1996)
Laos	BTA (2003); TIFA (2016)
Malaysia	TIFA (2004)
Myanmar	TIFA (2013)
Philippines	TIFA (1989)
Singapore	FTA (2003)
Thailand	TIFA (2002)
Vietnam	BTA (2000); TIFA (2007)
Other Countries	
Australia	FTA (2004)
China	Economic and Trade Agreement (Phase One trade deal) (2020)
India	n/a
Japan	Trade Agreement (2019); Digital Trade Agreement (2019)
Korea	FTA (2007); Amendments (2018)
New Zealand	TIFA (1992)
Taiwan	TIFA (1994)

BTA: Bilateral Trade Agreement (including the US-Cambodia Trade Relations & Intellectual Property Rights Agreement and the US-Laos Bilateral Trade Relations Agreement); **FTA**: Free Trade Agreement; **TIFA**: Trade and Investment Framework Arrangement/Agreement

As Table 5.1 above demonstrates, the United States signed FTAs with only three Asia-Pacific countries (Australia, Singapore and South Korea). Over thirty years, multiple TIFAs with ASEAN and Asia-Pacific

[40] *See generally* Office of the United States Trade Representative (USTR), *Trade Agreements*, https://ustr.gov/trade-agreements (last visited Nov. 6, 2020); Enforcement and Compliance, https://tcc.export.gov/Trade_Agreements/All_Trade_Agreements/index.asp (last visited Nov. 6, 2020); USTR, *Fact Sheet: Economic and Trade Agreement between the United States of America and the People's Republic of China* (2000), at 1; Cathleen D. Cimino-Isaacs, *US-Japan Trade Agreement Negotiations*, CRS in Focus (2000), at 1; Simon Lester et al., *Trump's First Trade Dal, Free Trade Bulletin*, No. 73 (2019), at 1–2; USTR, *United States and Taiwan Hold Dialogue on Trade and Investment Priorities*, Oct. 6, 2016, https://ustr.gov/about-us/policy-offices/press-office/press-releases/2016/october/united-states-and-taiwan-hold (last visited Nov. 6, 2020).

countries have mostly facilitated dialogues and resulted in piecemeal government and business initiatives. During the Trump presidency, the conclusion of the United States-Mexico-Canada Agreement (USMCA) and US agreements with Korea and Japan indicated the strong focus on market access for goods rather than WTO-plus issues.

Trump's first "success" to change FTAs was to renegotiate the US-Korea FTA by imposing restrictions on Korea's steel products, increasing the export of US-made vehicles and changing Korean rules on medicine pricing and customs procedures.[41] The twenty-five-year-old NAFTA was updated to the USMCA.[42] The changes include the increase of rules of origin's regional value contents for automobiles from 62.5 percent to 75 percent, greater labor protection clauses including higher minimum salaries for Mexican workers, and access to Canadian dairy markets.[43]

In 2019, the United States signed the separate Trade Agreement and Digital Trade Agreement with Japan. The Trade Agreement is not considered a comprehensive FTA. With the focus on reducing or eliminating tariffs on agricultural and industrial goods, the pact encompasses merely eleven articles, two annexes and six side letters.[44] This unconventional approach departs from past US FTA practice, the 2018 broad-ranging negotiating objectives for the US-Japan trade talks, and the GATT's "substantially all the trade" requirement.[45]

During Japan's 2020 Trade Policy Review, several WTO members such as China and the EU challenged the US-Japan Trade Agreement's compliance with Article XXIV of the GATT.[46] As Canada pointed out, other than the Trade Agreement, Japan and the United States produced no "outcomes from the second round of negotiations."[47] Japan's response was that as Article 5(1) of the Trade Agreement obliges parties to "improve market access in accordance with Annex I or Annex II," the

41 Lester et al., *supra* note 40, at 2–4.

42 Simon Lester & Inu Manak, *The Rise of Populist Nationalism and Renegotiation of NAFTA*, 21(1) J. Int'l Econ. L. 151, 160–67 (2018); Jen Kirby, *USMCA, Trump's New NAFTA Deal, Explained in 600 words*, July 1, 2020, VOX, www.vox.com/2018/10/3/17930092/usmca-mexico-nafta-trump-trade-deal-explained (last visited Nov. 20, 2020).

43 Kirby, *supra* note 42.

44 USTR, *US-Japan Trade Agreement Text*, https://ustr.gov/countries-regions/japan-korea-apec/japan/us-japan-trade-agreement-negotiations/us-japan-trade-agreement-text (last visited Nov. 20, 2020).

45 Cimino-Isaacs, *supra* note 40, at 1–2; USTR, *United States-Japan Trade Agreement (USJTA) Negotiations: Summary of Specific Negotiating Objectives* (2018), at 1–14.

46 *E.g.*, World Trade Organization (WTO), Trade Policy Review, Japan: Minutes of the Meeting: Addendum, WT/TPR/M/397/Add.1 (2020), at 83 & 98.

47 *Id.* at 202.

pact is consistent with Article XXIV.[48] Arguably, Japan's implicit position is that the Trade Agreement can be construed as "an interim agreement" within the meaning of Article XXIV:5.[49] This corollary suggests that the parties may violate WTO obligations to have "a plan and schedule for the formation of" the FTA if Biden does not continue negotiations with Japan's Yoshihide Suga government.[50]

C *Facing Xi's New China: The US-China Trade War*

The trade strategy based on inherent bilateralism culminated in Trump's approach to China, which presented the multifaceted "China challenge" to the unipolar moment of American hegemony.[51] The China challenge was not exceptional to Trump. What was unique was Trump's unilateral, escalating actions against Beijing, premised on the alleged nexus between America's trade loss and China's "economic aggression" and "unfair trading practices."[52] Trump was perceived to utilize the China factor to drive populist protectionism-based trade policy and to unleash public outrage against the White House's poor handling of COVID-19.

In the present-day context, Sino-US relations serve as the most crucial bilateral ties for the global security and economy. As Graham Allison averred, China and the United States risk falling in "Thucydides's Trap," which envisions an inevitable war that occurs when a rising power threatens to displace the existing hegemon.[53] Singapore Prime Minister Lee Hsien Loong emphasized that regardless of the forms and scale, confrontations between the two powers will endanger the Asian century.[54] Undoubtedly, the US-China trade war, Biden's position on the CPTPP, as well as Beijing's membership in the RCEP and potential accession to the CPTPP, are pivotal to new Asian regionalism.[55]

[48] *E.g.*, *id.* at 8, 83, 202–23.
[49] General Agreement on Tariffs and Trade (1994) (GATT), art. XXIV:5.
[50] GATT, art. art. XXIV:5(c).
[51] Office of the Secretary of State, *The Elements of the China Challenge* (2020), at 4–7.
[52] President of the United States, *supra* note 34, at i–25.
[53] Graham Allison, *Destined for War: Can America and China Escape Thucydides's Trap* xvi–xvii (2017).
[54] Lee Hsien Loong, *The Endangered Asian Century: America, China and the Perils of Confrontation*, 99(4) Foreign Aff. 52, 52–61 (2020).
[55] *Full Text of Chinese President Xi Jinping's Remarks at the 27th APEC Economic Leaders' Meeting*, Nov. 20, 2020, www.xinhuanet.com/english/2020-11/20/c_139531308.htm (Nov. 23, 2020).

US-China relations have undergone fundamental changes. America was a close ally of the Kuomintang-led Republic of China (ROC) during World War II. Roosevelt's aspiration for postwar order was for the ROC to be the essential pillar in the Far East. In 1949, the Chinese Communist Party founded the People's Republic China (PRC). The division between the PRC on Mainland China and the ROC on Taiwan resulted in long-lasting issues of the "Taiwan question" and the "one-China policy."[56] President Richard Nixon's normalization process with the PRC in the 1970s proclaimed the strategic transfer of Washington's Cold War containment to engagement policy on Beijing.

Nixon characterized the United States as "the greatest power" and Communist China as "Asia's most immediate threat."[57] However, he believed that America "cannot afford to leave China forever outside the family of nations" because "[t]he world cannot be safe until China changes."[58] Based on this engagement stance, Clinton granted Permanent Normal Trade Relations (PNTR) status to the PRC, paving the way for its accession to the WTO in 2001.[59] Among various reasons, Clinton justified the PNTR decision by claiming that it would accelerate China's political reform and ease its tensions with Taiwan.[60]

China's overtaking of Japan as the world's second largest economy in 2010 and Xi's aggressive pursuit of "the Chinese dream" by seeking "the dominant position" posed unprecedented challenges to Obama and subsequent administrations.[61] In particular, departing from Deng Xiaoping's doctrine of "hide your capacities and bide your time" (韬光养晦), Xi's assertive approach of "Major Country Diplomacy" has attempted to reinforce China's new great power status.[62]

56 Pasha L. Hsieh, *The Taiwan Question and the One-China XE "China, People's Republic of China (PRC)" Policy: Legal Challenges with Renewed Momentum*, 84(3) Die Friedens-Warte: J. Int'l Peace & Organ. 59, 59–66 (2009).

57 Richard M. Nixon, *Asia After Viet Nam*, 46(1) Foreign Aff. 111, 112–19 (1967).

58 *Id.* at 121.

59 *Full Text of Clinton's Speech on China Trade Bill*, Mar. 9, 2000, www.iatp.org/sites/default/files/Full_Text_of_Clintons_Speech_on_China_Trade_Bi.htm (last visited Nov. 23, 2020).

60 *Id.*

61 Yen Nee Lee, *Here Are 4 Charts that Show China's Rise as a Global Economic Superpower*, Sept. 23, 2019, CNBC, www.cnbc.com/2019/09/24/how-much-chinas-economy-has-grown-over-the-last-70-years.html (last visited Nov. 19, 2020); Office of the Secretary of State, *supra* note 51, at 4 & 36.

62 Office of the Secretary of State, *supra* note 51, at 34–35; Congyan Cai, *New Great Powers and International Law in the 21st Century*, 24(3) Eur. J. Int'l L. 775, 775–90 (2013).

Has America's engagement with China prompted its change? The "China reckoning" became the bipartisan consensus – China indeed changed but in an unexpected direction.[63] Contrary to what Nixon and Clinton had envisioned, the PRC neither transformed into a democracy accepted by the Western alliance nor reduced its military threat to the Asia-Pacific.[64] On the contrary, China has become more authoritarian at home and militarily aggressive against its neighbors, including Taiwan and South China Sea claimants.[65] Astonishingly, China's mercantilist-Leninist economic policy has galvanized its industrial dominance in strategic areas such as 5G networks and space technology, which in turn has modernized the Chinese military.[66] As the Belt and Road Initiative and the Asian Infrastructure Investment Bank evidence, China's modernization advances and institutional initiatives inevitably threaten US competitiveness and leadership.

Ironically, over the past half-century, the US-led trade regime provided legitimacy and policy space for China's economic power. In my view, China has seldom challenged international economic law shaped by the West. As a key beneficiary of the world trading system, Beijing has sought to augment its power of discourse in interpreting existing rules. The United States, which built the Bretton Woods system, came to realize that current rules cannot constrain China. Trump's unilateral actions against Beijing were thus based on the belief that WTO rules were "unfair" to America and accorded China "advantages."[67]

The trade war that Trump launched encompasses multiple aspects. The foremost conflict is the imposition of additional tariffs on Chinese exports without the WTO's authorization. From 2018 to 2020, average US tariffs on Chinese exports escalated over six times, from 3.1 percent to 19.3 percent, and China retaliated by increasing tariffs on US goods from 8 percent to 20.3 percent.[68] In 2020, the WTO panel found that US tariff

63 Kurt M. Campbell & Ely Ratner, *The China Reckoning: How Beijing Defied American Expectation*, 97(2) Foreign Aff. 60, 60–63 (2018); *Remarks Delivered by Secretary of State Michael R. Pompeo, July 23, 2020, in* Trump on China: Putting America First 89, 91–95 (2020).

64 Allison, *supra* note 53, at 219–20.

65 Office of the Secretary of State, *supra* note 51, at 9–18.

66 *Id.*

67 Reuters Staff, *Trump Says US Treated Unfairly vs China at WTO: Tweet*, Apr. 6, 2018, Reuters, www.reuters.com/article/us-usa-trade-china-trump-idUSKCN1HD224 (Nov. 24, 2020).

68 Chad P. Brown, *US-China Trade War Tariffs: An Up-to-Date Chart*, Feb. 14, 2020, PIIE Charts, www.piie.com/research/piie-charts/us-china-trade-war-tariffs-date-chart (last visited Nov. 19, 2020).

measures violated Articles I and II of the GATT and did not fall within the "necessary to protect public morals" exception under Article XX(a).[69]

On the security ground, the Trump administration also restricted the access of Huawei and ZTE to US technology and banned two Chinese apps, TikTok and WeChat.[70] The WTO decision on *Russia – Traffic in Transit* makes it difficult to envision that US measures can be justified by the security exceptions under Article XXI of the GATT.[71] In particular, the WTO panel found that Article XXI(b)(iii) is subject to objective determination and is by no means purely "self-judging."[72] Furthermore, in response to Beijing's imposition of draconian National Security Law on Hong Kong, Trump revoked Hong Kong's special status because it is no longer "sufficiently autonomous."[73] This change requires the origin of Hong Kong-produced goods to be marked as "China" rather than "Hong Kong" and prompted the territory to file a WTO complaint against Washington in 2020.[74]

Did the trade war yield tangible results during Trump's presidency? The US-China Bilateral Investment Treaty (BIT) has been negotiated since 2008 but made no breakthroughs in the Trump era, particularly compared to the progress of the EU-China Comprehensive Agreement on Investment.[75] The US-China BIT that includes investment protection is also critical to China because Chinese foreign direct investment (FDI) in America has surpassed US FDI in China since 2011.[76] Instead of finalizing the BIT, the Trump administration focused on the US-China

[69] Panel Report, *United States – Tariff Measures on Certain Goods from China*, WT/DS543/R (2020), paras. 8.1–8.2.

[70] Shelly Banjo et al., *Trump Backs Threats Against China with TikTok, WeChat Bans*, Sept. 18, 2020, Bloomberg, www.bloomberg.com/news/articles/2020-09-18/u-s-to-block-some-wechat-tiktok-transactions-as-of-sunday (last visited Nov. 24, 2020).

[71] Panel Report, *Russia – Measures Concerning Traffic in Transit*, WT/DS512/R (2019), paras. 7.66–7.77. & 7.102–03.

[72] *Id.*; Mona Pinchis-Paulsen, *Trade Multilateralism and US National Security: The Making of the GATT Security Exceptions*, 41 Mich. J. Int'l L. 109, 112–17 (2020).

[73] Request for Consultations by Hong Kong, China, *United States – Origin Marking Requirement*, WT/DS597/1, G/L1365, G/RO/D/8, G/TBT/D/53 (2020), at 1–2.

[74] *Id.*

[75] Kong Qingjiang, *US-China Bilateral Investment Treaty Negotiations: Context, Focus, and Implications*, 7(1) Asian J. WTO & Int'l Health and Policy 181, 183–89 (2012); Joshua P. Meltzer and Neena Shenai, *The US-China Economic Relationship: A Comprehensive Approach*, Brookings Policy Brief (2019), at 18; European Commission, *Key Elements of the EU-China Comprehensive Agreement on Investment* (2020), at 1–2.

[76] Lauren Gloudeman & Nargiza Salidjanova, *Policy Considerations for Negotiating a US-China Bilateral Investment Treaty*, US China Economic and Security Review Commission Staff Research Report (2016), at 5.

Economic and Trade Agreement (the Phase One trade deal), which was concluded in 2020.[77] Unlike an FTA with comprehensive coverage, this agreement encompasses seven chapters that cover selected issues ranging from intellectual property (IP) to exchange rates.

The "expanding trade" commitments of the Phase One trade deal are particularly remarkable, as they oblige China to purchase $200 billion of services and agricultural, manufactured and energy goods in the two-year period.[78] Arguably, these purchase commitments would benefit "red states," which are strongholds for Republicans. Yet, US trade deficits that Trump's tariff measures sought to remedy remained largely unchanged. The deficits with China rose to a peak of $418.9 billion in 2018 and fell to $345.6 billion in 2019, comparable to the amount in 2014.[79]

US tariffs disrupted the regional supply chain but did not necessarily benefit US labor force. To illustrate, tariffs on furniture drove businesses to move their manufacturing bases from China to ASEAN rather than the United States. Chinese tariffs on steel did "create" job opportunities in America, but the same tariffs forced closure of US-based automotive factories. Statistics also demonstrate that the actual amount of China's purchases have lagged much behind the expected progress pursuant to Article 6.2 of the Phase One trade deal.[80]

Based on the analysis above, Trump's "America first" measures proved to be "confrontational without being competitive."[81] Even worse, the global leadership vacuum created by Trump gave Xi an exceptional opportunity. Beijing portrays itself as the guardian of the multilateralism and endeavors to "make China proud again" by

[77] *See generally* Economic and Trade Agreement between the Government of the United States of America and the Government of the People's Republic of China (2020) (US-China Agreement).

[78] *Id.* art. 6.2 & annex 6.1. As of November 2020, China has only met 76 percent, 58 percent and 35 percent of commitments for purchasing US agricultural, manufactured and energy products, respectively. Chad P. Brown, US-China Phase One Tracker: China's Purchases of US goods: As of November 2020, Dec. 23, 2020, PIIE Charts, www.piie.com/research/piie-charts/us-china-phase-one-tracker-chinas-purchases-us-goods (last visited Dec. 24, 2020).

[79] Kimberly Amadeo, *US Trade Deficit with China and Why It's So High*, Oct. 12, 2020, Balance, www.thebalance.com/u-s-china-trade-deficit-causes-effects-and-solutions-3306277 (last visited Nov. 24, 2020).

[80] US-China Agreement, *supra* note 77, art. 6.2(a)–(d); Chad P. Brown, *US-China Phase One Tracker: China's Purchases of US Goods*, Nov. 9. 2020, PIIE Charts, www.piie.com/research/piie-charts/us-china-phase-one-tracker-chinas-purchases-us-goods (last visited Nov. 24, 2020).

[81] Campbell & Ratner, *supra* note 63, at 70.

enhancing its agenda-setting and norm-shaping power.[82] This China challenge persists and confronts the Biden administration. Biden is expected to strengthen the trans-Atlantic alliance and continue "to get tough with China," which he deems as the "most serious competitor."[83] It is unlikely that the existing tariffs on Chinese imports and the Phase One trade deal will change instantly. Biden's approach to the US-China BIT and the CPTPP will inevitably reshape the normative development of new Asian regionalism and the NREO.

III ASEAN-US Strategic Partnership

Much later than the US engagement with major powers in Northeast Asia, Washington only began to interact with ASEAN in the 1970s. Bilateral relations have focused more on security than on trade, which has narrowly highlighted development assistance. Inherent bilateralism has galvanized US partnerships with selected ASEAN states. Compared with the strategies of China, the EU and Japan, the perceived failure of US policy is the lack of engagement with ASEAN "as a bloc" and the absence of compelling legal schemes such as an ASEAN Plus One FTA. The once Obama-led TPP, which includes only four ASEAN countries (Brunei, Malaysia, Singapore and Vietnam), cannot substitute for a comprehensive framework. It also contravenes US interests to solely situate ASEAN in the context of the US-China rivalry.

A Security and Economic Initiatives

The Biden administration's ASEAN policy should intertwine security with economic initiatives. Although the United States became ASEAN's Dialogue Partner in 1977, tangible progress was rather limited.[84] In 2005, ASEAN-US relations became an "enhanced partnership," which was later

[82] Allison, *supra* note 53, 121–26; *id.* at 68–69.
[83] White House, *Remarks by President Biden on America's Place in the World*, Feb. 4, 2021, www.whitehouse.gov/briefing-room/speeches-remarks/2021/02/04/remarks-by-president-biden-on-americas-place-in-the-world/ (last visited Feb. 8, 2021); Biden, *supra* note 6, at 65–76; Lia Eustachewich, *Joe Biden Calls Russia an "Opponent," China a "Competitor" during Town Hall*, Sept. 18, 2020, N.Y. Post, https://nypost.com/2020/09/18/joe-biden-calls-russia-an-opponent-and-china-a-competitor/ (last visited Nov. 26, 2020).
[84] US Mission to ASEAN, *US – ASEAN Timeline*, https://asean.usmission.gov/our-relationship/policy-history/u-s-asean-timeline/ (last visited Nov. 26, 2020); Joint Communique: The First ASEAN-US Dialogue (1977).

elevated to a "strategic partnership" in 2015.[85] On the sidelines of the APEC's Singapore meeting in 2009, Obama became the first US president to meet ASEAN leaders.[86] The ASEAN-US Summit, which forms part of the annual ASEAN Summit and Related Summits, is a forum for US presidents to directly engage ten ASEAN leaders. Other than these ASEAN-hosted meetings, Obama convened the first-ever stand-alone ASEAN-US Summit in Sunnylands, California, in 2016.[87]

Trump's Indo-Pacific strategy alleged to focus on Asia. Nevertheless, Trump only attended the ASEAN-US Summit in 2017 and skipped the following meetings, including the virtual summit in 2020.[88] The relatively low-level US representation disappointed ASEAN countries. Due to COVID-19, Trump's plan for hosting a separate summit in Las Vegas, Nevada was also cancelled.[89] These developments led to survey results showing that 59.1 percent of ASEAN stakeholders acknowledge the deterioration of the US global power and 68 percent of them deem US engagement with ASEAN to have substantially decreased.[90] It is for the Biden administration to convince ASEAN states that "America is back" to the region by proposing legal frameworks rather than political rhetoric or technical assistance-focused "partnerships."[91]

I do not challenge the significance of security in US diplomacy. The US Seventh Fleet guarantees the freedom of navigation in the South China Sea and America's resident power status, which is welcomed by Asian states (except China).[92] Washington's security promises are vital to the

[85] Joint Vision Statement on the ASEAN-US Enhanced Partnership (2005); Joint Statement on the ASEAN-US Strategic Partnership (2015).

[86] US Mission to ASEAN, *supra* note 84.

[87] *Id.*

[88] Hau Ding & Eileen Ng, *Trump Skips Southeast Asia Summit for Third Year in a Row*, Nov. 14, 2020, ABC News, https://abcnews.go.com/International/wireStory/trump-skips-southeast-asia-summit-year-row-74204278 (last visited Nov. 26, 2020).

[89] The US representative was National Security Adviser Robert O-Brien. In 2019, only three ASEAN heads of states (Thailand, Vietnam and Laos) met with him. *Id.* Linette Lai, *Regional Leaders Skip Asean-US Summit, Trump Calls for "Special Summit" in US Next Year*, Nov. 4, 2019, Straits Times, www.straitstimes.com/asia/regional-leaders-skip-asean-us-summit-trumps-representative-invites-leaders-to-special-summit (last visited Nov. 26, 2020).

[90] Tang Siew Mun et al., *Survey Report: State of Southeast Asia: 2019*, 1/2019 ASEAN Focus 6, 10–11 (2019).

[91] Charissa Yong, *"America Is Back": Biden's Picks for Cabinet Signal that Days of "America First" Are Over*, Nov. 25, 2020, Straits Times, www.straitstimes.com/world/united-states/america-is-back-bidens-picks-for-cabinet-signal-that-days-of-america-first-are (last visited Nov. 26, 2020).

[92] Lee, *supra* note 54, at 53–59.

realist balance of power in the region and the collective identity of the defense alliance with Asian partners. The hegemonic stability that America has provided ensures regional peace, which forms the essential geopolitical basis for Asian regionalism.

In Asia, US defense treaty allies include Australia, Japan, South Korea, the Philippines and Thailand.[93] In 2016, India was accorded a unique major defense partner status, which entitles New Delhi to certain treaty ally privileges including access to defense technology.[94] Trump's Indo-Pacific strategy also positioned Singapore, Taiwan and New Zealand as "reliable, capable, and natural partners."[95] The ASEAN countries and ASEAN Dialogue Partners listed above are inevitably at the core of ASEAN-US relations.[96]

The Asia Reassurance Initiative Act of 2018 (ARIA) provides the legal basis for the Indo-Pacific strategy and characterizes ASEAN as a "functional problem-solving regional architecture."[97] The United States reiterates that ASEAN is "central to" Asia because the bloc "is most effective when it speaks one voice about pressing political and security issues."[98] Indeed, ASEAN-led mechanisms, including the twenty-seven-member ASEAN Regional Forum (ARF), eighteen-party ASEAN Defense Ministers' Meeting Plus (ADMM+) and the eighteen-country East Asia Summit (EAS), enable high-level US participation in Asian affairs.[99] The ARF and the presumably more effective ADMM+ focus on security issues, whereas the EAS provides a venue for key economic initiatives such as the RCEP.[100]

The inadequacy of US policy on trade and investment agreements with ASEAN would undermine the US-Asia defense alliance and accelerate China-centered regionalism. The ARIA therefore obliges the US president "to develop to negotiate a comprehensive economic engagement

93 Bruce Vaughn, *U.S Strategic and Defense Relationship in the Asia-Pacific Region*, CRS Report (2007), at 15–16.
94 Department of Defense, *supra* note 29, at 34.
95 *Id.* at 30–33.
96 As of 2020, ASEAN has ten Dialogue Partners, including Australia, Canada, China, the European Union, India, Japan, South Korea, New Zealand, Russia and the United States. *ASEAN Dialogue Coordination July 2015-July 2024*, https://asean.org/asean/external-relations/asean-dialogue-coordinatorship/ (last visited Nov. 25, 2020).
97 Asia Reassurance Initiative Act of 2018 (2018) (ARIA), sec. 102(3).
98 Department of State, *supra* note 5, at 7.
99 Michael Green et al., *Powers, Norms, and Institutions: The Future of the Indo-Pacific from a Southeast Asia Perspective*, Results of a CSIS Survey of Strategic Elites (2020), at 25–26.
100 *Id.*

framework with" ASEAN.[101] In tandem with Trump's Indo-Pacific strategy, ASEAN adopted the ASEAN Outlook on the Indo-Pacific (AOIP) in 2019. While the AOIP does not create a new mechanism, it reaffirms the notion of ASEAN centrality and calls for functional economic cooperation.[102] The ARIA and the AOIP provide a new synergy for the United States and ASEAN to construct comprehensive frameworks.

I call for the ASEAN-US strategic partnership to consolidate and coordinate existing bilateral initiatives. In 2002, the US-proposed Enterprise of ASEAN Initiative (EAI) became the first foundation for bilateral economic relations.[103] ASEAN Economic Minister and the United States Trade Representative (USTR) also launched consultations in the same year.[104] The EAI focuses on bilateral FTAs with individual ASEAN countries, thereby forming a network of FTAs and enhancing ASEAN integration.[105] Pursuant to the EAI, two conditions for a prospective FTA are that an ASEAN country must first accede to the WTO and then sign a TIFA with the United States.[106] As a precursor to a full-fledged FTA, a TIFA provides a senior-level consultative mechanism for resolving outstanding trade and investment obstacles and strengthening economic reform in the potential FTA partner.[107]

The 2012 US-ASEAN Expanded Economic Engagement (E3) Initiative provides "a new framework for economic cooperation."[108] The E3 Initiative centers on trade and investment facilitation with the goal of concluding a trade facilitation agreement and preparing ASEAN countries for meeting the TPP's high standards.[109] At the 2016 Sunnylands Summit, Obama launched the US-ASEAN Connect Initiative, which fortifies the public-private partnership to implement "a whole-of-US

[101] ARIA, sec. 303.

[102] ASEAN Outlook on the Indo-Pacific (2019), paras. 5 & 20.

[103] USTR, *Enterprise for ASEAN Initiative*, https://ustr.gov/archive/Trade_Agreements/Regional/Enterprise_for_ASEAN_Initiative/Section_Index.html (last visited Nov. 26, 2020).

[104] Informal Consultations between the ASEAN Economic Ministers and the United States Trade Representative (AEM-USTR) (2002).

[105] USTR, *supra* note 103.

[106] *Id.*

[107] USTR, *Trade & Investment Framework Agreements*, https://ustr.gov/trade-agreements/trade-investment-framework-agreements (last visited Nov. 26, 2020).

[108] White House, *Fact Sheet: The US-ASEAN Expanded Economic Engagement (E3) Initiative*, Nov. 19, 2012, https://obamawhitehouse.archives.gov/the-press-office/2012/11/19/fact-sheet-us-asean-expanded-economic-engagement-e3-initiative (last visited Nov. 26, 2020).

[109] *Id.*

approach to economic engagement" with ASEAN.[110] This initiative, which involves US enterprises and government agencies, covers projects ranging from agribusiness and clean energy to financial technology.[111]

To buttress the economic pillar of the Indo-Pacific strategy, investment by US government agencies exceeded $2.8 billion.[112] In particular, the United States has assisted ASEAN countries in creating the ASEAN Single Window, a key project of the ASEAN Economic Blueprint 2025 to accelerate customs procedures and facilitate a "more unified market" for goods.[113] Bilateral negotiations for linking the ASEAN Single Window with the US customs system were also launched.[114] Additional new connectivity initiatives include the smart cities network that addresses urbanization and cybersecurity issues and the Mekong power partnership, which develops ASEAN-based energy infrastructure with Japan.[115] The new Plan of Action for the ASEAN-US strategic partnership (2021–25) will continue to be based on the ASEAN-US TIFA, the E3 work plan and the Connect Initiative.[116]

B TIFA and FTAs

Multifaceted US initiatives emphasize attention on ASEAN. However, most projects are preoccupied with economic cooperation, trade facilitation and investment. Compared to Chinese, European and Japanese strategies toward ASEAN, a key flaw of ASEAN-US economic relations is the lack of upgraded and integrated legal frameworks that expand trade and investment liberalization. Washington concluded the TIFA with ASEAN in 2006 and separate bilateral TIFAs with nine ASEAN countries by 2016.[117] None

[110] US Mission to ASEAN, *US-ASEAN Connect Initiative*, https://asean.usmission.gov/our-relationship/policy-history/usaseanconnect-2/ (last visited Nov. 26, 2020).

[111] *Id.*

[112] Department of State, *2019 Indo-Pacific Business Forum Showcases High-Standard US Investment*, Nov. 3, 2019, www.state.gov/2019-indo-pacific-business-forum-showcases-high-standard-u-s-investment/ (last visited Nov. 27, 2020).

[113] US Mission to ASEAN, *The United States and ASEAN: Expanding the Enduring Partnership*, Nov. 3, 2019, https://asean.usmission.gov/the-united-states-and-asean-expanding-the-enduring-partnership/ (last visited Nov. 27, 2020); ASEAN Economic Blueprint 2025 (2015), para. 10(iii)(b).

[114] US Mission to ASEAN, *supra* note 113.

[115] *Id.*

[116] Plan of Action to Implement the ASEAN-United States Strategic Partnership (2021–25), paras 2 & 4. Previous initiatives are included in the Plan of Action to Implement the ASEAN-US Strategic Partnership (2016–20) and the Plan of Action to Implement the ASEAN-US Enhanced Partnership for Enduring Peace and Prosperity (2011–15).

[117] USTR, *supra* note 107.

of these TIFAs evolved to be US FTAs with ASEAN or individual ASEAN states.

The only "success" was the US-Singapore FTA. Uniquely, US-Singapore FTA negotiations were conducted under neither the EAI nor the TIFA.[118] It was Singapore Prime Minister Goh Chok Tong who proposed the FTA to Clinton at a golf game during the Brunei-hosted APEC summit in 2000.[119] Subsequent negotiations led to the signing of America's first FTA with an Asian country in 2003.[120] "Fast-track" negotiations of this FTA were due to Singapore's duty-free trade regime and its limited agricultural sector, making the island state very different from other ASEAN states.

The United States concluded BTAs with Cambodia, Laos and Vietnam before signing respective TIFAs.[121] Unlike FTAs, the BTAs formed part of the postwar normalization process and contain relatively short provisions on trade in goods and services, IP rights and investment issues.[122] Under Section 402 of Title IV of the Trade Act of 1974 (the Jackson-Vanik amendment), concluding a BTA is a necessary step for the United States to restore most-favored-nation treatment to selected socialist countries.[123] The BTAs facilitated the accession of these three ASEAN countries to the WTO and further economic relations with the United States.

Other than the US-Singapore FTA and BTAs, several attempts for trade agreements failed. The United States and Thailand launched FTA negotiations in 2004.[124] Relying on the US-Singapore FTA as the model, obstacles

118 There was no Trade and Investment Agreement between the United States and Singapore. *See also* Dean A. DeRosa, *US Free Trade Agreements with ASEAN*, *in* Free Trade Agreements: US Strategies and Priorities 117, 117 ft 1 (Jeffrey J. Schott ed. 2004) ("The negotiations of the US-Singapore FTA began before November 2002 – that is, the US-Singapore FTA was negotiated outside the EAI.").

119 *Statement of Tommy Koh*. Ministry of Trade and Industry, Video of the FTA Symposium 2019, www.youtube.com/watch?v=IiAoCLqcnGI&feature=youtu.be&fbclid=IwAR2dFQUT_gGjgOmAHZC3M2h-pDP5N6prGu1TzlAKCbNthE8VdGsJbe8gLvA (last visited Nov. 27, 2020).

120 USTR, *supra* note 40.

121 Note that the US-Cambodia agreement is called the Trade Relations & Intellectual Property Rights Agreement. Enforcement and Compliance, *supra* note 40.

122 Specialist in Asian Affairs & Specialist in International Trade and Finance, *Vietnam PNTR Status and WTO Accession Issues and Implications for the United States*, CRS Report (2007), at 10–13.

123 Analyst in Asian Affairs, Foreign Affairs, Defense, and Trade Division, *The Vietnam-US Bilateral Trade Agreement*, CRS Report (2002), at 2–7.

124 Raymond J. Ahearn & Wayne M. Morrison, *US-Thailand Free Trade Agreements*, CRS Report (2006), at 1.

arose when it came to agricultural goods and IP rights.[125] Due to Thailand's military coup, FTA negotiations were suspended in 2006 and have yet to resume.[126] The US-Malaysia FTA talks commenced in 2006, but were halted in 2008 because of Washington's support for Israel's military operation in Gaza.[127] Economically, what surfaced as a main hurdle was Malaysia's procurement policy that favors ethnic Malays (known as *Bumiputera*).[128] The potential change to the country's New Economic Program that accords a certain share of government projects to them made it difficult for Malaysia to open the public procurement market.[129] In 2010, the Obama administration notified the Congress that FTA talks with Malaysia would shift to bilateral negotiations within the TPP context.[130]

As for Vietnam, the US-Vietnam BTA urges both parties to negotiate a BIT "in good faith within a reasonable period of time" and implementing the BTA forms part of the TIFA's work program.[131] The BIT negotiations were launched in 2008, but additional negotiations have not been scheduled since 2010 arguably because of the same TPP reason for the US-Malaysia FTA.[132] Trump's withdrawal from the TPP essentially made "upgraded" economic pacts with these ASEAN countries impossible.

Interestingly, to enhance the security alliance with the Rodrigo Duterte government and to "prevent" the Philippines from siding with China, the Trump administration intended to commence FTA negotiations after finalizing the USMCA in 2019.[133] Although the US-Philippines FTA may become America's second FTA with an ASEAN country, the actual progress for the talks was limited. Biden's cautious attitude toward FTAs also diminishes the chance for concluding the US-Philippine FTA.

125 *Id.* at 6–11.

126 Emma Chanlett-Avery et al., *Thailand: Background and US Relations*, CRS Report (2015), at 8–9.

127 Michael F. Martin, *The Proposed US Malaysia Free Trade Agreement*, CRS Report (2008), at 2 & 5–6.

128 *Id.* at 1 fn. 4.

129 *Id.* at 9–10.

130 Ian F. Fergusson & Bruce Vaughn, *The Trans-Pacific Partnership Agreement*, CRS Report (2011), at 4–5.

131 US-Vietnam BTA (2000), art. 13; US-Vietnam TIFA (2007), annex.

132 Michael F. Martin, *US-Vietnam Economic and Trade Relations: Issues in 2019*, CRS: In Focus (2019), at 2.

133 Elijah Felice Rosales, *US, PHL to Open Talks on Free-trade Deal*, Nov. 25, 2019, BM, https://businessmirror.com.ph/2019/11/25/us-phl-to-open-talks-on-free-trade-deal/ (last visited Nov. 30, 2020).

IV From the TPP to the CPTPP

Rather than focusing on ASEAN, the Obama administration's TPP initiative underpinned the rebalance or the pivot to Asia strategy. The TPP built on the Trans-Pacific Strategic Economic Partnership (P4 Agreement), which took effect between four Pacific Rim countries including Singapore, New Zealand, Chile and Brunei in 2006.[134] After the Bush administration indicated its intention to join the negotiations of the extended P4 Agreement in 2008, Obama notified the Congress to negotiate the renamed TPP in the following year.[135] The framework for the mega-FTA was decided at the sideline of the APEC Ministerial Meeting in 2011 and Japan's participation in negotiations in 2013 significantly magnified the economic scale of the TPP.[136]

A Evolution and Accession Process

In 2016, twelve TPP parties, including the United States, signed the landmark agreement in Auckland, New Zealand.[137] The United States was "never" a party to the TPP. Obama suspended the efforts for the US Congress to ratify the TPP due to insufficient congressional support and the "unexpected" Trump's election victory.[138] In January 2017, the Trump administration notified the depositary of the TPP, New Zealand, that America "does not intend to become a party to the" TPP and hence bears "no legal obligations arising from its signature."[139]

Trump's decision frustrated US allies in Asia. However, under the leadership of Australia, Canada and Japan, the new CPTPP (known as TPP-11) was signed in Santiago, Chile in 2018.[140] A key driver for concluding the CPTPP is

[134] Elms & Lim, *supra* note 38, at 21–22.
[135] Fergusson & Williams, *supra* note 5, at 1.
[136] *Id.* 1–2.
[137] Australian Government: Department of Foreign Affairs and Trade (DFAT), *CPTPP News*, www.dfat.gov.au/trade/agreements/in-force/cptpp/news/Pages/cptpp-news (last visited Dec. 7, 2020).
[138] David Lawder, *Obama Administration Suspends Pacific Trade Deal Vote Effort*, Nov. 12, 2016, Reuters, https://fr.reuters.com/article/us-trade-tpp-idUSKBN13629G (last visited Dec. 7, 2020).
[139] Letter from María L. Pagán, Acting United States Trade Representative, to the Trans-Pacific Partnership Depositary, Jan. 30, 2017.
[140] DFAT, *supra* note 137; Ralph Jennings, *How an Australia-Canada-Japan Led TPP-11 Trade Deal Compares to China's Alternative*, Mar. 13, 2019, Forbes, www.forbes.com/sites/ralphjennings/2018/03/13/how-japan-australia-and-nine-friends-will-resist-china-in-world-trade/?sh=297e2a777dd6 (last visited Dec. 8, 2020).

the competition from the RCEP, whose parties finalized negotiations for seven out of twenty chapters in the same year.[141] Under international law, the CPTPP is a treaty separate from the TPP but incorporates original TPP contents with the exception of twenty-two provisions that were suspended under the CPTPP Annex.[142] While the CPTPP entered into force in 2018, Brunei, Chile, Malaysia and Peru have yet to ratify the pact as of 2020.[143]

The CPTPP Commission has convened since 2019 and the parties stressed the significance of the pact expediting post–COVID-19 economic recovery.[144] They also noted "the interest shown by several economies to accede to the CPTPP" and to comply with its "high standards."[145] The accession process for "an aspirant economy" mandates informal engagement with existing signatories and the subsequent formal process including the creation of an accession working group.[146] The CPTPP Commission will decide the application outcome "by consensus."[147]

Countries such as Taiwan and Thailand had previously indicated their intention to join the CPTPP and the United Kingdom applied to accede to the mega-FTA in 2021.[148] PRC President Xi also announced that China "will favorably consider joining the" CPTPP at the 2020 virtual APEC summit.[149] His declaration echoes Beijing's 14th Five-Year Plan that calls for "building a high-standard free trade area network with global reach" in order to achieve the "basic socialist modernization" objective under the Vision 2035.[150] China's stance prompted Korea to announce its interest in

141 Joint Leaders' Statement on the RCEP Negotiations (2018).

142 DFAT, *supra* note 137; Jennings, *supra* note 140; Comprehensive and Progressive Agreement for Trans-Pacific Partnership (2018), arts. 1–2; see Deborah Elms, *Understanding the CPTPP*, 6/2017 ASEAN Focus 8, 8 (2017) ("Overall, approximately 28 total pages have been frozen from the 622 pages of rules.").

143 DFAT, *supra* note 137.

144 CPTPP Statement on the Occasion of the Third Commission Meeting (2020), at 2.

145 *Id.* at 3.

146 Comprehensive and Progressive Agreement for Trans-Pacific Partnership (CPTPP) Accession Process, Annex to CPTPP/COM/2019/D002, paras. 1–3.

147 *Id.* para. 4.1.

148 Ben Blanchard, *Taiwan Talks up Trans-Pacific Trade Pact after Exclusion from New Deal*, Nov. 16, 2020, Reuters, https://cn.reuters.com/article/taiwan-trade-idINKBN27W0BG (last visited Dec. 8, 2020); Department for International Trade & The Rt Hon Elizabeth Truss MP, UK Applies to Join Huge Pacific Free Trade Area CPTPP, Jan. 30, 2021, www.gov.uk/government/news/uk-applies-to-join-huge-pacific-free-trade-area-cptpp (last visited Feb. 4, 2021).

149 *Full Text of Chinese President Xi Jinping's Remarks at the 27th APEC Economic Leaders' Meeting*, *supra* note 55.

150 中共中央关于制定国民经济和社会发展第十四个五年规划和二〇三五年远景目标的建议 [The Central Committee of the Chinese Community Party's Proposals for

joining the CPTPP because Seoul's membership will no longer "upset" Beijing and will upgrade trade ties with existing FTA partners in ASEAN.[151]

The potential accession of China and other US allies to the CPTPP is a wake-up call for the Biden administration. In Obama's words, the original "TPP allows America – and not countries like China – to write the rules of the road in the 21st century."[152] The TPP's comprehensive contents were set as benchmarks for US FTAs. In practice, the Obama administration transplanted the US approach to FTAs into the TPP and enhanced its standards to maximize US economic interests. Trump's decision to pull the United States out of the TPP substantially decreased the share of gross domestic product (GDP) of the pact from 38.2 percent to 13.5 percent, lower than half of that of the RCEP.[153] What the Biden administration needs to consider is the leverage that China may gain from its CPTPP membership. More fundamentally, America's exclusion from the CPTPP will deprive the United States from rule-shaping leadership in new Asian regionalism.

B Key Features and Challenges

Claimed as a twenty-first-century trade agreement, the TPP's thirty chapters encompass rules beyond tariffs, services and investment.[154] The independent chapters on state-owned enterprises (SOEs), anti-corruption, labor and environmental protection, which the RCEP omits, buttress the CPTPP's impact on constructing the NREO. For its economic and geopolitical salience, the CPTPP is perceived as a novel "megaregulation," which represents extensive regulatory governance on a transregional scale.[155] In terms of market access for goods, the CPTPP will eliminate 99 percent of tariff lines of goods traded

Formulating the 14th Five-Year Plan (2021–25) for National Economic and Social Development and the Long-Range Objectives through the Year 2035] (2020), www.gov.cn/zhengce/2020-11/03/content_5556991.htm (last visited Dec. 10, 2020).

151 Jung Suk-yee, *South Korea Moving to Join CPTPP*, Dec. 9, 2020, Bus. Korea, www.businesskorea.co.kr/news/articleView.html?idxno=56443 (last visited Dec. 9, 2020).

152 Statement by the President on the Signing of the Trans-Pacific Partnership (2016).

153 Yasu Ota & Shuichi Maruyama, *Ocean's Eleven*, 2018–12–18 Nikkei Asian Rev. 10, 16 (2018); *see* Summary of the Regional Comprehensive Economic Partnership Agreement (2020) ("RCEP participating countries account for about 30% of the global GDP . . . .").

154 C. L. Lim et al., *What Is "High-Quality, Twenty-First Century" Anyway? in* The Trans-Pacific Partnership: A Quest for a Twenty-first-Century Trade Agreement 3, 8–10 (C. L. Lim et al. eds. 2012).

155 Benedict Kingsbury et al., *Introduction: The Essence, Significance, and Problems of the Trans-Pacific Partnership, in* Megaregulation Contested: Global Economic Ordering after TPP 1, 2–3 (Benedict Kingsbury et al. eds. 2019).

among eleven parties, whereas the RCEP's tariff liberalization rate is 92 percent.[156] There exists a degree of flexibility in implementing the CPTPP. Tariff schedules accord lengthier periods for countries to cut tariffs on selected products. For instance, the agreement allows sixteen years for Japan to eliminate tariffs on seafood and for Malaysia to make wine duty free.[157]

The CPTPP will shift the regional supply chain. In Asia, commonly traded goods are electronic products, which are mostly covered by the WTO's Information Technology Agreement (ITA) that enables zero tariff. As the ITA does not cover mobile phones, manufacturers in one CPTPP country such as Vietnam will likely import components from, and export final products to, CPTPP parties.[158] A related controversial issue involves the CPTPP's rules of origin. The CPTPP incorporates "yarn-forward" rules under which only apparel made with imported textile inputs from CPTPP parties qualify for duty-free status.[159] These rules, which were included in US FTAs, are what the US textile industry preferred. However, the rules have posed challenges to Vietnam's garment industry because it heavily relies on yarns and fabrics from non-CPTPP parties including China, Korea and Taiwan.[160]

As for services commitments, the CPTPP adopts the progressive negative list approach. Three trade in services-related chapters incorporate provisions on financial services, the temporary entry for business persons, and professional services such as architectural, engineering and legal services.[161] In the area of investment protection, most attention has focused on the CPTPP's investor-state dispute settlement (ISDS). The TPP's ISDS provisions are modeled after the US BITs, which go beyond earlier BITs by including more detailed arbitration rules than the Convention on the Settlement of Investment Disputes between States

156 Government of Canada, *About Tariff Elimination under the CPTPP*, www.international.gc.ca/trade-commerce/trade-agreements-accords-commerciaux/agr-acc/cptpp-ptpgp/tariff-elimination-droits_de_douane.aspx?lang=eng (last visited Dec. 10, 2020); Ministry of Trade and Trade Industry Singapore, Regional Comprehensive Economic Partnership Signed (2020), at 4.

157 APL Logistics et al., *Understanding the TPP11: Market Access for Goods* (2017), at 6–9.

158 Asian Trade Centre, *Ten Benefits of the Comprehensive and Progressive Trans-Pacific Partnership (CPTPP)* (2018), at 5.

159 Fergusson & Williams, *supra* note 5, at 20–21.

160 Vu Dung, *Vietnam Imports US$6.6 billion in Textile-Garment Materials in H1*, Aug. 12, 2019, Saigon Times, https://english.thesaigontimes.vn/70513/vietnam-imports-us$66-billion-in-textile-garment-materials-in-h1.html (last visited Dec. 10, 2020).

161 Trans-Pacific Partnership (2016) (TPP), chs. 10–12.

and Nationals of Other States.[162] This type of US-style ISDS is incorporated in ASEAN Plus One FTAs and presents a different investment protection model from the EU's Investment Court System. Tellingly, ISDS caused concerns not just to ASEAN states but also to Australia and New Zealand. The *Philip Morris* case that Australia encountered led to the tobacco carveout clause of the TPP's arbitration rules.[163]

Following US withdrawal, CPTPP parties narrowed the scope of the TPP's ISDS by disallowing investors' claims based on private investment contracts and violations of the minimum standard of treatment pertinent to financial services.[164] New Zealand Prime Minister Jacinda Ardern took an even further step. In 2017, her cabinet announced that New Zealand will "ensure that no further free-trade agreements include ISDS clauses."[165] By signing side agreements with five CPTPP countries, New Zealand excludes ISDS entirely with those parties.[166]

The CPTPP incorporates additional landmark features of the TPP that makes it "a new type of trade deal."[167] To illustrate, electronic commerce provisions constitute a breakthrough to FTA norms on digital trade. The CPTPP includes notable rules that protect personal information and the free flow of data transfer, as well as prohibitions against members from requiring foreign companies to locate computing facilities in their territories.[168] As I pointed out in Chapter 4, Vietnam's Cybersecurity Law violates CPTPP rules on cross-border data flows and the prohibition on data localization. Although the CPTPP and Vietnam's side letters enable the socialist government to be immune from dispute settlement during grace periods, the law constitutes a bad-faith implementation and cannot be justified on "legitimate public policy" grounds.[169] Washington expressed concern

[162] Luke Nottage, *The Investment Chapter and ISDS in the TPP: Lessons from Southeast Asia*, ISEAS Yusof Ishak Institute Economics Working Papers, No. 2017-2 (2017), at 14–15.

[163] TPP, art. 29.5.

[164] DFAT, CPTPP Suspensions Explained (2019), at 1–2.

[165] Post-Cabinet Press Conference: Monday, Oct. 31, 2017 (2017), at 1.

[166] These countries include Australia, Brunei, Malaysia, Peru and Vietnam. New Zealand Foreign Affairs & Trade, *Comprehensive and Progressive Agreement for Trans-Pacific Partnership Text and Resources*, www.mfat.govt.nz/en/trade/free-trade-agreements/free-trade-agreements-in-force/cptpp/comprehensive-and-progressive-agreement-for-trans-pacific-partnership-text-and-resources/ (last visited Dec. 11, 2020).

[167] Statement by the President on the Signing of the Trans-Pacific Partnership, *supra* note 152.

[168] TPP, arts. 14.8, 14.11 & 14.13.

[169] TPP, arts. 14.11.3, 14.13.3, & 14.18.

about Cybersecurity Law, but it is clear that TIFA dialogues did not make Vietnam reconsider implementing the law.[170]

The chapter on SOEs ensures that states cannot accord SOEs favorable treatment in commercial considerations or noncommercial assistance.[171] The CPTPP's requirements on governments' dealings with SOEs would hinder China's accession application. In addition, the CPTPP also includes chapters on non-tariff barriers, which presently restrict trade no less than tariffs. Some exceptions are critical to Islamic countries such as Malaysia. For example, provisions on sanitary and phytosanitary measures do not prevent countries from imposing "halal requirements for food and food products in accordance with Islamic law."[172]

As only five CPTPP countries are parties to the WTO's Agreement on Government Procurement, the CPTPP helps enterprises to accede additional public procurement markets.[173] A deal-breaker issue for the US-Malaysia FTA was the *Bumiputera* policy. Malaysia was permitted to maintain the policy pursuant to its government procurement annex to the TPP.[174] Furthermore, the chapter on development that stresses sustainable development goals and the role of women "in the domestic and global economy" indicates the value-based components of the CPTPP.[175] Unlike development provisions that are excluded from dispute settlement, the chapters on labor and environmental protection are enforceable under the general dispute settlement mechanism.[176] The enforceability of these chapters reflects the US "sanctions" model and was surprisingly not suspended by the CPTPP.

V A Comprehensive Roadmap to Asia

At the inception of the Biden era, the White House is expected to focus on domestic issues rather than FTAs.[177] However, fundamental geopolitical changes should prompt the Biden administration to revitalize America's

170 US Chamber of Commerce, *The Next Stage of US-Vietnam Relations: A Blueprint to Deepen Trade and Investment Ties* (2019), at 8.
171 TPP, arts. 17.4 & 17.6.
172 TPP, art. 7.3.1.
173 Australia, Canada, Japan, New Zealand and Singapore are parties to the Agreement on Government Procurement. WTO, *Parties, Observers and Accessions*, www.wto.org/english/tratop_e/gproc_e/memobs_e.htm (last visited Dec. 11, 2020).
174 TPP, annex 15-A, Schedule of Malaysia, sec. G.1.
175 TPP, arts. 23.1.5 & 23.4.
176 TPP, arts. 19.15 & 20.23.
177 Biden, *supra* note 6, at 64–75.

strategy. An assertive, sustainable strategy will not only respond to the growing influence of China over global institutions and FTAs, but also restore US leadership in shaping norms of new Asian regionalism. I propose a two-pronged roadmap, which calls for Washington to reconsider joining the CPTPP and concluding the ASEAN-US FTA.

A US Accession to the CPTPP

As for the CPTPP, access to the US market will accord America sufficient leverage to expand existing members' commitments and elevate current standards. Rebuilding the CPTPP will make it a new US-led Asia-Pacific initiative.[178] The suspended provisions of the original TPP concentrate on ISDS and IP rights such as the term of protection for copyright.[179] The United States can be the pivotal force in shaping the CPTPP 2.0 by first bringing the CPTPP "back" to original TPP standards. The subsequent step will strengthen the standards of SOEs, labor and environmental protection, as well as expedite negotiations for additional commitments in areas such as government procurement.

`A concurrent step is to make the accession process more comprehensive, so that CPTPP 2.0 membership will be primarily for "democratic Asia." Among US allies, the CPTPP's further expansion is of particular importance to Taiwan. Beijing's political pressure has led to Taipei's exclusion from FTAs including the RCEP. For Japan, Taiwan's ban on food products from areas affected by the 2011 Fukushima Daiichi nuclear disaster has hindered Tokyo's support for Taipei's CPTPP accession.[180] Other CPTPP members' positions on Taiwan implicitly relate to China's potential accession to the pact. Hence, US policy on the CPTPP will be key to Taiwan.

The 1994 US-Taiwan TIFA has failed to yield substantive outcomes. The ARIA mandates that the US government develop "close economic, political, and security relationship" with Taiwan.[181] A new momentum for supporting the conclusion of a BTA with Taiwan is indicated by fifty

[178] Jeffrey J. Schott, *Rebuild the Trans-Pacific Partnership Back Better*, Trade and Investment Policy Watch, Nov. 30, 2020, www.piie.com/blogs/trade-and-investment-policy-watch /rebuild-trans-pacific-partnership-back-better (last visited Dec. 29, 2020).

[179] DFAT, *supra* note 164, at 1–6.

[180] Liang Pei-chi et al., *Interview/Taiwan's Ban on Japan's Fukushima Food Hindering CPTPP Bid: Minister*, Nov. 19, 2020, CNA, https://focustaiwan.tw/politics/ 202011190017 (last visited Dec. 15, 2020).

[181] ARIA, sec. 209(a)(1).

Senators' letter to the USTR in 2020.[182] Nevertheless, the USTR has yet to commence talks with Taipei presumably because of the concerns about the progress of the Phase One trade deal with Beijing.

Notable progress occurred in 2020 when the Department of State launched the US-Taiwan Economic Prosperity Partnership Dialogue (EPPD).[183] Rather than focusing on the BTA or FTA issues, the EPPD that coexists and complements the TIFA centers on industry cooperation in arenas such as 5G networks and supply chains. Moreover, the Tsai Ing-wen government's decision to permit US port imports containing ractopamine is seen as a step for "normalizing" bilateral trade.[184] These developments are positive for Washington's support of Taipei joining the US-led CPTPP 2.0. Taiwan's CPTPP membership will, in turn, reinforce the Biden administration's "rock-solid" commitments to Taiwan and engagement with Asia in response to the China challenge.[185]

B New Momentum for the ASEAN-US FTA

In addition to the CPTPP, the Biden administration should consider pursuing the ASEAN-US FTA, which functions as an ASEAN Plus One agreement. While the CPTPP aims at Asian countries ready for implementing high-standard commitments, the ASEAN-US FTA can follow an incremental, development-focused approach that consolidates and monitors existing initiatives. At present, all ten ASEAN countries are parties to the RCEP. Given that the CPTPP encompasses only four ASEAN members, the ASEAN-US FTA will better "offset" China's expanded power in the RCEP and ASEAN. Consequently, the CPTPP and the ASEAN-US FTA can collectively form America's comprehensive

182 Reuters Staff, *50 US Senators Call for Talks on Trade Agreement with Taiwan*, Oct. 2, 2020, Reuters, www.reuters.com/article/us-usa-taiwan-china/50-u-s-senators-call-for-talks-on-trade-agreement-with-taiwan-idUSKBN26M7HL (last visited Dec. 15, 2020); Schott, *supra* note 178.

183 US Department of State, *Inaugural US-Taiwan Economic Prosperity Partnership Dialogue*, Nov. 20, 2020, www.state.gov/inaugural-u-s-taiwan-economic-prosperity-partnership-dialogue/ (last visited Dec. 15, 2020).

184 Reuters Staff, *Thousands Join Taiwan Protest, Anger Focused on US Pork*, Nov. 22, Reuters, www.reuters.com/article/taiwan-protests-idINKBN28206Z (last visited Dec. 15, 2020).

185 US Department of State, *PRC Military Pressure Against Taiwan Threatens Regional Peace and Stability*, Jan. 23, 2021, www.state.gov/prc-military-pressure-against-taiwan-threatens-regional-peace-and-stability/ (last visited Feb. 4, 2021).

roadmap to Asia and accomplish Biden's goal of forging alliance and restoring US leadership.

The idea for the ASEAN-US FTA is not new. In 1989, the US International Trade Commission (USITC) deliberated the feasibility of the ASEAN-US FTA but came to the conclusion that the FTA would be premature for reasons such as "limited economic benefits to" America and ASEAN's insufficient negotiation resources.[186] In 2009 and 2011, Republican Senator Richard Lugar introduced bills to urge the USTR to "establish a strategy for initiating" FTA negotiations with ASEAN.[187] Lugar emphasized that while he supported Obama's TPP initiative, the ASEAN-US FTA would buttress US commitments to ASEAN leaders, who would otherwise pursue "comprehensive trade interaction" with countries such as China.[188] Lugar's prediction is accurate, as ASEAN significantly expedited the FTA progress with China and RCEP members.

The ASEAN-US FTA is no longer premature. The status of ASEAN has fundamentally changed, as ASEAN's economic benefits to the United States have become substantial. As the world's fifth largest economy, ASEAN is America's eleventh trade partner.[189] The fact that the United States accounts for 15.2 percent of ASEAN's FDI inflows makes America ASEAN's largest FDI source.[190] The creation of the ASEAN Economic Community and the conclusion of ASEAN Plus One FTAs and the RCEP have also fortified ASEAN's negotiation resources and experiences.

Given ASEAN centrality in Asia's security and trade initiatives, it is time for the United States to upgrade the 2006 TIFA with ASEAN to a full-fledged FTA. The ARIA, the legal basis for the Indo-Pacific strategy, also stresses the US-ASEAN strategic partnership and urges the White House to "negotiate a comprehensive economic engagement framework with" ASEAN.[191] The ASEAN-US FTA is the response to the ARIA mandate.

[186] United States International Trade Commission (USITC), *The Pros and Cons of Entering Into Negotiations on Free Trade Area Agreements with Taiwan, the Republic of Korea, and ASEAN, or the Pacific Rim Region in General: Reports to the Senate Committee on Finance on Investigation No. TA-332–259 under Section 332 of the Tariff Act of 1930, USITC Publications 2166* (1989), at 3-3–3-8.

[187] S. Res. 311 (111th Congress) (2009); S. Res. 218 (112th Congress) (2011). Both resolutions were not adopted.

[188] *Lugar Urges US-Asean FTA Negotiations*, Jun. 29, 2011, Nation, www.bilaterals.org/?lugar-urges-us-asean-fta&lang=es (last visited Dec. 15, 2020).

[189] ASEAN Secretariat, ASEAN Key Figures 2020 (2020), at 39; USTR, *supra* note 3.

[190] ASEAN Secretariat, *supra* note 189, at 57.

[191] ARIA, secs. 205 & 303.

1 EU Model

What should be the approach to achieving the ASEAN-US FTA? There are two models for the Biden administration to consider. The EU follows the building-block approach.[192] The EU prioritizes high-standard, bilateral agreements with individual ASEAN countries. These pathfinder agreements subsequently form a network of FTAs that serve as a basis for the ASEAN-EU FTA. EU agreements with Singapore and Vietnam also include important features that envision the region-to-region FTA, including particularly rules of origin for ASEAN cumulation. As the United Kingdom concluded FTAs with Singapore and Vietnam in 2020, London is expected to follow Brussels' building-block approach for the prospective ASEAN-UK FTA.[193] These Western allies' strategy for ASEAN Plus One agreements serves as a model for the United States.

The United States may also consider transplanting certain designs of the US-Singapore FTA to other bilateral agreements with ASEAN countries. To illustrate, the fact that the US-Singapore FTA covers Batam and Bintan Special Economic Zones in two Indonesian islands has facilitated Indonesian exports to America.[194] The US-Singapore FTA's rules of origin also incorporate an innovative mechanism, the Integrated Sourcing Initiative (ISI).[195] The ISI enables certain medical equipment and information technology products to count as Singapore goods.[196] The absence of the requirement to prove the origin of ISI products prompts ASEAN businesses to link to Singapore for the FTA's preferential treatment. Comparable to the purpose of ASEAN cumulation under EU FTAs, the features of the US-Singapore FTA create spillover economic benefits for other ASEAN states and benefit negotiations for the ASEAN-US FTA.

2 Asian Model

Distinct from the EU approach, Asia-Pacific countries follow the model of the ASEAN way for their respective FTAs with ASEAN. In particular,

[192] European Commission, *supra* note 15.

[193] *UK Strikes Singapore and Vietnam Trade Deals, Start of New Era of Trade with Asia*, Dec. 11, 2020, www.gov.uk/government/news/uk-strikes-singapore-and-vietnam-trade-deals-start-of-new-era-of-trade-with-asia (last visited Dec. 16, 2020).

[194] *See* Razeen Sally, *Southeast Asia in the WTO* 58–59 (2004) (stating that the agreement includes "innovative provisions for goods manufactured in Batam and Bintan, and trans-shipped through Singapore, to have duty-free access to the US market").

[195] Annex 3B of the US-Singapore FTA includes the list of products that are covered under the Integrated Sourcing Initiative.

[196] Ithnain Rossman, *The Goods Package, in* The United States-Singapore Free Trade Agreement: Highlights and Insights 61, 69 (Tommy Koh & Chang Li Lin eds. 2004).

China, Japan, India and Korea commenced their FTA negotiations based on the framework agreements, which constitute interim agreements under the GATT. The early harvest programs of the framework agreements that expedite tariff and services trade liberalization for less sensitive sectors help increase economic and political will to finalize FTA talks. Finally, subsequent agreements on trade in goods and services, investment and dispute settlement collectively form comprehensive FTAs.

US experts previously envisioned an "umbrella" framework agreement that includes key FTA components such as the rules of origin and dispute settlement mechanism.[197] Bilateral FTA negotiations can be conducted on the basis of the framework. I propose that the ASEAN-US TIFA be upgraded to an enhanced TIFA that functions as a framework agreement for FTA negotiations. As ASEAN has insisted that the FTA engage "ASEAN as a group," particular concerns may arise as to the inclusion of less-developed ASEAN countries in the ASEAN-US FTA.[198]

A challenge greater than diverse development stages relates to the human rights records of countries such as Cambodia and Myanmar because such records will be subject to the strict scrutiny of the US Congress in the FTA ratification process. The United States provides technical assistance to these ASEAN countries under the Lower Mekong Initiative.[199] Yet, it was argued that the financial support provided by the ARIA often ignores smaller states of ASEAN.[200] An alarming effect is that these ASEAN countries became economically and politically dependent on China. Beijing's vast military and economic support for authoritarian governments "pay off" when they advocate for Beijing's "core interests" in the South China Sea and the Taiwan question. Their ties with Beijing have shifted to what I call "neo-dependency," as China now functions like the neocolonial North in the presumably equal South-South relations.

The Biden administration should also be aware that the effect of the US and EU-preferred sanction approaches is doubtful. To respond to the

[197] USITC, *supra* note 186, at 3–4.

[198] Severino, *supra* note 26, at 328–29.

[199] Cambodia, Laos, Myanmar, Thailand, and Vietnam are the target countries of the Initiative. United States Agency for International Development, *Lower Mekong Initiative (LMI)*, Aug. 28, 2020, www.usaid.gov/asia-regional/lower-mekong-initiative-lmi#:~:text=The%20Lower%20Mekong%20Initiative%20(LMI,shared%20challenges%20in%20the%20region (last visited Dec. 16, 2020).

[200] Adrien Chorn, *The Asia Reassurance Initiative Act: Overlooking Smaller Players in Southeast Asia*, Apr. 25, 2019, CSIS, www.cogitasia.com/the-asia-reassurance-initiative-act-overlooking-smaller-players-in-southeast-asia/ (last visited Dec. 16, 2020).

Hun Sen government's human rights abuses, Brussels' partially suspended Cambodia's benefits under the EU generalized scheme of preferences.[201] However, the EU sanction expedited the conclusion of the Cambodia-China FTA, strengthening Chinese influences. Myanmar is another example. Following the victory of Aung San Suu Kyi's National League for Democracy (NLD) in the 2015 parliamentary election, Obama largely eased sanctions imposed on the previous military junta.[202]

In response to the Myanmar Armed Forces' "ethnic cleansing" in Rakhine State, Trump imposed visa and asset-related restrictions from 2017 to 2019.[203] Markedly, Beijing attempted to "help" Myanmar by blocking a UN Security Council briefing on the Rakhine crisis.[204] It also utilized COVID-19 aid to push for the China-Myanmar Economic Corridor, which will advance China's Belt and Road Initiative and counter US sanctions.[205] The Biden admiration's response to the military's detention of Aung San Suu Kyi and NLD leaders in 2021 represents additional geopolitical challenges to ASEAN-US relations and China-Myanmar ties.[206]

The cases of Cambodia and Myanmar demonstrate that Western sanctions have reinforced the China-centric alliance, thus undermining US geopolitical interests in the region. Hence, Washington should adopt a more pragmatic trade policy that facilitates constructive engagement with these countries. In my view, the enhanced ASEAN-US TIFA can cover all ASEAN countries, but the US FTA with ASEAN can be based on the flexible "ASEAN Minus X" formula, which the ASEAN Charter endorses.[207] Given the scale of the US export market, the potential trade diversion effect will induce countries including Cambodia and

[201] Shaun Turton, *China and Cambodia Sign FTA on Heels of EU Sanctions*, Oct. 12, 2020, Nikkei Asia, https://asia.nikkei.com/Economy/Trade/China-and-Cambodia-sign-FTA-on-heels-of-EU-sanctions (last visited Dec. 16, 2020).

[202] Michael F. Martin, *US Restrictions on Relations with Burma*, CRS Report (2020), at 3–4.

[203] *Id.* at 10–11.

[204] Michelle Nichols, *China Fails to Stop U.N. Security Council Myanmar Briefing*, Oct. 25, 2018, Reuters, www.reuters.com/article/us-myanmar-rohingya-un-idUSKCN1MY2QU (last visited Dec. 16, 2020).

[205] Jason Tower, *China Using Pandemic Aid to Push Myanmar Economic Corridor*, May 27, 2020, United States Institute of Peace, www.usip.org/publications/2020/05/china-using-pandemic-aid-push-myanmar-economic-corridor (last visited Dec. 16, 2020).

[206] US Department of State, *Briefing with Senior State Department Officials On the State Department's Assessment of Recent Events in Burma*, Feb. 2, 2021, www.state.gov/briefing-with-senior-state-department-officials-on-the-state-departments-assessment-of-recent-events-in-burma/ (last visited Feb. 4, 2021).

[207] Charter of the Association Southeast Asian Nations (2007), art. 21.2.

Myanmar to join the ASEAN-US FTA by complying with trade-plus requirements concerning human rights.

VI Conclusion

This chapter offered a detailed account of US-Asia economic agreements and pertinent legal issues. As a resident power in the Asia-Pacific, the United Stated provided hegemonic stability that made Asian integration feasible. Nevertheless, Washington's inactive response to the Asia Financial Crisis galvanized the financial and trade cooperation under the "ASEAN Plus Six" framework that excludes America. China's assertive stance on FTAs and Trump's unilateral trade policy, which led to the US withdrawal from the CPTPP and the US-China trade war, further deteriorated the unipolar moment of US hegemony. The postwar trade regime that the United States founded is giving way to the NREO.

Compared with practices of China, the EU and Japan, the fundamental flaw of US policy on Asia is the lack of a comprehensive, integral legal framework with ASEAN. Notwithstanding the emphasis on Asia under Obama's pivot to Asia strategy and Trump's Indo-Pacific strategy, US TIFAs with ASEAN and individual countries failed to achieve any meaningful trade agreements. Singapore remains the only ASEAN country with which the United States concluded an FTA. For the Biden administration to reunite Asian allies and restore US leadership, it is vital to focus on ASEAN "as a bloc" not only in security but also in trade initiatives. The chapter proposed the two-pronged roadmap. US accession to the CPTPP and the expansion of its membership will pave the way for the CPTPP 2.0 based on the enhanced TIFA international economic law.

6

The Marginalization or Rejuvenation of APEC?

I Introduction

After the founding of the Association of Southeast Asian Nations (ASEAN), the most significant milestone in Asian regionalism was the establishment of the Asia-Pacific Economic Cooperation (APEC) in 1989. Decided in 1994, APEC's Bogor Declaration aimed to accomplish "free and open trade and investment in the Asia-Pacific" for developed and developing economies by 2010 and 2020, respectively.[1] The so-called Bogor Goals therefore set ambitious targets for new Asian regionalism. Twenty-one APEC economies now account for more than 48 percent of global trade and 60 percent of the world's gross domestic product (GDP).[2] In addition, APEC members have concluded 189 free trade agreements (FTAs), representing 40 percent of global trade pacts.[3]

In the 1990s, APEC was widely perceived as the essential transregional economic architecture for the Asia-Pacific. However, since the world entered the Third Regionalism in the 2000s, APEC has encountered an "identity crisis" that has arguably undermined its role. First, distinct from ASEAN's transformation to the ASEAN Economic Community (AEC), APEC's *sui generis* status has rendered it neither an international organization nor a free trade zone as defined by World Trade Organization (WTO) law.[4] As an institution based on soft-law, APEC has primarily invigorated

[1] 1994 Leaders' Declaration (1994) (Bogor Declaration).

[2] Asia-Pacific Economic Cooperation (APEC) Policy Support Unit (PSU), *APEC in Charts 2019* (2019), at 2.

[3] *Id.* at 16; Regional Trade Agreements, www.wto.org/english/tratop_e/region_e/region_e.htm (last visited Jan. 27, 2020).

[4] For the legal basis for free trade agreements, refer to Article XXIV of the General Agreement on Tariffs and Trade (GATT), Article V of the General Agreement on Trade in Services (GATS) and the enabling clause.

economic cooperation and liberalization through nonbinding decisions and rules. Second, notwithstanding the significant "2020 target" of APEC's Bogor Goals, regional governments have prioritized FTA negotiations over APEC. Mega-FTAs, including the Comprehensive and Progressive Agreement for Trans-Pacific Partnership (CPTPP) and the Regional Comprehensive Economic Partnership (RCEP), have further crippled APEC's relevance.

Lastly, illustrated by the US-China hegemonic rivalry, geopolitical instability has overshadowed APEC's intended agenda. For the first time since APEC held its summit in 1993, APEC leaders failed to deliver the declaration at the Papua New Guinea meeting in 2018.[5] One bottleneck was conflicts between Washington and Beijing over the reference to "unfair trade practices."[6] Although 2019 marked APEC's thirtieth anniversary, it witnessed the first-ever cancellation of the APEC summit due to political unrest of Chile, the host state. Ironically, the cancellation delayed the presumably "more important" conclusion of US President Donald Trump's "phase-one" trade deal with China.[7]

Against this backdrop, a pivotal and timely query arises as to whether APEC will be marginalized or rejuvenated in new Asian regionalism. Unlike the conventional analysis from the viewpoint of international relations, the chapter assesses APEC's evolution from a legal perspective and examines the impact on Asian integration and the multilateral trading system. In particular, I argue that APEC's two cardinal principles, "open regionalism" and "concerted unilateral liberalization," have yielded a salient yet oft-ignored impact on trade liberalization in selected areas.[8] APEC's structured soft-law scheme has minimized states' "sovereign costs" and facilitated the making of extra and innovative commitments that galvanized WTO negotiations.[9] I nonetheless caution that APEC's institutional reforms are imperative

[5] Philip Wen et al., *APEC Fails to Reach Consensus as US-China Divide Deepens*, Reuters, Nov. 18. 2018, www.reuters.com/article/us-apec-summit-energy/apec-fails-to-reach-consensus-as-u-s-china-divide-deepens-idUSKCN1NN00M (last visited Jan. 27, 2020).

[6] *Id.* Instead of a "leaders' declaration," APEC issued the Chair's statement, which "reflects the chair's assessment of the prevailing views of all APEC member economies." The Chair's Era Kone Statement, the 26th APEC Economic Leaders' Meeting, Nov. 18, 2018.

[7] The "phase one" trade deal was subsequently signed in January 2020.

[8] For the detailed analysis of the two principles, see John Ravenhill, *APEC and the Construction of Pacific Rim Regionalism* 140–42 (2001); Ippei Yamazawa, *APEC: New Agenda in Its Third Decade* 11–14 (2012).

[9] The notion of sovereign costs, see Chris Brummer, *Why Soft Law Dominates International Finance – and Not Trade*, 13(3) J. Int'l Econ. L. 623, 623–24 (2010); Harmut Hillgenberg, *A Fresh Look at Soft Law*, 10(3) Eur. J. Int'l L. 500, 509.

even after the end of the Bogor Goals. The effective implementation of the post-2020 vision, known as the APEC Putrajaya Vision 2040, will enhance APEC's incubator role for a Free Trade Area of the Asia-Pacific (FTAAP), thus reinvigorating the forum's identity and gravity.[10] APEC will also enable developing countries to fortify their collective power to shape the new regional economic order (NREO) in the Third Regionalism.

The chapter will explore APEC's evolving process vis-à-vis regional and global regionalism. It will first shed light on the origin of APEC's transregional structure and operating mechanism, which is based on the 1995 Osaka Action Agenda designed to fulfil the Bogor Goals. It will also explain APEC's credibility crisis due to the failure of premature liberalization efforts and its inability to assist countries during the Asian financial crisis.[11] Furthermore, the chapter will provide insight into key APEC members' legal and political approaches that have affected APEC's evolution and agendas. For instance, the US Indo-Pacific strategy, China's Belt and Road Initiative (BRI) and ASEAN's AEC Blueprint 2025 have influenced APEC's current connectivity initiative involving infrastructure development.[12]

To evaluate APEC's incremental achievements, the chapter will center on APEC's FTA-related model measures, trade facilitation essential to the regional supply chain, and tariff liberalization for information technology (IT) and environmental products. Finally, taking into account the APEC Putrajaya Vision 2040, the chapter will provide recommendations for APEC's legal and institutional reforms that could buttress the capacity of the APEC Secretariat and the peer review process. The feasible pathways to the FTAAP, including the CPTPP and the RCEP, will also be examined in the context of new Asian regionalism and international economic law.

II APEC As a Transregional Economic Institution

The rapid integration of ASEAN, Europe and North America was a marked feature of the Second Regionalism in the 1980s and prompted the idea of establishing an Asia-Pacific economic institution. Australia and Japan played a critical role. Academics in the two countries initially proposed to create the Organization for Pacific Trade and Development (OPTAD), modeled after the Organization for Economic Cooperation

[10] APEC Vision Group, *Report of the APEC Vision Group – People and Prosperity: An APEC Vision to 2040* (2019), at 3–11; 2020 Leaders' Declaration (2020).

[11] Yamazawa, *supra* note 8, at 10.

[12] Annex D – APEC Connectivity Blueprint for 2015–2025, 2014 Leaders' Declaration (2014).

and Development (OECD).[13] The OPTAD proposal was tepidly received by the governments because of cold war divisions and their concerns about binding commitments.[14]

This new momentum resulted in the Pacific Economic Cooperation Conference (PECC) in 1980. As a tripartite organization, the PECC brings together academics, businesses and government representatives. The PECC has provided models and precedents for APEC such as holding high-level yet "informal" forums and enabling economic consultations across the Taiwan Strait.[15] In 1989, with Japan's robust support, Australian Prime Minister Bob Hawke's initiative led to the founding of APEC.[16] Other than APEC's twenty-one members, the ASEAN Secretariat and the PECC have participated in APEC meetings as official observers.

A APEC's Operation and Structure

Without a treaty that confers legal personality, APEC has operated as a de facto institution with established norms and procedures built on thirty years of practice. The diversity of APEC membership has contributed to its weaknesses and advantages. Absent a collective identity across the Pacific, a simplified constructivist understanding cannot explain the grouping of twenty-one members. Unlike ASEAN, geographic proximity is not a convincing factor that connects APEC. Moreover, the economic parity among APEC economies can be demonstrated by the GDP per capita of the United States being more than twenty-five times that of Vietnam.[17] These divergences have galvanized APEC to adopt and continue its nonbinding, consensus-based approach. This political compromise has also prevented APEC from transforming into an FTA or an international organization.

Nevertheless, it would be inaccurate to ignore APEC's incremental impact on economic integration. Albeit on a nonbinding basis, intra-APEC merchandise trade has soared eightfold since 1989, reaching more

[13] Notable figures include Professor Kiyoshi Kojima and Professor Peter Drysdale. The Organization for Pacific Trade and Development (OPTAD) was proposed at the Pacific Trade and Development (PAFTAD) conference. Ravenhill, *supra* note 8, at 41–52; Mark Borthwick, *Building Momentum: The Movement Toward Pacific Economic Cooperation Prior to 1980, in* The Evolution of PECC: The First 25 Years 1, 6 (2005).

[14] Christopher M. Dent, *East Asian Regionalism* 119–20 (2d ed. 2016); Andrew Elek, *Back to Canberra: Founding APEC, in* The Evolution of PECC: The First 25 Years 66, 71 (2005).

[15] Andrew Elek, *Overview, in* The Evolution of PECC: The First 25 Years xv, xx–xxi (2005).

[16] Ravenhill, *supra* note 8, at 41; Elek, *id.* at xxi.

[17] APEC Secretariat, *APEC Outcomes & Outlook 2018–2019* (2019), at 37.

than 70 percent.[18] This figure notably exceeds intra-regional trade in the European Union (EU) (64 percent) and North America (50 percent), which are legally binding trade blocs.[19] In addition, APEC has attempted to depoliticize its nature by designating its constituencies as "member economies" rather than states and addressing its annual summit as the "economic leaders' meeting." In my view, APEC's focus on economy has unintentionally elevated its geopolitical salience, as it provides a high-level forum for trans-Pacific dialogues pivotal to global governance. The topics of such dialogues range from North Korea to US-China trade discords. Countries have also utilized APEC meetings as opportunities to reach consensus on CPTPP and RCEP negotiations.

Commentators have characterized APEC as "A Perfect Excuse to Chat" due to its 63 working groups and 150 officials-level meetings every year.[20] While some discussions have yet to yield substantive results, others have benefited WTO-plus and extra areas, including customs procedures, e-commerce and the economic participation of women.[21] As APEC enables its members to pioneer selected issues, the sense of "ownership" has energized national contributions to regional capacity-building. As a current example, Singapore serves as the "champion economy" for improving construction permits for implementing the Ease of Doing Business Action Plan.[22] Moreover, the business community's direct involvement in APEC's decision-making process is an exception to intergovernmental organizations. The APEC Business Advisory Council, along with the tripartite PECC, has fortified APEC's commercial relevance.[23] Arguably, this pro-business scheme has influenced APEC's pragmatic priority to cut time to start a business, export and import, and enforce contracts.[24]

By their nature, APEC's declarations and decisions constitute political commitments instead of binding agreements. Nevertheless, these commitments are endorsed by economic leaders and taken as principal policy directions. Since 1989, soft-law rules have guided the governance of

[18] APEC PSU, *supra* note 2, at 8.

[19] World Trade Organization (WTO), *World Trade Statistical Review 2019* (2019), at 55

[20] Ravenhill, *supra* note 8, at 220; APEC Vision Group, *supra* note 10, at 29.

[21] APEC PSU, *APEC's Bogor Goals Progress Report* (2018), at 2–9; APEC PSU, *APEC Regional Trends Analysis: Counting What Counts* (2019), at 15–17.

[22] APEC PSU, *APEC's Ease of Doing Business – Final Assessment 2015–2018* (2019), at 4.

[23] The APEC Business Advisory Council (ABAC) was created by the APEC Economic Leaders in November 1995. Founding and Structure, www2.abaconline.org//page-content/2521/content (last visited Jan. 28, 2020).

[24] APEC PSU, *supra* note 22, at 9–33.

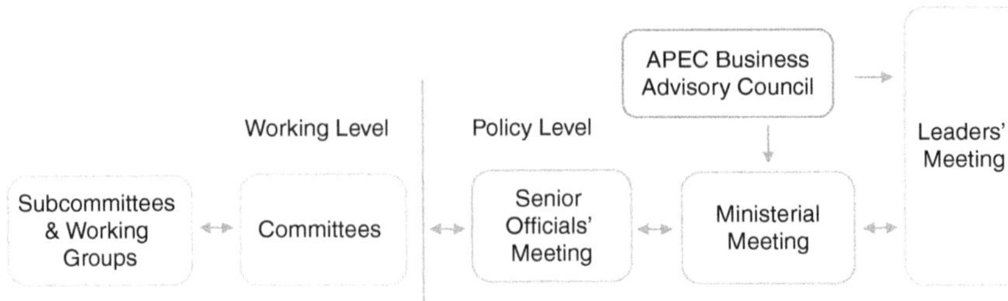

Figure 6.1 APEC's decision-making process[27]

APEC's meetings and institution-building.[25] APEC's structure encompasses policy and working levels and follows the coexisting top-down and bottom-up processes.[26] At the apex of the policy level, leaders or their representatives from twenty-one APEC members convene at the annual leaders' meeting and issue declarations that guide APEC's priorities. In practice, the agenda and priorities of the leaders' meeting are built upon the consensus forged at the ministerial meeting and recommendations by the APEC Business Advisory Council that is comprised of business leaders. Tellingly, the annual gatherings are not confined to foreign and trade ministers. In response to APEC's wide-ranging topics, ministers responsible for agriculture, finance and other APEC-related matters have also participated in sectoral ministerial meetings.

Convened four times each year, the Senior Officials' Meeting oversees four working-level committees that include subcommittees and working groups on specific areas, including business mobility, competition law and energy.[28] For strategic issues, the Senior Officials' Meeting has authority to form advisory bodies such as the APEC Vision Group tasked for envisioning APEC's post-2020 vision.[29] The meeting is supported by the APEC Secretariat, which administers APEC's annual budget and oversees more than 250 APEC-funded projects.[30] Today the agendas of working groups respond to fast-changing challenges confronting the

[25] *See e.g.*, APEC Secretariat, Guidelines for Hosting APEC Meetings (2017).
[26] APEC Secretariat, *supra* note 17, at 38.
[27] *Id.*; Francis A. Quimba & Mark Anthony A. Barral, *The Evolution of APEC and Its Role in the Philippine Trade and Investment*, PIDS Discussion Paper Series, No. 2019–07 (2019), at 13.
[28] Structure, www.apec.org/About-Us/How-APEC-Operates/Structure (last visited Feb. 17, 2020).
[29] APEC Vision Group, *supra* note 10, at 36.
[30] APEC Secretariat, www.apec.org/About-Us/APEC-Secretariat (last visited Feb. 18, 2020).

Asia-Pacific. For instance, the Health Working Group facilitated APEC governments' efforts to combat the coronavirus (COVID-19) outbreak and sought to minimize its economic impact.[31]

B *Three-Phased Evolution: 1989–2021*

In the past thirty years, APEC's development can be understood in three major phases, which are intertwined with the progress of Asian regionalism and the WTO. APEC's first phase commenced with its inception in 1989 and culminated with the Bogor Declaration, which specifies 2010 and 2020 as target years for achieving regional trade and investment liberalization. The Bogor Goals, which ignited Asian integration and high expectations of APEC, gave rise to the principle of "open regionalism." This principle unambiguously rejects the inward-looking notion of FTAs by encouraging APEC members to accord liberalization benefits to other countries on a most-favored-nation (MFN) basis.[32] The Bogor Goals also led to APEC's three-pillared agenda, including trade and investment liberalization, business facilitation, and economic and technical cooperation (ECOTECH) based on capacity-building initiatives.[33]

To implement the Bogor Goals, the 1995 Osaka Action Agenda and the 1996 Manila Action Plan for APEC devised the modality of "concerted unilateral liberalization."[34] Under this principle, APEC would rely on Individual Action Plans and Collection Action Plans. The Individual Action Plans mandate that APEC members periodically report on their implementation of seventeen areas such as non-tariff measures, customs procedures and FTAs.[35] These areas, including those identified in the

[31] Denis Hew, *The Economic Effects of the Coronavirus on the Asia-Pacific*, Feb. 17, 2020, www.apec.org/Press/Blogs/2020/0217_PSU (last visited Feb. 18, 2020).

[32] Dent, *supra* note 14, at 122; Ravenhill, *supra* note 8, at 138–40.

[33] Scope of Work, www.apec.org/About-Us/How-APEC-Operates/Scope-of-Work (last visited Feb. 18, 2020).

The Framework for Strengthening Economic Cooperation and Development (2016 Manila Declaration) introduced the APEC term, "economic and technical cooperation (ECOTECH)." Ippei Yamazawa, *APEC's Achievements and Tasks*, *in* APEC in the 21st Century 1, 16 (Riyana Miranti & Denis Hew eds. 2004).

[34] Yamazawa, *supra* note 33, at 4; The Osaka Action Agenda: Implementation of the Bogor Declaration, www.apec.org/Meeting-Papers/Leaders-Declarations/1995/1995_aelm (last visited Feb. 25, 2020); Manila Action Plan for APEC (MAPA): Volume 1, www.mofa.go.jp/policy/economy/apec/1996/mapa/vol1/index.html (last visited Feb. 18, 2020).

[35] Committee on Trade and Investment (CTI) Chair, The Individual Action Plan (IAP) and IAP Peer Review, 2011/SOM2/021anx2 (2011), at 1–2.

Osaka Action Agenda and subsequently added issues, aim to exert peer pressure on members and ensure unilateral liberalization in a concerted manner.[36]

Collection Action Plans also require reports on the status of APEC economies' joint actions in selected areas. These actions offer training on the best practices and enhance transparency by creating databases, such as the APEC Competition Policy and Law Database that Taiwan operates.[37] During this period, APEC's "success" was evidenced by members' support for the Information Technology Agreement (ITA), which Canada, Japan and the United States vigorously proposed.[38] With the objective of eliminating tariffs on IT products, this landmark agreement was adopted at the WTO's 1996 Singapore Ministerial Conference and highlighted APEC's global impact.

In its second phase ranging from 1997 to 2000, APEC suffered a credibility crisis that undermined its impetus for intended liberalization. Encouraged by the ITA's success, APEC's developed economies pushed for implementing more ambitious Early Voluntary Sectoral Liberalization (EVSL).[39] APEC's 1997 Vancouver meeting designated fifteen sectors where members would decrease tariffs, non-tariff and standards and conformance measures.[40] Unexpectedly, the multisector EVSL initiative made it difficult to replicate the approach to the single-sector ITA. The fact that EVSL shifted from a voluntary basis to WTO-style negotiations was met with the opposition from Japan and other Asian countries.[41] In particular, the fierce domestic resistance to EVSL's inclusion of fisheries and forest sectors and APEC members' vulnerability amid the Asian financial crisis ended early liberalization efforts.[42]

[36] The Osaka Action Agenda identified 15 areas to be reported. The current Individual Action Plan report deleted the area of "implementation of the Uruguay Round Outcomes" and added three areas: "transparency," "RTAs/FTAs" and "other voluntary areas." *Id.*; APEC PSU, *supra* note 21, at i; Hadi Soesastro, *Revamping APEC's Concerted Unilateral Liberalization, in* APEC at 20: Recall, Reflect, Remake 67, 68–69 (K. Kesavapany and Hank Lim eds. 2009).

[37] *E.g.*, Summary Report of Competition Policy and Law Group Meeting 2012, 2013/SOM1. CPLG/002 (2013), at 3.

[38] WTO, *15 Years of the Information Technology Agreement: Trade, Innovation and Global Production Networks* (2012), at 12–15.

[39] Yamazawa, *supra* note 33, at 7.

[40] *Id.* at 8.

[41] *Id.* at 9–10.

[42] Tatsushi Ogita, *Japan: The Structure of Complete Objection, in* Trade Liberalization and APEC 83, 97–98 (Jiro Okamoto ed. 2004).

EVSL is thus considered as APEC's "public relations disaster," resulting in "APEC adrift" pessimism.[43]

APEC's reforms and modernization are decisive to its third phase that coincides with the WTO Doha Development Round and new Asian regionalism. APEC has strived to recover from the EVSL failure and to reposition itself as an incubator for FTAs and innovative arenas. The 2001 Shanghai Accord signifies a turn back to concerted unilateral liberalization. The adoption of a pathfinder approach highlights flexible consensus by permitting "21 Minus X" APEC members to shepherd selected initiatives in tandem with the Bogor Goals.[44] Recent pathfinder initiatives encompass eleven to twenty APEC members and focus on diverse issues such as digital trade and supply chain connectivity.[45] Distinct from the "ASEAN Minus X" formula that precludes "free-riders," the APEC scheme conforms to open regionalism. This nondiscrimination principle on the Osaka Action Agenda clearly articulates that the benefits of trade and investment liberalization will be "not only among APEC economies but also between APEC economies and non-APEC economies."[46]

The third phase of APEC has encountered challenges from mega-FTAs. As APEC itself is not a forum for trade negotiations, its marginalization or rejuvenation will hinge on its incubator role for proliferating trade and investment pacts. In 2010, APEC leaders stressed that a twenty-one-member FTAAP should be "building on ongoing regional undertakings, such as ASEAN+3, ASEAN+6, and the Trans-Pacific Partnership, among others."[47] The CPTPP and RCEP are based on the original Trans-Pacific Partnership (TPP) and ASEAN Plus One FTAs, respectively, and thus fall within the ambit of the pathways to the FTAAP. APEC's post-2020 vision that galvanizes its leadership in shaping economic agreements will also revitalize APEC's identity and function.

III Legal and Political Strategies of Asia-Pacific Governments

The convergence and divergence of national interests among APEC's twenty-one members have influenced the ebbs and flows of APEC as

[43] Ravenhill, *supra* note 8, at 186–89.

[44] Appendix 1 – Shanghai Accord: APEC Economic Leaders' Declaration (2001); Man-jung Mignonne Chan, *APEC's Eye on the Prize: Participants, Modality, and Confidence-Building*, *in* APEC at 20: Recall, Reflect, Remake 41, 44–45 (K. Kesavapany and Hank Lim eds. 2009).

[45] Appendix 5 – 2019 CTI Pathfinder Initiatives, 2019 CTI Report to Ministers (2019).

[46] The Osaka Action Agenda: Implementation of the Bogor Declaration, *supra* note 34.

[47] 2010 Leaders' Declaration (2010).

a trans-Pacific institution. The states' legal and political strategies are closely linked to APEC's priorities and agendas. Moreover, the East-West division and the differences between developed and developing nations have prompted APEC to place an unequal emphasis on its three pillars – trade and investment liberalization, business facilitation and ECOTECH – during different periods. Since 2017, escalating national populism and US-China trade conflicts have threatened the global economy and APEC's relevance. Below I will examine the approaches of ASEAN, Australia, China, Japan and the United States and analyze their impact on APEC's evolution.

A ASEAN

ASEAN and APEC constitute twin engines for new Asian regionalism. Since its founding in 1967, the ten-member ASEAN has evolved from a loose security alliance to an indispensable trade bloc in Asia. The launching of the ASEAN Free Trade Area in 1993 and the AEC in 2015 are key milestones in trade liberalization of Southeast Asia. To keep ASEAN's collective power, ASEAN governments agreed on the 1990 Kuching Consensus, which formed the basis for ASEAN's participation in APEC.[48] They agreed that "ASEAN's identity and cohesion should be preserved" and that APEC will neither create "an inward-looking economic or trading bloc" nor adopt "mandatory directives."[49]

Mahathir Mohamad, who twice served as Malaysia's Prime Minister (1981–2003 and 2018–2020), played a significant role in APEC history. In 1990, he proposed to establish the East Asia Economic Group (EAEG) within APEC in order to prevent ASEAN from being dominated by APEC's "Caucasian" countries.[50] Although the EAEG proposal faced resistance from Indonesia, the United States and other members, such debates invigorated the establishment of the ASEAN Free Trade Area.[51] Tellingly, APEC's 2020 meeting hosted by Malaysia was necessary due to the end of Bogor Goals and the cancellation of the 2019 summit that Chile was supposed to host. Different from his skeptical stance thirty years ago, Mahathir agreed that APEC "remains relevant"

[48] Alice Ba, *(Re)Negotiating East and Southeast Asia: Region, Regionalism, and the Association of Southeast Asian Nations* 148–49 (2009); Elek, *supra* note 14, at 77–78.

[49] Appendix 5.2: Kuching Consensus, *in* Elek, *supra* note 14, at 82.

[50] Ravenhill, *supra* note 8, at 109–10.

[51] Ba, *supra* note 48, at 151–53.

and its work in pursuing regional integration "is now more important than ever."[52]

ASEAN's threefold influence on APEC has strengthened the legal and economic significance of the "ASEAN way" that underpins new Asian regionalism and the NREO. First, APEC includes seven ASEAN states (Brunei, Indonesia, Malaysia, the Philippines, Singapore, Thailand and Vietnam). Except for the EU and India, APEC comprises ASEAN's top trade partners.[53] In particular, ASEAN replaced the United States as China's second largest trade partner in 2019 and overtook the EU as China's largest trade partner in 2020.[54] The ASEAN-China FTA has therefore become the most important South-South agreement in APEC and augmented ASEAN's standing to represent developing countries.

Second, a critical pathway to APEC's FTAAP is the RCEP, which ASEAN introduced as "an ASEAN-led process."[55] RCEP parties similarly recognize the principle of "ASEAN centrality" in forging the mega-FTA.[56] Legally significant, the RCEP will be building on the AEC frameworks and existing "ASEAN Plus One" FTAs, which follow a building-block approach guided by the programmatic incrementalism. The RCEP and ASEAN-centered FTAs are expected to benefit "the unfinished business of the Bogor Goals" and the FTAAP under the APEC Putrajaya Vision 2040.[57]

Finally, known as the "concentric ring" effect, APEC and ASEAN, which is a subgroup and official observer of APEC, are mutually reinforcing because of their highly converged initiatives.[58] It is true that the "ASEAN way" has departed from APEC's pure soft-law approach by imposing hard-law obligations with flexibility. Nevertheless, similar to APEC's pathfinder

52 Mergawati Zulfakar, With APEC Cancelled, Focus is Now on ASEAN Summit, The Star, Nov. 1, 2019, www.thestar.com.my/news/nation/2019/11/01/with-apec-cancelled-focus-is-now-on-asean-summit (last visited Feb. 24, 2020).

53 Association of Southeast Asian Nations (ASEAN) Secretariat, *ASEAN Integration Report 2019* (2019), at 127–29.

54 *Id.* at 133; Xinha, *China-ASEAN Trade Continues to Boom Amid Global Growth Slowdown, Uncertainties*, Jul. 23, 2019, China Daily, www.chinadaily.com.cn/a/201907/23/WS5d367792a310d8305640082a.html (last visited Feb. 25, 2020); *ASEAN Becomes China's Largest Trading Partner*, Mar. 7, 2020, Global Times, www.globaltimes.cn/content/1181864.shtml#:~:text=Association%20of%20Southeast%20Asian%20Nations,external%20shockwaves%20like%20the%20coronavirus%2C (last visited Feb. 5, 2021).

55 ASEAN Framework for Regional Comprehensive Economic Partnership (2011).

56 Guiding Principles and Objectives for Negotiating the Regional Comprehensive Economic Partnership (2012) (RCEP Guiding Principles).

57 APEC Vision Group, *supra* note 10, at 12.

58 S. Pushpanathan, *ASEAN's Strategy Towards Its Dialogue Partners and ASEAN Plus Three Process*, Nov. 4, 2003, https://asean.org/?static_post=asean-s-strategy-towards-its-dialogue-partners-and-asean-plus-three-process-by-s-pushpanathan (last visited Feb. 25, 2020).

initiative, ASEAN has served as an "experimental laboratory" for wider APEC initiatives. Surprisingly, APEC and ASEAN leaders only held their first dialogue on potential cooperation in 2017, which marked the fiftieth anniversary of ASEAN.[59] Both institutions recognized that the topics covered in AEC Blueprint 2025 and the Bogor Goals are complementary. Comparable initiatives are particularly noteworthy in trade facilitation schemes such as the operationalization of single windows for customs procedures, electronic commerce (e-commerce) and mutual recognition arrangements.[60] As for development and capacity building, the ongoing Initiative for ASEAN Integration Work Plan III also benefits APEC's ECOTECH actions.

B Australia

Australia has been a keen proponent for APEC, which has underpinned the country's Asia-oriented policy. The birth of APEC was based on former Australian Prime Minister Bob Hawke's initiative and the first APEC ministerial meeting took place in Canberra in 1989. The proposal by the following Prime Minister Paul Keating to convene an APEC leaders' meeting was supported by US President Bill Clinton, leading to the first APEC summit in Seattle in 1993.[61]

As Hawke recognized, Australia's transformation to an open economy since the 1980s kept the nation from marginalization, about which Singapore Prime Minister Lee Kuan Yew had warned.[62] APEC members now account for 70 percent of Australia's trade in goods and services.[63] Furthermore, APEC has enabled Australia to increase its influence through setting regional agendas, data standards and

[59] The informal dialogue took place in Vietnam and the theme was "Partnering for New Dynamism for a Comprehensively Connected and Integrated Asia-Pacific." Secretary-General of ASEAN: ASEAN and APEC Can Achieve More by Working Together, Nov. 12, 2017, https://asean.org/secretary-general-of-asean-asean-and-apec-can-achieve-more-by-working-together/ (last visited Feb. 25, 2020).

[60] Akhmad Bayhaqi et al., *Trade Facilitation in APEC: Progress and Impact*, APEC PSU Policy Brief No. 25 (2019), at 1–2; ASEAN Secretariat, *supra* note 53, at 27–35 & 91–92.

[61] The idea was first proposed to US President George H. W. Bush during his visit to Australia in 1992. P. J. Keating, APEC: Australia's Biggest Seat at its Biggest Table, Aug. 23, 2007.

[62] Jonathan Pearlman, *"White Trash" Warning Spurred Australia to Be Better: Abbott*, Straits Times, Mar. 26, 2015, www.straitstimes.com/singapore/white-trash-warning-spurred-australia-to-be-better-abbott (last visited Feb. 27, 2020).

[63] Asia-Pacific Economic Cooperation (APEC), https://dfat.gov.au/trade/organisations/apec/Pages/asia-pacific-economic-cooperation-apec.aspx (last visited Feb. 25, 2020).

economic cooperation.[64] Complemented by Australia's FTAs with Asian countries such as ASEAN and China, APEC provides paramount institutional frameworks for upgrading economic links to Asia and securing Australia's sustainable growth.

In light of US-China conflicts, Canberra has used APEC forums to engage both Washington and Beijing. Australia has been cautious about unilateralism and "trade liberalization" that the United States advocated for in APEC and FTA negotiations.[65] It was inevitably disappointed by the Trump administration's decision to withdraw the United States from the TPP, for which President Barack Obama had advocated. Australia and Japan subsequently emerged as the pivotal forces to revive the TPP and concluded the 11-party CPTPP in 2018. In addition, Australia deems it to be imperative to counter foreign influences such as China's BRI projects on Pacific islands. Thus, although Australian Prime Minister Scott Morrison criticized "trade protectionism" at the 2018 APEC meeting, he endorsed the US Indo-Pacific vision as part of Australian foreign policy.[66] Supporting US initiatives in APEC benefits Australia's long-term strategic goals.

C China

Since Deng Xiaoping's economic reform in 1978, the People's Republic of China (PRC) has become the world's second largest economy. Chinese accession to APEC in 1991 broke the blockade after the Tiananmen Square protests and reintegrated the country into the global economic order. Following the PECC model, the "three Chinas" (the PRC, Hong Kong and Taiwan) simultaneously joined APEC. Before Beijing and Taipei joined the WTO, APEC was the sole intergovernmental forum that accommodated two rival governments. The Taiwan issue was "solved" in the memoranda of understanding (MoU) that China and Taiwan respectively signed with South Korea, the APEC chair in 1991.[67] Taiwan's APEC title

[64] Australia Government, *2017 Foreign Policy White Paper* (2017), at 46–64.
[65] Ravenhill, *supra* note 8, at 116–17.
[66] Katharine Murphy, *Scott Morrison to Take on Backlash against Trade Deals at APEC*, Guardian, Nov. 16, 2018, www.theguardian.com/australia-news/2018/nov/17/scott-morrison-to-take-on-backlash-against-trade-deals-at-apec (last visited Mar. 11, 2020); Address to APEC CEO Summit, Nov. 17, 2018 www.pm.gov.au/media/address-apec-ceo-summit-2018 (last visited Mar. 11, 2020).
[67] Philip Y. M. Yang, *Taiwan's Approaches to APEC: Economic Cooperation, Political Significance, and International Participation*, Nov. 14, 1997, http://club.ntu.edu.tw/~yang/apec-paper-2.htm (last visited Feb. 26, 2020).

would be "Chinese Taipei" rather than Taiwan or its official name, the Republic of China. Despite the technically nonbinding nature of MOUs, existing practices have excluded the participation of Taiwan's presidents and foreign ministers.[68]

Akin to ASEAN's position, China supports APEC's function as "economic cooperation" and is not in favor of APEC resulting in binding commitments. In light of Deng's low-profile diplomacy, China participated in international organizations, including APEC, in the 1990s and 2000s passively and proposed no conspicuous initiatives. Since 2013, PRC President Xi Jinping has ushered the country into a new era of pursuing an assertive approach to realizing the "Chinese dream" that will "make China great again."[69]

Xi's most noteworthy strategy is the BRI, which he announced in 2013 and which the PRC State Council adopted in 2015 as the guiding principle for Chinese FTAs.[70] The BRI centers on infrastructure financing and the exportation of Chinese goods, services and labor. It is expected to heighten Beijing's influence over countries incapable of obtaining loans from the World Bank or the Asian Development Bank. More profoundly, although the BRI lacks a treaty-based framework, the soft-law agreements will help China to form its hub-and-spoke network.[71] To promote the BRI, the Chinese government has been involved in the feasibility study on the FTAAP and the infrastructure-based APEC Connectivity Blueprint.[72]

While some consider the BRI China's Marshall Plan, others deem the BRI to be "debt-trap diplomacy" because Chinese projects made countries

[68] In practice, the Taiwan president will "receive invitations" from the APEC host country but will appoint a "leader's representative" to attend the summit, officially known as the APEC Economic Leaders' Meeting. The representative is usually a formal government official (such as former Vice President Lien Chang) or a business leader.

[69] Graham Allison, *Destined for War: Can America and China Escape Thucydides's Trap?* 116–22 (2017).

[70] State Council, 国务院关于加快实施 自由贸易区战略的若干意见 [Several Opinions of the State Council on Accelerating the Implementation of the Strategies for Free Trade Areas] (2015); Julien Chaisse & Mitsuo Matshshita, *China's "Belt and Road" Initiative: Mapping the World Trade Normative and Strategic Implications*, 52(1) J. World Trade 163, 165–84 (2018). The Belt and Road Initiative (BRI) is also commonly known as One Belt One Road (OBOR), which refers to China's development strategy for the Silk Road Economic Belt and the twenty-first-century Maritime Silk Road.

[71] Heng Wang, *China's Approach to the Belt and Road Initiative: Scope, Character and Sustainability*, 22(1) J. Int'l Econ. L. 29, 35–41 (2019).

[72] Annex A – The Beijing Roadmap for APEC's Contribution to the Realization of the FTAAP, 2014 Leaders' Declaration (2014); Assistant Foreign Minister Zhang Jun Publishes Signed Article on APEC Economic Cooperation, Nov. 14, 2018, www.fmprc.gov.cn/mfa_eng/wjbxw/t1612994.shtml (Feb. 25, 2020).

vulnerable to debt distress.[73] Given the neo-dependency relations that China may forge with developing nations, the BRI has raised concerns for APEC members. To counter the impact of China's BRI infrastructure projects, Australia and Japan have provided alternative funding to support land and maritime connectivity initiatives for APEC's developing economies.[74] The Trump administration adopted an even stronger stance against the BRI.

In a remarkable challenge to US Vice-President Mike Pence's criticism of Chinese trade practices at the 2018 APEC summit, Xi dismissed the debt-trap accusation and responded that US protectionism and unilateralism is "short-sighted and doomed to failure."[75] Additionally, APEC has helped Beijing bolster interactions with Latin American members (Chile, Mexico and Peru) and promote BRI projects in "America's backyard." As the coronavirus outbreak severely hit APEC economies such as China, Korea and Japan, the 2020 APEC meetings included discussions on pertinent economic issues. The impact of trade measures on the BRI remains to be assessed.

D *Japan*

Japan was arguably the first nation to propose Asian integration. Nonetheless, its "Greater East Asia Co-Prosperity Sphere" perished with the Japanese surrender in WWII. Japan's postwar economic ascendance and its need for expanding the manufacturing network led to the Fukuda Doctrine that guided Asia-oriented diplomacy in the 1970s.[76] Tokyo was APEC's key founding member and has supported APEC's consensus-based trade liberalization. Although Japan's direction was complicated by the institutional "turf" conflict between its foreign and trade ministries at the inception of APEC, the divergence was overcome.[77]

[73] John Pomfret, *China's Debt Traps around the World Are a Trademark of its Imperialist Ambitions*, Wash. Post, Aug. 27, 2018, www.washingtonpost.com/news/global-opinions/wp/2018/08/27/chinas-debt-traps-around-the-world-are-a-trademark-of-its-imperialist-ambitions/ (last visited Feb. 25, 2020); John Hurley, *Examining the Debt Implications of the Belt and Road Initiative from a Policy Perspective*, CGD Policy Paper (2018), at 12–27.

[74] APEC Secretariat, APEC Connectivity Blueprint (2014), at 34–36.

[75] Lim Yan Liang, *China's Xi Jinping Defends Its Development Path and Slams Protectionist Actions*, Straits Times, Nov. 17, 2018, www.straitstimes.com/world/chinas-xi-jinping-defends-its-development-path-and-slams-protectionist-actions (last visited Feb. 25, 2020).

[76] Sueo Sudo, *Japan's ASEAN Policy: In Search of Proactive Multilateralism* 18 & 69 (2015).

[77] Ravenhill, *supra* note 8, at 116–17; Elek, *supra* note 15, at 73.

To Japan, APEC is a "main thrust" for regional economic cooperation and offers "one venue with major players in the Asia-Pacific region."[78] Japan has operated active capacity building activities under economic cooperation chapters of trade agreements, including the ASEAN-Japan FTA. Built on its FTA experiences, Japan has concentrated on APEC's economic cooperation initiatives. As the largest donor for the Policy Support Unit (PSU), which is the "think tank" of the APEC Secretariat, Japan also contributes to APEC's research capacity and institution-building.[79]

In new Asian regionalism, Japan's leadership led to the conclusion of the CPTPP following the US withdrawal. Despite the suspension of certain provisions of the TPP, the CPTPP is essentially "TPP 2.0." that functions as a critical pathway to the FTAAP. Tokyo's support for expanding CPTPP to include countries such as the United Kingdom will augment the global impact of the mega-FTA.[80] Also, at the 2018 APEC summit, Prime Minister Shinzo Abe stressed that "Japan, Australia and the United States completely share a vision of a free and open Indo-Pacific based on the rule of law."[81] Abe's approach, which Prime Minister Yoshihide Suga has largely followed, is to provide alternatives to China's BRI. The US Indo-Pacific strategy that involves quality infrastructure based on transparency and fiscal soundness aligns with Japan's national interests.

Notably, there is another "trade war" between APEC members. After Korean courts ordered Mitsubishi and Nippon Steel to compensate wartime forced labor, Japan restricted the export of chemicals that are essential to Korea's semi-conductor companies.[82] In 2019, Seoul brought

[78] Speech Given by Minister for Foreign Affairs Yohei Kono at the Kansai Press Club, Japan's Foreign Policy in the Asia-Pacific, and the Significance of APEC, Nov. 15, 1995; What is APEC for Japan? Jan. 2003, www.mofa.go.jp/policy/economy/apec/what.html (last visited Feb. 27, 2020).

[79] APEC PSU, *Annual Report 2018* (2018), at 12.

[80] Michito Tsuruoka, *Britain in the Trans-Pacific Partnership After Brexit? It's Complicated, Diplomat*, Nov. 12, 2019, https://thediplomat.com/2019/11/britain-in-the-trans-pacific-partnership-after-brexit/ (last visited Feb. 25, 2020).

[81] Satoshi Iizuka, *Abe Fails to Bridge US-China Divide at APEC Summit, Diplomat*, Nov. 19, 2018, www.japantimes.co.jp/news/2018/11/19/business/abe-fails-bridge-u-s-china-divide-apec-summit/#.XliNcmgzayJ (last visited Feb. 26, 2020).

[82] Yuka Fukunaga, *Japan's Trade Policy in the Midst of Uncertainty*, Aise.Visions, No. 112 (2020), at 19; Satoshi Sugiyama, *Frustrated with South Korea, Japan Greenlights Curbs on Smartphone and Semiconductor Supplies*, Japan Times, Jul. 4, 2019, www.japantimes.co.jp/news/2019/07/04/business/frustrated-south-korea-japan-greenlights-curbs-smartphone-semi conductor-supplies/#.XlijlmgzayI (last visited Feb. 27, 2020); Joyce Lee, *South Korean Forced Labor Victims to Seek Japan's Mitsubishi Asset Sale*, Reuters, Jul. 16, 2019, www.reuters.com/

a WTO complaint against Japan because of its illegal export restrictions and Tokyo's defense relied on the national security exception under Article XXI of the General Agreement on Tariffs and Trade (GATT).[83] Outside the WTO framework, APEC meetings may be utilized to facilitate conciliation between two sides.

E United States

As the world's largest economy, the United States ensured hegemonic stability for the neo-liberal international order premised on the Bretton Woods system and the Washington Consensus.[84] The sharp turning point occurred with the inauguration of President Trump in 2017. His discarding of multilateralism and heightened containment of China are now predictable elements of unpredictable US policy. It also raises grave concerns about whether the US-China confrontation will result in "Thucydides's Trap," which envisions the inevitable conflicts "[w]hen a rising power threatens to displace a ruling power."[85] APEC is a rare regional bloc that includes three superpowers, America, China and Russia. The ideological and geopolitical differences between Washington's Indo-Pacific strategy and Beijing's BRI, which Moscow supports, risk bifurcating APEC members and agendas. The Joe Biden administration's strategy toward China and Russia will inevitably influence the development of APEC.

From a historical perspective, US involvement significantly shaped APEC's direction. President Clinton's hosting of the first APEC leaders' meeting in 1993 gave rise to the custom that twenty-one APEC leaders take a group photo wearing the traditional costume of the host country. Washington conceived of APEC as leverage against European states in the Uruguay Round negotiations and considered it vital for APEC not to pursue Mahathir's EAEG proposal excluding America.[86] After APEC adopted its Non-Binding Investment Principles and the failure of the EVSL, US interests in achieving meaningful liberalization through APEC

article/us-southkorea-japan-laborers-mhi/south-korean-forced-labor-victims-to-seek-japans-mitsubishi-asset-sale-idUSKCN1UB0HO (last visited Mar. 1, 2020).

83 DS590: Japan – Measures Related to the Exportation of Products and Technology to Korea; Fukunaga, *supra* note 82, at 18.

84 *See generally* Michael C. Webb & Stephen D. Krasner, *Hegemonic Stability Theory: An Empirical Assessment*, 15 Rev. Int'l Stud. 183, 183–84 (1989).

85 Allison, *supra* note 69, at vii–viii.

86 Sung-Hoon Park & Jeong Yoen Lee, *APEC at Crossroads: Challenges and Opportunities*, 33(2) *Asian Persp.* 97, 108 (2009); Ravenhill, *supra* note 8, at 93–95.

deteriorated.[87] In 2001, APEC regained the White House's attention, as President George W. Bush utilized the APEC summit to garner support for the US-led "War on Terror" following the September 11 terrorist attacks.[88] For the first time, APEC introduced a nontrade issue into its agenda. Importantly, APEC's counterterrorism actions have expanded to cover secure supply chains, travel, finance and infrastructure.[89]

Concluding the US-led TPP was the trade priority of the Obama administration. APEC was the key forum through which Washington enhanced ties with ASEAN and "marketed" the TPP as the most feasible pathway to the FTAAP.[90] Trump replaced Obama's pivot to Asia strategy with a new "free and open Indo-Pacific" vision that stresses "[f]ree, fair, and reciprocal trade."[91] Although Trump announced the Indo-Pacific strategy at the 2017 APEC summit in Vietnam, he did not attend the 2018 Papua New Guinea meeting. Different from the "Asia-Pacific," the "Indo-Pacific" emphasizes the participation of India, which is not an APEC member. The new strategy is in response to Xi's assertive policy. Represented by US Vice President Pence, Washington's disagreement with Beijing in 2018 resulted in APEC's first-ever chair's statement rather than a leaders' declaration.[92]

Tellingly, the US Congress passed the Asia Reassurance Initiative Act of 2018 to reiterate the US diplomatic priority to support APEC and enhance engagement with ASEAN, Japan, Korea and Taiwan.[93] The 2019 APEC summit in Chile was cancelled. However, the United States reaffirmed the importance of APEC, which advances the Indo-Pacific vision and benefits US companies, as seven of America's top fifteen markets for goods exports are in APEC.[94] As Table 6.1 shows, APEC will continue to be an indispensable institution to promote the development of regional trade initiatives. APEC will also provide windows of opportunity for US and Chinese leaders to

[87] Ravenhill, *supra* note 8, at 94–97.
[88] 2001 Leaders' Declaration (2001).
[89] APEC Counter-Terrorism Working Group Strategic Plan 2018–2020 (2017), at 5–6.
[90] Remarks by President Obama at APEC CEO Summit, Nov. 10, 2014, https://obamawhitehouse.archives.gov/the-press-office/2014/11/10/remarks-president-obama-apec-ceo-summit (last visited Mar. 2, 2020).
[91] Department of Defense, *Indo-Pacific Strategy Report: Preparedness, Partnerships, and Promoting a Networked Region* (2019), at 3–4.
[92] The Chair's Era Kone Statement, *supra* note 6.
[93] S.2736 – Asia Reassurance Initiative Act of 2018, secs. 102(3) & 205–06.
[94] Office of the Spokesperson, US 2019 APEC Outcomes, Dec. 19, 2019.

Table 6.1 *APEC member economies' participation in regional initiatives*[95]

Member Economies	ASEAN	CPTPP	RCEP	China's BRI	US FTA
Australia		√	√		√
Brunei Darussalam	√	√	√	√	
Canada		√			√
Chile		√		√	√
China			√	√	
Hong Kong, China				√	
Indonesia	√		√	√	
Japan		√	√		√
Korea			√	√	√
Malaysia	√	√	√	√	

[95] ASEAN Member States, https://asean.org/asean/asean-member-states/ (last visited Jan. 21, 2020); Comprehensive and Progressive Agreement for Trans-Pacific Partnership (CPTPP), https://dfat.gov.au/trade/agreements/in-force/cptpp/Pages/comprehensive-and-progressive-agreement-for-trans-pacific-partnership.aspx (last visited Jan. 21, 2020); RCEP Overview, www.mfat.govt.nz/en/trade/free-trade-agreements/agreements-under-negotiation/regional-comprehensive-economic-partnership-rcep/rcep-overview/#countries (last visited Jan. 21, 2020); The Belt and Road Initiative: Country Profiles, http://china-trade-research.hktdc.com/business-news/article/The-Belt-and-Road-Initiative/The-Belt-and-Road-Initiative-Country-Profiles/obor/en/1/1X000000/1X0A36I0.htm (last visited Jan. 21, 2020); Free Trade Agreements, https://ustr.gov/trade-agreements/free-trade-agreements (last visited Jan. 21, 2020); Japan Free Trade Agreement, www.cbp.gov/trade/free-trade-agreements/japan (last visited Jan. 21, 2020).

Table 6.1 (*cont.*)

Member Economies	ASEAN	CPTPP	RCEP	China's BRI	US FTA
Mexico		√			√
New Zealand		√	√	√	
Papua New Guinea				√	
Peru		√		√	
Philippine	√		√	√	
Russia				√	
Singapore	√	√	√	√	√
Taiwan (Chinese Taipei)					
Thailand	√		√	√	
United States					
Vietnam	√	√	√	√	

directly engage and minimize the detrimental effect of a large-scaled trade war.

IV APEC's Soft-Law Approach and Incremental Achievements

Converged trade priorities of key APEC members such as ASEAN, Australia, China, Japan and the United States have fortified their support for APEC. Undeniably, diverging national interests have prevented APEC from modeling itself after ASEAN's legalization. Much criticism about APEC's nonbinding approach centers on how APEC meetings merely result in initiatives based on the least common denominator. The ill-defined soft-law principle was APEC's birth defect. The Bogor Declaration failed to define the objective of "free and open trade and investment." The principles in the Osaka Action Agenda, which intended to elaborate on the Bogor Goals, lack clarification and contradict each other in practice. To illustrate, it is inconceivable to reconcile the principle of flexibility "in the liberalization and facilitation process" with the principle of comprehensiveness.[96] There is actually no consensus on the principle of nondiscrimination, commonly known as open regionalism, or even on the concept of APEC consensus that may not equate unanimity.[97]

While acknowledging the weaknesses of the soft-law approach, I argue that APEC's thirty-year incremental achievements in WTO-plus and "Singapore issues" should not be ignored.[98] Commentators aver that soft-law has functioned efficiently in the field of international financial regulations such as the Basel Accords.[99] For several reasons, the APEC mechanism has demonstrated the positive impact of soft-law on certain areas of international trade law. In reality, countries are more motivated to make WTO-plus and extra "soft" commitments. Although they are not legally binding, the peer review mechanism under the Individual Action Plans involves reputational costs and buttresses voluntary compliance. In practice, developing countries

96 The Osaka Action Agenda: Implementation of the Bogor Declaration, *supra* note 34.

97 Vinod K. Aggarwal & Elaine Kwei, *Asia-Pacific Economic Cooperation (APEC): Transregionalism with a New Cause?*, *in* Interregionalism and International Relations 67, 73 (Heiner Hänggi et al. eds. 2006); Akiko Yanai, *Characteristics of APEC Trade Liberalization: A Comparative Analysis with the WTO*, *in* Trade Liberalization and APEC 9, 22–24 (Jiro Okamoto ed. 2004).

98 Singapore issues refer to four subjects (trade and investment, competition policy, transparency in government procurement and trade facilitations) decided at the WTO Ministerial Conference in Singapore in 1996.

99 *E.g.*, Chris Brummer, *Soft Law and the Global Financial System: Rule Making in the 21st Century* 60–114 (2012).

have referred to APEC model measures and "internalized" peer pressure against domestic protectionism. More significantly, APEC's soft-law rules are perceived as international standards and have subsequently been transformed into hard-law obligations in the WTO and FTAs. Reaching consensus among APEC members will also accelerate multilateral trade negotiations.

A Model Rules and Nonbinding Principles

In 2010, APEC leaders stressed the role of APEC "as an incubator of an FTAAP by providing leadership and intellectual input into the process."[100] An approach to achieving the incubator role is to develop model rules that reflect best practices and provide guidance for regulatory components of FTAs. Consequently, APEC members have deliberately drafted model and nonbinding rules as if they were binding. These initiatives are of particular significance to APEC members because 36 percent of their trade agreements were intra-APEC.[101]

A cardinal example is the Best Practice for RTAs/FTAs in APEC, which stipulates mandates for trade agreements, including WTO-plus commitments and simplified rules of origins.[102] APEC members, Korea and Chile, also sent the Best Practices to the WTO for reference.[103] In addition, APEC has developed various model measures on FTAs' specific chapters ranging from trade facilitation to the environment.[104] Have APEC governments adhered to these nonbinding rules? FTA's dispute resolution provisions exemplify a case of noncompliance. APEC's Best Practices call for "avoiding duplication with the WTO dispute settlement mechanism."[105] The dispute involving the WTO/FTA conflicting jurisdiction actually occurred in the seminal case of *Mexico – Soft Drinks*.[106]

[100] 2010 Leaders' Declaration (2010).

[101] APEC PSU, *Trends and Developments in Provisions and Outcomes of RTA/FTAs Implemented in 2018 by APEC Economies* (2020), at 2; APEC PSU, *Trends and Developments in Provisions and Outcomes of RTA/FTAs Implemented in 2017 by APEC Economies* (2018), at 4.

[102] Best Practice for RTAs/FTAs in APEC (2004).

[103] Communication from Chile and the Republic of Korea, Best Practices for FTAs/FTAs in APEC, TN/RL/W/187, Sept. 12, 2005.

[104] Fifteen model measures were developed between 2005 to 2008. CTI Report to Ministers, Collective Strategic Study on Issues Related to the Realization of the FTAAP (2016), at 129; APEC PSU, *The Mutual Usefulness between APEC and TPP* (2011), at 12–13.

[105] Best Practices for RTAs/FTAs in APEC (2004).

[106] *Id.*; Appellate Body Report, *Mexico – Tax Measures on Soft Drinks and Other Beverages*, WT/DS308/AB/R (2006) (*Mexico – Soft Drinks*).

According to the Appellate Body, the WTO cannot decline its jurisdiction due to the FTA's exclusion clause.[107] In other words, FTA provisions do not bar the jurisdiction of the WTO panel. Despite the Best Practices and WTO jurisprudence, most FTAs still have overlapping jurisdiction designs. The China-Singapore FTA even allows parties to use multiple mechanisms for a "particular dispute" if "[p]arties expressly agree."[108] The agreement is nonetheless silent on potentially divergent decisions rendered by different tribunals.

In new Asian regionalism, a critical issue is the harmonization of overlapping rules of origin, which result in the "spaghetti bowl" or "noodle bowl" syndrome that has caused a loss of 55.6 percent of the trade creation effect of FTA.[109] Following APEC's 2007 model measures on rules of origin and origin procedures, ASEAN changed from applying only the 40 percent Regional Value Content rule to also permitting the Change in Tariff Classification rule in 2008.[110] This more flexible coequal rule has been consistently adopted in newer FTAs, such as the 2015 ASEAN-China FTA Upgrading Protocol that amends the rules of origin in the original bilateral FTA.[111] Empirical research also reveals FTAs' higher degree of conformity to APEC model measures on customs administration and trade facilitation, as well as competition policy.[112]

Other than bilateral investment treaties, contemporary Asia-Pacific FTAs now commonly include investment chapters. The 1994 APEC Non-Binding Investment Principles reflect members' desire to follow common standards of practice. As constitutional provisions and domestic laws encompass different rules for expropriation and compensation, the Principles provide guidance for regional and international standards.[113] APEC updated the original Principles in 2011. The new version incorporates additional provisions mandating the consistency of laws and rules and regulatory protections,

[107] *Mexico – Soft Drinks*, paras. 42–53.

[108] Free Trade Agreement between the Government of the People's Republic of China and the Government of the Republic of Singapore (2008), art. 92(7).

[109] CTI Report to Ministers, *supra* note 104, at 123. The "spaghetti bowl" syndrome is also known as the "noodle bowl" effect in the context of Asian regionalism. Richard Baldwin & Masahiro Kawai, *Multilateralizing Asian Regionalism*, ADBI Working Paper, No. 431 (2013), at 11

[110] Yamazawa, *supra* note 8, at 76; Stefano Inama & Edmund W. Sim, *Rules of Origin in ASENA: A Way Forward 27* (2015).

[111] A Guide to Understanding the ASEAN-China Free Trade Area Update (2016), at 2.

[112] APEC PSU, *supra* note 101, at 12–13 & 19.

[113] United Nations Conference for Trade and Development (UNCTAD) Secretariat, Core Elements of International Investment Agreements in Domestic Investment Frameworks in the APEC Region (2011), at 11 & 40–43.

which prohibit the relaxation of health, labor and environmental regulations to induce foreign investment.[114]

These model measures and nonbinding principles on WTO-plus issues can offer reference for FTA negotiations, as well as capacity-building actions and trade policy dialogues under APEC's FTA sharing mechanism.[115] Moreover, for APEC countries' domestic reforms, the model rules provide roadmaps to new legislation. APEC's 2018 nonbinding principles for domestic regulation of the services sector and 2019 model procedural rules for online dispute resolution further illustrate APEC's forward-looking dimensions.[116]

B Trade Facilitation and Supply Chain Connectivity

Trade facilitation is no longer confined to customs procedures that involve the clearance of goods, but also include non-tariff barriers or behind-the-border measures that affect investment, infrastructure and e-commerce.[117] As one of four "Singapore issues," trade facilitation became part of the Doha Development Agenda work program, known as the "July Package."[118] The WTO's adoption of the 2014 Trade Facilitation Agreement (TFA) was a rare breakthrough amid the Doha Round impasse. Trade facilitation, which involves regulatory cooperation and harmonization and is incorporated into contemporary FTAs, could reduce trade costs by more than 14 -percent.[119] As of 2018, all APEC members have notified the acceptance of the TFA and have implemented 96.3 percent of the required measures.[120]

114 APEC Non-Binding Investment Principles (2011). The 1994 version of the Principles, see Annex 3, in *id.* at 85–87.

115 APEC endorsed the APEC Information Sharing Mechanism on FTAs/RTAs in 2014. CTI Report to Ministers, *supra* note 104, at 133–34; CTI Chair, Annex 4 – The Conduct of the Trade Policy Dialogue on WTO-Plus Elements of RTAs/FTAs and the Trade Policy Dialogue Outcomes Report, 2017/SOM2/018anx04 (2017), at 2–3.

116 APEC Non-Binding Principles for Domestic Regulation of the Services Sector (2018), which is built upon APEC Principles for Cross-Border Trade in Services (2009). The model procedural rules for online dispute resolution are included in Hong Kong, China, APEC Collaborative Framework for Online Dispute Resolution of Cross-Border Business-to Business Disputes – Endorsed, 2019/SOM3/EC/022 (2019). This Framework was supported by APEC leaders on a pilot basis in 2019.

117 WTO, World Trade Report 2015 (2015), at 35–36.

118 Text of the "July Package" – the General Council's Post-Cancún Decision, Aug. 1, 2004, www.wto.org/english/tratop_e/dda_e/draft_text_gc_dg_31july04_e.htm (last visited Mar. 1. 2020).

119 WTO, *supra* note 117, at 45–46; Bayhaqi et al., *supra* note 60, at 1.

120 APEC PSU, *supra* note 21, at 6; Bayhaqi et al., *supra* note 60, at 2.

After the EVSL's failed attempt for trade liberalization, APEC's two-phased Trade Facilitation Action Plans commenced after the 2001 leaders' meeting in Shanghai.[121] Unlike trade liberalization, trade facilitation seldom involves "deal-breaker" concessions. APEC's soft-law approach has pioneered innovative trade facilitation initiatives. In line with APEC's Bogor Goals and post-2020 vision, the APEC Supply Chain Connectivity Framework Action Plan (2017–20) and the APEC Connectivity Blueprint (2015–25) expanded previous action plans.[122]

APEC's trade facilitation actions have benefited the TFA and ASEAN. For instance, APEC's "single window" plan consolidates customs procedures and the "authorized economic operator" scheme implements the counter-terrorism and secure trade strategy in the supply chain.[123] These initiatives facilitate compliance with Articles 7 and 10 of the TFA.[124] Also, both the APEC Connectivity Blueprint and the Master Plan on ASEAN Connectivity 2025 focus on physical, institutional and people-to-people connectivity.[125] This reinforces my previous analysis of the "concentric ring" effect between APEC and ASEAN.

Physical connectivity denotes the development of "quality infrastructure for sustainable economic growth," which APEC leaders stressed in 2017.[126] This initiative is in tandem with the prospective evolution of the United Nations (UN) Sustainable Development Goals to develop "resilient infrastructure," as well as the Indo-Pacific strategy and the BRI.[127] To augment the soft-law function, APEC developed the Guidebook that ensures quality infrastructure and investment based on the public-private partnership.[128] Pursuant to the Guidebook, APEC initiated the peer review process that started with three ASEAN countries.[129] This process helps enhance

[121] APEC developed two Trade Facilitation Action Plans (TFAPs), including TFAP I (2001–06) and TFAP II (2007–10). APEC Secretariat, APEC's Second Trade Facilitation Action Plan (2007), at 3–4; Bayhaqi et al., *supra* note 60, at 1.

[122] APEC PSU, APEC Supply-Chain Connectivity Framework Action Plan 2017–2020: Interim Review of External Indicators (2019), at iv to 5.

[123] Bayhaqi et al., *supra* note 60, at 6–7.

[124] Trade Facilitation Agreement (2014), arts. 7(7) and 10(4).

[125] The APEC concept of three-pillar connectivity was defined in the 2013 Leaders' Declaration. APEC Secretariat, APEC Connectivity Blueprint (2014), at 12–13; ASEAN Secretariat, Mater Plan on ASEAN Connectivity 2025 (2016), at 19–21.

[126] 2017 Leaders' Declaration; APEC PSU, *supra* note 122, at 7–8.

[127] Sustainable Development Goals, *in* United Nations General Assembly, Transforming our world: the 2030 Agenda for Sustainable Development, A/Res/70/1 (2015), goal 9.1.

[128] *See generally* APEC Secretariat, *APEC Guidebook on Quality of Infrastructure Development and Investment (Revision)* (2018).

[129] The Philippines, Vietnam and Indonesia. APEC PSU, *supra* note 122, at 7.

transparency and capacity building. For instance, the peer review report on the Philippines acutely identified its legal weaknesses, such as the constitutional restriction on foreign equity and the vague notion of "just compensation" under the law on land acquisition.[130]

Moreover, an important area of institutional connectivity is to foster regulatory coherence of e-commerce laws. In 2020, 80 percent of countries worldwide passed e-transactions laws and 73 percent of them enacted cybercrime laws, whereas only 64 percent and 52 percent of these countries have legislation on consumer protection and data privacy, respectively.[131] In comparison, almost all APEC members have enacted comprehensive legal frameworks for e-commerce.[132] APEC's Cross-Border E-Commerce Framework has concentrated on improving the legal approach to assisting smaller enterprises and data privacy.[133]

Finally, as for people-to-people connectivity, a WTO-extra flagship scheme is the five-year valid APEC Business Travel Card, which enables precleared business travelers short-term entry to participating economies.[134] Nineteen APEC members have fully implemented the scheme, whereas Canada and the United States are transitional members.[135] From a constructivist perspective, the APEC fast-track lane at airports enhances the shared identity of APEC citizens. Practically, the scheme has expedited business mobility by enabling more than 270,000 cardholders to cut time spent at immigration checkpoints in half.[136] It

130 APEC PSU, Peer Review and Capacity Building on APEC Infrastructure Development and Investment: The Philippines (2017), at 6–7.

131 UNCTAD, Summary of Adoption of E-Commerce Legislation Worldwide, https://unctad.org/en/Pages/DTL/STI_and_ICTs/ICT4D-Legislation/eCom-Global-Legislation.aspx (last visited Mar. 17, 2020).

132 A notable exception is Brunei, which is yet to enact laws on data protection and privacy. APEC PSU, *supra* note 122, at 16–17.

133 *See generally* CTI Chair, Annex 2 – APEC Cross-Border E-Commerce Facilitation Framework, 2017/SOM3/027anx02 (2017).

134 The APEC Business Travel Card to be Further Modernized, Mar. 5, 2019, www.apec.org/Press/News-Releases/2019/0306_ABTC (last visited Mar. 2, 2020). In 2014, the APEC Business Mobility Group decided to extend the validity of the APEC Business Travel Card from three to five years. APEC Secretariat, *Supporting Continued Growth in Trade and Facilitation: End to End Review of the APEC Business Travel Card Scheme Final Report* (2014), at 5.

135 Frequently Asked Questions for APEC Business Travel Card Clients, www.apec.org/Groups/Committee-on-Trade-and-Investment/Business-Mobility-Group/ABTC/FAQ (last visited Mar. 3, 2020).

136 The APEC Business Travel Card to be Further Modernized, *supra* note 134; APEC's Achievements in Trade Facilitation in 2007–2010: Final Assessment of the Second Trade Facilitation Action (TFAP II) (2012), at 1.

therefore benefits temporary movement of natural persons (known as Mode 4) under the General Agreement on Trade in Services, thus illustrating the best practice for other trade blocs.

C *Information Technology Agreement and Tariff Cuts on Environmental Goods*

Tariff liberalization within APEC has made significance progress since its inception in 1989. As the average MFN tariffs of APEC members have decreased from 16 percent to 5.3 percent, the remaining challenges are in the area of tariffs on agricultural products and non-tariff measures.[137] It may be argued that tariff elimination is only due to WTO or FTAs rather than APEC. I disagree with this argument. Illustrated by China's tariff cuts in its pre-WTO period, APEC economies' commitments during the Osaka Leaders' Meeting led to APEC-wide tariff liberalization.[138] The peer review process under the Individual Action Plan, which covers tariffs as the first reporting element, has expedited the process. More profoundly, APEC's sectoral tariff reductions for IT and environmental goods have energized the transformation from soft-law commitments to hard-law obligations at the WTO. The rapid flow of these innovative products, in turn, contributes to Sustainable Development Goals and APEC's post-2020 vision.

Except for the EU, all of the world's top ten exporters of IT products are APEC members.[139] APEC played a pivotal role in shaping the WTO's first sectoral, plurilateral agreement, the ITA, which now covers 97 percent of global trade in IT products.[140] The main components of the ITA, including its product coverage and formulas for reducing tariffs, were first decided in the 1996 APEC ministerial meeting.[141] Built upon their consensus, the "APEC caucus" then pushed for the binding ITA at the WTO in the same year.

137 APEC PSU, *supra* note 21, at 2.

138 The Osaka Initial Actions, www.mofa.go.jp/policy/economy/apec/1995/initial.html (last visited Mar. 10, 2020).

139 The top ten exporters include China, the European Union (EU), the United States, Singapore, Korea, Taiwan, Japan, Vietnam, Malaysia and Mexico. WTO, *20 Years of the Information Technology Agreement: Boosting Trade, Innovation and Digital Connectivity* (2017), at 28.

140 *Id.* at 6.

141 Catherine Mann & Xuepeng Liu, *The Information Technology Agreement: Sui Generis or Model Stepping Stone?, in* Multilateralizing Regionalism: Challenges for the Global Trading System 182, 189 (Richard Baldwin & Patrick Low eds. 2009).

Given the fast-moving IT development, expanding the ITA coverage became urgent and necessary.[142] As the post-ITA talks ("ITA II" negotiations) stalled in 1998, APEC's 2011 decision to "[p]lay a leadership role in" the process again led to the WTO's 2015 ITA Expansion Declaration that applies to 201 products.[143] The parties to the ITA have grown from twenty-nine to eighty-two members.[144] As ITA commitments are on an MFN basis, developing countries yet to accede to the ITA are entitled to duty-free treatment, therefore buttressing their IT industries.

In tandem with the APEC Putrajaya Vision 2040 to develop a digital economy and technology, I urge APEC to initiate and facilitate "ITA III" talks. The WTO case of *EC-IT Products* well illustrates the legal challenges involving uncertainties of the ITA due to technological advances and the consistent need for expanding and clarifying ITA coverage.[145] IT products today have developed multiple functions, which initial ITA signatories in the 1990s could have never anticipated. For example, the 1996 ITA did not include popular consumer electronic products such as global positioning systems and MP3 players. The Harmonized System tariff nomenclature on which the ITA coverage was based also underwent significant changes.[146]

The WTO dispute involves challenges by three APEC economies, the United States, Japan and Taiwan, against the EU because it imposed 6–14 percent tariffs on three types of multifunctional machines.[147] Complainants argued that the flat panel displays, set-top boxes with communication functions, and multifunction digital machines should be duty-free because they were covered by the ITA.[148] The WTO panel did not accept Brussels' defense that these products' new functions justified reclassification.[149]

[142] Reasons for expanding the agreement, see Carlos Kuriyama & Azul Ogazon, *Expanding the Information Technology Agreement*, APEC PSU Brief No. 6 (2013), at 2–4.

[143] 2011 Leaders' Declaration (2011); WTO, *supra* note 139, at 59–65.

[144] WTO, *supra* note 139, at 6.

[145] Panel Report, *European Communities and Its Member States – Tariff Treatment of Certain Information Technology Products*, WT/DS375/R, WT/DS376/R, WT/DS377/R, Aug. 16 2010 (*EC-IT Products*).

[146] WTO, *supra* note 139, at 59–60; Concept Paper for the Expansion of the ITA, Communication from Canada, Japan, Korea, the Separate Customs Territory of Taiwan, Penghu, Kinmen and Matsu, Singapore and the United States, G/IT/W/36, May 2, 2012, at 1.

[147] *EC-IT Products*, paras. 7.119, 7.766 & 7.1138.

[148] Paola Conconi & Robert Howse, *Panel Report on EC-IT Products*, 11:2 World Trade Rev. 223, 223–24 (2012).

[149] *Id.*; Han-Wei Liu & Shin-Yi Peng, *Managing Trade Conflicts in the ICT Industry: A Case Study of EU-Greater China Area*, 19(3) J. Int'l Econ. L. 629, 651–52 (2016).

The panel found that as these products fell within the EU concessions, the tariff imposition contravened the ITA and Article II:1(a) and Article II:1(b) of the GATT.[150] Nevertheless, the panel did caution that multi-functional devices should be determined "on a case-by-case basis" and that they may become dutiable should their "principal function" significantly alter.[151] This case and the panel's reasoning provide the rationale for ITA II and prospective ITA III negotiations. Moreover, given the unprecedented demand for IT resources that enable "working from home" during the COVID-19 outbreak, APEC's leadership in the ITA remains critical.

Similar to tariff elimination on IT products, APEC members' tariff reduction on environmental goods also demonstrates APEC's success in the sectoral approach and its impact on the WTO. After APEC's EVSL that incorporated the environmental sector failed in 1997, the Doha Ministerial Declaration mandated the reduction of tariffs on environmental goods.[152] Although this trade initiative is essential to the goal of tackling rapid climate change under the Paris Agreement and the Sustainable Development Goals, the WTO's progress has been sluggish.

In comparison with the WTO and other trade blocs, APEC leaders made a breakthrough at the 2011 Honolulu summit, pledging to advance "green growth" by reducing applied tariffs on environmental goods to 5 percent or less by 2015.[153] Notably, the host country, the United States, was also the nominating economy to include the environmental sector in the previous EVSL.[154] In 2012, APEC governments agreed on the tariff reduction list of fifty-four environmental goods such as gas turbines and purifying machinery.[155] Based on their tariff rates, APEC economies have met the 5 percent goal and have thus

150 *E.g.*, *EC-IT Products*, paras. 8.3–8.11.

151 *E.g.*, *EC-IT Products*, paras. 7.734, 7.986 & 7.1501; paras. 7.1308 & 7.1397. See generally Tsai-Yu Lin, *Systemic Reflection on the EC-IT Product Case: Establishing an "Understanding" on Maintaining the Product Coverage of the Current Information Technology Agreement in the Face of Technological Change*, 45(2) J. World Trade 401, 417–19 (2011).

152 Yamazawa, *supra* note 33, at 8; Doha Ministerial Declaration, WT/MIN(01)/DEC/1, 20 Nov. 2001, art. 31(iii).

153 2011 Leaders' Declaration (2011).

154 Other nominating economies include Canada, Japan and Taiwan. Yamazawa, *supra* note 33, at 8.

155 Annex C – APEC List of Environmental Goods, Sept. 8, 2012, www.apec.org/Meeting-Papers/Leaders-Declarations/2012/2012_aelm/2012_aelm_annexC.aspx (last visited Mar. 18, 2020).

promoted clean technologies and global trade worth more than $500 billion.[156] More importantly, following the ITA model, eleven APEC members have engaged in negotiating the WTO Environmental Goods Agreement since 2014.[157] Due to the MFN design, other WTO members will be entitled to the spillover benefits. The agreement will further reinforce APEC's capacity to transform the regional soft-law consensus to multilateral hard-law obligations.

V Reforming APEC in New Asian Regionalism

New Asian Regionalism has encountered daunting challenges posed by mega-FTAs, nationalist protectionism, and global travel and trade restrictions following the COVID-19 pandemic. Will APEC be marginalized or rejuvenated in the new era? It depends on APEC's constructive implementation of its post-2020 vision, which aims to finalize unfinished actions of the Bogor Goals and galvanize regional integration.[158] Core agendas should focus on reforms of the APEC Secretariat, the PSU and the peer review process, and APEC's active incubator role for advancing the FTAAP.

A *Professionalizing the APEC Secretariat*

APEC and ASEAN shared similar loose organizational structures when they were formed. While APEC continues to be a soft-law alliance, ASEAN's legalization made significant progress when the ASEAN Charter conferred legal personality on the bloc as an intergovernmental organization.[159] The establishment of the AEC further crystalized ASEAN's economic goals and imposed hard-law obligations without changing the decision-making process premised on consensus. In contrast, APEC lacks a founding document. The earliest agreement on APEC's structure was the 2012 Bangkok Declaration, which provided the legal basis for setting up the APEC Secretariat in Singapore.[160] According to the advisory opinion of the International Court of Justice, it may be contended that a separate legal

[156] CTI Report to Ministers, *supra* note 104, at 129; APEC Cuts Environmental Goods Tariffs, Jan. 28, 2016, www.apec.org/Press/News-Releases/2016/0128_EG.aspx (last visited Mar. 18, 2020).

[157] There are eighteen negotiating parties, including the EU. Environmental Goods Agreement (EGA), www.wto.org/english/tratop_e/envir_e/ega_e.htm (last visited Mar. 18, 2020).

[158] *E.g.*, APEC Vision Group, *supra* note 10, at 10–13.

[159] Charter of the Association of Southeast Asian Nations (2007), art. 3.

[160] Bangkok Declaration on Asia-Pacific Economic Cooperation (APEC) (1992).

personality of an international organization from its members can be conferred or inferred.[161] The argument does not extend to APEC, as member economies have made it clear in declarations and in practice that the *sui generis* status remains unchanged.

Singapore law rather than an APEC treaty grants the APEC Secretariat "the legal capacities of a body corporate" and "inviolability of official archives and premises."[162] Singapore law confines privileges and immunities of the APEC Secretariat and its staff to the country.[163] APEC officials are neither entitled to travel documents comparable to UN laissez-passers nor are they accorded privileges and immunities in other APEC economies.[164] These practical hurdles have jeopardized the meaningful impact of the APEC Secretariat. ASEAN provides a model. The legal capacity and inviolability of the Jakarta-based ASEAN Secretariat were once only recognized under Indonesian law.[165] However, based on the mandate of the ASEAN Charter, the 2009 ASEAN agreement reinforces privileges and immunities to the ASEAN Secretary-General and staff of the ASEAN Secretariat.[166] APEC members should enact an ASEAN-like agreement in order to strengthen the legal status and capacity of the Secretariat.

Other than legal issues, financial and human resources are pivotal to any international institution. Notably, the APEC Secretariat has an annual budget of only $5 million (approximately a quarter of the ASEAN Secretariat's budget), but the number of staff has increased from thirteen to sixty since 1993.[167] As Table 6.2 demonstrates, the scale of the APEC Secretariat is rather

161 Advisory Opinion, *Reparation for Injuries Suffered in the Service of the United Nations*, ICJ Reports (1949), at 118–79.

162 The International Organizations (Immunities and Privileges) (APEC Secretariat) Order 1993, arts. A.3 & A.4.

163 *Id.*; Agreement between the Government of Singapore and the Secretariat of the Asia Pacific Economic Cooperation Organization Relating to the Privileges and Immunities of the APEC Secretariat (1993); Supplemental Agreement between the Secretariat of the Asia-Pacific Economic Cooperation Organization (APEC) Relating to the Privileges and Immunities of the APEC Secretariat (2005).

164 Convention on the Privileges and Immunities of the United Nations (1946), art. VII

165 Agreement between the Government of Indonesia and ASEAN Relating to the Privileges and Immunities of the ASEAN Secretariat (1979), arts. 2 & 3.

166 Agreement on Privileges and Immunities of the Association of Southeast Asian Nations (2009), art. 4.

167 *"No Reforms" for ASEAN Anytime Soon*, Jarkata Post, Sept. 25, 2017, www.thejakartapost.com/seasia/2017/11/25/no-reforms-for-asean-anytime-soon.html (last visited Mar. 20, 2020); Carlo Closa & Lorenzo Casni, *Comparative Regional Integration: Governance and Legal Models* 285–86 (2016); Frequently Asked Questions, www.apec.org/FAQ (last visited Mar. 20, 2020); APEC – A Multilateral Economic Forum, www.apec.org/About-Us/How-APEC-Operates (last visited Mar. 20, 2020).

Table 6.2 *Selected information on international institutions*[168]

Institution	Secretariat: Number of Staff	Number of Member States/Economies
EU	European Commission: 32,000	27 (after Brexit)
OECD	Secretariat: 3,300	36
WTO	Secretariat: 625	164
ASEAN	Secretariat: 300	10
APEC	Secretariat: 60 & PSU: 13	21

limited in comparison with secretariats of other international and regional organizations.

Arguably, major expenses for holding APEC meetings are borne by host economies and APEC projects are often funded by individual members. However, it cannot be ignored that an insufficient budget and staff of professionals of the APEC Secretariat have confined its function to passive coordination. Unlike the European Commission and the OECD Secretariat, the APEC Secretariat has seldom exerted leadership in APEC initiatives. Other than locally recruited personnel, seventeen staff members are career diplomats seconded from and salaried by their respective governments.[169] These diplomats usually serve as program directors but will only work at the Secretariat for three years.[170] The Executive Director of the APEC Secretariat can neither discipline nor promote them.

[168] Commission Staff, https://ec.europa.eu/info/about-european-commission/organisational-structure/commission-staff_en (last visited Jan. 22, 2020); EU Member Countries in Brief, https://europa.eu/european-union/about-eu/countries/member-countries_en (last visited Jan. 22, 2020); Organisational Structure, www.oecd.org/about/structure/ (last visited Jan. 22, 2020); Member Countries, www.oecd.org/about/members-and-partners/ (last visited Jan. 22, 2020); Overview of the WTO Secretariat, www.wto.org/english/thewto_e/secre_e/intro_e.htm (last visited Feb. 2, 2021); Members and Observers, www.wto.org/english/thewto_e/whatis_e/tif_e/org6_e.htm (last visited Jan. 22, 2020); Evan Laksmana, *Time to Consider Refinancing Options for the ASEAN Secretariat*, Nov. 10, 2017, www.aspistrategist.org.au/time-to-consider-refinancing-options-for-the-asean-secretariat/ (last visited Jan. 22, 2020); Asian Development Bank Institute, ASEAN 2030: Toward a Borderless Economic Community 201 (2014); Frequently Asked Questions, *supra* note 167; PSU Staff, www.apec.org/About-Us/Policy-Support-Unit/PSU-Staff (last visited Jan. 22, 2020).

[169] Frequently Asked Questions, *supra* note 167.

[170] APEC Secretariat, www.apec.org/ContactUs/APECSecretatriat (last visited Mar. 20, 2020).

APEC members have proposed reforms of the Secretariat since 2002.[171] In 2010, a key result was to create a three-year Executive Director position, open to applicants from qualified professionals rather than only government nominees.[172] Previously, Executive Directors and Deputy Executive Directors rotated between APEC economies.[173] The fact that the Secretariat was headed by these ambassador-level officials for merely two years made long-term plans and possible reforms difficult. For these reasons, it is imperative to increase professional positions, which will enhance professionalism and institutional memory at the APEC Secretariat. The strengthened capacity of the Secretariat will better bridge the link among APEC's three-pillared actions and evaluate proliferating yet fragmented ECOTECH initiatives.[174]

B Policy Support Unit and APEC's Peer Review Process

Another significant reform of the APEC Secretariat was the creation of the PSU in 2008.[175] Based on its Governance Arrangements, the mandate for the PSU is to assist APEC economies in implementing their structural reforms and APEC measures.[176] Although the PSU forms a part of the APEC architecture, it is technically independent of the APEC Secretariat. Different from career diplomats at the APEC Secretariat, the PSU Director and staff members are not affiliated with APEC governments. The budget of the APEC Secretariat relies on members' mandatory contributions, whereas the PSU is supported by voluntary contributions.

The PSU was initially designed as a temporary structure. Nonetheless, "an ongoing mandate was granted to the PSU from" 2018 if it receives sufficient financial resources.[177] Seven APEC members provided financial contributions to the PSU, including Japan, the United States and Australia as the

[171] Closa & Casni, *supra* note 167, at 286–87.

[172] Dr Rebecca Fatima Sta Maria, www.apec.org/Press/Blogs/Dr-Rebecca-Fatima-Sta-Maria (last visited Mar. 31, 2020).

[173] The Executive Director came from the member that hosted the APEC meetings in that year and the Deputy Executive Director, who would become the next executive director, came from the next host economy. Ravenhill, *supra* note 8, at 131.

[174] *E.g.*, SOM Steering Committee on Economic and Technical Cooperation, 2018 Senior Officials' Report on Economic and Technical Cooperation (2018), at 19–20.

[175] Policy Support Unit, www.apec.org/About-Us/Policy-Support-Unit (last visited Mar. 23, 2020).

[176] APEC Policy Support Unit Governance Arrangements (2018), at 3.

[177] *Id.* at 10.

largest donors.[178] With its reports on various dimensions of the Bogor Goals, the PSU has strengthened APEC's analytical capacity and identity. In my view, the PSU should be incorporated into the APEC Secretariat as a permanent unit and its budget should be supported by all members. To realize APEC's post-2020 vision, the PSU should contribute more to the peer review process, thus buttressing APEC's soft-law impact and its incubator role for the FTAAP.[179] The PSU's analysis will also help meet APEC governments' urgent need to assess their potential entry into CPTPP and RCEP negotiations.

Undoubtedly, the PSU has enhanced Individual Action Plans that require periodic reports on seventeen specific areas from APEC members, including those identified in the Osaka Action Agenda and additional issues.[180] According to the principle of concerted unilateral liberalization, APEC commenced the voluntary peer review system in 1998 and the system became compulsory in 2002.[181] From 2012 to 2020, all APEC economies were obliged to submit reports on their progress every two years.[182] The review meeting occurs in a special session of the Senior Officials' Meeting. Discussions are based on observations of two independent experts' visits to review economies, the PSU's short report, and questions by other members and the APEC Business Advisory Council.[183] In addition to these regular reviews, the PSU was tasked to function as "the ad-hoc review team secretariat for" APEC's new infrastructure development and investment initiative.[184] Hence, the peer review system has become APEC's key mechanism to exert peer pressure on members and facilitate the best practices and capacity building.

178 Australia, the United States, Japan provided 30 percent, 21.6 percent and 20.6 percent, respectively, of the total contributions that the PSU received. APEC PSU, *supra* note 79, at 12.

179 PSU projects, see APEC Secretariat, APEC Secretariat's 2019 Operational Plan (2019), at 3; APEC PSU Five-Year Strategic Plan 2013–17 (2013), at 4.

180 CTI Chair, The Individual Action Plan (IAP) and IAP Peer Review, 2011/SOM2/021anx2, May 17–18, 2011, at 1–2.

181 Soesastro, *supra* note 36, at 74–75.

182 APEC members would report in 2012, 2014, 2016, 2018 and 2020, which was the final assessment for the end of the Bogor Goals. CTI Chair, *supra* note 180, at 2.

183 *Id.* at 2–3; Geoffrey Woodhead, *The Role of Peer Reviews in APEC, First OECD-South East Asia Regional Forum: Peer Review Mechanisms – Macroeconomic Policies, Regional Economic Integration and Economic Development* (2007), at 2– 4; APEC Secretariat, IAP Peer Review: Review Teams, Timeline and List of Experts, 2008/SOM1/014, Mar. 2–3, 2008, at 3–5.

184 APEC PSU, *supra* note 79, at 4.

A comparative scheme is the WTO's trade policy review mechanism. WTO members are required to submit government reports and answer questions from other members during the review meeting. The WTO Secretariat will publish final reports, which will be made available on the WTO website and serve as reference documents to understand different trade regimes. At the WTO, only the top "four trading entities" will be reviewed every two years, so that most APEC members will only be subject to the WTO review every four to six years.[185]

Presumably, APEC's more frequent reviews and their WTO-plus coverage will invigorate transparency and liberalization. However, the weaknesses of the APEC review procedure should be remedied. First, as it stands now, the review process involves independent experts, who are primarily academics nominated by governments and work with the APEC Secretariat on a contract basis.[186] In practice, different review teams, including independent experts, have often led to divergent levels of assessment.[187] Second, although APEC aimed to make peer review reports more accessible to the public, those reports can hardly be found on the APEC website.[188] The rare "publicly available" reports derived from the review process are the PSU's stocktaking reports on the Bogor Goals progress.[189]

Lastly, as WTO reports become more comprehensive, the added value of APEC reports that cover limited WTO-plus issues has diminished. The fact that the WTO mechanism is perceived to be more stringent has inevitably induced members to simply "copy and paste" their WTO reports for the APEC review. For these reasons, I recommend that the prospective review process rely more on PSU professionals rather than ad-hoc experts. To standardize their format, APEC review reports can be modeled after WTO Secretariat reports. The coverage of APEC reports is advised to include additional WTO-plus issues such as the status of e-commerce legislation and regulations on infrastructure projects. The reports should also identify the deviation from APEC's model rules and measures, thus reinforcing their soft-law impact on the post-2020 vision.

[185] Trade Policy Review Mechanism (TPRM), www.wto.org/english/docs_e/legal_e/29-tprm_e.htm (last visited Mar. 24, 2020).

[186] APEC Secretariat, *supra* note 183, at 3–6.

[187] Yamazawa, *supra* note 8, at 15; APEC Secretariat, *supra* note 183, at 2–3.

[188] The e-IAP website does not work. Action Plans, www.apec.org/About-Us/How-APEC-Operates/Action-Plans (last visited Mar. 22, 2020).

[189] *E.g.*, APEC PSU, *supra* note 21, at 1–9.

C APEC As the Incubator for Mega-FTAs and the FTAAP

The reformed APEC Secretariat and the peer review process will collectively contribute to APEC's intellectual leadership. More significantly, APEC's incubator role in developing mega-FTAs as feasible pathways to the twenty-one-party FTAAP will determine APEC's marginalization or rejuvenation in new Asian regionalism. For APEC governments, understanding the development of mega-FTAs is pivotal because currently seven APEC members are parties to both the CPTPP and the RCEP.[190]

In 2004, the APEC Business Advisory Council propounded the FTAAP in order to revitalize APEC amid proliferating trade and investment agreements.[191] APEC leaders adopted the FTAAP vision in 2006 and identified ASEAN-plus frameworks and the TPP as the basis of the FTAAP in 2010.[192] The precursor to the TPP is the P4 agreement that four smaller APEC economies (Brunei, Chile, New Zealand and Singapore) finalized during the 2015 APEC meeting.[193] In 2009, the Obama administration's decision to join TPP negotiations that expanded the P4 agreement secured the TPP's status as the most feasible pathway to the FTAAP.[194] Although twelve TPP countries signed the agreement in 2016, the Trump administration withdrew the United States from the TPP in 2017.[195] Some TPP members, including particularly Japan, salvaged this agreement. Having suspended twenty-two controversial provisions of the thirty-chapter TPP, such as those related to investor-state dispute settlement and extended intellectual property rights, the remaining eleven parties concluded the new CPTPP, which came into force in 2018.[196]

The RCEP has been seen as the competing mega-FTA with the TPP. Based on ASEAN's 2012 Guiding Principles for the RCEP, the first round of

[190] These members include Australia, Brunei, Japan, Malaysia, New Zealand, Singapore and Vietnam. CTI Report to Ministers, *supra* note 104, at 157.

[191] APEC News Release, Asia Pacific Business Leaders to Press APEC Leaders to Accelerate Regional Economic Integration, Feb. 14, 2014, at 1.

[192] *Id.*; 2010 Leaders' Declaration (2010).

[193] The official title of the P4 agreement is the Trans-Pacific Strategic Economic Partnership Agreement (TPSEP). Deborah K. Elms & C. L. Lim, *An Overview and Snapshot of the TPP Negotiations, in* The Trans-Pacific Partnership: A Quest for a Twenty-First-Century Trade Agreement 21, 21–22 (C. L. Lim el. eds. 2012).

[194] *Id.* at 26–27.

[195] CTI Report to Ministers, *supra* note 104, at 166.

[196] Annex II – List of Suspended Provisions, www.international.gc.ca/trade-commerce/trade-agreements-accords-commerciaux/agr-acc/cptpp-ptpgp/annex2-annexe2.aspx?lang=eng (last visited Mar. 25, 2020); CPTPP, *supra* note 95; Meredith Kolsky Lewis, *The Origin of Plurilateralism in International Trade Law*, 20 J. Inv. & Trade 633, 639–40 (2019).

negotiations took place in 2013 and sixteen countries, including India, outlined the contents for the RCEP in 2017.[197] RCEP parties agreed on the twenty chapters in 2019 and signed the agreement in 2020.[198] Strikingly, Indian Prime Minister Narendra Modi decided not to join the RCEP presumably because escalating trade deficits with China and other RCEP countries would severely hinder the domestic industry.[199] Beijing's support for the RCEP is easily understood, as key proponents for the CPTPP are close US allies that may undermine Chinese influence in the region.

It may be averred that the RCEP is built upon "ASEAN Plus Six" FTAs that APEC leaders envisioned in 2010. In fact, the RCEP first appeared in the 2014 Beijing Roadmap for the FTAAP, in which APEC economies articulated the TPP and the RCEP as potential pathways to the FTAAP.[200] Beijing conducted a two-year collective strategic study on the FTAAP, which APEC leaders endorsed in their Lima Declaration in 2016.[201] According to the Declaration, the CPTPP and the RCEP are considered as essential building blocks for the FTAAP.

The open accession clauses of the two mega-FTAs also make their potential expansion to twenty-one APEC members legally possible. Such clauses that allow the accession of other countries have been incorporated in plurilateral and bilateral FTAs within APEC such as the P4 agreement and the Australia-US FTA.[202] Significantly, the CPTPP is open to "any State or separate customs territory," subject to terms and conditions set by current parties.[203] A similar open accession clause is

[197] Outline of the RCEP Agreement (as at November 2017), *in* Joint Leaders' Statement on the Negotiations for the Regional Comprehensive Economic Partnership (RCEP) (2017).

[198] Joint Leaders' Statement on the Regional Comprehensive Economic Partnership (RCEP) (2019); Joint Leaders' Statement on the Regional Comprehensive Economic Partnership (RCEP) (2020).

[199] Rahul Mazumdar, *India Should Hold Off on RCEP Agreement*, Business Line, Nov. 1, 2019, www.thehindubusinessline.com/opinion/india-should-hold-off-on-rcep-agreement/article29856854.ece (last visited Mar. 22, 2020).

[200] Annex A – The Beijing Roadmap for APEC's Contribution to the Realization of the FTAAP (2014); CTI Report to Ministers, *supra* note 104, at 2–3.

[201] 2014 Leaders' Declaration (2014); Annex A: Lima Declaration on FTAAP (2016).

[202] Asia-Pacific FTAs with open accession clauses, see Shintaro Hamanaka, *Accession to TPP: Veto Power and "Opt-Out" Option*, *in* Paradigm Shift in International Economic Law Rule-Making: TPP as a New Model for Trade Agreements? 435, 439–41 (Julien Chaisse et al. eds. 2017). For instance, Australia-US FTA permits the participation of a "[a]ny country or group of countries" and the P4 agreement, which is open to "any APEC Economy and other States." Australia-United States Free Trade Agreement (2004), at 23.1; TPSEP (2005), art. 20.6.

[203] CPTPP (2018), art 5. The CPTPP clause amended the accession clause, article 30.4 of the Trans-Pacific Partnership that makes the accession of "a member of APEC" easier.

also included in the RCEP.[204] Other APEC members have been evaluating their accession to the CPTPP and the RCEP. Consequently, APEC's incubator and leadership role should be fortified by providing insight into the convergence and divergence of the two mega-FTAs.

VI Conclusion

As a de facto transregional institution, APEC's nonbinding approach based on consensus has been subject to criticism. The chapter provided the most updated insight into APEC's soft-law mechanism and implications for emerging mega-FTAs. It contended that the impact of APEC's two cardinal principles, open regionalism and concerted unilateral liberalization, should not be ignored. To understand APEC's development and agendas, the chapter deciphered the legal and trade strategies of key APEC stakeholders, including Australia, ASEAN, China, Japan and the United States. While the divergence of their priorities led to different emphases on APEC's three pillars, the convergence of national interests contributed to the incremental achievements of APEC.

In the past thirty years, APEC's model measures and trade facilitation actions provided the best practices for members' structural reforms. The success of ITA and tariff elimination on environmental goods further demonstrate APEC's salient influence over WTO agreements that imposes hard-law obligations. In line with the APEC Putrajaya Vision 2040, APEC governments are advised to enhance the capacity of the APEC Secretariat and fortify the peer review process. More importantly, reasserting APEC's intellectual leadership in developing the CPTPP and the RCEP will rejuvenate the impetus of APEC in new Asian regionalism.

[204] RCEP Guiding Principles, *supra* note 56, princ. 6; RCEP (2020), art. 20.9.

7

Conclusion

With the arrival of the Asian century, proliferating trade and investment agreements in the Asia-Pacific have attracted tremendous academic and government attention. The book represents the first systematic examination of new Asian regionalism as a paradigm shift in international economic law. It argued that new Asian regionalism has emerged amid the Third Regionalism and contributed to the New Regional Economic Order (NREO), which reinvigorates the role of developing countries in shaping international trade norms.

To substantiate the claims and promote interdisciplinary dialogues, the book introduced theoretical lenses and assessed major regional economic initiatives and institutions, as well as trade policies of Asian powers, the European Union (EU) and the United States. New Asian regionalism is defined as a new normative integration process, which has evolved with the Association of Southeast Asian Nations (ASEAN) Plus Six framework that underpins Asia's ascending economic power. Distinct from the conventional country-specific approach to understanding regionalism, the book built the analysis on the ASEAN Plus Six framework and its international implications. Building on case studies in preceding chapters, this final chapter summarizes key findings and recommendations for the Global South and the multilateral trading system.

Chapter 1 illuminated key concepts of the Third Regionalism, which denotes the third wave of global regionalism, and the NREO that demonstrates developing countries' changing strategy after their failed attempt to establish the New International Economic Order (NIEO). As modern Asia-Pacific agreements illustrate, the unique characteristics of the Third Regionalism include the rapid development of South-South free trade agreements (FTAs), mega-FTAs, interregional and comprehensive agreements.

The most critical normative development in Asia is the ASEAN-centered regime that transformed from the ASEAN Plus Three structure into the ASEAN Plus Six framework. Unlike the Washington or Beijing Consensus, the ASEAN Consensus facilitated the multilateralization of the ASEAN way and became an operational notion recognized by Asia-Pacific economies. Consequently, the book's focus on the legal regimes of new Asian regionalism filled a major literature gap and remedied the weaknesses of regionalism studies preoccupied with European experiences. The empirical investigations also support political scientists' theoretical arguments for the new regionalism approach, comparative regionalism and the new dependency theory.

Following Chapter 1's introduction, Chapter 2 examined the legalization of the ASEAN Economic Community, which has intersected with ASEAN's internal and external pacts. The chapter found it incorrect to simply characterize the ASEAN way as a pure political or soft-law concept. Against the backdrop of the AEC Blueprint 2025 and its "Global ASEAN" agenda, the ASEAN way has gradually shifted to hard-law obligations with structured flexibility. It exhibits a model of pragmatic incrementalism that reflects Asia's legal culture and practice and departs from the Western perception of legalization. As the chapter discovered, ASEAN's legal and structural differences from the EU have in reality minimized the "sovereign cost" and energized developing countries with divergent levels of development to pursue regionalism.

Although ASEAN's tariff elimination schedules accorded ASEAN's least developed country members extra flexibility, intra-ASEAN tariff liberalization became the most successful arena of ASEAN integration. The ASEAN way also influenced the services liberalization approach, which encompasses the "packages" structure, the "ASEAN Minus X" formula, and Mutual Recognition Arrangements to facilitate Mode 4 liberalization for selected sectors. Although these structured flexibilities are by no means perfect, they proved to be feasible for a South-South FTA.

ASEAN shared the anti-litigation tradition with East Asia. The state-to-state dispute resolution system is modeled after the World Trade Organization (WTO), but no ASEAN countries have resorted to the system. ASEAN's investor-state dispute settlement (ISDS) scheme is based on the US Model Bilateral Investment Agreement and has only been utilized once. ASEAN's internal FTA experiences, including the implementation of electronic commerce (e-commerce) and development provisions, have a salient impact on ASEAN's external FTAs that form the basis of the ASEAN Plus Six framework. Instead of concluding one single FTA similar to the EU and US pacts, multiple agreements negotiated under the framework agreement facilitated the building of confidence and led to a comprehensive FTA over time. With structured reviews and updates, the levels of liberalization of ASEAN Plus One FTAs are expected to be comparable to agreements that follow the "Western" approach.

To reinforce the multilateralization of the ASEAN way, Chapter 3 offered an up-to-date account of the legal structure of the Regional Comprehensive Economic Partnership (RCEP). As the world's largest FTA by economic scale, the RCEP represents Asia's collective response to the US-China trade war and the COVID-19 recession. As the chapter stressed, the RCEP has been an ASEAN-led process rather than a China-dominated pact. Commentators should not underestimate the potential influence of the RCEP due to its omission of contents that are incorporated into the Comprehensive and Progressive Agreement for Trans-Pacific Partnership (CPTPP), such as ISDS, state-owned enterprises (SOEs) and sustainable development provisions. Both mega-FTAs are competing and complementary.

In essence, the RCEP makes the horizontal expansion of trade rules easier for developing countries to accept. The RCEP ought to be deemed as a framework agreement. The chapter asserted that the RCEP's tariff elimination over twenty years will not yield an immediate impact on the regional supply chain. Nonetheless, the consolidation of rules of origin alone will bring substantial benefits to enterprises. Furthermore, akin to the CPTPP, the RCEP will coexist with instead of supersede current agreements, so that it will only reduce the "noodle bowl" syndrome on a de facto basis.

The RCEP's hybrid services schedule, which is poised to convert to the more progressive negative list approach, also demonstrates the pragmatic incrementalism approach. While the RCEP's soft-law rules on government procurement and e-commerce have a limited regulatory impact, they indicate an increasing consensus among Asia-Pacific states. The RCEP's potential normative conflicts with the WTO, other FTAs and BITs, as well as the institutionalization of the RCEP Secretariat, will be critical to legal research. At the core of the NREO, the RCEP serves as a more development-friendly and politically amenable model alternative to neoliberal EU and US trade agreements.

The book emphasized both endogenous and exogenous impacts on new Asian regionalism and identified the transformation of North-South relations leading to the NREO in the Third Regionalism. While I shared political scientists' concerns about the Euro-centric methodology of regionalism research, I observed that Asian countries' interregional FTAs with Brussels and Washington have shaped Asia-Pacific agreements. Chapter 4 concentrated on the EU's new Asia strategy and recent agreements with Asian countries. As for East Asia, the EU signed FTAs with Korea and Japan. In 2020, the EU also concluded in principle the negotiations for a Comprehensive Agreement in Investment with China, but the ratification of the agreement will likely be delayed due to Brussels' and Beijing's impositions of tit-for-tat sanctions over forced labor issues in Xinjiang. In the same year, the EU elevated its relationship with ASEAN to a strategic partnership, which provided an extra impetus for the ASEAN-EU FTA. This development also enriched theoretical debates of interregionalism. In my view, contemporary ASEAN-EU ties represent what I refer to as the "Third Interregionalism" amid the global wave of the Third Regionalism.

Based on EU agreements with Singapore and Vietnam following the Opinion 2/15 of the Court of Justice of the EU, the chapter provided insight into the EU's building-block approach to realizing the region-to-region FTA. Tellingly, these bilateral, pathfinder FTAs should be understood in tandem with Investment Protection Agreements (IPAs) and the Partnership and Cooperation Agreements (PCAs). EU FTAs are EU-only agreements, whereas IPAs and PCAs are mixed agreements and require ratification from the European Parliament and twenty-seven national parliaments. The chapter noted that the key textual differences between Singapore and Vietnam agreements revealed the EU's flexibility in negotiating trade pacts. There are unique, different characteristics related to ASEAN cumulative rules of origin under two EU FTAs, which in turn benefit ASEAN integration. Other significant differences exist in the arenas of copyright protection, geographical indications and SOEs.

In terms of ISDS, the two EU IPAs incorporate the two-tiered Investment Court System, but the two IPAs differ in the number and appointment of adjudicators. I doubted the acceptance of this system by other ASEAN members. Nevertheless, the IPAs' elaborate mediation rules complement the Singapore Convention on Mediation, contributing to the new foundation for resolving investor-state disputes through mediation, which is appealing to Asian and developing countries.

As for politically sensitive FTA and PCA provisions on human rights and sustainable development, Brussels' negotiations with Singapore and Vietnam showed a more lenient stance on the former. Different from the conventional understanding, it is unlikely that the EU will bring complaints against Vietnam in the near future, as its government had largely complied with similar requirements under the CPTPP. Notwithstanding these pathfinder agreements, I cautioned that the EU's palm oil disputes with Indonesia, as well as sanctions again Myanmar for the military coup, will continue to pose challenges for ASEAN-EU FTA negotiations.

On the other side of the Atlantic, the Bill Clinton and Barack Obama administrations enabled the United States to play an indispensable role in constructing the Asia-Pacific economic architecture. EU and US agreements with Asian countries have expedited enforceable obligations concerning labor and environmental standards. Chapter 5 evaluated US trade policy on Asia and focused on the strategic changes during the Donald Trump and Joe Biden presidencies. The chapter considered the Asia-Pacific Economic Cooperation (APEC) and the Trans-Pacific Partnership, the precursor to the CPTPP, to be the critical initiatives proposed and led by Washington. The US negotiation approach has been premised on inherent bilateralism. Yet, most US Trade and Investment Framework Agreement yielded limited success, including FTAs with Australia, Korea and Singapore.

The "China reckoning" culminated in Trump's trade war with China. Various attempts such as the imposition of tariffs on Chinese goods failed to achieve the intended result of decreasing trade deficits. As Vietnam illustrates, selected developing countries ironically became beneficiaries of US-China tensions that prompted supply chain restructuring. The Biden administration is expected to continue the tougher position on an increasingly assertive China but change Trump's unilateralism to forge alliances in Europe and Asia. Amid the efforts to combat COVID-19 and growing Chinese influences, the chapter suggested that the White House reconsider the ASEAN-US FTA, which will buttress the strategic partnership with the bloc. Asian countries are also advised to persuade the United States to accede to and elevate the standards of the CPTPP. These initiatives will revitalize the US pivot to Asia in a tangible way and fortify the US status in the NREO.

Given emerging Asia-Pacific agreements, APEC's role is often perceived to be marginalized. Based on the findings in the previous chapters, Chapter 7 shed light on different angles of APEC's structural evolution. Different from the legalization of the ASEAN way and hard-law obligations under EU and US FTAs, APEC has remained a soft-law institution operating under key principles of "open regionalism" and "concerted unilateral liberalization." These principles, which converged on the policies of key stakeholders including ASEAN, Australia, China, Japan and the United States, formed the foundation for new Asian regionalism.

APEC's incremental achievements should not be ignored. The chapter observed that APEC's model rules and trade facilitation initiatives have been incorporated into FTAs and national agendas. APEC also directly contributed to the WTO Information Technology Agreement and current WTO negotiations on reducing tariff on environmental goods. These experiences have not only enriched the ASEAN Plus Six framework, but have also provided valuable lessons for other regions and developing countries.

To realize the APEC Putrajaya Vision 2040 and rejuvenate APEC's role beyond the Third Regionalism, I recommended that APEC strengthen its Singapore-based Secretariat and the peer-review process. To achieve the APEC-based Free Trade Area of the Asia Pacific, APEC should strengthen its incubator role for expanding the CPTPP and the RCEP under their open accession clauses. Along with rapid developments of ASEAN, mega-FTAs and EU and US trade agreements with Asian partners, APEC's reforms will further fertilize new Asian regionalism in international economic law.

SELECT BIBLIOGRAPHY

Journal Articles and Working Papers

Acharya, Amitav, *Foundations of Collective Action in Asia: Theory and Practice of Regional Cooperation*, ADBI Working Paper Series, No. 344 (2012)

Aggarwal, Vinod K. & Jonathan T. Chow, *The Perils of Consensus: How ASEAN's Meta-regime Undermines Economic and Environmental Cooperation*, 17 (2) Rev. Int'l Pol. Econ. 262 (2010)

Araujo, Billy Melo, *Labour Provisions in EU and US Mega-regional Trade Agreements: Rhetoric and Reality*, 67 Int'l & Com. L. Q. 233 (2018)

Archarya, Amitav, *Ideas, Identity, and Institution-Building: From the "ASEAN Way" to the "Asia-Pacific Way"?* 10 (3) Pac. Rev. 319 (1997)

Ba, Alice, *Institutional Divergence and Convergence in the Asia-Pacific? ASEAN in Practice and in Theory*, 27 (2) Cam. Rev. Int'l Aff. 295 (2014)

Baldwin, Richard, *A Domino Theory of Regionalism*, NBER Working Paper Series, No. 4465 (1993)

Baldwin, Richard & Masahiro Kawai, *Multilateralizing Asian Regionalism*, ADBI Working Paper Series, No. 431 (2013)

Balganesh, Shyamkrishna, *The Pragmatic Incrementalism of Common Law Intellectual Property*, 63 (6) Vanderbilt L. Rev. 1543 (2010)

Bhagwati, Jagdish, *Regionalism versus Multilateralism*, 15 World Econ. 535 (1992)

Biden, Joseph R., Jr., *Why America Must Lead Again: Rescuing U.S. Foreign Policy After Trump*, 99 (2) Foreign Aff. 64 (2020)

Blyde, Juan & Natalia Sinyavskaya, *The Impact of Liberalizing Trade in Services on Trade in Goods: An Empirical Investigation*, 11 (3) Rev. Dev. Econ. 566 (2007)

Bradford, Anu, *The Brussels Effect*, 107 (1) NW. Univ. L. Rev. 1 (2012)

Brummer, Chris, *Why Soft Law Dominates International Finance – and Not Trade*, 13 (3) J. Int'l Econ. L. 623 (2010)

Cai, Congyan, *New Great Powers and International Law in the 21st Century*, 24 (3) Eur. J. Int'l L. 755 (2013)

Campbell, Kurt M. & Ely Ratner, *The China Reckoning: How Beijing Defied American Expectation*, 97 (2) Foreign Aff. 60 (2018)

Camroux, David, *Interregionalism or Merely a Fourth-Level Game? An Examination of the EU-ASEAN Relationship*, 27 E. Asia 57 (2010)

Chaisse, Julien & Jamieson Kirkwood, *Chinese Puzzle: Anatomy of the (Invisible) Belt and Road Investment Treaty*, 23 (1) J. Int'l Econ. L. 245 (2020)

Chaisse, Julien & Mitsuo Matshshita, *China's "Belt and Road" Initiative: Mapping the World Trade Normative and Strategic Implications*, 52 (1) J. World Trade 163 (2018)

Cho, Sungjoon, *Breaking the Barrier between Regionalism and Multilateralism: A New Perspective on Trade Regionalism*, 42 (2) Harv. Int'l L. J. 419 (2001)

Cho, Sungjoon & Jurgen Kurtz, *Legalizing the ASEAN Way: Adopting and Reimagining the ASEAN Investment Regime*, 66 Am. J. Com. L. 233 (2018)

Claussen, Kathleen, *Dispute Settlement under the Next Generation of Free Trade Agreement*, 46 (3) Ga. J. Int'l & Com. L. 611 (2018)

Clinton, Hillary, *America's Pacific Century*, 189 Foreign Pol'y 56 (2011)

Conconi, Paola & Robert Howse, *Panel Report on EC-IT Products*, 11 (2) World Trade Rev. 223 (2012)

Cremona, Marise, *Shaping EU Trade Policy Post-Lisbon: Opinion 2/15 of 16 May 2017*, 14 Eur. Cont'l L. Rev. 231 (2018)

Dang, Le Ngoc et al., *State-owned Enterprises Reform in Viet Nam: Progress and Challenges*, ADBI Working Paper Series, No. 1071 (2020)

Das, Sanchita Basu et al., *Can ASEAN+1 FTAs be a Pathway towards Negotiating and Designing the Regional Comprehensive Economic Partnership (RCEP) Agreement?*, 50 (2) J. World Trade 253 (2016)

deLisle, Jacques, *China's Rise, the U.S., and the WTO: Perspectives from International Relations Theory*, 2018 Univ. Ill. L. Rev. 57 (2018)

Desierto, Diane A., *ASEAN's Constitutionalization of International Law: Challenges to Evolution under the New ASEAN Charter*, 49 Colum. J. Transnat'l L. 268 (2010–11)

Durán, Gracia Marín, *Sustainable Development Chapters in EU Free Trade Agreements: Emerging Compliance Issues*, 57 Common Market L. Rev. 1 (2020)

Elms, Deborah, *Understanding the CPTPP*, 6/2017 ASEAN Focus 8 (2017)

Freiber, Arie, *Therapeutic Jurisprudence in Australia: Paradigm Shift or Pragmatic Incrementalism?* 20 (2) L. in Context 6 (2003)

Fukunaga, Yoshifumi, *Assessing the Progress of ASEAM MRAs on Professional Services*, ERIA Discussion Paper Series (2015)

Fukunaga, Yoshifumi & Hikari Ishido, *Assessing the Progress of Services Liberalization in the ASEAN-China* Free *Trade* Area *(ACFTA)*, ERIA Discussion Paper Series (2013)

Fukunaga, Yoshifumi & Ikumo Isono, *Taking ASEAN+1 FTAs towards the RCEP: A Mapping Study*, ERIA Discussion Paper Series (2013)

Fukunaga, Yuka, *Japan's Trade Policy in the Midst of Uncertainty*, Aise.Visions, No. 112 (2020)

Galbraith, Jean, *United States Continues to Block New Appellate Body Members for the World Trade Organization, Risking the Collapse of the Appellate Process*, 113 (4) Am. J. Int'l L. 822 (2019)

Garzón, Jorge F., *Multipolarity and the Future of Economic Regionalism*, 9 (1) Int'l Theory 101 (2016)

Gilman, Nils, *The New International Economic Order: A Reintroduction*, 6 (1) Humanity 1 (2015)

Gilson, Julie, *New Interregionalism? The EU and East Asia*, 27 (3) Eur. Integration 307 (2005)

Ginsburg, Tom, *Eastphalia Asian Regionalism*, 44 UC Davis L. Rev. 859 (2010–11)

Ginsburg, Tom, *Authoritarian International Law*, 114 (2) Am. J. Int'l L. 221 (2020)

Goh, Evelyn, *Great Powers and Hierarchical Order in Southeast Asia: Analyzing Regional Securities Strategies*, 32 (3) Int'l Security 113 (2007/08)

Guzman, Andrew T. & Timothy L. Meyer, *International Soft Law*, 2 (1) J. Legal Analysis 171 (2010)

Hamanaka, Shintaro & Sufian Jusoh, *Understanding the ASEAN Way of Regional Qualification Governance: The Case of Mutual Recognition Agreements in the Professional Service Sector*, 12 (4) Reg. & Governance 486 (2018)

Hathaway, Oona A., *International Delegation and State Sovereignty*, 71 (1) L. & Contemp. Problems 115 (2008)

Hettne, Björn, *Beyond the "New" Regionalism*, 10 (4) New Pol. Eco 543 (2005)

Hillgenberg, Harmut, *A Fresh Look at Soft Law*, 10 (3) Eur. J. Int'l L. 500 (1999)

Hoang, Ha Hai, *Normative Power Europe through Trade: Vietnamese Perceptions*, 30 (2) Int'l Rel. 176 (2015)

Hoang, Ha Hai & Daniela Sicurelli, *The EU's Preferential Trade Agreements with Singapore and Vietnam: Market vs. Normative Imperatives*, 23 (4) Contemp. Pol. 369 (2017)

Hofmann, Claudia et al., *Horizontal Depth: A New Database on the Content of Preferential Trade Agreements*, Policy Research Working Paper, No. 7981 (2017)

Hradilová, Kateřina & Ondřej Svoboda, *Sustainable Development Chapters in the EU* Free Trade *Agreements: Searching for Effectiveness*, 52 (6) J. World Trade 1019 (2018)

Hsieh, Pasha L., *The Taiwan Question and the One-China Policy: Legal Challenges with Renewed Momentum*, 84 (3) Die Friedens-Warte: J. Int'l Peace & Organ. 59 (2009)

Hsieh, Pasha L., *The China-Taiwan ECFA, Geopolitical Dimensions and WTO Law*, 14 (1) J. Int'l Econ. L. 121 (2011)

Hsieh, Pasha L., *Reassessing the Trade-Development Nexus in International Economic Law: The Paradigm Shift in Asia-Pacific Regionalism*, 37 (2) NW J. Int'l L. & Bus. 321 (2017)

Ikenberry, G. John, *The End of International Order?* 94 (1) Int'l Aff. 7 (2018)

Ikenberry, G. John, *The Next Liberal Order: The Age of Contagion Demands More Internationalism, Not Less*, 99 (4) Foreign Aff. 133 (2020)

Ing, Lili Yan et al., *How Do Exports and Imports Affect the Use of Free Trade Agreements? Firm-level Survey Evidence from Southeast Asia*, ERIA Discussion Paper Series (2016)

Kang, David, *South Korean and Taiwanese Development and the New Institutional Economics*, 49 (3) Int'l Organ. 555 (1995)

Kawai, Masahiro & Kanda Naknoi, *ASEAN Economic Integration through Trade and Foreign Direct Investment: Long-Term Challenges*, ADBI Working Paper Series, No. 545 (2015)

Kelsey, Jane, *The Risks for ASEAN of New Mega-Agreements that Promote the Wrong Model of e-Commerce*, ERIA Discussion Paper Series (2017)

Kikuchi, Tomoo et al., *The Effects of Mega-Regional Trade Agreements to Vietnam*, 55 J. Asian Eco. 4 (2017)

Kim, Dong-Young, *Adapting the MGA for Negotiating with South Korean Counterparts*, Asialink Bus. (2015)

Kim, Samuel S., *Regionalization and Regionalism in Asia*, 4 (1) J. E Asian Stud. 39 (2004)

Kleimann, David & Gesa Kübek, *The Signing, Provisional Application, and Conclusion of Trade and Investment Agreements in the EU: The Case of CETA and Opinion 2/15*, 45 (1) Legal Issues Eco. Integration 13 (2018)

Kojima, Kiyoshi, *The "Flying Geese" Model of Asian Economic Development: Origin, Theoretical Extensions, and Regional Policy Implications*, 11 J. Asian Econ. 375 (2000)

Kong, Qingjiang, *U.S.-China Bilateral Investment Treaty Negotiations: Context, Focus, and Implications*, 7 (1) Asian J. WTO & Int'l Health and Policy 181 (2012)

Krauthammer, Charles, *The Unipolar Moment*, 70 Foreign Aff. 23 (1990–91)

Lamy, Pascal, *Unlocking the Potential of the ASEAN-EU Partnership: The Role of Singapore*, 2 Asia Eur. J 485 (2004)

Lee, Hsien Loong, *The Endangered Asian Century: America, China and the Perils of Confrontation*, 99 (4) Foreign Aff. 52 (2020)

Lee, Seungjoo, *Institutional Balancing and the Politics of Mega-FTAs in East Asia*, 56 Asian Survey 1055 (2016)

Lester, Simon & Inu Manak, *The Rise of Populist Nationalism and Renegotiation of NAFTA*, 21 (1) J. Int'l Econ. L. 151 (2018)

Leutert, Wendy & Zachary Haver, *From Cautious Interaction to Mature Influence: China's Evolving Engagement with the International Investment Regime*, 93 (1) Pac. Aff. 59 (2020)

Lewis, Meredith Kolsky, *The Origin of Plurilateralism in International Trade Law*, 20 J. Inv. & Trade 633 (2019)

Lim, Darren J. & Zack Cooper, *Reassessing Hedging: The Logic of Alignment in East Asia*, 24 (4) Sec. Stud. 696 (2015)

Lim, Paul Joseph, *ASEAN's Relations with the EU: Obstacles and Opportunities*, EU External Aff. Rev. 46 (2012)

Limenta, Michelle, *Palm Oil for Fuels: WTO Rules and Environmental Protection*, 15 (7) Global Trade & Customs J. 321 (2020)

Lin, Justin Yifu, *From Flying Geese to Leading Dragons New Opportunities and Strategies for Structural Transformation in Developing Countries*, Policy Research Working Paper, No. 5702 (2011)

Lin, Tsai-Yu, *Systemic Reflection on the EC-IT Product Case: Establishing an "Understanding" on Maintaining the Product Coverage of the Current Information Technology Agreement in the Face of Technological Change*, 45 (2) J. World Trade 401 (2011)

Liu, Han-Wei & Shin-Yi Peng, *Managing Trade Conflicts in the ICT* Industry: *A Case Study of EU–Greater China Area*, 19 (3) J. Int'l Econ. L. 629 (2016)

Magiera, Stephen L., *International Investment Agreements and Investor-State Disputes: A Review and Evaluation for Indonesia*, ERIA Discussion Series (2017)

Manea, Maria-Gabriela, *Human Rights and the Interregional Dialogue between Asia and Europe: ASEAN-EU Relations and ASEM*, 21 (3) Pac. Rev. 369 (2008)

Manners, Ian, *Normative Power Europe: A Contradiction in Terms?*, 40 (2) J. Common Market Stud. 235 (2002)

Manners, Ian & Richard Whitman, *The "Difference Engine": Constructing and Representing the International Identity of the European Union*, 10 (3) J. Eur. Pub. Pol'y 380 (2003)

Mansfield, Edward D. & Etel Solingen, *Regionalism*, 13 Ann. Rev. Pol. Sci. 145 (2010)

Mansfield, Edward D. & Helen V. Milner, *The New Wave of Regionalism*, 53 (3) Int'l Organ. 589 (1999)

Marhold, Anna-Alexandra, *Externalising Europe's Energy Policy in EU Free Trade Agreements: A Cognitive Dissonance between Promoting Sustainable Development and Ensuing Security of Supply*, 3 (1) Eur & World: A L. Rev. 1 (2019)

Mattoo, Aaditya et al., *Trade Creation and Trade Diversion in Deep Agreements*, Policy Research Working Paper, No. 8206 (2017)

McKenzie, Lachlan & Katharina L. Meissner, *Human Rights Conditionality in European Union Trade Negotiations: The Case of the EU-Singapore FTA*, 55 (4) J. Common Market Stud.832 (2017)

McLaughlin, Mark, *Defining a State-Owned Enterprise in International Investment Agreements*, 34 (3) ICSID Rev. 595 (2020)

Medalla, Erlinda M. & M. Supperamaniam, *Suggested Rules of Origin Regime for EAFTA*, Philippine Inst. for Dev. Stud. Discussion Paper Series No. 2008–22 (Rev.) (2009)

Mercurio, Bryan, *Trade Liberalisation in Asia: Why Intra-Asian Free Trade Agreements Are Not Utilised By the Business Community*, 6 (1) Asian J. WTO & Int'l Health L. & Pol. 109 (2011)

Mitchell, Jonathan, *An Unconventional but Essential Marriage: Pro-Poor Tourism and the Mainstream Industry*, Private Sector & Dev., No. 7 (2010)

Moranda, Noel M., *Europe and Southeast Asia: ASEAN-EU Interregionalism between Pluralist and Solidarist Societies*, 4 (3) Rev. Eur. Stud. 89 (2012)

Morris-Sharma, Natalie Y., *The Singapore Convention is Live, and Multilateralism, Alive*, 20 (4) Cardozo J. Conflict Resol. 1009 (2019)

Nguyen, Trang (Mae), *International Law as Hedging: Perspectives from Secondary Authoritarian States*, 114 Am. J. Int'l L. Unbound 237 (2020)

Nixon, Richard M., *Asia After Viet Nam*, 46 (1) Foreign Aff. 111 (1967)

Nottage, Luke, *The Investment Chapter and ISDS in the TPP: Lessons from Southeast Asia*, ISEAS Yusof Ishak Institute Economics Working Papers, No. 2017–2 (2017)

Ong, Bernard, *Recognizing Regions: ASEAN' Struggles for Recognition*, 25 (4) Pac. Rev. 513 (2012)

Orakhelashvili, Alexander, *Article 30 of the 1969 Vienna Convention on the Law of Treaties: Application of the Successive Treaties Relating to the Same Subject-Matter*, 31 ICSID Rev. 344 (2016)

Ota, Yasu & Shuichi Maruyama, *Ocean's Eleven*, 2018–12–18 Nikkei Asian Rev. 10 (2018)

Pakrashi, Debayan & Paul Frijters, *Takeoffs, Landing, and Economic Growth*, ADBI Working Paper Series, Nov. 641 (2017)

Park, Sung-Hoon & Jeong Yoen Lee, *APEC at Crossroads: Challenges and Opportunities*, 33 (2) Asian Persp. 97 (2009)

Petri, Peter A. & Michael G. Plummer, *East Asia Decouples from the United States: Trade War, COVID-19, and East Asia's New Trade Blocs*, PIIE Working Paper (2020)

Pinchis-Paulsen, Mona, *Trade Multilateralism and U.S. National Security: The Making of the GATT Security Exceptions*, 41 Mich. J. Int'l L. 109 (2020)

Price, Adrian Hyde, *"Normative" Power Europe: A Realist Critique*, 13 (2) J. Eur. Pub. Pol'y 217 (2006)

Quimba, Francis A. & Mark Anthony A. Barral, *The Evolution of APEC and Its Role in the Philippine Trade and Investment*, PIDS Discussion Paper Series, No. 2019–07 (2019)

Roberts, Anthea et al., *Toward a Geoeconomic Order in International Trade and Investment*, 22 J. Int'l Econ. L. 655 (2019)

Robles, Alfred C., Jr, *An EU-ASEAN FTA: The EU's Failure as an International Actor*, 13 Eur. Foreign Aff. Rev. 541 (2008)

Ruggie, John Gerard, *International Regimes, Transactions, and Change: Embedded Liberalism in the Postwar Economic Order*, 36 (2) Int'l Organ. 379 (1982)

Santos, Theotonio Dos, *The Structure of Dependence*, 60 Am. Econ. Rev. 231 (1970)
Shaffer, Gregory & Henry Gao, *A New Chinese Economic Order?* 23 (3) J. Int'l Econ. L. 607 (2020)
Singh, Surendar & Ram Singh, *Domestic Sources of India's Trade Policy References in RCEP Negotiations*, 54 (4) J. World Trade 503 (2020)
Söderbaum, Fredrik & Luk Van Langenhove, *Introduction: The EU as a Global Actor and the Role of Interregionalism*, 27 (3) Eur. Integration 249 (2005)
Suse, Andrei & Jan Wouters, *Exploring the Boundaries of Provisional Application: The EU's Mixed Trade and Investment Agreements*, 53 (3) J. World Trade 395 (2019)
Tang, Siew Mun, *Is ASEAN Due for a Makeover*, 39 (2) Contem. Southeast Asia 239 (2017)
Tang, Siew Mun, *ASEAN's Hard Look at Indo-Pacific*, 3/2018 ASEAN Focus 6 (2018)
Tang, Siew Mun et al., *Survey Report: State of Southeast Asia: 2019*, 1/2019 ASEAN Focus 6 (2019)
Tham, Siew Yean, *ASEAN Trade in Services* Agreement *(ATISA: Advancing Services Liberalization for ASEAN?* 54 Persp. 1 (2019)
Tho, Tran Van, *The Middle-Income Trap: Issues for Members of the Association of Southeast Asian Nations*, ADBI Working Paper Series, No. 421 (2013)
Tong, Goh Chok, *Asia – Catalyst for Global Economic Integration*, 2 Asia Eur. J. 1 (2004)
Urata, Shujiro, *Constructing and Multilateralizing the Regional Comprehensive Economic Partnership: An Asian Perspective*, ADBI Working Paper Series, No. 449 (2013)
Vandewalle, Laurence, *The ASEAN Inter-Parliamentary Assembly (AIPA): A Privileged Interlocutor for the European Parliament in South East Asia* (2015)
Walt, Stephan M., *Alliance Formation and the Balance of Power*, 9 (4) Int'l Sec. 3 (1985)
Wang, Heng, *China's Approach to the Belt and Road Initiative: Scope, Character and Sustainability*, 22 (1) J. Int'l Econ. L. 29 (2019)
Webb, Michael C. & Stephen D. Krasner, *Hegemonic Stability Theory: An Empirical Assessment*, 15 (2) Rev. Int'l Stud. 183 (1989)
Wendt, Alexander, *Collective Identity Formation and the International State*, 88 (2) Am. Pol. Sci. Rev. 384 (1994)
Williamson, John, *The Strange History of the Washington Consensus*, 27 (2) J. Post Keynesian Eco.195 (2004)
Wilson, Jeffery D., *Mega-Regional Trade Deals in the Asia-Pacific: Choosing Between the TPP and RCEP?*, 45 (2) J. Contemp. Asia 343 (2015)
Wong, Benjamin, *Data Localization and ASEAN Economic Community*, 10 Asian J. Int'l L.158 (2020)

Woon, Walter, *Resolving Territorial Disputes in ASEAN*, 30 Chinese (Taiwan) YB Int'l L. & Aff. 1 (2012)

Zhong, Zewei, *The ASEAN Comprehensive Investment Agreement: Realizing a Regional Community*, 6 (1) Asian J. Comp. L. 1 (2011)

Books and Book Chapters

Abrenica, Joy et al., *The Future of Trade in Services for Developing Countries, in* Trade and Poverty Reduction in the Asia-Pacific Region: Case Studies and Lessons from Low-Income Communities (Andrew L. Stoler et al. eds. 2009)

Acharya, Amitav, *The Making of Southeast Asia: International Relations of a Region* (2000)

Acharya, Amitav, *The Quest for Identity: International Relations of Southeast Asia* (2000)

Acharya, Amitav, *Whose Ideas Matter? Agency and Power in Asian Regionalism* (2009)

Acharya, Amitav, *Constructing a Security Community in Southeast Asia: ASEAN and the Problem of Regional Order* (3d 2014)

Acharya, Amitav, *Regionalism beyond EU-Centrism, in* The Oxford Handbook of Comparative Regionalism (Tanja A. Börzel & Thomas Risse 2016)

Aggarwal, Vinod K. & Edward A. Fogarty, *Between Regionalism and Globalism: European Union Interregional Trade Strategies, in* EU Trade Strategies: Between Regionalism and Globalism (Vinod K. Aggarwal & Edward A. Fogarty eds. 2004)

Aggarwal, Vinod K. & Elaine Kwei, *Asia-Pacific Economic Cooperation (APEC): Transregionalism with a New Cause?, in* Interregionalism and International Relations (Heiner Hänggi et al. eds. 2006)

Allison, Graham, *Destined for War: Can America and China Escape Thucydides's Trap* (2017)

Ba, Alice, *(Re)Negotiating East and Southeast Asia: Region, Regionalism, and the Association of Southeast Asian Nations* (2009)

Beth, Vivienne & Luke Nottage, *International Investment Agreement and Investor-State Arbitration in Asia, in* Handbook of International Investment Law and Policy (Julien Chaisse et al. eds. 2020)

Bhagwati, Jagdish, *Termites in the Trading System: How Preferential Agreements Undermine Free Trade* (2008)

Borthwick, Mark, *Building Momentum: The Movement Toward Pacific Economic Cooperation Prior to 1980, in* The Evolution of PECC: The First 25 Years (2005)

Börzel, Tanja A. & Thomas Risse, *Introduction: Framework of the Handbook and Conceptual Clarifications, in* The Oxford Handbook of Comparative Regionalism (Tanja A. Börzel & Thomas Risse 2016)

Bradford, Anu, *The Brussels Effect: How the European Union Rules the World* (2020)

Breslin, Shaun et al., *Regions in Comparative Perspective, in* New Regionalism in the Global Political Economy: Theories and Cases (Shaun Breslin et al. eds. 2002)

Brown, Chester & Phoebe Winch, *The Confidentiality and Transparency Debate in Commercial and Investment Mediation, in* Mediation in International Commercial and Investment Disputes (Catherine Titi & Katia Fach Gómez eds. 2019)

Brummer, Chris, *Soft Law and the Global Financial System: Rule Making in the 21st Century* (2012)

Bull, Cavinder, *Enhancing the Rule of Law in Investor-State Dispute Settlement, in* The ASEAN Law Conference 2018: A Compendium of Speeches, Papers, Presentations and Reports (2019)

Cardoso, Fernando Henrique & Enzo Faletto, *Dependency and Development in Latin America* (Marjory Mattingly Urquidi trans., 1979)

Chaisse, Julien, *The ACIA: Much More Than a BIT of Protection for Foreign Investors, in* ASEAN Law in the New Regional Economic Order (2019)

Chaisse, Julien & Sufian Jusoh, *The ASEAN Comprehensive Investment Agreement: The Regionalisation of Laws and Policy on Foreign Investment* (2016)

Chan, Man-jung Mignonne, *APEC's Eye on the Prize: Participants, Modality, and Confidence-Building, in* APEC at 20: Recall, Reflect, Remake (K. Kesavapany and Hank Lim eds. 2009)

Chen, Christopher, *ASEAN Financial Integration and the Belt and Road Initiative: Legal Challenges and Opportunities for China in Southeast* Asia, *in* International Governance and the Rule of Law in China under the Belt and Road Initiative (Yun Zhao ed. 2018)

China in the International Economic Order: New Directions and Changing Paradigms (Lisa Toohey et al. eds. 2015)

Chow, Michael Ewing & Ranyta Yusran, *The ASEAN Trade Dispute Settlement Mechanism, in* The Legitimacy of International Trade Courts and Tribunals (Robert Howse et al. eds. 2018)

Closa, Carlo & Lorenzo Casni, *Comparative Regional Integration: Governance and Legal Models* (2016)

Coicaud, Jean Marc, *Legitimacy and Politics: A Contribution to the Study of Political Right and Political Responsibility* (2002)

Cremona, Marise, *Distinguished Essay: A Quiet Revolution – The Changing Nature of the EU's Common Commercial Policy, in* 2017:8 Eur. YB Int'l Econ. L. (Marc Bungenberg et al. eds. 2017)

Crozier, Andrew J., *The Trade and Aid Policy of the European Union: A Historical Perspective, in* EU-ASEAN: Facing Economic Globalisation (Paul J. J. Welfens et al. 2009)

Dent, Christopher M., *East Asian Regionalism* (2d. ed. 2016)

DeRosa, Dean A., *US Free Trade Agreements with ASEAN*, *in* Free Trade Agreements: US Strategies and Priorities (Jeffrey J. Schott ed. 2004)

Dothan, Shai & Joanna Lam, *A Paradigm Shift? Arbitration and Court-Like Mechanism in Investors' Disputes*, *in* 2020 Eur. YB Int'l Econ. L. (Güneş Ünüvar et al. eds. 2020)

Dowdle, Michael W. et al., *Dialogus de Beijing Consensus*, *in* The Beijing Consensus? How Chian Has Changed Western Ideas of Law and Economic Development (Weitseng Chen ed. 2017)

Elek, Andrew, *Back to Canberra: Founding APEC*, *in* The Evolution of PECC: The First 25 Years (2005)

Elek, Andrew, *Overview*, *in* The Evolution of PECC: The First 25 Years (2005)

Elms, Deborah K. & C. L. Lim, *An Overview and Snapshot of the TPP Negotiations*, *in* The Trans-Pacific Partnership: A Quest for a Twenty-first-Century Trade Agreement (C. L. Lim et al. eds. 2012)

Flaaen, Aaron et al., How to Avoid Middle-Income Traps? Evidence from Malaysia, World Bank: Economic Premise, No. 120 (2013)

Frost, Ellen L., *Asia's New Regionalism* (2008)

Fukunaga, Yoshifumi, *Challenges of ASEAN MRAs on Professional Services*, *in* ASEAN Law in the New Regional Economic Order: Global Trends and Shifting Paradigms (Pasha L. Hsieh & Bryan Mercurio eds. 2019)

Gathii, James Thuo, *African Regional Trade Agreements as Legal Regimes* (2011)

Gilbert, Alan, *Must Global Politics Constrain Democracy? Great-Power Realism, Democratic Peace, and Democratic Internationalism* (1999)

Gold, Thomas Baron, *State and Society in the Taiwan Miracle* (1986)

Gu, Weixia, *China's Arbitration Modernisation under Judicial Efforts and Marketisation Waves*, *in* The Developing World of Arbitration: A Comparative Study of Arbitration Reform in the Asia Pacific (Anselmo Reyes & Weixia Gu eds. 2018)

Haggard, Stephan, *Developmental States* (2018)

Hamanaka, Shintaro, *Accession to TPP: Veto Power and "Opt-Out" Option*, *in* Paradigm Shift in International Economic Law Rule-Making: TPP as a New Model for Trade Agreements? (Julien Chaisse et al. eds. 2017)

Hänggi, Heiner, *Interregionalism as a Multifaceted Phenomenon: In Search of a Typology*, *in* Interregionalism and International Relations: A Stepping Stone to Global Governance? (Jürgen Ruland et al. 2005)

Hettne, Björn, *The New Regionalism: Implications for Development and Peace*, *in The New Regionalism: Implications for Global Development and International Security*, UNU/WIDER World Institute for Development Economics Research (Björn Hettne & András Inotai 1994)

Hoa, Tran Van, *Globalisation, Crises and the Emergence of New Asian Regionalism: Genesis and Current Development*, *in* New Asian Regionalism: Responses to Globalisation and Crises (Tran Van Hoa & Charles Harve eds. 2003)

Hsieh, Pasha L., *China-Taiwan Free Trade Agreement*, *in* Bilateral and Regional Trade Agreements: Case Studies (Simon Lester et al. eds. 2d ed. 2015)

Hsieh, Pasha L., *Transnational Legal Services in Asia: Legal Implications of the AEC and the CPTPP*, *in* ASEAN Law in the New Regional Economic Order: Global Trends and Shifting Paradigms (Pasha L. Hsieh & Bryan Mercurio 2019)

Hsu, Locknie, *EU-ASEAN Trade and Investment Relations with a Special Focus on Singapore*, *in* 2015:6 Eur. YB Int'l Econ. L. (Christoph Herrmann et al. eds. 2015)

Hurell, Andrew, *Regionalism in Theoretical Perspective*, *in* Regionalism in World Politics: Regional Organization and International Order (Louise Fawcett & Andrew Hurrell eds. 1995)

Inama, Stefano & Edmund W. Sim, *Rules of Origin in ASEAN: A Way Forward* (2015)

Ing, Lili Yang et al., NTMs in ASEAN: *Ways toward Regulatory Convergence*, *in* Regional Integration and Non-Tariff Measures in ASEAN (Lili Yan Ing et al. eds. 2019)

Jetschke, Anja et al., *Asia*, *in* The Oxford Handbook of Comparative Regionalism (Tanja A. Börzel & Thomas Risse 2016)

Jusoh, Sufian, *Investment Liberalization in ASEAN: Moving Myths to Reality*, *in* ASEAN Law in the New Regional Economic Order: Global Trends and Shifting Paradigms (Pasha L. Hsieh & Bryan Mercurio 2019)

Karton, Joshua, *Beyond the "Harmonious Confucian": International Commercial Arbitration and the Impact of Chinese Cultural Values*, *in* Legal Thoughts between the East and the West in the Multilevel Legal Order: Liber Amicorum in Honor of Professor Herbert Han-pao Ma (Chang-fa Lo et al. eds. 2016)

Katzenstein, Peter J., *Introduction: Asian Regionalism in Comparative Perspective*, *in* Network Power: Japan and Asia (Peter J. Katzenstein & Takashi Shiraishi eds. 1997)

Kawai, Masahiro & Ganeshan Wignaraja, *Main Findings and Policy Implications*, *in* Asia's Free Trade Agreements: How is Business Responding? (2011)

Kiang, Lim Hng to Anand Sharma, *Special Scheme for Registration of Generic Medicinal Products from India* (2010)

Kingsbury, Benedict et al., *Introduction: The Essence, Significance, and Problems of the Trans-Pacific Partnership*, *in* Megaregulation Contested: Global Economic Ordering after TPP (Benedict Kingsbury et al. eds. 2019)

Kirshner, Jonathan, *Realist Political Economy: Traditional Themes and Contemporary Challenges*, *in* Routledge Handbook of International Political Economy (IPE): IPE as a Global Conversation 36 (Mark Blyth ed. 2009)

Kissinger, Henry, *World Order* (2014)

Koh, Tommy, *The United States and Southeast Asia, in* America's Role in Asia, Asian and American Views: Recommendations for U.S. Policy from Both Sides of the Pacific (2008)

Kuijper, Peter Jan et al., *From Treaty-Making to Treaty-Breaking: Models for ASEAN External Trade Agreements* (2015)

Lakatos, Csilla & Lars Nilsson, *The EU-Korea Free Trade Agreement: Anticipation, Trade Policy Uncertainty and Impact, Chief Economist Note* (2015)

Lenz, Tobias & Gary Marks, *Regional Institutional Design, in* The Oxford Handbook of Comparative Regionalism (Tanja A. Börzel & Thomas Risse 2016)

Leong, Susanna H. S., *European Union-Singapore Free Trade Agreement: A New Chapter for Geographical Indications in Singapore, in* Geographical Indications at the Crossroads of Trade, Development, and Culture: Focus on Asia-Pacific (Irene Calboli & Wee Loon Ng-Loy eds. 2017)

Lester, Simon et al., *Trump's First Trade Dal, Free Trade Bulletin*, No. 73 (2019)

Lim, C. L. et al., *What is "High-Quality, Twenty-First Century" Anyway? in* The Trans-Pacific Partnership: A Quest for a Twenty-first-Century Trade Agreement (C. L. Lim et al. eds. 2012)

Liu, Han-Wei, *Data Localization and Digital Trade Barriers: ASEAN in Megaregionalism, in* ASEAN Law in the New Regional Economic Order (2019)

Lincoln, Edward J., *East Asian Economic Regionalism* (2004)

Mahbubani, Kishore & Jeffery Sng, *The ASEAN Miracle: A Catalyst for Peace* (2017)

Mahoney, James et al., *Dependency Theory, in* The Oxford Handbook of the Politics of Development (Carol Lancaster & Nicolas van de Walle 2018)

Mann, Catherine & Xuepeng Liu, *The Information Technology Agreement: Sui Generis or Model Stepping Stone?, in* Multilateralizing Regionalism: Challenges for the Global Trading System (Richard Baldwin & Patrick Low eds. 2009)

Mattoo, Aaditya & Gianni Zanini, *Services Trade Agreements and Negotiations: An Overview, in* Handbook of Trade Policy for Development (Arvid Lukauskas et al. eds. 2013)

Megaregulation Contested: Global Economic Ordering after TPP (Benedict Kingsbury et al. 2019)

Minh Hue Nguyen et al., *The ASEAN Trade in Goods Agreement: Evolution and Regional Implications, in* ASEAN Law in the New Regional Economic Order: Global Trends and Shifting Paradigms (Pasha L. Hsieh & Bryan Mercurio eds. 2019)

Mohan, Mahdev, *The European Union's Free Trade Agreement with Singapore – One Step Forward, 28 Steps Back? in* International Investment Treaties and Arbitration Across Asia (Julien Chaisse & Luke Nottage eds. 2018)

Natalegawa, Marty, *Does ASEAN Matter? A View from Within* (2018)
Network Power: Japan and Asia (Peter J. Katzenstein & Takashi Shiraishi eds. 1997)
Nikomborirak, Deunden & Supunnavadee Jitdumrong, *ASEAN Trade in Services, in* The ASEAN Economic Community: A Work in Progress (Sanchita Basu Das ed. 2013)
Ogita, Tatsushi, *Japan: The Structure of Complete Objection, in* Trade Liberalization and APEC (Jiro Okamoto ed. 2004)
Ostry, Sylvia, *The Uruguay Round North-South Grand Bargain: Implications for Future Negotiations, in* The Political Economy of International Trade Law: Essays in Honor of Robert E. Hudec (Daniel L. M. Kennedy & James D. Southwick eds. 2002)
Paradigm Shift in International Economic Law Rule-Making: TPP as a New Model for Trade Arrangements? (Julien Chaisse et al. eds. 2017)
Peet, Richard & Elaine Hartwick, *Theories of Development: Contentions, Arguments, Alternatives* (3d ed. 2015)
Pempel, T. J., *Transpacific Torri: Japan and the Emerging Asian Regionalism, in* Network Power: Japan and Asia (Peter J. Katzenstein & Takashi Shiraishi eds. 1997)
Rashid, Zakariah et al., *Regional Market for Goods, Services, and Skilled Labor, in* Realizing the ASEAN Economic Community: A Comprehensive Assessment (Michael G. Plummer & Chia Siow Yue eds. 2009)
Ravenhill, John, *APEC and the Construction of Pacific Rim Regionalism* (2001)
Rodrik, Dani, *Straight Talk on Trade: Ideas for a Sane World Economy* (2018)
Rolland, Sonia E., *Development at the WTO* (2012)
Roloff, Ralf, *Interregionalism in Theoretical Perspective: State of the Art, in* Interregionalism and International Relations: A Stepping Stone to Global Governance? (Jürgen Ruland et al. 2005)
Romanchyshyna, Iulianna, *Tackling Technical Barriers to Trade in EU "New Generation" FTAs: An Example of Open or Conflicting Regionalism? in* Global Politics and EU Trade Policy: Facing the Challenges to a Multilateral Approach, Special Issue: Eur. YB Int'l Econ. L. (Wolfgang Weiß & Cornelia Furculita eds. 2020)
Rossman, Ithnain, *The Goods Package, in* The United States-Singapore Free Trade Agreement: Highlights and Insights (Tommy Koh & Chang Li Lin eds. 2004)
Ruland, Jürgen, *Interregionalism: An Unfinished Agenda, in* Interregionalism and International Relations: A Stepping Stone to Global Governance? (Jürgen Ruland et al. 2005)
Sally, Razeen, *Southeast Asia in the WTO* (2004)
Sally, Razeen, *ASEAN FTAs: State of Play and Outlook for ASEAN's Regional and Global Integration, in* The ASEAN Economic Community: A Work in Progress (Sanchita Basu Das et al. eds. 2013)
Sasradipoera, Kanya Satyani, *ASEAN Trade in Goods Agreement (ATIGA), in* ASEAN: Life after the Charter (S. Tiwari ed. 2010)

Severino, Rodolfo C., *Southeast Asia in Search of an ASEAN* Community: *Insights from the Former ASEAN Secretary-General* (2006)

Severino, Rodolfo C., *Japan's Relations with ASEAN, in* ASEAN-Japan Relations (Takashi Shiraishi & Takaaki Kojima eds. 2014)

Siong, David Chin Soon, *ASEAN's Journey towards Free Trade, in* Economic Diplomacy: Essays and Reflections by Singapore's Negotiations (C. L. Lim & Margaret Liang eds. 2011)

So, Alvin Y., *Social Change and Development: Modernization, Dependency, and World-System Theories* (1990)

Söderbaum, Fredrik, *Rethinking Regionalism* (2016)

Söderbaum, Fredrik, *Old, New, and Comparative Regionalism: The History and Scholarly Development of the Field, in* The Oxford Handbook of Comparative Regionalism (Tanja A. Borzel & Thomas Risse 2016)

Soesastro, Hadi, *Revamping APEC's Concerted Unilateral Liberalization, in* APEC at 20: Recall, Reflect, Remake (K. Kesavapany and Hank Lim eds. 2009)

Sudo, Sueo, *Japan's ASEAN Policy: In Search of Proactive Multilateralism* (2015)

Telò, Mario, *Introduction: Globalization, New Regionalism and the Role of the European Union, in* European Union and New Regionalism: Competing Regionalism and Global Governance in a Post-Hegemonic Era (Mario Telò ed. 2014)

Tham Siew Yean & Sanchita Basu Das, *Introduction: The ASEAN Economic Community and Conflicting Domestic Interests, in* Moving the AEC Beyond 2015: Managing Domestic Consensus for Community-Building (Tham Siew Yean & Sanchita Basu Das eds. 2016)

Thomas, Chantal & Joel P. Trachtman, *Editors' Introduction, in* Developing Countries in the WTO Legal System (Chantal Thomas & Joel P. Trachtman eds. 2009)

The China-Australia Free Trade Agreement: A 21st Century Model (Colin B. Picker et al. eds. 2018)

Titi, Catherine, *Recent Developments in International Investment Law, in* 2018:9 Eur. YB Int'l Econ. L. (Marc Bungenberg et al. eds. 2019)

Townsend, Belinda, *Update on the Regional Comprehensive Economic Partnership Agreement – NGO Briefing* (2015)

Venzke, Ingo and Li-Ann Thio, *The Internal Effects of ASEAN External Relations* (2016)

Voon, Tania & Elizabeth Sheargold, *Australia, China and the Co-Existence of Successive International Investment Agreements, in* The China-Australia Free Trade Agreement: A 21st Century Model (Colin B. Picker et al. eds. 2017)

Weiler, J. H. H., *ASEAN Law, the ASEAN Way and the Role of Domestic Courts, in* The ASEAN Law Conference 2018: A Compendium of Speeches, Papers, Presentations and Reports 43 (2019)

Wohlforth, William C., *Realism*, *in* The Oxford Handbook of International Relations 131 (Christian Reus-Smit & Duncan Snidal eds. 2008)

Woon, Walter, *The ASEAN Charter: A Commentary* (2016)

Yamazawa, Ippei, *APEC's Achievements and Tasks*, *in* APEC in the 21st Century (Riyana Miranti & Denis Hew eds. 2004)

Yamazawa, Ippei, *APEC: New Agenda in Its Third Decade* (2012)

Yanai, Akiko, *Characteristics of APEC Trade Liberalization: A Comparative Analysis with the WTO*, *in* Trade Liberalization and APEC (Jiro Okamoto ed. 2004)

Yeo, Lay Hwee, *EU-ASEAN Security Cooperation*, *in* EU Security Strategies: Extending the EU System of Security Governance (Spyros Economides & James Sperling eds. 2018)

Documents of Governments, International Organizations and Think Tanks

Ahearn, Raymond J. & Wayne M. Morrison, *U.S.-Thailand Free Trade Agreements*, CRS Report (2006)

AIPO, Resolution of the Ninth General Assembly of AIPO on the ASEAN-EC Economic Cooperation, WC/GA9/88/KL/29/6 (1988)

Analyst in Asian Affairs, Foreign Affairs, Defense, and Trade Division, *The Vietnam-U.S. Bilateral Trade Agreement*, CRS Report (2002)

APEC Counter-Terrorism Working Group Strategic Plan 2018–2020 (2017)

APEC Economic Leaders' Declaration (2001)

APEC Non-Binding Investment Principles (2011)

APEC Non-binding Principles for Domestic Regulation of the Services Sector (2018)

APEC Policy Support Unit Governance Arrangements (2018)

APEC PSU, *Annual Report 2018* (2018)

APEC PSU, *APEC in Charts* 2019 (2019)

APEC PSU, *APEC Regional Trends Analysis: Counting What Counts* (2019)

APEC PSU, APEC Supply-Chain Connectivity Framework Action Plan 2017–2020: Interim Review of External Indicators (2019)

APEC PSU, *APEC's Bogor Goals Progress Report* (2018)

APEC PSU, *APEC's Ease of Doing Business – Final Assessment 2015–2018* (2019)

APEC PSU Five-Year Strategic Plan 2013–2017 (2013)

APEC PSU, Peer Review and Capacity Building on APEC Infrastructure Development and Investment: The Philippines (2017)

APEC PSU, *The Mutual Usefulness between APEC and TPP* (2011)

APEC PSU, *Trends and Developments in Provisions and Outcomes of RTA/FTAs Implemented in 2017 by APEC Economies* (2018)

APEC Secretariat, *APEC Guidebook on Quality of Infrastructure Development and Investment (Revision)* (2018)

APEC Secretariat, *APEC Outcomes & Outlook 2018–2019* (2019)

APEC Secretariat, APEC Secretariat's 2019 Operational Plan (2019)

APEC Secretariat, APEC's Second Trade Facilitation Action Plan (2007)

APEC Secretariat, Guidelines for Hosting APEC Meetings (2017)

APEC Secretariat, IAP Peer Review: Review Teams, Timeline and List of Experts, 2008/SOM1/014, March 2–3, 2008

APEC Secretariat, *Supporting Continued Growth in Trade and Facilitation: End to End Review of the APEC Business Travel Card Scheme Final Report* (2014)

APEC Vision Group, *Report of the APEC Vision Group – People and Prosperity: An APEC Vision to 2040* (2019)

APEC's Achievements in Trade Facilitation in 2007–2010: Final Assessment of the Second Trade Facilitation Action (TFAP II) (2012)

ASEAN, ASEAN Economic Community 2025 Consolidated Strategic Action Plan (2017)

ASEAN, *ASEAN Integration Report 2019* (2019)

ASEAN, *ASEAN Key Figures 2019* (2019)

ASEAN, *ASEAN Key Figures 2020* (2020)

ASEAN, *ASEAN Mutual Recognition Arrangement on Tourism Professionals (MRA): Handbook* (2013)

ASEAN, *ASEAN Services Report 2017: The Evolving Landscape* (2017)

ASEAN, *Investing in ASEAN: Association of Southeast Asian Nations* (2019/2020)

ASEAN, Master Plan on ASEAN Connectivity 2025 (2016)

ASEAN and the EU Through the Years, *in* 6/2016 ASEAN Focus 12 (2016)

ASEAN Business Advisory Council & EU-ASEAN Business Council, *Non-Tariff Barriers (NTBs) in ASEAN and Their Elimination from a Business Perspective* (2019)

ASEAN Comprehensive Investment Agreement: A Guidebook for Businesses & Investors (2d 2015)

ASEAN Framework for Regional Comprehensive Economic Partnership (2011)

ASEAN Historical Timeline, *in* 50 Years of ASEAN and Singapore (Tommy Koh et al. eds. 2017)

ASEAN-EU Vision Group, *Report of the ASEAN-EU Vision Group: Transregional Partnership for Shared and Sustainable Prosperity* (2006)

ASEAN Secretariat, A Historic Milestone for FDI and MNEs in ASEAN (2017)

ASEAN Secretariat, *ASEAN Integration Report 2019* (2019)

ASEAN Secretariat, *ASEAN Key Figures 2020* (2020)

ASEAN Secretariat & World Bank, *ASEAN Integration Monitoring Report* (2013)

ASEAN & UNCTAD, *ASEAN Investment Report 2019: FDI in Services: Focus on Health Care* (2019)

ASEAN +3 Macroeconomic Research Office, *Theme: ASEAN+3 Region 20 Years after the Asian Financial Crisis*, ASEAN+3 Regional Economic Outlook 2017 (2017)

Asian Development Bank, *Asia 2050: Realizing the Asian Century: Executive Summary* (2011)

Asian Development Bank, *Regional Comprehensive Economic Partnership Agreement: Overview and Economic Impact*, ADB Brief, No. 164 (2020)

Asian Development Bank Institute, ASEAN 2030: Toward a Borderless Economic Community 201 (2014)

Asian Trade Centre, *Ten Benefits of the Comprehensive and Progressive Trans-Pacific Partnership (CPTPP)* (2018)

Aspirations, Opportunities and Challenges in 2015 and Beyond, IOM-MPI Issues in Brief, No. 11 (2014)

Australia Government, 2017 Foreign Policy White Paper (2017)

Bayhaqi, Akhmad et al., *Trade Facilitation in APEC:* Progress *and* Impact, APEC PSU Policy Brief No. 25 (2019)

Best Practices for RTAs/FTAs in APEC (2004)

Boustany, Charles W. Jr. & Aaron L. Freidberg, *Answering China's Economic Challenge: Preserving Power, Enhancing Prosperity*, NBR Report, No. 76 (2019)

Centre for Economics and Business Research, *World Economic League Table 2021* (2020)

Chanlett-Avery, Emma et al., *Thailand: Background and U.S. Relations*, CRS Report (2015)

Cimino-Isaacs, Cathleen D., *Labor Enforcement Issues in U.S. FTAs*, CRS: In Focus (2000)

Clifford Chance, *The EU-Japan Economic Partnership Agreement: A Different Kind of Treaty?* (2018)

Commission of the European Communities, A New Partnership with South East Asia, COM(2003) 399 final (2003)

Commissions of the European Communities, Communication from the Commission: A New Partnership with South East Asia, COM (2003) 399 final (2003)

Commission of the European Communities, Creating a New Dynamic in EU-ASEAN Relations, COM(96) 314 final (1996)

Commission of the European Communities, Europe and Asia: A Strategic Framework for Enhanced Partnerships, COM(2001) 469 final (2001)

Commission of the European Communities, Report on the State of Play of the FTA Negotiations with ASEAN, India, the Andean Community and Central America, SEC(2009) 681 final (2009)

Commission of the European Communities, Towards a New Asia Strategy, COM(94) 314 final (1994)

Committee on Trade and Investment (CTI) Chair, The Individual Action Plan (IAP) and IAP Peer Review, 2011/SOM2/021anx2 (2011)

Communication from Chile and the Republic of Korea, Best Practices for FTAs/FTAs in APEC, TN/RL/W/187, Sept. 12, 2005

Concept Paper for the Expansion of the ITA, Communication from Canada, Japan, Korea, the Separate Customs Territory of Taiwan, Penghu, Kinmen and Matsu, Singapore and the United States, G/IT/W/36, May 2, 2012

Coper, William H., *The EU-South Korea Free Trade Agreement and Its Implications for the United States*, CRS Report (2011)

CPTPP Statement on the Occasion of the Third Commission Meeting (2020)

CTI Chair, Annex 2 – APEC Cross-Border E-Commerce Facilitation Framework, 2017/SOM3/027anx02 (2017)

CTI Chair, Annex 4 – The Conduct of the Trade Policy Dialogue on WTO-Plus Elements of RTAs/FTAs and the Trade Policy Dialogue Outcomes Report, 2017/SOM2/018anx04 (2017)

CTI Chair, The Individual Action Plan (IAP) and IAP Peer Review, 2011/SOM2/021anx2, May 17–18, 2011

CTI Report to Ministers, Collective Strategic Study on Issues Related to the Realization of the FTAAP (2016)

Delegation of the European Union to Vietnam, *Guide to the EU-Vietnam Trade and Investment Agreements* (2016)

Department of Defense, *Indo-Pacific Strategy Report: Preparedness, Partnerships, and Promoting a Networked Region* (2019)

Department of State, *A Free and Open Indo-Pacific Advancing a Shared Vision* (2019)

DFAT, *CPTPP Suspensions Explained* (2019)

DFAT, *Regional Comprehensive Economic Partnership: Outcomes: Services and Investment* (2020)

DFDL, *Investment Guide: Vietnam 2020* (7th ed. 2020)

Dominican Republic-Central America FTA, Arbitral Panel Established Pursuant to Chapter Twenty, In the Matter of Guatemala – Issues Relating to the Obligations Under Article 16.2.1(a) of the CAFTA-DR, Final Report of the Panel (2017)

EU Intellectual Property Office (EUIPO), *Geographical Indications in the ASEAN* Region: *A* Booklet *on ASEAN* Geographical Indications *Procedure and Products* (2019)

EU-ASEAN Business Council, *2020 EU-ASEAN Sentiment Survey* (2020)

European Chamber of Commerce in Vietnam (EuroCham), *2019 EVFTA Report: The EU-Vietnam Free Trade Agreement: Perspectives from Vietnam* (2019)

European Commission, *Cambodia Loses Duty-Free Access to the EU Market over Human Rights Concerns* (2020)

European Commission, Client and Supplier Countries of the EU 27 in Merchandise Trade (Value %) (2019, Excluding Intra-EU Trade) (2019)

European Commission, *Consultation Strategy: Impact Assessment on the Establishment of a Multilateral Investment Court for Investment Dispute Resolution* (2016)

European Commission, Europe's Moment: Repair and Prepare for the Next Generation, COM(2020) 456 final (2020)

European Commission, *EU-China Geographical Indications* (2020)

European Commission, *EU-Mercosur Trade Agreement: Building Bridges for Trade and Sustainable Development* (2019)

European Commission, *EU-UK Trade and Cooperation Agreement: A New Relationship, with Big Changes* (2020)

European Commission, EU-Vietnam Trade Agreement Enters into Force (2020)

European Commission, *Factsheet : A New EU Agreement with Japan* (2018)

European Commission, *Global Europe: Competing in the World* (2006)

European Commission, *Human Rights and Sustainable Development in the EU-Vietnam Relations with Specific Regard to the EU-Vietnam Free Trade Agreement* (2016)

European Commission, *Key Elements of the EU-China Comprehensive Agreement on Investment* (2020)

European Commission, *Overview of FTA and Other Trade Negotiations* (Updated Aug. 2020)

European Commission, Report from the Commission to the European Parliament, the Council, the European Economic and Social Committee and the Committee of the Regions on Implementation of Free Trade Agreements: 1 January 2016 – 31 December 2016, COM(2017) 654 final (2017)

European Commission, Report from the Commission to the European Parliament, the Council, the European Economic and Social Committee and the Committee of the Regions: Report on the Implementation of the Trade Policy Strategy Trade for All: Delivering a Progressive Trade Policy to Harness Globalisation, COM (2017) 491 final (2017)

European Commission, State of the Union Address 2020 (2020)

European Commission, *Trade for All: Towards a More Responsible Trade and Investment Policy* (2015)

European Commission, *Trade in Services Agreement (TiSA): Factsheet* (2016)

European Commission, *2020 Strategic Foresight Report* (2020)

European Commission & High Representative of the Union for Foreign Affairs and Security Policy, *EU-China – Strategic Outlook*, Joint (2019) 5 final (2019)

European Ombudsman, Decision in Case 1409/2014/MHZ on the European Commission's Failure to Carry Out a Prior Human Rights Impact Assessment of the EU-Vietnam Free Trade Agreement (2016)

European Parliament, CJEU Opinion on the EU-Singapore Agreement (2017)

European Parliament, *Driving Trade in the ASEAN Region: Progress of FTA Negotiations* (2016)

European Parliament, European Parliament Resolution on Regional Free Trade Areas and Trade Strategy in the European Union (2002/2044(INI)), P5_TA (2003)0237 (2003)

European Parliament, European Parliament Resolution of 25 November 2010 on Human Rights and Social and Environmental Standards in International Trade Agreements, P7(2010)0434 (2010)

European Parliament, European Parliament Resolution of 17 April 2014 on the State of Play of the EU-Vietnam Free Trade Agreement, P7_TA(2014)0458 (2014)

European Parliament, European Parliament Resolution of 7 October 2020 on the Implementation of the Common Commercial Policy – Annual Report 2018, P9_TA-PROV(2020)0252 (2020)

European Parliament, EU-Singapore Partnership and Cooperation Agreement (Resolution), P8-TA(2019)0093 (2019)

European Parliament, *Factsheet on the European Union: The Treaty of Lisbon* (2020)

European Parliament, *Free Trade Agreement between the EU and the Republic of Singapore – Analysis* (2018)

European Parliament, *Human Rights in EU Trade Agreements: The Human Rights* Clause *and* its *Application* (2019)

European Parliament, Legislative Train 09.2020 (2020)

European Parliament, Resolution on the Situation in South-East Asia, A3-0219/91 (1991)

European Parliament, *Southeast Asia, Fact Sheets on the European Union* (2020)

European Parliament, *The Generalised Scheme of Preferences Regulation (No 978/ 2012): European Implementation Assessmen*t (2018)

European Services Forum, Letter to the Commissioner for Trade, 12 July 2020

Evaluation Unit et al., *Evaluation of EC Co-Cooperation with ASEAN: Final Report*, vol. 2 (2009)

EU, *EU-Vietnam Free Trade Agreement Enters into Force as of 1 August 2020* (2020)

FDI in Services: Focus on Health Care (2019)

Fergusson, Ian F. & Brock R. Williams, *The Trans-Pacific Partnership (TPP): Key Provisions and Issues for Congress*, CRS Report (2016)

Fergusson, Ian F. & Bruce Vaughn, *The Trans-Pacific Partnership Agreement*, CRS Report (2011)

Foreword by Singapore Minister for Communications & Information and Minister-in-Charge of Trade Relations S Iswaran, *in* European Commission & MTI, *European Union – Singapore Trade and Investment Agreements* (2019)

General Council Decision, TRIPS Non-Violation and Situation Complaints Moratorium, WT/L/1080, Dec. 1, 2019

Gloudeman, Lauren & Nargiza Salidjanova, *Policy Considerations for Negotiating a U.S.-China Bilateral Investment Treaty*, U.S. China Economic and Security Review Commission Staff Research Report (2016)

Google et al., *SEA Internet Economy Report 2019* (2019)
Green, Michael et al., *Powers, Norms, and Institutions: The Future of the Indo-Pacific from a Southeast Asia Perspective*, Results of a CSIS Survey of Strategic Elites (2020)
Guiding Principles and Objectives for Negotiating the Regional Comprehensive Economic Partnership (2012)
Hsu, Locknie et al., *Improving Connectivity between ASEAN's Legal Systems to Address Commercial Issues* (2018)
Hurley, John, *Examining the Debt Implications of the Belt and Road Initiative from a Policy Perspective*, CGD Policy Paper (2018)
ISEAS-Yusof Ishal Institute, *The State of Southeast Asia: 2020 Survey Report* (2002)
Joint Leaders' Statement on the Regional Comprehensive Economic Partnership (RCEP) (2019)
Joint Local Statement on the Death Penalty Case of Moad Fadzir bin Mustaffa in Singapore (2020)
Kuriyama, Carlos & Azul Ogazon, *Expanding the Information Technology Agreement*, APEC PSU Brief No. 6 (2013)
Letter from María L. Pagán, Acting United States Trade Representative, to the Trans-Pacific Partnership Depositary, Jan. 30, 2017
Martin, Michael F., *The Proposed U.S. Malaysia Free Trade Agreement*, CRS Report (2008)
Martin, Michael F., *U.S. Restrictions on Relations with Burma*, CRS Report (2020)
Martin, Michael F., *U.S.-Vietnam Economic and Trade Relations: Issues in 2019*, CRS: In Focus (2019)
Mckinsey Global Institute, *Digital Globalization: The New Era of Global Flows* (2016)
Meltzer, Joshua P. and Neena Shenai, *The US-China Economic Relationship: A Comprehensive Approach*, Brookings Policy Brief (2019)
Ministry of Trade and Trade Industry Singapore, Regional Comprehensive Economic Partnership Signed (2020)
MTI, *A Guide to Understanding the ASEAN-China Free Trade Area Upgrade* (2016)
Murrill, Brandon J., *The WTO's Appellate Body Loses Its Quorum: Is This the Beginning of the End for the "Rules-Based Trading System"?* CRS Legal Sidebar (2019)
New Zealand Foreign Affairs & Trade, *Regional Comprehensive Economic Partnership: National Interest Analysis* (2020)
New Zealand's CPTPP Investor-State Dispute Settlement Side Letters with Australia, Brunei, Malaysia, Peru and Vietnam (2018)
Office of the Secretary of State, *The Elements of the China Challenge* (2020)
Office of the Spokesperson, U.S. 2019 APEC Outcomes, Dec. 19, 2019
Organisation for Economic Co-operation and Development, *Leveraging Digital Trade to Fight the Consequences of COVID-19* (2020)

Outline of the RCEP Agreement (as at November 2017), *in* Joint Leaders' Statement on the Negotiations for the Regional Comprehensive Economic Partnership (RCEP) (2017)

Possible reform of Investor-State dispute settlement (ISDS): Comments by the Government of Indonesia: Note by the Secretariat, A/CN.9/WG.III/WP.156, Nov. 9, 2018

Post-Cabinet Press Conference: Monday, Oct. 31, 2017 (2017)

Presence of Natural Persons (Mode 4), S/C/W/301, Sept. 15, 2009

President of the United States, *National Security Strategy of the United States of America* (2017)

PWC, *The Long View: How Will the Global Economic Order Change by 2050?* (2017)

Rana, Pradumna B & Ji Xianbai, *BRI's "Debt Trap Diplomacy,"* RISI Commentary, No. 191 (2020)

RCEP: A Guide to the World's Largest Trade Agreement, Asia House Advisory Briefing (2020)

Report of the East Asian Vision Group II (EAVGII) (2012)

Resolution of the Sixth AIPO General Assembly on ASEAN-EC Economic Cooperation, 6 GA/RES.11/83 (1983)

S. Res. 311 (111th Congress) (2009)

S. Res. 218 (112th Congress) (2011)

Sajjanhar, Ashok, *Taking Stock of India's "Act East Policy,"* ORF Issue Brief, No. 142 (2016)

Schnepf, Randy, *WTO Doha Round: Implications for U.S. Agriculture*, CRS Report (2014)

Sharma, Sachin Kumar et al., *A Quantitative Assessment of India's Withdrawal from RCEP: Issues and Concerns* (2020)

Singapore Customs, *Application Procedures for a Certificate of Origin via TradeNet and Related Administrative Matters* (2020)

Singapore International Chamber of Commerce, *Plain English Guide to the European Union-Singapore Free Trade Agreement* (2020)

Singapore International Commercial Court Users Guide (2019)

Singapore International Dispute Resolution Academy, *SIDRA International Dispute Resolution Survey: 2020 Final Report* (2020)

Spak, Gregory et al., *Overview of Chapter 4 (Rules of Origin) of the US-Mexico-Canada Trade Agreement* (2018)

Special Issue: UNCITRAL and Investment Arbitration Reform: Matching Concerns and Solutions (Malcolm Langford et al. eds.) *in* 21: 2–3J. World Invest. & Trade (2020)

Specialist in Asian Affairs & Specialist in International Trade and Finance, *Vietnam PNTR Status and WTO Accession Issues and Implications for the United States*, CRS Report (2007)

Statement by the President on the Signing of the Trans-Pacific Partnership (2016)

State Council, 国务院关于加快实施自由贸易区战略的若干意见 [Several Opinions of the State Council on Accelerating the Implementation of the Strategies for Free Trade Areas] (2015)

Sugiyarto, Guntur & Dovelyn Rannveig Agunias, *A "Freer" Flow of Skilled Labour within ASEAN: Aspirations, Opportunities and Challenges in 2015 and Beyond*, IOM-MPI Issues in Brief, No. 11 (2014)

Summary of the Regional Comprehensive Economic Partnership Agreement (2020)

Summary Report of Competition Policy and Law Group Meeting 2012, 2013/SOM1.CPLG/002 (2013)

Sustainable Development Goals, *in* United Nations General Assembly, Transforming our world: the 2030 Agenda for Sustainable Development, A/Res/70/1 (2015), goal 9.1

The European Community and ASEAN, *in* Europe Information: External Relations, 16/79 (1979)

Trans-Pacific Partnership Leaders Statement (2015)

UNCTAD, *ASEAN at 50: Achievements and Challenges in Regional Integration* (2017)

UNCTAD, *International Classification on Non-Tariff Measures* (2019)

UNCTAD, *Investment Trends Monitor* (2021)

UNCTAD, *Non-tariff Measures: Evidence from Selected Developing Countries and Future Research Agenda: Developing Countries in International Trade Studies* (2010)

UNCTAD, *RCEP Agreement as a Potential Boost for Investment in Sustainable Post-COVID Recovery*, *Investment Trends Monitor* (2020)

UNCTAD, *The Asian Developmental State and the Flying Geese Paradigm*, No. 213 (2013)

UNCTAD, *World Investment Report 2019* (2019)

UNCTAD, *World Investment Report 2020* (2020)

UNCTAD Secretariat, Core Elements of International Investment Agreements in Domestic Investment Frameworks in the APEC Region (2011)

UNESCAP, *Asia-Pacific Trade and Investment Report 2016: Recent Trends and Development* (2016)

UNESCAP, Complementarities between the ASEAN Community Vision 2025 and the United Nations 2030 Agenda for Sustainable Development: A Framework for Action (2017)

UNESCAP & UNCTAD, *Asia-Pacific Trade and Investment Report 2019: Navigating Non-tariff Measures towards Sustainable Development* (2019)

United Nations, *South-South Trade in Asia: The Role of Regional Trade Agreements* (2008)

U.S. Chamber of Commerce, *The Next Stage of US-Vietnam Relations: A Blueprint to Deepen Trade and Investment Ties* (2019)

USITC, *The Pros and Cons of Entering Into Negotiations on Free Trade Area Agreements with Taiwan, the Republic of Korea, and ASEAN, or the Pacific Rim Region in General: Reports to the Senate Committee on Finance on Investigation No. TA-332–259 under Section 332 of the Tariff Act of 1930, USITC Publications 2166* (1989)

USTR, *Fact Sheet: Economic and Trade Agreement between the United States of America and the People's Republic of China* (2000)

USTR, *National Trade Policy for 2017* (2017)

USTR, *United States-Japan Trade Agreement (USJTA) Negotiations: Summary of Specific Negotiating Objectives* (2018)

Vaughn, Bruce, *U.S. Strategic and Defense Relationship in the Asia-Pacific Region*, CRS Report (2007)

Vietnam Ministry of Industry and Trade, *Vietnamese-German Cooperation Research Projects on Wind Power* (2017)

White House, Interim National Security Strategic Guidance (2021)

Williams, Brock R. & Nicolas Cook, *The African Continental Free Trade Area (AfCFTA)*, CRS: In Focus (2020)

Woodhead, Geoffrey, *The Role of Peer Reviews in APEC, First OECD-South East Asia Regional Forum: Peer Review Mechanisms – Macroeconomic Policies, Regional Economic Integration and Economic Development* (2007)

World Bank, *Vietnam: Deepening International Integration and Implementing the EVFTA* (2020)

WTO Appellate Body Report, *Mexico – Tax Measures on Soft Drinks and Other Beverages*, WT/DS308/AB/R (2006)

WTO Appellate Body Report, *Peru – Additional Duty on Imports of Certain Agricultural Products*, WT/DS457/AB/R (2015)

WTO, *Background Note by Secretariat, Council for Trade in Services: Mode 3 – Commercial Presence*, S/C/W/314 (2010)

WTO, DS590: Japan – Measures Related to the Exportation of Products and Technology to Korea

WTO, European Union – Certain Measures concerning Palm Oil and Oil Palm Crop-based Biofuels, WT/DS593/1, G/L/1348, G/TBTB/D/52, G/SCM/D128/1 (2019)

WTO, Mode 3 – Commercial Presence, S/C/W/314, Apr. 7, 2010

WTO, Panel Report, *European Communities and Its Member States – Tariff Treatment of Certain Information Technology Products*, WT/DS375/R, WT/DS376/R, WT/DS377/R, Aug. 16, 2010 (*EC-IT Products*)

WTO, Panel Report, *Russia – Measures Concerning Traffic in Transit*, WT/DS512/R (2019)

WTO, Panel Report, *United States – Tariff Measures on Certain Goods from China*, WT/DS543/R (2020)

WTO, Request for Consultations by Hong Kong, China, *United States – Origin Marking Requirement*, WT/DS597/1, G/L1365, G/RO/D/8, G/TBT

WTO, *Trade in Medical Goods in the Context of Tackling COVID-19* (2020)

WTO, *Trade in Services in the Context of COVID-19* (2020)

WTO, Trade Policy Review, Japan: Minutes of the Meeting: Addendum, WT/TPR/M/397/Add.1 (2020)

WTO, Trade Policy Review, Report by India, WT/TPR/G403 (2020)

WTO, Trade Policy Review: Report by the Secretariat: European Union, WT/TPR/S/395 (2019)

WTO, Trade Policy Review, Report by the Secretariat: The Philippines, WT/TPR/S/368 (2018)

WTO, Trade Policy Review, Report by the Secretariat, Singapore, WT/TPR.S.343 (2016)

WTO, *World Trade Report* 2011: *The WTO and Preferential Trade Agreements: From Co-existence to Coherence* (2011)

WTO, *World Trade Report 2015* (2015)

WTO, *World Trade Report 2019: The Future of Services Trade* (2019)

WTO, *World Trade Statistical Review 2019* (2019)

WTO, *World Trade Statistics Review 2020* (2020)

WTO, *15 Years of the Information Technology Agreement: Trade, Innovation and Global Production Networks* (2012)

WTO, *20 Years of the Information Technology Agreement: Boosting Trade, Innovation and Digital Connectivity* (2017)

INDEX

Lightning Source UK Ltd.
Milton Keynes UK
UKHW010846061221
395124UK00004B/30

9 781108 845601